THE NEW MIDDLE AGES

BONNIE WHEELER, *Series Editor*

The New Middle Ages is a series dedicated to
transdisciplinary studies of medieval cultures, with
particular emphasis on recuperating women's
history and on feminist and gender analyses.
This peer-reviewed series includes both
scholarly monographs and essay collections.

PUBLISHED BY PALGRAVE:

*Women in the Medieval Islamic World:
Power, Patronage, and Piety*
  edited by Gavin R. G. Hambly

*The Ethics of Nature in the Middle Ages:
On Boccaccio's Poetaphysics*
  by Gregory B. Stone

*Presence and Presentation:
Women in the Chinese Literati Tradition*
  by Sherry J. Mou

*The Lost Love Letters of Heloise and Abelard:
Perceptions of Dialogue in Twelfth-Century
France*
  by Constant J. Mews

Understanding Scholastic Thought with Foucault
  by Philipp W. Rosemann

*For Her Good Estate:
The Life of Elizabeth de Burgh*
  by Frances A. Underhill

*Constructions of Widowhood and Virginity in
the Middle Ages*
  edited by Cindy L. Carlson and
  Angela Jane Weisl

*Motherhood and Mothering in
Anglo-Saxon England*
  by Mary Dockray-Miller

*Listening to Heloise:
The Voice of a Twelfth-Century Woman*
  edited by Bonnie Wheeler

The Postcolonial Middle Ages
  edited by Jeffrey Jerome
  Cohen

*Chaucer's Pardoner and Gender Theory:
Bodies of Discourse*
  by Robert S. Sturges

*Crossing the Bridge: Comparative Essays
on Medieval European and Heian Japanese
Women Writers*
  edited by Barbara Stevenson and
  Cynthia Ho

*Engaging Words: The Culture of Reading
in the Later Middle Ages*
  by Laurel Amtower

*Robes and Honor: The Medieval World of
Investiture*
  edited by Stewart Gordon

*Representing Rape in Medieval and Early
Modern Literature*
  edited by Elizabeth Robertson and
  Christine M. Rose

*Same Sex Love and Desire Among Women
in the Middle Ages*
  edited by Francesca Canadé Sautman and
  Pamela Sheingorn

*Sight and Embodiment in the Middle Ages:
Ocular Desires*
  by Suzannah Biernoff

CHARLEMAGNE'S MUSTACHE AND OTHER CULTURAL CLUSTERS OF A DARK AGE

Paul Edward Dutton

CHARLEMAGNE'S MUSTACHE AND OTHER CULTURAL CLUSTERS OF A DARK AGE
© Paul Edward Dutton

First published 2004 by
PALGRAVE MACMILLAN™
175 Fifth Avenue, New York, N.Y. 10010 and
Houndmills, Basingstoke, Hampshire, England RG21 6XS
Companies and representatives throughout the world

PALGRAVE MACMILLAN is the global academic imprint of the Palgrave Macmillan division of St. Martin's Press, LLC and of Palgrave Macmillan Ltd. Macmillan® is a registered trademark in the United States, United Kingdom and other countries. Palgrave is a registered trademark in the European Union and other countries.

ISBN 1–4039–6223–5 (cloth)

Library of Congress Cataloging-in-Publication Data
Dutton, Paul Edward, 1952–
        Charlemagne's mustache / Paul Edward Dutton.
            p. cm. — (The New Middle Ages)
        Includes bibliographical references and index.
        ISBN 1–4039–6223–5 (cloth)
            1. Charlemagne, Emperor, 742–814. 2. France—History—To 987.
3. Carolingians—History. 4. Civilization, Medieval, I. Title. II. New Middle Ages (Palgrave Macmillan (Firm))

DC73.D87 2004
944'.014—dc22   2003062223

A catalogue record for this book is available from the British Library.

Design by Newgen Imaging Systems (P) Ltd., Chennai, India.

First edition: May 2004
10 9 8 7 6 5 4 3 2 1

Printed in the United States of America.

For my parents

CONTENTS

LIST OF ILLUSTRATIONS

PREFACE

For those who like and need such things, there is a theory or perhaps just an observation that underlies this collection of essays and it is this: that cultures are not fixed, but fluid; that they are made and reconfirmed daily, coalescing around people, places, and ideas; and that it would be better for us (however reductive it might at first seem) to study pieces or, as I have called them, clusters rather than wholes. But perhaps that is how cultural historians are forced to proceed most of the time anyway, since cultural history can never be known in the same way as political or eventful history, which asks the simpler questions of who did what, when, and why. Such linearity and exactness escapes cultural histories, which are dogged by their complex, composite, and changeable natures. The whole of a culture may never exist in any comprehensible form, since transience, ill-defined borders, shifting ideas, and a continually changing cast of characters make any larger cultural entity as difficult to grasp as a slippery and wriggling brook trout in a swift flowing stream.

Cultures contain people, things, ideas, places, memories, monuments, rituals, and institutions, but those are all in motion and often moving at different speeds. One day Alcuin was a fixture at the court of Charlemagne and the next he was gone and with him went a set of ideas, recollections, and influences that could not be replaced. And Alcuin was a role player and never the center of cultural cohesion that Charlemagne had been in his time. But even the emperor stood on the margins of the literary activity of his own court. No person, I suspect, can ever fully participate in the complete culture of a time; nor should s/he wish to, for we are all engaged all the time in making cultural choices.

Indeed, how knowable is a culture either to its participants or to those of us at great distance from it in space and time? Even if one knew everything about a given time (all the thoughts and emotions of all its people, all the physical facts, all the events) its cultural wholeness would still escape us because it was lived and in motion, never fixed and frozen. Cultural history may not be so much indefinable as uncatchable and unstoppable. How, for instance, could we ever recreate the particular smell of the past? And cultures do encompass sensory realms that we can only (and even then but rarely) imagine and never supply: the perspiration of seldom bathing meat-eaters, the candles, smoke from fire, the scent of cooked and rotten food are all gone. When the stolen relics of the martyrs Marcellinus and Peter were returned to Einhard in Aachen, he described with some amazement the sweet smell that drifted softly over the city and announced to all that his saints had come home. The aroma of a saint meant something to Einhard and his world that we can never experience or fully appreciate today. Too often we intellectualize the cultures we seek to recover, neglecting all the while the human and sensory experiences that once so enlivened them, that made them them.

The best we may ever achieve is to gain some insight into cultural segments, parts that intimate the larger world that once existed around them or, at least, alert us to its dizzying complexities. Even cultural clusters are not comprehensible wholes, for they form and disappear, extend over time and are themselves agents and elements of change; and there are circles of cultural change within larger circles and they are not all moving at the same speed. *Tempora mutantur, nos et mutamur in illis* was the motto Matthias Borbonius laid upon Lothar I: "The times are changing and we ourselves are changing in them." In that suggestive epigram I prefer to see some awareness that external and internal changes (or at least their speed) may move separately; "in them" but not necessarily "with them." Individuals exist within a time, but may not always be of it or keep pace with its cultural changes and influences. Old scribes, we may usefully recall, were still writing late Caroline minuscule long after the new Gothic script had taken hold.

The fragility of the court cultures (and perhaps we should always speak in the plural) of the Carolingians was a product of their newness and their limited resources and conception. No wonder that Einhard and Walahfrid Strabo worried about the impermanence of their times. Cultural life in those high places must have seemed perilously unstable since it was laid so thinly on the ground. Medieval monasticism supplied an antidote of sorts since its prime method was to regularize and make permanent a life of prayer; the Monk (that is, all monks) should pass through all his years with a sempiternal, world-denying sameness of life and thought. But monks and monasteries changed too, even if they added heavy ballast to the second great generation of Carolingian thought.

My hope in what follows is to explore but a few of the cultural clusters of the Carolingian age. I would not claim that they were the most important such assemblages, and indeed know that they were not, but thinking about them may help us to cast a weak light into still obscure corners of the Carolingian experience. The 'Dark Age' of the title is only partly ironical since Carolingian intellectuals themselves, men again such as Einhard and

Walahfrid Strabo, thought they saw darkness closing in all around them and they made dangerous forays into its ever-lengthening shadows. A compelling case could be made that the Carolingians invented the very concept of the Dark Ages long before Edward Gibbon and Charles Oman got to it, but that would be another essay and there are already enough of those in this book.

Most of these essays began as lectures given over many years to such groups as the Institute of Historical Research at the University of London, the Centre for Medieval Studies at the University of Toronto, the University of British Columbia's medieval workshop, the Canadian Society of Medievalists, the medieval seminar at Harvard University, and the Comparative Court Cultures group to which I belong. Whether I have succeeded in transforming deliverable lectures into readable essays is for the reader to judge. The last three essays have also been published before, but they appear here in revised and, in two cases, renamed and substantially reworked form. In all but a few cases, which are noted, the translations are mine, but I have often supplied readers with an indication of where a full translation of a given work may be found should they wish to read the whole work in translated form.

The many friends and colleagues who have helped me to pursue leads and avoid mistakes are thanked for specific contributions throughout the collection, but as far as possible I would like to thank them here as a group for their many unselfish kindnesses in steering me forward even if I have not always followed their wise advice. To Édouard Jeauneau, John Contreni, Bruce Eastwood, Herbert Kessler, David Ganz, Michael Lapidge, Mary Garrison, Richard Hodges, Courtney Booker, the late Donald Bullough, Derryl MacLean, Paul Cobb, David Knechtges, Alan Rudrum, John Shinners, Del Sweeney, Ralf Stammberger, John Craig, Patrick Geary, Johannes Heil, Michelle Lucey-Roper, Paul Fouracre, Eugene Vance, Christopher McDonough, Richard Landes, Jacqueline Murray, Paul Meyvaert, Mary-Ann Stouck, Bryan Ward-Perkins, Giles Constable, Eric Goldberg, and Michael McCormick I extend my deepest thanks. Joan MacDonald kindly retyped one of the essays, Greg Kozak proofread the notes, Tammy McCurry worked on the index, my daughter Laura took one of the photographs, and Ron Long and Greg Ehlers of instructional resources at Simon Fraser worked on the rest. I am also extremely grateful to the institutions and libraries that have allowed me to print plates of their precious objects and to the libraries that have assisted me and allowed me the use of their holdings, in particular, the Pontifical Institute of Mediaeval Studies, the University of British Columbia, and Simon Fraser University and its ever helpful Interlibrary Loans office. The Social Sciences and Humanities Research Council of Canada and Simon Fraser University provided welcome time and assistance so that I might pursue my many inquiries.

Essays, as the word *essayer* implies, are but attempts; mine, at least, harbor no hope of being definitive or comprehensive; they are instead merely exploratory. Hence I am conscious, as I learned while working on "Whispering Secrets," that to the ninth century *exploratores* were spies. The historian is a spy: s/he visits an alien past in order to report back to readers on the lie of the land, its peoples, their thoughts and customs. Occasionally the information brought back is simply wrong or misleading and it is all too often misunderstood by the receiver, this one in particular, and so I can only hope that others will extend and challenge, improve and finish my small spyings.

In many ways the topics taken up were just ones that interested me at the time, but they hang together, I suppose, the way the floating figures in a Chagall painting do, however displaced and unjointed they might at first seem. From the Charlemagne essays with which the collection begins to the weather essay with which it ends, the objects under consideration are almost too large to be seen whole. Hence, the reader will often find me doubling back to take up already treated matters in the light of a new context. Like the shimmering tesserae of a Ravenna mosaic, images change as the light does in diurnal passage; Theodora and Justinian need to be studied both in the morning and afternoon as the sunlight shifts around San Vitale.

Borges once wondered about the possibility of writing biography without a subject, history without events. I harbor no such subversive thoughts here, for I was just seeking sightlines into complex matters in the hope that the edges of some larger map might appear and that some view of a way forward might at last come to me out of the enveloping mist.

As an inducement to read on I leave the reader with seven questions:

Why did Charlemagne have a mustache?
Why peacocks?
What and, more importantly, why was Charlemagne writing in bed?
How did one become a medieval star?
How were secrets kept and conveyed in the early Middle Ages?
Does the world age with the aged?
And, why did early medieval peoples believe in hailmakers, their own equivalent of the African rainmaker?

These were the questions with which I began, but were not in all cases the ones with which I ended.

humanas actiones non ridere, non lugere, neque detestari, sed intelligere

—Spinoza, *Tractatus politicus*

non semper ea sunt, quae uidentur

—Phaedrus, *Fabulae*

CHAPTER 1

CHARLEMAGNE'S MUSTACHE

On Christmas day 800 Charlemagne, dressed in a majestic Greek garment, processed solemnly into St-Peter's in Rome. One can almost hear, twelve hundred years later, the rustle of his long tunic, see his pointed Roman shoes, and smell the incense that burned that day as he was crowned emperor. Amid all the pomp and ceremony of that high moment, few people probably stopped to study Charlemagne's mustache. I would like to think that had I been there that is just what I would have done.

Hair matters, but it may have mattered more to the early Middle Ages than it does to us today.[1] Anthropologists shaped by the shaggy 1960s and current students of popular culture have closely studied head hair,[2] but historians have long neglected it, perhaps thinking it a trivial and unhistorical concern. But hair is the most historical member of the human body, for if human bodies have remained substantially unchanged throughout recorded history, hair because of its mutability has been a historically defining and differentiating part of the body. With a quick glance we can assign a photograph or painting to a specific period of time because hair and clothes allow us to locate them in time and space. Hair is a signature of history.

Yet hair and nails are paradoxical members of the human body, living, but dead; disposable, but always with us. An old Roman riddle remembered by Petronius captures something of the deep mystery of hair: "I am one who comes out of us in length and breadth: untangle me."[3] Human beings are uneasy about parts of their bodies that are transitory, that stick to us, but are not quite of us, that leave us though we continue on complete without them, that seem to grow out of us but lack feeling. Hair is a raveling riddle of symbolism, insensation, and corporal tenuity; it is also the only member of the body that we can easily and effectively change.

That humans can manipulate hair, which is all prominence, lying head high and eye-level, makes it the most expressive part of our bodies. The relatively recent phenomenon of young men and women shaving words onto their heads should remind us, in the spirit of their graphic bluntness, that human hair has always had a communicative capacity, has always, as it were, talked. One clever character in the ancient world sent a secret message by shaving a slave's head, tattooing words onto his scalp, and then allowing the slave's hair to grow back before sending him on his way. If by this novel means of concealment Histiaeus could not send his message quickly or easily employ the same surface twice, he was nevertheless experimenting with the communicative possibilities of the hairy head and it is a most malleable medium.[4] Medievalists would do well to listen more closely to this symphony of hair, which had not just social, but political songs to sing.[5] At one time its importance was historically immense.

Late antiquity was a battleground of hairstyles, which today we can hardly appreciate and so tend to dismiss as a primitive and bizarre aspect of the past.[6] But to visit a Volksmuseum in Germany today and to look into one of the glass cases that house objects from a time when the Germanic tribes were roaming outside the Roman empire is to peer into a world of fine ivory combs, shears, and hair pins. Both male and female Franks seem, when we gaze through that dusty glass, to have been obsessed with their hair. A gravestone from Niederdollendorf depicts a dead warrior in the very act of grooming himself (figure 1.1). Most of us would hardly wish to be remembered for all eternity fussing with our hair, but this man's hair like his sword spoke of who he was to his world and of his continuing vitality in the next.

Merovingian coins convey a certain hirsute *grauitas* whether it be Childeric I's hair flowing onto his shoulders on a likeness on his now lost golden signet ring (figure 1.2) or Dagobert I's implausible bun on one of his coins (figure 1.3). Even on pieces that reduce the human form to mere geometry, it is the hair and beard that remain most striking, for together they outline and contain the essence of the German king: the hair makes the man (figure 1.4).

All the Germanic peoples who came to occupy the Roman empire were makers of such hairy statements. Paul the Deacon was convinced, for instance, that the root meaning of Lombard or Longobard was "long beard"[7] and on the bronze Agilulf Visor from around 600 the Lombard king sits on his throne, his long beard and hair flowing (figure 1.5).[8] On an impressive gold medallion Theoderic the Great may be dressed in Roman clothes and flanked by a symbol of victory, but his hair is everything and it is not some Caesar's cropped and thinning strands that we see, but an impressive construction of curls that proudly proclaimed that he was a Germanic king and no clipped Roman (figure 1.6). By comparison the portrait of Theoderic cut into amethyst is a shocking piece, for in contrast to the highly formalized medallion portrait, we see here a hairy German

1.1   A tombstone of a Germanic warrior from Niederdollendorf (Rheinisches Landesmuseum Bonn).

prince as he must have wanted his own people to view him. The hair that sweeps around his head is thick and matted, but it perfectly complements his rugged face (figure 1.7).[9]

The Germanic males whom Tacitus describes in his *Germania* were engaged in hairy rites of passage. When the boys of the Chatti reached puberty they were no longer allowed to cut their facial or head hair, but had to grow it into a mass of hair that would cover their faces. Only when they had finally killed an enemy were they allowed to show their faces to the world again and to cut their blood beards.[10]

1.2 Childeric I's hair flows onto his shoulders on a plaster cast of his now lost golden signet ring (Ashmolean Museum, Oxford).

1.3 A coin of Dagobert I (Cabinet des Médailles, Bibliothèque Nationale, Paris).

1.4 A gold coin from Chalon of a Merovingian king (Cabinet des Médailles, Bibliothèque Nationale, Paris).

1.5 The bronze Agilulf Visor from around 600 (Museo Nazionale del Bargello, Florence).

We need at this point to think for a moment about the color of this warrior hair.[11] Many ancient writers had spoken of the long blond hair of the Germans, and wicked Juvenal had gone so far as to describe them as forever playing with it, twisting it into greasy curls.[12] Tacitus, however, claimed that as a people the Germans had "red hair" (*rutilae comae*) and Isidore spoke of the blood-red curls of the Goths.[13] But was their hair generally and naturally red? In the *Histories*, Tacitus relates in some detail the

1.6   A gold medallion of Theoderic the Great (Museo Nazionale Romano, Rome).

1.7   Portrait of Theoderic on an amethyst gem (Antikensammlung Bern: photo K. Buri, Harry N. Abrams Inc.).

history of Julius Ciuilis who led a campaign in A.D. 69 against Vitellius and the Roman forces of the Rhine.[14] Ciuilis, despite his Roman name, was a Batavian, an offshoot tribe of the Chatti, and of royal descent. According to Tacitus, he swore an oath in the German fashion to let his hair grow down (*propexum*) and to dye it red (*rutilatum*) until he had achieved the destruction of the Roman legions.[15] Many Germans "regularly dyed their hair red."[16] Red was, after all, the color of the enemy's sweet flowing blood and the case of Ciuilis and the blood beards of the Chatti helps us to locate the symbolism.

Not just length and color, but the presentation of hair conveyed meaning to this Germanizing world. The Suebi and the men of their allied tribes swept their long hair to the sides of their heads. They did this chiefly, says Tacitus, in order to distinguish themselves from other Germans and "the free man from the slave."[17] But something else was also at work, for the Suebi twisted back their hair until it stood erect and knotted on the tops or sides of their heads. Their chiefs had an even more ornamental style of presentation, but Tacitus was quick to note that their concern with hair was altogether innocent. For these were not lovelocks designed to attract women, but an effect designed to enhance the warriors' height and make them appear even more terrifying to their enemies in the midst of battle.[18]

With our eyes fixed on the top or side-knot of the Suebi we can begin to spy something of the deeper strategic significance of hair, whose value was a relative one, signaling differences between the free and unfree, Suebi and Chatti, chiefs and tribesmen, men and women, Germans and their enemies. Hair length, style, and color were all mutable signs of distinction. All the males of the German tribes seem to have kept their hair relatively long,[19] but there is some evidence that within many tribes the chiefs and their families came to regard their own hair as special. Thus on the Agilulf Visor only the king has a long beard and the leaders of the Suebi worked special effects on their own hair. Tacitus, even from the comfortable study where he read the German briefs written by others, sensed something of the physiognomic quality and symbolism of Germanic power.

Most imperial Romans simply despised Germanic long hair. Now some of this was, as Patrick Amory would have it, merely a classicizing topos, the hairy barbarian being an easy way for Romans to type Germans even if in reality the appearance of their head and facial hair was varied and individual.[20] But we should be cautious about dismissing cultural clichés, which often serve as tightly bound kernels of characterization, compacting difference and disgust into a few words and forceful images that free their users from seeking some deeper knowledge of a thing. For clichés are also artifacts of a culture and inside hard kernels lie layers that matter and mean. Julian the Apostate ran up against one such small, but stubborn cultural fact with his defense of long hair and beards in the *Misopogon, The Beard Hater*, which startled his fellow Romans who did not share his studied admiration of bearded Greek philosophers.[21] More in tune with the values of his Roman readers, the poet Sidonius Apollinaris made bitter fun of the hairiness of the peoples who disturbed his elegant Gallic life. To a friend he wrote (here in Helen Waddell's delightful translation):

> How should I, even if I could,
>   Write you an Epithalamium,
> Set down among these hairy hordes
>   And suffering their German?
> I dine with them and with wry face
>   Praise all they choose to utter,
> They sing full-fed Burgundian songs,
>   And oil their head with butter.[22]

And action may flow from commonplace convictions. In the *Codex Theodosianus*, the emperors, worried by the prospect of creeping barbarism, simply outlawed excessively long hair, for short hair had come to be a visible sign of the civilized Roman, long hair a Germanic affectation and affront.[23] The Germanic peoples may not have objected to being so typed since hair likely played some part along with religion and law in their determination to resist assimilation, to preserve their visible otherness from the great sea of *Romanitas* always threatening to wash them away.

The Romans knew this, of course, and also played at the highly symbolic politics of hair and haircutting. When the Sigambri submitted to the emperor Honorius, they were compelled to cut their hair. After spreading their golden locks on the ground before the emperor, they were allowed to enter his army as mercenaries.[24] Stilicho, the famous defender of the western empire, was himself a German, but the short-haired and lightly bearded figure who stares out at us from his ivory diptych along with his family has become part of the establishment (figure 1.8). His hair tells us that he is a Romanized German, a mercenary. Cut hair, thus, became a symbol of Germanic submission, not the outstretched neck that other peoples had traditionally offered to the Roman boot or the Roman sword.[25] Centuries later Pope Hadrian I found himself still living in the same symbolic universe of meaningful hair when he agreed to have the Lombards of Spoleto shaved in Roman fashion as a sign of their submission to his protection.[26] Notker the Stammerer from the hairy north in the late ninth century poked fun at a Carolingian deacon, who, imitating the Italians, wished to be bald, and had his hair chopped off (*decurtauit*) until he resembled the rotund idol a carpenter might make in planing and smoothing a piece of

1.8   An ivory diptych of Stilicho and his family (Museo del Duomo di Monza).

wood. For the monk of St-Gall, this deacon, who also bathed incessantly and cleaned his fingernails, had dared to defy nature, but nature in the form of a lethal spider bit him back.[27]

The Merovingian kings have become for us the most famous of the long-haired Germanic kings, the *reges criniti*.[28] They wore their hair parted in the middle of their foreheads and swept back over and around their heads until it spilled onto their backs, the very style we see on the preserved image of King Childeric I.[29] Gregory of Tours said that when the Franks crossed the Rhine they had set up long-haired kings, who were chosen from the first family, in each *ciuitas* of the empire they occupied.[30] The remarkable part of his testimony is not the long hair itself, but the plural *reges*. For Gregory here associates long hair with a ruling family of Frankish kings whose power was in this, its first imperial phase, diffuse and familial.

He does not claim that other Franks were short-haired, but informs us that the Merovingian family itself possessed long hair as its distinguishing characteristic.

And Gregory was not alone. His contemporary, the Byzantine historian Agathias, noted that when the Burgundians in a battle against the Franks caught sight of the long-flowing hair of a slain enemy they realized that they had killed the Frankish chief himself.

> For it is the practice of the Frankish kings never to have their hair cut. It is never cut from childhood onwards and each individual lock hangs right down over the shoulders, since the front ones are parted on the forehead and hang down on either side. It is not, however, like that of the Turks and Avars, unkempt, dry and dirty, and tied up in an unsightly knot. On the contrary they treat it with all kinds of soap and comb it very carefully. Custom has reserved this practice for royalty as a sort of distinctive badge and prerogative. Subjects have their hair cut all round, and are strictly forbidden to grow it any longer.[31]

The Burgundians cut off and displayed King Chlodomer's head with its long flowing hair in order to sow fear among the Franks.

Better than Gregory, then, Agathias helps us to appreciate that a distinction needs to be drawn between the special long hair of royal Franks and the still long, but once-cut or shorter hair of others. A good deal of evidence suggests that virtually the whole of the Frankish world of the sixth and seventh centuries thought of a full head of hair as the generic symbol of a free man.[32] Even to provide a criminal or slave with a wig so that he might pass as a free man was a serious offense[33] and to cut off the hair of free-born boys and girls without the permission of their guardians was almost as grave an offense as to kill them. It was, in the eyes of the wider Frankish world, to steal their freedom, to take away the visible sign of their standing as free Franks. It was also to subject and humiliate them and their families.[34] In a world in which visible presence, rich ornament, and public display were critical to establishing one's standing within a group, enforced shearing was a source of great shame and its result was there for all to see, visually documenting the powerlessness of self and family.

There was then a hierarchy of hair that ran from the bald or nearly bald slave at the bottom of society all the way up to the long-haired Merovingian family at its summit. Gregory repeatedly returns, like some dog to its lost breakfast, to royal hair in part because this dynamic sign of social standing seemed so strange to his disapproving Gallo-Roman eyes and in part because it was a tangible feature, an official marker, of the Merovingian persona in an age that lacked sure proofs of place and identity. He tells us that after the murder of one young king, his uncle,

King Guntram, went looking high and low for his dead nephew. A commoner reported that he thought he had finally found the body. The man explained that he had constructed a trap in the Marne River to catch fish and had instead caught a king. At first he was not sure whose corpse he had dragged up, but when he saw the body's long hair he knew that it was young King Clovis as did the king when he spied the hair still spilling down onto his nephew's shoulders.[35] To hide dead Germans decapitation was the best solution, since otherwise their long hair might give them away.[36]

Free Franks situated below the royal family had relatively long hair, but these men were apparently not allowed, by strict prohibition, to grow it to royal length, according to Agathias. Instead they had it trimmed, probably so that it did not fall onto their shoulders. But they too invested much in the maintenance of their relatively long hair. When the merchant Eufronius was tonsured against his will, he moved to another city and let his hair grow back before he would return home.[37] The fact that a bishop had ordered Eufronius's tonsure in order to steal his property should alert us, as Germanic law does, to the importance of hair as a marker of place in Frankish society. Subjects had longish hair and tried to keep it so because it affected their legal standing and, as Eufronius's case shows, because it was an essential aspect of the face they wished to turn outward upon society. Public shame and retreat from court or the village's all-inquiring eye were the painful results of the unwanted removal of hair, just as they had once been for King David's men (2 Kings 10:5).

At the heights of Merovingian society the implications of haircutting were even more profound, for on it turned issues of life and death, political power and degradation. The royal family itself in its competing lines exercised a coercive tonsorial power over enemies and defeated family members. After Clovis I captured the Salian king Chararic and his son, he immediately had their hair cut and ordered them to enter the church, one as a priest, the other as a deacon. When the father burst into tears at the utter humiliation of it all, his son said in a strange, but moving speech:

> These shoots have been cut off of living wood [and] are not yet dried out [and dead]. Rather they will quickly sprout and begin to grow; I wish that the man who did this might die just as quickly.[38]

The imagery is striking, for it begins in Scripture with Luke 23:31, the words that Jesus spoke to the grieving women who watched as he was led to Golgotha carrying his own pieces of green wood. Chararic's son (or his recorder Gregory) twisted Christ's metaphor, but in both we find an intimation of resurrection. Moreover, the Germanic peoples of the early medieval world still retained their fascination with the power and vitality of trees,[39] so that it was natural for a shorn Salic king and his son to think in their moment of low disgrace of the regenerative force of trees.

Northern Europe in the early Middle Ages was still covered with old and intractable trees and many of these gnarled giants seemed eternal; some like the great oak Irminsul were thought to hold up the very vaults of heaven. Chararic and his son may have thought that their hair, once long and living, contained something of the divine vigor of an eternal tree. But to talk of defoliated trees budding again, even if just to revive the spirit of a despairing father, was dangerously foolish. When Clovis heard that these shorn kings were threatening to grow back their hair and wished him dead, he had their heads cut off as his own final act of pruning.

Within the Merovingian family a tonsorial imperative of sorts was maintained; it was one of several techniques for depriving others of power and the promise of power. King Chilperic I had his son Merovech tonsured and sent to a monastery.[40] But did the shearing of a royal Frank in and of itself render him once and for all ineligible for kingship or did it symbolize something closer to a tonsure and a coerced career change? The case of Chararic suggests that the victims viewed enforced shearing as humiliating, as a sign of present but perhaps not permanent powerlessness. For the sheared, as Chararic's son proclaimed, could overcome with time and the return of their hair the humiliation laid upon them. Merovech and many others did just that. The deposed and tonsured Theuderic III was allowed to hide in the monastery of St-Denis until his locks grew back.[41] It was shame that led him to hide himself from public view, not that his fall from power was final.

Nor can we overlook the religious significance of shearing, whether voluntary or not, since for many it signaled renunciation of the world and entry into the church. Christian monks had long demonstrated their subordination to God and their manifest commitment to the religious life through the tonsure. To shave the top of one's head was a mark of submission and enslavement to the overlordship of God.[42] It was a daily reminder to monks that they had submitted themselves to a higher power and had renounced the world and its enduring animalities.

The religious connotations of hair-shaving were very old and not the exclusive domain of Christianity. Lucius Apuleius, the Antonine novelist, was apparently besotted with the allure and seductive magic of women's hair. In the *Golden Ass* his eponymous narrator Lucius openly confesses his obsession with women's hair, which he deemed the most significant and conspicuous feature of the human body. He would not, he claims, give a bald Venus the time of day, but devotes himself to describing the voluptuous hair of the slave Fotis, whom he was trying to seduce.[43] She dabbled in the magical arts of her mistress and finally, and accidentally, transformed Lucius into an ass. The rest of the story concerns poor Lucius's pathetic attempts as a hairy, braying ass to become human again. Only, at the end of the novel does the transformation occur, when in a moment of transcendent bliss on a beach, Lucius finally sees the great goddess Isis rise from the sea, her long and lustrous hair falling in ringlets upon her shoulders. The handmaidens who devoutly followed her constantly pantomimed the act of combing her hair, while her male priests went about completely bald as a sign of their utter submission to her long locks. Thus, Lucius himself went from being a hairy beast to the bald priestling of a lustrous goddess.[44] So, as strange as it may seem, the tonsure of Christian monks belonged to a code of religious subordination whose significance even the pagan Apuleius would have immediately recognized.

This religious symbolism played perfectly into the long-standing Germanic assumption that long hair designated a free man, short hair a slave. When Clovis converted he was careful to retain his long hair, but Bishop Avitus praised him for keeping his royal hair, which had been bathed in holy oil, tucked under his helmet during the ceremony.[45] The Frankish royal family went one step further, as we have seen, by effectively prescribing the hair styles of its kingdom and internally running a brutal barbershop for fallen family members. Royal shearing was itself a rite of passage, even if it led down and out. When King Childebert I was worried about the royal future that lay ahead for two nephews, he famously asked his brother whether they ought to cut off the boys' hair and so reduce them to the status of ordinary individuals or should they have them killed and then divide up their brother's kingdom equally between themselves?[46] After the scheming uncles had lured the boys away from their protective grand-mother, they sent a representative to the queen mother with a pair of scis-sors in one hand and a sword in the other. She was given the dreadful choice of having to decide whether she would prefer to see her grandsons sheared or dead. In a moment of powerful melodrama, Clotild answered that if they could not be kings, she would rather see them dead than shorn. And so they died.

A third grandson, Chlodovald, known to us as Saint Cloud, voluntarily cut his own hair and entered the church.[47] His was a model followed by other kings who wished to drop out. Dagobert III, after a severe bout of the night sweats, chewed off his fingernails and in the morning ordered his long hair cut off, thus voluntarily abandoning his kingship.[48]

It would probably be wrong to think of Merovingian shearing as some gentle haircut. Even if we may continue to puzzle over the meaning of such words as *decaluare* and *tondere/tundere*, there is no hard proof that the Merovingians practiced scalping. Nonetheless, the process could be a bru-tal one. Droctulf, a Frank who had conspired against the king, had both his ears and his hair cut off, which is suggestive of the violence involved.[49] Still, no matter the brutality, shearing was a punishment that might save the condemned from execution; that was the choice her sons gave Clotild. Her decision to choose execution rather than shearing for her grandsons was a complex one, based not just on royal pride, impulse, and anger, as Gregory would have it, but on a realistic reading, in a moment of searing intensity and suddenness, of the politics of tonsure and, perhaps, some general awareness that the tonsure itself was a form of torture and shameful mutilation.[50] Gregory goes to some trouble to portray Clotild as a kind and Christian woman and her sons as savage murderers, but then he did not try very hard to understand the dynamic nature of the Merovingian belief in the power of hair or Clotild's informed decision to avoid the enforced shearing of her grandsons at all costs.

The Merovingian family used scissors and razor as a way to trim royal rivals from the family tree, some permanently, some temporarily. The Pippinid mayors of the palace, from whom Charlemagne's line descended, seem to have watched all of this carefully and to have played along, at least for a time. In fact, around 656, Grimoald, the early Carolingian mayor of Austrasia, made a bold, but premature move to graft his own family onto the Merovingian line upon the death of King Sigebert III. He ordered Sigebert's son Dagobert tonsured and sent to a monastery in Ireland and, at the same time, elevated his own son Childebert to the throne.[51] The sources are silent on whether he ordered his own young son to grow his hair long, but it would have been in keeping with other aspects of the coup. Grimoald's son ruled under a Merovingian name and claimed Sigebert as his adoptive father.

Still the length of his hair may not have been a critical issue since at that point in their history the Pippinids were themselves long-haired, even if not as long-haired as the males of the royal family. Indeed, when Theuderic III and his mayor, Ebroin, were overthrown in 673, both were shorn, though not long afterward the mayor grew his hair back and abandoned his monastic prison.[52] Grimoald's daring attempt to attach his family to the Merovingian line startled other Neustrian nobles, who overthrew him and, in time, his son. Neither the Merovingians nor Carolingians were yet finished with this politics of shearing, as contending forces continued to depose Merovingian kings and to cut their hair.

Despite Grimoald's failure to replace from the inside a Merovingian king with a Pippinid one, the Carolingians remained over the next century the dominant mayoral force of Francia and slowly transformed the Merovingians into the infamous do-nothing family of French history, remembered so cruelly in the nursery rhyme, *Le bon roi Dagobert*. When the Carolingian family was finally prepared to overthrow the Merovingian monarchy, it moved on an almost dizzying number of fronts to make sure the line was once and for all finished and its own claims validated.[53]

Pepin the Short asked the pope the famous, but thoroughly loaded question about who ought to rule, he who had the real power or he who presently held the empty title of king. With the Catholic church on side, the Carolingians employed symbols of royal ordination such as anointing that the manifestly royal Merovingians had never needed. But if the elevation of a new family to royal rank was wrung round with innovation and experiment, we need to notice that the deposition of the old family was traditional and entirely Merovingian in execution. Surely that was the point: to overthrow the last representative of the old line according to its own standards. Pepin the Short had King Childeric III's hair cut off and then had him imprisoned in a monastery. Einhard would relate all of this later in a devastatingly effective, if unfair, portrait, for nothing was left to the last Merovingian king to do "except sit on his throne with his hair long and his beard uncut, satisfied [to hold] the name of king only and pretending to rule."[54] Einhard drew a sketch of the Merovingian family's utter enfeeblement. Childeric used to be hauled from his one meager estate to the royal assembly called by the mayor in an ox cart led by a rustic herdsman.[55] As Einhard presents it, one almost feels that the Carolingians were doing the spent Merovingian line a favor by putting it out of its misery.

Yet there is an important matter here that no contemporary source treats. When did the Carolingians themselves become short-haired? In the seventh century, along with other free Franks, their family was likely still, and relatively speaking, long-haired. While the Merovingian dynasty had been vigorous and dominant it had doubtless insisted, as Agathias noted, on its subordinates keeping their hair shorter than their own. Yet as its power ebbed away in the eighth century was the same tonsorial mandate still enforceable? If we may suppose that Grimoald's son Childebert had necessarily grown his hair out when he assumed power, might Charles Martel, the great innovator, have done the same? For a time he even ruled without a Merovingian royal figurehead and took the title of *princeps*. At that stage he could presumably have grown his hair to any length he wished. Einhard's emphasis, however, on the long hair of the last Merovingian king, puppet though he was, may suggest that the old hair code was still in place and that much more impressive late in the history of the Merovingian dynasty because of its capacity to distinguish the royal from the common. It is likely that the mayors of the palace, as they both enfeebled and propped up their Merovingian kings, continued to see hair length as a point of useful distinction in the first half of the eighth century. The purely symbolical potency of Merovingian long hair may even have been exaggerated by them as real royal power slipped away.

It would be wrong to think, as some seem to have, that the Carolingians abandoned the politics of hair, for they continued to play the game with the same relish, though in the long run they would work to change the value of its signs. The pivotal chapter in the story of Frankish hair was, I suspect, being written in the 740s and 750s by Pepin the Short and his circle. And here we have a fascinating piece of information about the moment just prior to the great hirsute turn. Between 735 and 738, when Pepin was already in his early twenties,[56] his father sent him to the Lombard king, with whom the Franks were allied, so:

> that [Liutprand] might take his hair according to custom. And [the king], cutting his hair, became a father to him and sent him back to his father enriched with many kingly gifts.[57]

This ceremony, a variation on the Roman *barbatoria*, is a complex one, both in its meaning and origins. It mixed elements of a rite of passage and one of subordination and was Roman in its background. Roman boys when reaching manhood had submitted their first growth of facial hair, their beards, to the gods, their parents, or the emperor.

The Germanic peoples had initially, I suspect, received a deformed version of the *barbatoria*, since they were often adults when they underwent the rite and they were not always asked to submit their beards, but more often their long hair to their Roman superiors; not then a *barbatoria*, but a *capillaturia* or ritual hair-cutting, though both were often fused together as rites of hair taking.[58] Pepin's case is noteworthy since he surrendered his head hair (called both *capillus* and *caesaries*) and to a German king, not a Roman emperor. Among the Germans, it was this aspect of demonstrating or acknowledging superiority and spiritual fatherhood that came to prevail and to which Liutprand's taking of Pepin's hair belongs. By this ritual the Lombard king and Pepin created, even if they were unaware of its ancients roots, an adoptive family bond; one that Roman fathers and sons had once achieved when they surrendered the boy's first shavings to some superior such as the emperor, who effectively became their *paterfamilias*.[59]

Such token submission hanging on a ritual of hair giving was familiar enough. Alaric, king of the Visigoths, had earlier established his peace with Clovis by insisting that he "touch Clovis's beard and become his godfather."[60] Another account of the same incident replaced the word *tangerit* with *detonderet*, that is, that Alaric cut Clovis's previously uncut beard and became his godfather.[61] The distinction is an important one, for the former describes a mock and largely symbolic ceremony, a pantomime shave, while the latter represents an actual one. Given the relative equality of the two enemies, it is hard not to suspect that the former is closer to the mark; that

Clovis submitted to a symbolic act and not the deed itself. A century later, Gregory, the patrician of the Romans, promised Taso, the duke of the Forum Julii, that "he would cut his beard for him, as is the custom, and make him his son." Instead he had him hunted down and ordered the head of the slaughtered Taso brought to him and, though "caught in a lie, cut off his beard as he had promised."[62]

In Pepin the Short's case, which was the last and in some ways most unusual of the cases of the German *barbatoria/capillaturia*,[63] his father was in need of allies to help him resist the Muslim raids on southern Gaul and so had turned to the king of the Lombards for help. Adrevald of Fleury's ninth-century account of Pepin's haircut, which depends on Paul the Deacon's, says that Charles:

> reached an agreement (*foedus*) with Liutprand, the king of the Lombards, and sent his son Pepin to him so that in the manner of faithful Christians he might be the first to cut his hair and be a spiritual father to him.[64]

By insisting upon taking Pepin's hair as part of the negotiated agreement, King Liutprand demonstrated his royal superiority and Charles Martel's inferior status and subordination. This was less, then, a rite of passage into adulthood for the twenty to twenty-four-year-old Pepin than it was a rite of homage. Frankish boys normally became men at twelve years of age. By the ninth century, Carolingian laymen would exchange the initiatory *barbatoria/capillaturia* for investing their sons with arms, thus oddly for them, as Pierre Riché pointed out, replacing a Roman practice with an even older Germanic one.[65] As the importance of long hair leached away in the Carolingian age, the turn toward investiture was a natural one that followed the shifting locus of power. But beyond the politics of Pepin's shearing, we can see that as late as the 730s Charles and Pepin still subscribed to the Germanic hair code, however variable it was on the ground.[66] Here then we see a magnate family of Ripuarian Franks submitting their hair to a king precisely as an acknowledgment of his royal standing and seniority.

In the light of this ceremony, one has to wonder if in the seventh century the Carolingian mayors of the palace had ritually submitted their own hair, at least once in a lifetime, to their Merovingian superiors. Was Pepin's hair previously uncut (as Adrevald said) because there was no effective Merovingian king to submit it to? The *barbatoria/capillaturia* in Pepin the Short's case was not just a rite of passage into adulthood, but into political power, thus fusing fealty and symbolical sonship. Agathias maintained that the Franks had forbidden others to keep their hair long, and Alaric and Liutprand, in order to confirm pacts, had insisted upon ritual control of the hair of their nominal inferiors. It would probably not surprise us to learn that even as the Pippinids pushed their way up the Merovingian chain of command they willingly submitted their hair to their kings or that those kings demanded the right, at least at some symbolic level, to shear their powerful subjects and royal officials. Would that we had a single description of such an event.

To go further, one might also wonder if the Pippinids as the aiders and abettors of the majesty of Merovingian power actually worked for a time to promote the king's shearing rights and to enhance the magic of his long royal hair. A royal figurehead was that much more useful the more potent he seemed, especially if that potency lay in majestic symbol and not military might. If this were true, then when the Carolingians turned against their long-haired kings and the power of their hair, they were also turning against a policy they themselves had once protected and promoted. Vassalage as an institution ran a similar cycle, since what had served the pioneering mayors may have proved uncomfortable as a source of secure support once they were kings. Some effort was invested by the Carolingians, once royal, in undoing the subversive bonds and institutions that their Pippinid predecessors had employed to undermine Merovingian royal power in the first place.

By the middle of the eighth century Pepin and his advisors had begun to reevaluate the significance of long hair. There were already several famous examples of the rejection of worldly locks within their own family history. Pepin I had intended to marry off his long-haired daughter, Geretrud, but died before a match could be arranged. In the wake of the mayor's death his widow and daughter founded the convent of Nivelles, whereupon the mother cut her daughter's long hair so that she could not be dragged back into the world.[67]

Closer to the great changeover itself, Pepin's own brother Carloman voluntarily tonsured himself, became a monk, and withdrew from public life in 747, a short four years before the day of usurpation.[68] The incident has, however, always been wrapped in its own mysteries and many have searched for an explanation. A century later the matter was still something of a surprise. Adrevald speculated that Carloman had been frightened into monastic life after learning that a visionary had seen his father, Charles Martel, suffering horribly in some hellish purgatorial realm for his worldly greed.[69]

The official line on Carloman's retreat was that it had been a voluntary abandonment of public life for spiritual reasons: *se totondit*, said the house annals, thus emphasizing with the reflexive pronoun Carloman's individual will and agency in choosing tonsure. Said Einhard:

> Carloman walked away from the oppressive chore of governing an earthly kingdom. It is not clear why he did this, but it seems that he was driven by a desire to lead a contemplative life.[70]

Still, Einhard's reluctance to supply more information or to speculate, the same attitude he took when discussing problem points in Charlemagne's career such as his childhood and his sudden divorce of Desiderius's daughter, cannot but arouse suspicion that there was more to Carloman's act than he was prepared to report. If Carloman was forced into monastic retirement, then his tonsure would effectively be another late instance of Merovingian shearing, but now within a mayoral family that was on the very edge of denying the potency of royal hair; if not, then Carloman simply opted out, as others had, in order to retire from the cares of the world into an enshrouding monastic quiet he never quite found.

Thus, two tonsures (Carloman's and Childeric's) and not just one led Pepin to kingship; and the first of these was the more important one, for if two brother mayors had held fast in Francia it is unlikely Pepin would ever have become king. The second tonsure, Childeric III's, was effective, but a largely symbolic gesture; Carloman's was the crucial event in clearing the way for Pepin's elevation and the centralization of power within a single continuing line of Charles Martel's family.

It remains remarkable, then, how often hair played a critical role in the events of those years. Hair mattered almost as much as it had two centuries before, even though the conditions of life and rule had perceptibly changed by the mid-eighth century. The Merovingians, who had ruled in Gaul in old Roman territory, had in part preserved their long hair as a hedge against assimilation, as a badge of *Germanitas* against the predominant Roman style of "ordinary people" (as King Childebert had called them). But this anxiety and racial insecurity had doubtless faded over time north of the Rhine in lands outside the old empire. The Carolingians were not only not afraid to Romanize, they embraced it, as Theoderic the Great once had, at least under Cassiodorus's comforting hand. By the 740s short hair appealed to the Carolingians not just because it was un-Merovingian, but also because it was both more Christian and more Roman.

Pepin's counselors, men like Boniface and Fulrad of St-Denis, both of whom were themselves tonsured monks, promoted a rejection of what they perceived as pagan practices in all fields. To the degree to which the Merovingian line had, with the support of its mayors, convinced the Frankish world that its long hair was potent Germanic magic, it had also produced the very conditions that would lead to the pointed Christian rejection of it. An early form of that backlash had come from Gregory of Tours. His general disdain for long hair would finally have its complementary response in Pepin and his circle of monks.

It was with the deposition of the last Merovingian that the Carolingian rejection of long hair as an essential basis for kingship was publicly announced. The argument put to the pope was one centered on a question of merit—that kingship was not just a matter of being, but of doing. If long hair was the sign of the former, energy and activity were proofs of the latter. And how easy it must have seemed to destroy the former sign of royal being by a public act of ritual shearing.

The overthrow of Childeric was brilliantly orchestrated. Pepin did not have Childeric killed, but tonsured and put away. By this act the Carolingians seem, on the surface at least, to have subscribed one last time to the notion that symbolic, if not real power had resided in the long hair of the Merovingian kings. The fusion of a real and ritual deposition was a powerful public statement, for the shearing of Childeric belonged to a symbolical language all the Franks still understood. The Carolingians now held the power to shear their subordinates. But the important point was that a long-haired Merovingian was not succeeded by a long-haired Carolingian; instead it was the end, at least in terms of royal head hair, of a specific code of royal symbolism and legitimation. Thus, it was probably in the 740s and early 750s that Pepin and his line cropped their own long hair once and for all and their hair-shortening was infinitely more important than the public shearing of the last Merovingian, but no one seems to have noticed or said a word. In Pieter Bruegel's *Fall of Icarus*, the herdsman studies the sky and the fisherman fishes, but no one hears the splash or sees the feet and feathers sinking into the green sea.

We shall never encounter a long-haired Carolingian king. I even went so far for a brief time as to wonder whether Pepin's later epithet "the Short" might refer to his hair, rather than his height. It did not seem at first such a farfetched idea when one remembers that one of his grandsons would be called "the Bald." And there might have been some confusion of identification caused by Pepin the Hunchback, who was *nanus et gipperosus*, a dwarf and hunchbacked.[71] But at this juncture, and without further evidence, it seems impossible to get beyond Notker the Stammerer's legends about Pepin's small size, which were probably the source of the epithet.[72] Still, perhaps it would be better now to think of the king as Pepin the Short-Haired since he deliberately wore his hair short, but could do nothing whatsoever about his height.

Pepin's royal line would be consistently short-haired, and that was to be a deliberate statement about the nature of their power and its source. Not only did their short hair stand as a visible rejection of the previous dynasty and its hirsute hocus-pocus, but it also stood as a sign of the more complete Christian orientation of their house. Still one has to wonder if the Carolingian preoccupation with regalia, as studied so intimately by Percy Schramm, was not a form of compensation for their lack of powerful locks. No Carolingian king would ever be depicted without a radiant crown on his head as Childeric and Agilulf, both possessors of long hair, had earlier been.[73] Perhaps symbols never truly die but just shift in form; in this case from long locks to glorious crowns.

Boniface and Fulrad may have been the architects and advocates of a new set of symbols, one that was biblically based.[74] Psalm 67:22 had promised David that God would "crush the skulls of the enemy, the hairy heads of those who walk in sin," which is a passage that may lurk behind Gregory of Tours's fixation on Merovingian locks; or perhaps it was Saint Paul's warning to the Corinthians that it was both unnatural and shameful for a man to grow his hair long (1 Cor. 11:14). Boniface's rightful successor as the conscience of the Carolingian court was Alcuin and he was adamant in his Christian rejection of long hair. In 793 when he was attempting to comprehend why God had been so angered with the Northumbrians that he had allowed or caused the Northmen to sack Lindisfarne, he scolded King Ethelred and his nobles for their pagan backsliding:

> Consider the dress, hair, and luxurious ways of both rulers and people. Look at your hair, which you have wished to be like that on pagan beards and pagan heads. Does the terror of those, whose hair you would imitate, not hang over us even now?[75]

Thus, the Carolingians were also to have another powerful reason for keeping their hair short in the ninth century, for their enemies were a long and blond-haired pagan people. Centuries later Scandinavians would still think of rulers as a type as long-haired, for the king pieces among the Lewis chessmen, which were carved from walrus tusks in twelfth-century Christian Norway, have (in all cases but one) hair that spills down onto their backs in tresses.[76] Long hair, along with crowns and full beards, still denoted the royal person in the far north. Theodulf of Orléans fantasized that one day all foreign peoples—the Arabs with their long flowing hair and the Huns with their hair long and braided—would come to serve Christ and drop to their knees, necks outstretched, before Charlemagne.[77] But he never imagined that these peoples would offer up their hair to Charlemagne. For Theodulf, writing toward the end of Charlemagne's reign, hair had become a point of descriptive and, perhaps, ethnic difference between the Christian Carolingians and the heathen other.

Nor could the Carolingians quite forget the stories of Samson undone by Delilah or Nisus by Scylla when she took a lock of his hair,[78] but they found ways to dismiss the supposed potency of hair. It was slowly stripped of its infused potency. Hrabanus Maurus spoke of Samson's profound mistake in believing that his power lay in his hair, "for God does not care about our hair."[79]

Thus, when Charlemagne proceeded into St-Peter's on that momentous Christmas day and became the emperor of Rome, he fulfilled a Romanizing and Christianizing destiny to which his family had been tending for a half century, and not the least part of that tending was his short hair and mustache.

There are no contemporary painted portraits of Charlemagne, so we must turn to coins, the image on his lead seal or *bulla*, and a much compromised mosaic to judge his appearance. The few coins bearing an image of the emperor were minted after Roman imperial types, so that they both reinforce and exaggerate the theme of Charlemagne's Roman persona as on them he wears a laurel wreath and toga (figure 1.9).[80] But he also sports short hair and a mustache and these traits were not copied after some imperial model, for no Roman coin depicts a mustachioed emperor.[81] Rather, they reflected Charlemagne's own chosen style, which became the preferred style of his royal house. In giving Charlemagne his mustache, the minter proceeded as did other Carolingian image-makers by working with ancient models, but choosing to honor contemporary cultural facts.[82] The image of Charlemagne preserved on one of his lead *bullae* (the one bearing on the obverse the inscription RENOVATIO ROMAN. IMP.) depicts the short-haired emperor with a drooping mustache, diadem, *paludamentum* or military cloak, and lance (figure 1.10).[83] His direct descendants were also to be

1.9   An imperial coin portrait of Charlemagne (Staatlichen Museen, Berlin).

1.10 Drawing after F. Le Blanc, 1689, of the image of Charlemagne on one of his lead *bullae*; the obverse bears the inscription RENOVATIO ROMAN. IMP.

shown with official mustaches: on Louis the Pious's gold coins, on a gold medallion of Lothar I, on a seal of Louis the German, and the seals of the emperors.[84]

An early-seventeenth-century antiquarian said that the mosaic depiction of Charlemagne in the Lateran Palace in Rome, which was still visible at the time, showed that Charlemagne's "chin is shaven. On the upper lip he has two twisted mustaches in the fashion of the Turks or Franks."[85] One can see what he meant in the various drawings and reconstructions of the Lateran mosaic in which we do not quite see a Salvador Dali mustache, but one markedly different from the other Carolingian mustaches to be seen in northern Carolingian art. Had the mosaicist given Charlemagne's image an Italian twist?

But why a mustache? It is hard not to suspect that by wearing a mustache Charlemagne was deliberately imitating Theoderic the Great. If we may judge by the gold medallion portrait and the amethyst gem the Ostrogothic king's short, but bushy mustache was something of a novelty (figures 1.6 and 1.7). The Romans never wore mustaches without accompanying beards or at least they are never depicted or described as doing so. Yet Theoderic (and his successor Theodahad in imitation of him) took up a style that was relatively unusual even among the Germans, many of whom wore full beards with mustaches.[86] Sidonius tells us that Theoderic II, king of the Goths, was careful each day to have the barber remove the bristles that grew beneath his nose.[87] Latin, it should be pointed out here, has no perfectly satisfactory word for "mustache" since the uneconomical *labri superioris capilli* seems a definition rather than a simple signifier.[88] Many a *barba* must have hidden within it a mustache, the latter being an understood part of a greater hairy whole. Indeed, the very lack of a Latin word for mustache may have resulted from the fact that it was not common for Roman males to have a mustache without a beard, and yet Theoderic chose just such a distinctive style, probably in order to distinguish himself once again from the Romans whom he ruled.

And Charlemagne apparently chose to adopt that singular style. We do not know whether his father Pepin ever wore a mustache, so that it may well have fallen to Charlemagne himself to set a house style for facial hair, one that his heirs would honor in imitation of his importance. He could not have followed the Merovingian style since the Carolingians had soundly rejected the long hair and beards of the line they had usurped, and so he took up Theoderic's mustache. How Charlemagne learned of the Ostrogoth's mustache we may never know. The gold medallion and amethyst gem were unlikely to have come his way, but Charlemagne visited Ravenna several times and after becoming emperor had the large bronze statue of Theoderic transported to Aachen and set up in his court-yard.[89] Sadly despite two contemporary descriptions of the statue we cannot be sure the statue actually depicted Theoderic, though his name was affixed to it, or know anything about the appearance of the head upon it.[90] Perhaps the bronze figure, if it was Theoderic, did sport a mustache and on-the-shoulder hair, which would be a test of the statue's authenticity if we knew more about it, or Charlemagne may have seen some other now lost image of the Ostrogoth or had simply heard stories of the king's mustache.

If Charlemagne's mustache does evoke Theoderic's it opens up for us a fascinating set of cultural resonances. For this would lead us to that other Charlemagne, the Germanic one whom we know less well, who loved to listen to songs of the warrior deeds of great Germans and who embraced Rome as Theoderic had while also attempting to preserve a careful distance from it. This would be a Charlemagne who rejected things Merovingian, but still sought out a superior Germanic model in Theoderic. The Ostrogoth, despite the dark reputation that later haunted his name in the Carolingian west, likely seemed to Charlemagne the first German to govern Rome and, therefore, his immediate precursor as a Germanic emperor.[91] Looming behind all of this was the powerful impression that Ravenna and its architecture had made on him. To carry back to Aachen the monumental statue of Theoderic was one expression of Charlemagne's admiration for the great one; to wear a mustache may have been another.

Charlemagne and his heirs would all maintain short (or medieval military) mustaches as part of their dynastic style, but these seem to have been largely decorative in effect, having no divine significance. In the game of riddles Alcuin played with the emperor's son, the question arose, "What is a beard?" To which Alcuin said, "A difference between the sexes, a mark of age."[92] All divinity had been stripped from both beard and hair. Einhard, in his famous portrait of Charlemagne did not even mention the emperor's mustache; he simply said that the king's hair was gray and his head handsome and round.[93]

1.11   Charlemagne portrait, *Retable du Parliament de Paris* (Permission RMN).

Ironically, in a direct reversal and misunderstanding of the Carolingian house style, the later image of Charlemagne that would survive in statues, portraits, and prose would cover him with hair (figure 1.11). Even in the *Song of Roland*, which contains the distillation of an image of Charlemagne that had been fermenting for three hundred years, the old king is bearded

1.12   Reliquary of Charlemagne, mid-fourteenth century (Domschatz Aachen, photo: Ann Munchow).

and fussily stokes his beard and mustache in worry. By the fourteenth century, on his splendid reliquary, Charlemagne's head is absolutely radiant and his beard and mustache carefully manicured (figure 1.12). Outside Notre Dame cathedral in Paris today, one can see the statue that was made for the Universal Exposition mounted in Paris in 1867. The Eiffel Tower, that tinker-toy construction of aggressive modernity, was made for the exposition in 1889. But Louis Rochet's statue is all wrong for the sculptor imagined a hairy old Charlemagne accompanied by his two shaggy retainers, Roland and Oliver. His Charlemagne belongs entirely to the *Song of Roland* and not to the ninth century (figure 1.13), but then the Middle

1.13   Drawing after Vétault of Louis Rochet's statue of Charlemagne, Roland, and Oliver from 1867, which now stands outside the Cathedral of Notre Dame in Paris.

Ages itself soon forgot Charlemagne's own hair preferences and pictured him instead with a full beard and long hair.

The Carolingian family was to pride itself on its accomplishments and its Christianity, not the length of its locks. In the ninth-century paintings that adorned the palace at Ingelheim, as described by Ermold, the exiled poet, the martial acts of Charles Martel, Pepin, and Charlemagne were celebrated, but the poet made no mention of hair at all. When Theodulf of Orléans paused to distinguish two of Charlemagne's sons, he did so by noting that the elder one had a youthful growth of hair on his face.[94] This, we should note, was Alcuin's *honor aetatis* and not the blood beard of the Chatti.

If Charlemagne's mustache was deliberately understated, it was still, if one thinks about it, a powerful statement about who he and these new Carolingian kings were or, rather, what they were not. They were not the hairy, half-Christian Merovingian kings of Gregory of Tours's caricaturing; they were Christian, civilized, short-haired, mustachioed, and still German. A mustache might also, in the ninth century, distinguish a noble from a churchman. Though monks and priests in the ninth century on occasion had beards as does the old gray beard from St-Martin of Tours seen in the First Bible of Charles the Bald, mustaches by themselves belonged particularly to kings (figure 1.14). Even the poor seem to have generally gone about clean shaven, at least as they are portrayed in manuscripts (see figure 7.1). If the two noble looking individuals in the first register of the painting of the Labors of the Months, who represent falconry and the hunting of small game, which were the aristocratic pastimes of February and March, have traces of beards, that too was in keeping with the beards that many noble Franks wore. In an age when shaving must have been a scabrous experience, perhaps only the well-off could command a decent shave. An early ninth-century fresco in the monastic church of San Benedetto in Malles high in the Italian Alps shows a short-haired, bearded layman, probably the patron of the church.[95] It was this noble hair style that Frederick Barbarossa, he of the red beard, adopted in the twelfth century. But everything suggests that Carolingian kings had mustaches and not beards.

Long Germanic hair or, at least, its symbolic significance largely disappeared in the ninth century. But the long hair of the Merovingian world had had some value in the earlier Frankish politics of shear or be sheared, since it had been a quick and effective way to shape dynastic destinies. The Carolingians did not entirely give up on cutting the hair of the rebellious and the displaced. A story was still circulating late in ninth-century Italy that before Charlemagne would agree to the petition of some Beneventan magnates to allow Grimoald III to succeed his father as the Lombard duke

1.14 Presentation Miniature from the First Bible of Charles the Bald (Paris, Bibliothèque Nationale, ms. lat. 1, fol. 423r).

of Benevento in 788, he insisted that they shave off their beards and insert his name on their charters and coins.[96] If the incident actually occurred, one might still ask whether Charlemagne was just dealing with the Beneventan nobility in terms of their own expectations about what constituted symbolic submission or if he was actually trying to impose upon them the new Carolingian hair code.

For its part the Carolingian dynasty would continue a now delimited form of political tonsure, one that made no claims about royal power springing from long locks, but still wanted rivals securely put away. What mattered to them was effective monastic imprisonment. In a world largely without jails, the monastery was the next best thing; an institution filled with monastic guards who seemed never to sleep. Pepin the Hunchback, the eldest, if less than fully legitimate son of Charlemagne, rose up in revolt, but was tonsured and eventually placed in the monastery of Prüm by his father.[97] When Louis the Pious began to worry about revolt within his extended family, he ordered his illegitimate half-brothers tonsured and placed under "free custody" in monasteries.[98] In 830 his own sons tried to force him to receive the tonsure and thus reject the world and its highest office.[99] Between 849 and 852 Charles the Bald had two troublesome family members tonsured and put in monasteries.[100] He had committed his own son Carloman to the monastery of St-Médard of Soissons in order to prevent him from succeeding to the throne.[101]

But Carolingian kings soon discovered, now that hair was no longer magically imbued with power, that simple tonsure and monastic confinement were not always enough and so they turned throughout the ninth century to the more brutal removal of rivals, rebels, and the unwanted by blinding them. For surely, they thought, a blind man could never be an effective king in a peripatetic age, since he could not safely ride a horse. So when Bernard of Italy rose up in rebellion against Louis the Pious, he was not tonsured, but rather (as custom suggests) a red hot stiletto was put to his eyes and he soon died.[102] Louis may have wept, but Bernard was no longer a threat to his direct dynastic line. His son, Charles the Bald, worked the same brutal punishment upon one of his own rebellious sons and another king called Louis the Blind bore the very name of his punishment as he tried to preserve some slender portion of power.[103] The blind losers of these dynastic disputes would surely have been better served by a simple shearing, but too often the medieval monastery proved to be an insecure gaol.

The Carolingian kings who peer out at us from painted manuscripts and a few pieces of sculpture seem at first glance remarkably similar. Louis the Pious, in the famous painting of him as a Christian hero in Hrabanus Maurus's *On the Praises of the Holy Cross*, seems almost to lack a mustache.[104] But I suspect that the artist meant to depict it and hence the drooping lines below his nose are probably the outlines of a mustache rather than the line of his upper lip (figure 1.15). The same technique was used on the famous portrait of Lothar I that appears in the Gospel book made for him at St-Martin of Tours (figure 1.16). The very fact that the written sources are silent on Louis's facial hair and that of all other Carolingian rulers is in itself revealing; Carolingian poets and historians just no longer paid much attention to hair. It had ceased to be a matter of any great symbolic importance. Still the mustache did identify and it is unlikely that the mysterious portrait of a ruler being crowned in the Sacramentary

1.15   Portrait of Louis the Pious in a manuscript of Hrabanus Maurus's *On the Praises of the Holy Cross* (Vatican City, Bibliotheca Apostolica Vaticana, Reg. lat. 124, fol. 4v).

Fragment of Metz (Paris, B.N. lat. 1141, fol. 2v) depicts some Carolingian king, since the figure lacks a mustache. By the same standard, the figure's short hair should also count Clovis out of the running (figure 1.17).[105] Would we then be left with Constantine, who was depicted as short-haired and clean shaven on his arch, monumental head, and coins, or just with the likeness of a royal type, a youthful, universal Christian king?

The paintings do not mislead us about Louis the Pious's sons, all of whom wore mustaches. Lothar I in two famous portraits has the distinct and characteristic Carolingian head hair—short hair, mustache, beardless

1.16   Portrait of Lothar I in the Gospels of Lothar (Paris, Bibliothèque Nationale, ms. lat. 266, fol. 1v).

(figures 1.16 and 1.18). Charles the Bald is similarly portrayed. In his Psalter, which contains the most unusual portrait of the king, Charles's hair and mustache are gray; indeed, his mustache is difficult to pick out, but it is there (figure 1.19). A different, more idealized and sharper portrait of the king is to be found in his First Bible, which was painted in 845 at Tours

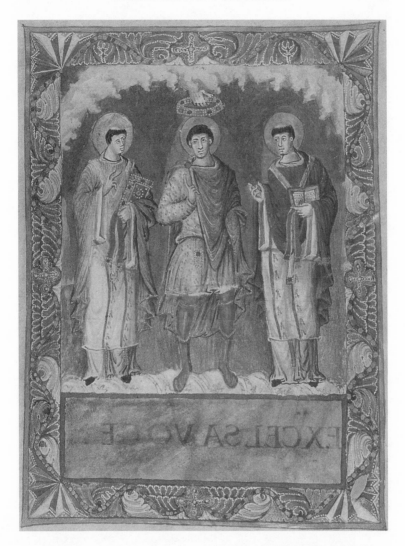

1.17   Crowning in the Sacramentary Fragment of Metz (Paris, Bibliothèque Nationale, ms. lat. 1141, fol. 2v).

(figure 1.14).[106] The same type is seen in the Codex Aureus of St-Emmeram from 869–870 (figure 4.1),[107] and in the Bible of San Paolo, where apparently his new wife, Richildis, stands at his side (figure 1.20). In these portraits the mustaches are full and black.

On the small equestrian statue long thought to depict Charlemagne and now attributed by most to Charles the Bald,[108] we again see the same

1.18   Lothar I enthroned, Lothar Psalter (British Library, Addit. ms. 37768, fol. 4r).

mustache (figure 1.21), as we do also on the wood and ivory throne of Saint
Peter, which was given to the pope and upon which popes were to sit for
centuries (figure 1.22).[109]

Was Charles in fact bald? His crown-covered head in the surviving illuminations disguises what was there or not there. The king's pate on the
equestrian statuette does possess a clear design of hair and below the crown
a full fringe of short hair that surrounds the back of the rider's neck but
never touches his shoulders (figure 1.23).[110] And Janet Nelson and others
have suggested that the epithet may be ironical, that in fact Charles, the
grandson of Charlemagne, may have been extremely hairy.[111] If that were
true, it would be exceedingly strange that no one from Charles's chirpy
court ever commented on his hairiness. And, indeed, the so-called
Genealogy of Frankish Kings, a text that comes from Fontanell perhaps as
early as 869, does explicitly state that Louis was the father and Judith the
mother of "Karolus caluus" and it is a source without a trace of irony.[112] By
the end of the tenth century, Richer of Rheims and his near contemporary

1.19   Psalter of Charles the Bald (Paris, Bibliothèque Nationale, ms. lat. 1152, fol. 3v).

Adhemar of Chabannes would both call Charles "the Bald," but only that one Carolingian source seems to talk about Charles's hair and it is unlikely that it was the source of the later use of the epithet. If Charles's baldness was ironical and he was, in fact, a strikingly hairy Carolingian, why do we not find even one Carolingian poet making sport of the comic imagery of it all? If he was actually bald, why did disapproving enemies such as the east Frankish annalists ignore the epithet entirely? Instead they preferred to call him a tyrant, but why would they have missed the opportunity? In any

1.20 Charles the Bald enthroned (Rome, Bible of San Paolo fuori le mura, fol. 334v: Istituto Poligrafico e Zecca dello Stato S.p.A., Rome).

event, the Carolingians seem to have largely ceased thinking that hair was a source of powerful symbolic importance.

We may never know whether Charles II was bald, but we can be sure that baldness itself was a subject of some interest to medieval men and women. Perhaps the strangest poem written in the ninth century can help

1.21   Bronze equestrian statue of Charlemagne or Charles the Bald (Musée du Louvre).

us to tie together the few strands that remain to this study. A Carolingian monk wrote a poem of 146 hexameter lines on the theme of baldness, but each word also begins with C, the first letter of *caluus* or bald.[113] Richard Sullivan said that, "It would take a congress of eminent psychiatrists to explain what prompted Hucbald of Saint-Amand to write" such a poem.[114] Perhaps, we do not need psychiatrists after all, but an understanding of the shifting interest in hair in the early Middle Ages. When Hucbald was a young monk he had known Charles the Bald, but he wrote his poem not for that emperor, who died in 877, but for Hatto, the archbishop of Mainz, who did not assume office until 891. Hucbald's uncle, Milo, also of St-Amand, had written an elaborate and lengthy poem on sobriety for

1.22   Charles the Bald on the Cathedra Petri, the wood and ivory throne of Saint Peter (St. Peter's Basilica, Vatican City: permission Fabbrica di San Pietro in Vaticano).

1.23   Detail of the top and back of the head of the equestrian statue (Paris, Musée du Louvre: photo Laura Dutton).

Charles the Bald, but when he died in 872, it had fallen to his nephew to forward that sobering poem to the king.

In the preface he added to his uncle's poem, Hucbald had already begun to explore the possibilities of alliteration and panegyric, but no youthful experimentation could compare with the alliterative excess and wicked irony to be found in the mature *Eclogues on Bald Men*, which he composed twenty or more years later. The poet does not, as one might have expected, simply sing the praises of tonsured priests and monks (see figure 1.24), but rather of all the world's bald men. The poem's refrain is:

> Carmina, clarisonae, caluis cantate, Carmenae,

which, with allowances made for the attempt to recapture the 'initial' effect, one could render as:

> Sing songs, sweet sounding spirits, celebrating society's shorn.

Despite being great fun and a display of technical virtuosity, Hucbald's poem has a serious side to it, for he thought that the shorn stood closer to Christ and to heaven than the hairy and nothing and no position had been

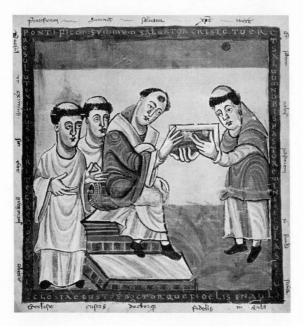

1.24 Hrabanus Maurus presents his *On the Praises of the Holy Cross* to Pope Gregory IV (Vienna, Österreichische Nationalbibliothek, Cod. 652, fol. 2v: Bildarchiv d. ÖNB, Wien).

denied them in the past [lines 15–23]. Bald men had risen to the highest ranks of the church [25–33], had been among the most learned [35–43], and had been judges [45–53], warriors [55–63], and doctors [65–73]. In response to the world's jeers, bald men had learned humility and chastity [75–93]. To encourage them, Hucbald celebrated famous bald men such as the Apostle Paul[115] and he lashed out at the laughing mob [95–133]. For him bald men and their wise counsel stood at the very center of the circuit of heaven [135–43].

Whether Hucbald was aware of it or not, his praise of bald men belonged to a continuing medieval debate on the meaning of hair. The Byzantine theologian Synesius of Cyrene in the late fourth century had written an extended praise of baldness in response to its maligners.[116] And in the twelfth century, the Cistercian monk Burchard of Bellevaux would write an elaborate and lengthy praise of beards, which the lay-brothers of his order wore in order to distinguish themselves from monks.[117] But Hucbald's discussion of hair belongs to the final phase of Carolingian history.

If in the early Frankish period, important hair had been royal, by the late ninth century it or its absence had taken on a largely ecclesiastical meaning. The Carolingian family had as mayors of the Merovingian palace played along with the politics of shearing and had validated it one last time in 751 when they overthrew the last of the Merovingian kings. But after that, they went their own way as short-haired, mustachioed kings. By the end of the ninth century, hair like so much else had become a symbol invested with meaning by churchmen, not kings. In the hands of poets, its symbolic importance came to circle around the issue of patronage. Hucbald introduced his alliterative tour de force on baldness with a fifty-four line poetic plea for the patronage of Archbishop Hatto. The question he put to his patron was a straightforward one: if patronage dried up, who would compose beautiful poems for bald men. He called on Hatto [lines 2–3], as "the smooth summit and glory of bald men," to come to his aid [34–35]. For what had finally happened, of course, to the Carolingian world was the death of the royal court. By the late ninth century, bishops and abbots had become the best and surest sources of patronage—they were the holders of the only courts in town, and theirs was a circle occupied by the hairless. A king's head hair now mattered less to clients than a bishop's lack of it.

So if we began with long hair and with blood beards, watched as Pepin the Short and his successors cropped their own long hair, and saw Charlemagne and his heirs cultivate Theoderican mustaches, we end with hairless bishops and tonsured monks, for that is where we are left at the end of the early Middle Ages, bald and waiting for our hair to grow back.

CHAPTER 2

CHARLEMAGNE, KING OF BEASTS

On the cold and freshly cut edge of a new millennium Otto III, that most precocious of Ottonian emperors, opened Charlemagne's tomb, refreshed his Carolingian predecessor's body with oil, and clothed it in white vestments. Before closing the sarcophagus, he wrapped the corpse in a purple cloth decorated with elephants.[1] Otto knew what we, who have been too influenced by Einhard's confining categories, have forgotten: that Charlemagne was also king of the beasts. He was "the lion who reigns over all living creatures and wild beasts."[2] When encountering hyperbolic praise, as we do in Alcuin's animal boast, we should try not to hurry past the obvious: here that Charlemagne's power was thought to extend over both the human and animal worlds. Otto's elephantine winding-sheet said the same, if more softly.

Unlike Orpheus, Saint Francis, and Dr. Dolittle most of us today are strangely alienated from the animal world to which we properly belong. The cat curled up on the couch and the tethered dog barking in the distance make the case since they are living artifacts of the human world that we as a species have been making and remaking daily for the last ten thousand years. Most of us no longer compete with other animals, but eat them, fence them in, work them, kill them for sport or as vermin, protect them in reserves, collect them as curiosities and companions, and transform them into icons of our own aggressively inclusive imaginations.[3]

As far back as we can see it has been thus, but we need to recognize that the nature and balance of the human engagement with the animal world in the early Middle Ages was different from ours, being both more intense and immediate.[4] Early medieval men and women lived in the midst of a *habitatio animalium*, a haunt of animals, yet little of that primary fact of animal existence surfaces in the written record of human affairs. Peasants and animals may have numerically dominated the past, but for the most part they fell outside the narrow range of learned attention.

For too long animals have been regarded as ahistorical beings and natural history, strangely enough, as having no history because it has no documents. Paleontology and the unraveling of the animal genome (perhaps the most marvelous document of them all) may at last surrender a confident chronological sequence, but of such long-range dimensions that we may never fit it comfortably into the tiny temporal dimensions of human history.

The Germanic world out of which the northern Carolingian peoples came was a world of dark forests and vigorous animality, which today we can best sense through its surviving art, an art of animal figures twisting for all time on bronze brooches, of the wolf assistants on the Sutton Hoo pendant stretching their mouths around Odin's head as though caught in mid-whisper, of the sinuous Uroboros-like animal forms forever nibbling on each other's body parts on manuscript pages and church trumeaux, of dragon-headed ships (both Viking and Carolingian), and of the ballooning, fire-breathing dragon banner leading soldiers into battle on a page of the Golden Psalter of St-Gall.[5] Long before all of that, paleolithic cave painters had not so much reduced their world to a stark dichotomy of humans and animals as begun there, their reddish and ochre drawings animated by things alive and in motion, landscape understood, individuality absent. That was a matter of circumstance and attention. And the Carolingians would not so much reject the long proto-European obsession with animals as complicate and enrich it, humanize and civilize it, for they were moving off in new directions.

They were to have a less simple and codified relationship with animals than their predecessors had as they left behind some of the elemental relationships known to their hunter–gatherer forebears. In their world the boundaries between the animal and the human were becoming increasingly indistinct and some people were worried. What were they to make of reports of strange creatures and disturbing natural events inside and outside their shifting borders? The old values had, of course, not entirely passed away. In 846 a man was discovered fornicating with a mare and was sentenced to be burned alive.[6] Sex was one of the age-old barriers solidly set down between human and beast and the harsh judgment of Frankish customary law fulfilled the unforgiving prohibitions against bestiality laid out by the Old Testament (Lev. 20:15, Exod. 22:18). Thus, one familiar and unmoveable line drawn between humans and animals continued to hold, but few such certainties remained as the Carolingian peoples began to ponder the wider world in which they lived.[7] Dicuil, an Irish scholar at the courts of Charlemagne and then his son, had learned that the Neuri, a tribe living on the Dnieper, were in the habit of transforming themselves into wolves during the summer months and returning to human form in the fall.[8]

Monsters seemed to be abroad in this world. Dicuil's wide horizon was filled with fabulous creatures: with ferocious unicorns that could run victims through with razor-sharp, four-foot-long horns, with paralyzing, hypnotic-eyed hyenas, and with enormous worms that could drag even elephants down to their deaths.[9] Ratramnus of Corbie had heard old tales of the monstrous births of calves and snakes to women and yet still tried to reconcile two contradictory notions: that only humans could come from humans and that the monstrous offspring of humans still lacked human souls.[10] Yet even monsters lay within the divine plan, for "these [creatures] do not arise against the law of nature, but arise by divine arrangement, for in fact the law of nature is an arrangement of the divine."[11] Here we encounter Carolingian thought at its most challenging: with its practical acceptance of the given as the starting point for intellectual inquiry, but without sufficient awareness that the given itself might be misapprehended and that it was not entirely sound for the end points of any investigation to lie in the untested realm of received opinion.

Ratramnus's reflections are found in the letter he sent to Rimbert, Anskar's missionary successor to the far north, about the classification of the *Cynocephali* or dog-headed creatures.[12] Were they, he wondered, the descendants of Adam or animals proper, a question earlier raised by Augustine in the *City of God*?[13] In bringing the matter to the attention of his friend, Rimbert revealed his own gnawing anxiety over the nature of the beings who occupied the extra-Carolingian world, for even if the Gospels had commanded him to preach the word to all creatures (Mark 16:15) it still made sense for a missionary to want to know what he was likely to confront out there in strange lands.

Rimbert's unease may not have been all of his own making. The warrior peoples of the far north had long waged a low-grade campaign of disinformation in order to instill fear in their enemies, one that came to serve as a counterforce to the aggressive missionary message assaulting them from the south. Rimbert and his brothers had heard disturbing stories that the *Cynocephali* lived in the north.[14] But these tales of dog-headed men were not utter inventions, for various Scandinavian peoples did wear wolf masks in their rituals and dances. Deformed tales of their pagan rites may have slipped south to unsettle peoples who could not hope to verify or understand them.[15]

Yet Ratramnus's task as a cloistered monk was not to determine in the field whether the *Cynocephali* actually existed, but to examine by reason and authority the status of these creatures and their particular place in the scheme of God's wide creation. He approached the matter as though it were one of those examinable questions that had been considered in eso-teric debate at Charlemagne's court; the issue over whether darkness and night were something or nothing was the most famous of these, but there were others.[16]

Ratramnus denied that the barking of the *Cynocephali* or the shape and position of their canine heads automatically made them animals. Instead he looked for evidence of human reason. He learned from his sources that these creatures reputedly possessed laws, lived in villages, cultivated and harvested crops, and did not go around naked as did other beasts. In presenting their virtues and customs in these terms, Ratramnus was defining the human or, at least, a Carolingian version of it; hence, to the monk, the importance of prudent vesture as one test of moral decency. In following laws, living by common consent in villages, and farming together, the *Cynocephali* manifested both reason and an evident grasp of the moral economy of settled life.

Behind agriculture and clothing Ratramnus also saw the possession of art or skill, which he thought belonged exclusively to the rational human soul.

> But it has never been heard or believed that animals of one kind [can] by themselves take care of [other] animals, especially those of a domestic kind, keep them and force them to obey rules and follow regular routines. But since the *Cynocephali* are said to possess a multitude of domestic animals, then animal savagery does not fit them because they tame their domestic beasts with gentleness.[17]

Here he set out a relational definition of humanity: humans are not animals because they keep animals. Hence he could not but conclude that the dog-headed men were part of an extended human family, descendants all of Adam and Eve.

Still things remained fuzzy at the extreme edges of Ratramnus's rough science of classification, as pygmies, Macrobii (giants from Ethiopia), and hippopodes (horse-footed humans) pressed against the comfortable compartments of Noah's ark.[18] Even Saint Christopher was reputed to have been a dog-headed man or a giant, further evidence of the elasticity of the human as a category. For Ratramnus, then, it was not just appearance, but rationality and rational behavior that defined the human. His understanding of what humans were was categorically centered, but anatomically and culturally plastic. If Augustine had deemed the *Cynocephalus* more animal than human and Isidore had thought of him as a wild man,[19] Ratramnus boldly came to think of the dog-headed as human and civilized, no matter how animal-like in appearance.

Lines of a different kind between the human and animal were already faint, both within Christianity where three of the evangelists have animal symbols and at the Carolingian royal court where members of Charlemagne's immediate circle took animal nicknames.[20] Theodulf proudly called himself a clan wolf (*gentilupus*), fierce wolf (*trux lupus*), and lazy wolf (*lupus inertis*), thus dressing himself in the metaphorical skin of animals and animal powers.[21] In one deliberately mystifying poem meant for decoding by his fellow, puzzle-solving courtiers, Theodulf leaves us as external readers almost entirely at sea.[22] He begins with the swirling of birds (swans, ravens, magpies, a parrot, a diving bird [*mergulus*], and a crow), who represent people at court, before returning us to the drier land of nicknamed court figures such as Charlemagne (David), Alcuin (Flaccus), and Einhard (Bezaleel). For his learned friends at court half the humanist fun was in figuring out who was who and what was meant. Pieter Bruegel almost eight hundred years later would play a similar game of buried references, this time in paint, for his humanist viewers.[23]

Alcuin too was fond of animal sport and wrote one riddling poem to a friend about a two-headed, multi-toothed beast (a comb) that had fallen into his possession.[24] He also delighted in animal nicknames and called his friends and students by such names as the eagle, cuckoo, calf, and animal.[25] Most intriguing of all is the animal-likenesses letter he wrote in September 799 to Adalhard, the abbot of Corbie.[26] Behind the menagerie of animal nicknames with which he loads the letter lie the people and dramatic events of that pregnant year. Late in April Pope Leo III had been assaulted in Rome and after escaping had been brought to Paderborn to seek the protection and support of the king. It was a famous meeting since it led to Charlemagne's expedition to Rome and the imperial coronation of the next year. In September Alcuin was desperate to know where things stood and so wrote in animal code to the prominent and well-connected Adalhard. He wanted to know, with all the rumors flying about, what the eagle [Leo] and the lion [Charlemagne] had agreed upon. Adalhard was a cock, now silent, whom the wolf or devil had silenced;[27] Alcuin a sparrow placidly waiting for the cock to crow. The sparrow accused the rooster of having been transformed into a cuckoo, a bird known to fall silent under the blistering heat of the summer sun. Unidentified ravens, doves, partridges, and an ibis flit through the letter, but Charlemagne and the lupine devil are its only mammals; the ecclesiastics are all birds as they probably were in Theodulf's poem as well.[28]

Charlemagne's court was then and on set occasions a mock haunt of animals and the stock qualities of animals were assigned and played off against each other for the amusement of learned courtiers and royal watchers. Boethius had long before reduced people by their virtues and vices to animal types and Machiavelli much later would urge the prince to draw on the animal as well as the human sides of his nature.[29]

Often in the ninth century these animal associations were negative. Thus Theodulf impugned those whispering words of bribery (as the serpent once had to Eve) as serpents, reptiles, and horned snakes.[30] And he urged his fellows to rise above the animal:

> O genus, exemplum fugito, mortale, ferarum,
>   Nec homo sit homini quod fera torua ferae.[31]
>
> [O mortals, flee from the example of the wild beasts,
>   Let no human be to human what cruel beast is to beast.]

Hrabanus Maurus thought of wicked judges as restless wolves seizing everything and leaving nothing for the poor.[32] Tyrants were foul dragons[33] and rebels, overcome by their animal excitement, acted like greedy dogs and birds.[34]

If the modern world has had a tendency to anthropomorphize animals, earlier ages had at times an inclination to animalize humans.[35] Name and essence shifting of this sort speaks not just to a closer physical proximity to animals, but to the well-stocked repertory of animal images that filled the minds of early medieval men and women. Animals meant more to them and occupied a larger part of their vocabulary of the world than they do for us.

Despite the playfulness of an animal court with its nicknames and free-flowing animal insults, the Carolingian world was one chiefly devoted to agriculture, particularly to the cultivation of grain crops: "Give us our daily bread," all could be heard to say. In moving beyond an earlier Germanic dependence on hunting and gathering, early medieval men and women were also slowly transforming their attitudes toward the animal world, at least to a degree. Perhaps this shift from the animal to the agricultural in part accounts for the troubling blurring of species lines in the ninth century; the Carolingians may, because of recent dislocations, have been on the cusp of a new ordering of human relations with the natural world, but there were social lags.

Hunting, for one thing, was on its way to becoming a socially specialized activity and would remain so for much of the Middle Ages.[36] Civil and royal law increasingly kept commoners out of the forests and sharply prohibited poaching,[37] while ecclesiastical law forbade churchmen from "going about in the woods with dogs" or hunting with falcons.[38] At the end of the Middle Ages Erasmus would turn his cutting wit against the aristocratic ritual of the hunt with all its highly formalized sticking and dismembering of animals by commoners who played in the woods at living like kings. Hunting became in the Middle Ages the right and passion of the powerful and propertied, much as fox hunting continues to be so slotted in England today.[39]

Carolingian kings and their aristocrats stood near the start of the reserving of forests as game preserves for private use.[40] The wild was increasingly being separated off from the civilized, the forest from the farm. The annual agendas of the rich and elevated in the ninth century were punctuated by hunting seasons, chiefly in the autumn. Even in the final fall of his life, Charlemagne still insisted on going hunting "as was his custom," though he did not stray far from his palace at Aachen.[41] He and his son Louis liked nothing better than to take to their forests in the autumn when boars were fat and stags carried impressive racks of antlers. In an account that can disturb the modern reader, Ermold the Black lovingly lingers over his description of Charles the Bald as a child aching to join a royal hunt and with juvenile joy assaulting the trembling back of a tiny doe laid before him by some young hunters.[42]

The royal hunt was not about provisioning or even killing; it was about aristocratic being and begetting, social and personal bonding, and longed-for escape from the civilized confines of a domesticating court. These hunts, with women left behind and men organizing themselves and their control of nature into recognizable human hierarchies, mirrored the underlying forces, structures, and strains of high Carolingian society. Still the royal hunt could be decidedly dangerous. Notker claimed that Charlemagne had been gored on one outing and young King Carloman, the son of Louis the Stammerer, lost his life on a boar hunt, apparently from a misdirected spear.[43]

In a hierarchical world of competing forces it was necessary for kings to demonstrate their superior control of animals. Charlemagne was said to have cowed some eastern emissaries by having them witness a western hunt against the immense beasts of the Carolingian forest.[44] Notker also relates a revealing story about Pepin the Short as master of animals and men. At a point when he was suffering from the demeaning disrespect of his own magnates, Pepin like some Roman magnate set up a *uenatio*, a staged combat, between a lion and a huge and ferocious bull.[45] If the point of Pepin's spectacle was to show his haughty magnates that size was not everything,[46] for the small lion readily killed the immense bull, he ended by demonstrating his own royal superiority. When his men refused to extract the lion from the bull's bleeding back, Pepin slew the lion with his sword and then decapitated the bull. By dominating fierce animals the king, small though he was, had proved to all that he was manifestly powerful and courageous. The legendary Pepin of this story was also a fitting symbol for the ever-striving Carolingian royals who felt the constant need to prove themselves against their aristocratic doubters; not being royal in distant descent, they needed to be presently and manifestly royal in deed and symbol. To his doubting men Pepin had finally revealed his impressive supremacy "over beasts and humans."[47]

And animals, even the small and insignificant, were still thought to be lethal or at least they were so if God wished them to be. For his anti-episcopal king, Charles the Fat, Notker happily told a story of a spider that descended upon a dissolute and imprudent deacon and killed him on the spot.[48] To less skeptical eyes than ours the early Middle Ages seemed awash with divine power, sometimes evident in the thunderous and catastrophic, sometimes in the small and miraculous. Animals played their part, for they too were thought to be the agents and active expressions of supernatural power. Hence, it was natural to assume that some divine force had passed fatal judgment on the puffery of the deacon. In another Notker story, we encounter a devil who transformed himself into a mule in order to mock and unseat a pompous bishop. The mule, with the flawed churchman on his back, galloped into a whirlpool in a hell-bent effort to drown the stupid man.[49] God too used animals to assist the holy. In trying to protect some persecuted herdsmen, Saint Remigius caused a stampede among the animals and a riot among men.[50]

Stories such as these would have been dismissed outright by few, since most were convinced that God communicated with the world through all his creation. Like the ancient haruspex, men and women looked to the nat-ural world and its moments of sudden rupture to discern the underlying rhythms of the divine will. Melancholy Theodulf of Orléans, worrying his late exile as Ovid once had his, wrote a poem about several great battles of birds and the startling desiccation of a river.[51] Behind his examples lay the assumption that disturbances in the divine mind would manifest themselves through the broken music of the natural world. Beasts, now unconstrained by the confining regularities of animal life, could quarrel and riverbeds dry because God had let them or even caused them to do so; the very whirling of the heavens depended on his steady hand, so that all dissonance above and below was his doing and spoke like thunder to the alert.

Now it would be a mistake, I suspect, to pursue the hunt, despite its vast and enlivening importance, as the only animal show of the early Middle Ages, since it would be to take the formulaic and ritualistic as the chief engagement with animals, and it was far from. Losing ourselves in the woods with Charlemagne might mean missing some of the other revealing features of his haunt of animals. Instead we should look more closely at some of the animals that occupied his world. In so doing we may creep closer and chance to see just how rich and complex a relationship existed between humans and animals in the early Middle Ages or, at least, in Charlemagne's small world. It is to the ideas of the animal world that he carried about in his energetic head that we now need to turn.

I have, for instance, always wondered why Charlemagne kept peacocks. He commanded his stewards, *pro dignitatis causa*, to keep swans (*etlehas*), peacocks, pheasants, ducks, pigeons, partridges, and turtle doves on his estates.[52] And in the sample or exemplary inventories that survive in another capitulary, we find that in fact twenty-two peacocks were kept on one royal estate and eight on another.[53] But why keep peacocks at all? The capitulary De uillis is, for the most part, a rigorously practical document, setting out in minute detail the administration of the king's property and the care and maintenance of his domesticated animals. Stallions were, for instance, not to be kept too long in one pasture and, if they were feeble, the king himself was to be notified before they were sent out among the mares. Mares were to be taken away from their colts at due season and fillies, when their numbers justified it, were to be separated off to start their own herds.[54] Even the rearing of puppies fell within the special purview of the king and queen.[55] If we can without too much trouble see the economic, military, and social purposes of the care and upkeep of horses, dogs, stocked fishponds, draft animals, chickens, sheep, and pigs on royal estates, we are still left to wonder about the purpose of the peacocks and the king's other pretty birds.

Isidore said that peacocks took their name from the sound of their panicked cry, that is, that *pauo* came from *pauor* or terror.[56] But, although peacocks wail when attacked,[57] they were not apparently used as an early warning system on Carolingian estates. Isidore also said that their flesh was so hard that it did not seem to suffer deterioration (hence the popular belief in the peacock's purchase on immortality) and that it was difficult to cook.[58] Still Apicius had supplied the Romans with recipes for preparing peacock, Saint Augustine ate a portion of one in Carthage and kept the rest for over a month to test its speed of putrefaction, and a thousand years later the merchant of Prato deemed the bird a "great delicacy."[59] But Charlemagne does not seem to have been stocking his estates with pea-cocks for consumption; he preferred roasts of wild meat and had hunters whose job it was to supply fresh meat from his forests.[60] Nor did Charlemagne claim that his collection of birds had any particular useful-ness; rather, they should be kept "for the sake of dignity." Several translators have rendered this phrase as "for the sake of ornament," but that may express the translators' own search for the meaning of these ornamental birds.[61] The phrase *pro dignitatis causa* weighs heavily here, for its extra-ordinary point (since commands and not reasons are principally given in the De uillis) was to alert the stewards that the king wanted them to stock beautiful, if mostly useless, birds on his estates.

Looked at broadly, the De uillis represents more than just an attempt to regulate the king's domestic economy in an age when the king still had to live of his own; to insure that his supply lines were kept open and flowing; and to restrain from a great distance stewards who might take advantage of the king's absence to gain economic advantage and power of their own. Indeed, early in the document the king forbade stewards to receive animals (horses, oxen, cows, pigs, sheep, piglets, lambs) as gifts, but granted them permission to accept gifts of wine, vegetables, fruit, chickens, and eggs.[62] The king may not have wanted his stewards bribed with large domestic animals, but he may also have been worried that they would set up their own pasturing operations, thus distracting them from the care of his own animals and leading them to intrude upon his own finite resources of labor and pasture. But there were also social barriers to preserve: large or unusual animals belonged to the king, not his gross inferiors. That too was an aspect of the dignity at stake.

Notker poked fun at pompous churchmen who wished to possess their own exotic animals. One pretentious and manifestly silly bishop spent a fortune buying a scented and painted mouse reputed to have come from Judaea and advertised as the costliest creature ever seen.[63] Another tumid bishop (or rather the caricature of one) was tricked into believing that one of his retainers had stopped a fox in its tracks by calling out to him in the bishop's name. The Carolingian confidence man of this legend presented the attentive fox to the bishop who took the obedience of the creature to be a singular confirmation of his own specialness: "Now my holiness is manifest. Now I know who I am; now I see what I shall become."[64] In the bishop's natural world, as sketched by Notker, God might speak through his creatures for what separated humans from full discourse with the animals was the Fall and the severing of complete and Adamic understanding between man and beast. The real Charlemagne would have been as shocked as the legendary one was by the bishop's pride and pomposity, but most of all by his treading on the king's own special mastery of animals. For Alcuin and the courtiers Charlemagne's control of and communication with animals was not a shared gift.

The *De uillis* aims high. It lays out the details and operations of an ideal society consisting of a commanding and possessing king, reliable and scrupulous resident stewards, and the king's resources of both real and living estate. Charlemagne's real genius, after all, as both warrior and lord, was organizational and logistical. He won numerous wars, wore down the Saxons, and was able to invade Spain and other distant lands because he was good at putting more men into the field and marching them greater distances, year after year, than his enemies ever could. His were victories of planning and purpose, not daring-do.

In ordering his estates in such meticulous detail, Charlemagne was also stealing a march on nature. Reading the *De uillis* reminds one of some of the other ideal constructions of the age such as the famous St-Gall diagram of a monastery laid out with precision and rectilinear certitude on a piece of cold parchment.[65] How close these plans came to achievement is unclear, but we may suspect that the realities of life on royal estates with their drunken and abusive stewards, stolen grain, diseased and neglected animals, withheld taxes, floods, pilfering, and fires were quite other than the high goals laid down by the king.

There are clauses in the *De uillis* that inventory the ideal. The very last chapter (which some have suspected was a later addition to the document) lists the plants that an estate should have in its gardens and orchards: seventy-three different kinds of vegetables and herbs, plus the leeks that were to be grown on the gardener's plot, sixteen different trees, four different kinds of apple trees, and three or four of pear.[66] Walahfrid Strabo would later catalogue in verse the various medicinal plants that he grew in his garden while taking an enforced sabbatical from the political troubles of his world. "Many are the rewards of a tranquil life," he said in his *Hortulus*, a sentiment that one would have thought a professional creed for all but the most political and worldly of monks.[67] When Walahfrid turned to his garden after a winter of dead stillness, with life (both his own and that of the plants) having retreated deep underground, he found nettles barbed and tinged with poison blocking his way and his small plot crowded with willow branches and mole tunnels. Walahfrid's pastoral thoughts in his depoliticized garden were therapeutic, but they were still about his troubled world, all the more so by their very avoidance of the overtly political, for the act of avoiding implies an object to be avoided and not talking about a thing can be the noisiest act of all. At the very heart of the monastic mission lay the notion that one engaged by disengaging, spoke by not speaking. And the pastoral, as it had been for Virgil, was a foil for greater things.

The Carolingians were more aware than we generally are of the quiet possibilities of discourse, their language so often full of care, silence, and indirection. Notker, for instance, relates the strikingly sad story of Pepin the Hunchback, who, after rebelling against his father Charlemagne, was tonsured and sent to a monastery. When another rebellion broke out, the king sent an emissary to ask his disgraced son for his opinion on what to do with these new rebels. He found Pepin cutting down nettles and working a meager monastic garden. The captive monk, irritable as are all deformed people, according to the storyteller, refused to answer his father and grumpily told the agent to report only what he was doing, removing weeds so that the good plants might grow. Charlemagne saw the point of the message: he executed the conspirators and rewarded the faithful with their lands.[68] Notker's account of Pepin the Hunchback's talk in plants and vegetable truths, and Charlemagne's unknotting of his riddled discourse are examples of the pastoral politics of an earlier age,[69] one that assumed the existence of a human garden, the good garden of the civilized world the Carolingians were planting and harvesting. In the metaphor was the model.

Control and not conquest of the natural world was the Carolingian goal. Charlemagne's bridge over the Rhine and the great canal he attempted to dig between the tributaries of the Danube and Rhine rivers were finally failures,[70] but the poets celebrated smaller triumphs achieved in civilizing the countryside. Conques, said one, had once been completely wild and overrun by beasts and birds, but with the rise of the Carolingian house it had become fit for a throng of Christian monks to inhabit.[71]

But let us return to those royal peacocks, for the gorgeous birds of Charlemagne's estates speak to his conception of the natural world as something to be shaped and humanized. Strangely, for all its presence as a Christian symbol, the peacock is a bird scarcely mentioned in the Vulgate, though King Solomon himself collected them.[72] And yet the peacock was taken as a standard symbol in Christian art for immortality and a token of paradise on earth, and sometimes in literature as a figure of pride. Charlemagne himself may have seen the stunningly resplendent mosaic peacock in San Vitale when he passed through Ravenna and perhaps also the intricate peacock carved in relief on a marble ambo in the church of San Salvatore in Brescia.[73]

The Carolingians liked to think about the meaning of peacocks almost as often as have modern evolutionary theorists.[74] The peacock's gorgeous coloring and fanciful feathers have always wanted an explanation and in the Middle Ages that meant a symbolical reading. Eriugena famously saw in the variegated colors of the peacock's exotic feathers a likeness of the richness and variability of biblical hermeneutics.[75] Scripture was as polysemous as the decoration of a peacock's tail feathers with their hypnotic eyes of shifting hues. An alphabet poem from St-Gall about hawks and peacocks valiantly struggles to capture something of the multivalence of the peacock, but no poem could contain or exhaust the *pauo*.[76] Theodulf went for a lighter, but caustic touch when he lampooned the *mergulus*, the diving riverbird or Loire poet now haunting the Brie woods, who dared to think of himself as a strutting peacock when he praised the king. But while his wail was like the peacock's, his feathers were pale and entirely devoid of shimmering ornament.[77]

On the sample inventories of royal estates that survive we do not find the other ornamental birds of the *De uillis*, only chickens, geese, and peacocks; two birds to eat and one to look at. To find the exotic birds of the *De uillis* we need to look at the *Fons uitae* paintings of two manuscripts made for Charlemagne.[78] The Godescalc Evangelistary was created for Charlemagne and his wife Hildegard between 781 and 783.[79] On a page preceding the commencement of the Gospels, the illuminators painted a fountain of life set in a walled garden. The octagonal fount has four pairs of columns that evoke the evangelists who were the vessels through which the divine word spilled over the earth (figure 2.1). Around the fountain are the ornamental birds of paradise, fourteen birds in all:[80] cocks pursue hens (or some other bird) on each side of the cruciate pinnacle of the fountain, below them a pheasant on each side, a peacock on each side, a drake and duck, and in the lower parts of the page one small bird on one side and a female ibis on the other (above the stag), then a male ibis across from the stag, and finally on our left at the bottom what may be a partridge.[81] Some of the birds on the top half of the page are paired and the peacocks with their tails fanned out mimic the curving roofline of the fountain. The stag and most of the birds are browsing on the plants growing around the fountain. The four birds in the bottom half of the illumination below the roofline of the temple each represent a separate species, as does the stag who fulfills the words of the psalmist who had likened his soul to one thirsting for the Lord just as the deer drinks "ad fontes aquarum," at the water's source (Ps. 41:2).

Twenty years later at Charlemagne's court another painting of the fountain of life was produced in the sumptuously painted Gospels of St-Médard of Soissons (figure 2.2). It is often assumed that this painting was a copy of the one in the Godescalc Evangelistary, but it is sufficiently different to lead one to doubt that it was a direct copy. The Soissons painting is more elaborate, supplying a rich architectural setting, and the animals that surround the fountain are more numerous, though essentially the same species. Twenty-one birds and four deer inhabit the scene. Again cocks follow hens (or again some other bird) at the top of the fountain, blue peacocks flank the steeple, pairs of what may be cranes are found at the level of the roofline, pheasants come next and below them doves, pigeons, or partridges, with white doves in flight high inside the fountain, a belled stag and deer at the next level, an ibis on one side and swan on the other, and finally two resting and belled deers at the bottom of the octagonal fountain.[82]

In the two fountain-of-life illuminations we meet a set of paradisiacal aspirations that were also expressed, though in less obvious form, on Charlemagne's estates. The pretty birds on his estates were not merely ornamental; they too were birds of paradise: swans, peacocks, pheasants, doves and pigeons, partridges, and turtledoves. This was not, then, some random collection of birds, but one with a deeper meaning. *Dignitas*, in this light, conjures up the grandeur of nature in primitive harmony, prestige, purity, and perfection. There is also a suggestion here of Charlemagne cast as a new Adam returning his estates to that prelapsarian state of perfection in which God had begun it before Eve ate of the fruit and farmer Cain killed shepherd Abel. To go further: in the *De uillis* by the royal act of naming the

2.1   The Godescalc Evangelistary, Fountain of Life (Paris, Bibliothèque Nationale, Nouv. acq. lat. 1203, fol. 3v).

plants and animals Charlemagne reminds us of Adam's god-given right and duty to name the creatures of Eden, the ones the Lord granted him in his garden (Gen. 2:19–20). To name them was to possess and control them, as the king instinctively understood. Charlemagne was, in miniature imitation, stocking his estates with God's creatures like some Noah and naming them as had Adam.

2.2   Gospels of St-Médard of Soissons, Fountain of Life (Paris, Bibliothèque Nationale, ms. lat. 8850, fol. 6v).

For the ancients paradise was a lush animal park, which is the root meaning of that Persian word,[83] and Carolingian poets wrote of Aachen as though it too were some earthly paradise. Alcuin's nostalgic *O mea cella* begins with a description of the glory that Aachen once was, for it had contained a wonderful wood, flowering trees, green pastures with curative herbs, a brook with its happy fisher, apple orchards, and birds that greeted each day with praise of the Lord.[84] The poet of *Karolus Magnus et Leo Papa* imagined Aachen even more expansively as an earthly paradise of woods and green lawns, birds aplenty, wandering deer, and wild beasts in the king's forest.[85] Ermold the Black too wrote of an Aachen surrounded by woods wonderfully filled with birds and wild beasts, which the king could hunt at his leisure.[86]

In a still more profound way, Walahfrid, in his *De imagine Tetrici*, characterized Aachen as a paradise laid out by Charlemagne and now ruled by his Moses-like son Louis:

> Tu uero in populis paradysi ad amoena uocatis
> Templa regis fundata sacris, rex magne, lapillis,
> Quorum pensa pater quondam tibi magnus adauxit…[87]
>
> [You, O great king, rule among a people summoned
> To the delightful temples of paradise built with sacred stones,
> Whose weight your father (once dear to you) consecrated.]

Walahfrid saw the world outside the great chapel of St-Mary reflected on its window panes; it possessed a remarkable forest and a stream rushing through a green meadow. This was not some wilderness, but an earthly paradise, that longed-for world in which wild and tame animals frolicked together as did all things fierce and timid. Walahfrid said that if Louis should will it, he could fill his paradise with exotic beasts: with lions, bears, boars, panthers, wolves, lynxes, elephants, rhinoceroses, tigers, and even domesticated dragons. They would live in peace with domestic animals and all "animal strife" would be put aside, and high in the trees birds would harmoniously serenade the pacific world below.[88] Behind Walahfrid's vision lay the biblical promise of peace with the animals (Gen. 1:28), a world in which humans would not fear even the most ferocious animals (Job 5:22) and would hold dominion over them all (Gen. 1:28). Ovid, the city man, had also imagined a first world all aflower and bursting with fruit, but without animals.[89] The Carolingians would fill their paradises with animals. Walahfrid saw his not directly but on the reflected glass of a chapel, as though through a glass religiously, for this was a reflection of God's original design before humans ruined the innocent garden of the world.

But there was little peace in Louis's own life and any earthly paradise soon seemed beyond his reach. In the *Vision of the Poor Woman of Laon*, which circulated while he still lived, he was condemned for the crime of killing a nephew to stand outside paradise.[90] An immensely high wall stretching to the heavens blocked his entrance while his name, inscribed on it alongside the others who would enter, grew fainter by the day.

The existence of that pleasureful paradise (*terrestris paradisus*) just beyond the effacing wall was a powerful rebuke of the Pious and of his dreams of good government and Christian redemption. The animals of paradise were just beyond that wall waiting, the lion lying down with the lamb, the elephant and the stag at play; beyond that wall too was the very peace and good order lacking in his temporal kingdom of competing aristocrats, hard decisions, and compromised Christianity.

Elephants belonged to this creative imagining of paradise.[91] A large elephant with its trunk raised in triumphant bellow dominates the bottom register and Adam and Eve at the moment of their temptation face each other in the top register of the back side of the Areobindus Diptych.[92] We are there just a moment away from the disordering of the natural world that waited on the first sin. Of either Byzantine or Carolingian origin, this ivory carving with its crowded paradise of animals was once employed as a Carolingian bookcover.[93] The beast also figured on Gospel concordance pages such as those of the First Bible of Charles the Bald where two anatomically imperfect bull elephants face each other in medallions (Paris, BN lat. 1, fol. 327v).[94] On other canon table pages in that gorgeous book, we encounter a pegasus, peacocks, griffins, and a horned and winged sea-creature set in the upper corners in medallions or quasi-medallions. In the so-called Bible of Alcuin (Bamberg, Staatsbibliothek, Misc. class. Bibl. 1, fol. 7v), which was actually produced at Tours around 840, on the first panel of the Genesis frontispiece, the Lord creates Adam, who, then, at the Lord's command names the animals (Gen. 2:19–20).[95] A mound of animals, an impressively chaotic heap of them, is piled up before Adam: six birds on high (including a duck and ibis), nine mammals in the middle (including a stag, camel, lion, elephant, and pig or boar), and three small creatures at the bottom (a snake and, perhaps, a cat and dog). All of nature by this pictorial synedoche (in this case, the parts for the whole) was assembled before Man for his naming, organization, command, and employment.

Charlemagne himself wanted an elephant for his earthly paradise and went to some considerable trouble to obtain one. It was an animal that belonged to the wider world of animals he had come to imagine. In Maccabees the elephant is the great engine of war and for the Romans it was an imperial beast even represented on Caesar's coins.[96] Why Charlemagne wanted an elephant may be less directly determinable than the means by which he obtained one, but Einhard explicitly stated that it was Charlemagne's own idea: he asked Hārūn al-Rāshid for an elephant.[97] A much later Arabic source claimed that the elephant had passed from an Indian rājā to the Caliph al-Mahdī and, thence, presumably to his successor Hārūn for disposition.[98] Whether this story is true or a mere legend, it does seem likely that the elephant came from India, though an African origin cannot be ruled out. Einhard's claim that Abul Abaz was Hārūn's only elephant can be, since he lacked the means to make or obtain an inventory of Hārūn's menagerie. His purpose was rather to demonstrate the caliph's special devotion to the Frankish king.

The *Royal Frankish Annals* claims that Charlemagne had sent two emissaries to the king of Persia in 797 along with Isaac the Jew, who may have been their guide and translator. The purpose of the mission was complex, including as Roger Collins has suggested a forewarning of Charlemagne's approaching elevation as emperor.[99]

Charlemagne and Hārūn both had their own complicated relations with the Byzantine empire and with Umayyad Spain to consider in their dealings with each other. In 801 two Muslim emissaries, one a Persian and the envoy of Hārūn himself and the other a Saracen and the envoy of the governor of Egypt, arrived at the port of Pavia and were brought to Charlemagne, who at that point had begun his gradual return to Francia after his imperial coronation in Rome. When the emissaries caught up with him he and his train were between Vercelli and Ivrea. According to the annalist, the emissaries reported that Isaac was on his way bearing various gifts, but that Charlemagne's own ambassadors to the east, Lantfrid and Sigimund, had died on their mission. The emperor sent his notary Ercenbald to prepare ships on which the elephant and the other gifts might be transported. Meanwhile Charlemagne left Ivrea late in June. Isaac and the elephant disembarked at Portovénere on the west coast of Italy near modern La Spéza in October, but because of the oncoming snows they wintered at Vercelli before crossing the Alps.[100] Finally in July 802:

> Isaac arrived with the elephant and the other presents, which were sent by the king of the Persians, and he delivered them all to the emperor at Aachen. The elephant's name was Abul Abaz.[101]

According to Einhard, Hārūn on a second occasion also sent gifts to Charlemagne including robes, spices, and other riches of the east.[102] We do not hear about Abul Abaz again until 810 when Charlemagne was about to undertake what would prove to be his last campaign, this time against the Danish king. He went to meet his troops at Lippeham on the Rhine River and there the elephant suddenly died.[103]

There are many unanswerable questions about Charlemagne's elephant: what, for instance, did its Arabic name mean (see appendix 1) and did Charlemagne take it on other campaigns or only on this one and was it used merely to impress? But it would be better for us to explore the known.

The gift itself and the mission of the emissaries to and from the east may have been related to Charlemagne's harassment of the Umayyad rulers of

Spain, against whom Hārūn was happy to have some support. But, as F.W. Buckler (in his unjustifiably neglected monograph) establishes, this gift exchange meant different things to the two sides: for Hārūn the extension of his vast empire with Charlemagne as his western supporter or even subordinate, while for Charlemagne and his biographer Hārūn's act signaled his recognition of the Frank's singular power over the Roman west.[104] It may not be an utter coincidence that the arrival of Hārūn's representatives was followed by the successful siege of Barcelona, an account of which the annalist cleverly sandwiched between the arrival of the emissaries and the arrival of the sought-after elephant. It would be far-fetched to suppose that Charlemagne waged a campaign against Umayyad Spain in order to obtain an elephant, but Abul Abaz remains a striking token of Franco-Islamic contact and shared interests.

For our purposes, the one element that underlies all the others, at least according to Einhard's witness, is that Charlemagne wanted an elephant,[105] we may suppose, *pro dignitatis causa*. The external significance of the elephant as a sign of the relations between the Franks and Islam, of the Franks and Spain, and the hard evidence of long-distance travel and trade,[106] pales here in the light of Charlemagne's animal wants. The elephant and peacock were status animals and belonged to Charlemagne's conception of his royal and now imperial dignity.[107]

This king was the universal master of both men and animals.[108] Hence, as we saw in the *De uillis*, his inferiors were not allowed to own major domestic animals, let alone exotic wild ones. Those belonged to a king's overriding prerogative[109] and as legend or, at least, Notker would have it Charlemagne's haul of foreign animals included a Marmorican lion, a Numidian bear, and some monkeys.[110] Royal woods were the same: they were the private property of the king, his personal preserve, which he used to impress foreign emissaries with his ferocious northern beasts. And he and Hārūn, traded animals, Charlemagne sending Spanish horses, mules, and hunting dogs that could even run down lions and tigers.[111]

The two rulers also sent each other *uestes* or cloaks.[112] Buckler suggested that these may represent the granting of the *malbūs khās* or *uestis praecipua*, the enrobing of an inferior with a gown once worn by a superior.[113] It is hard to believe that the Carolingians did not understand the symbolism of these gifts of gowns, since they too gave previously worn royal robes to those within their care, even in the pope's name.[114] And Charlemagne, as though to balance or, perhaps, to cancel out vestimentary claims, may have sent Hārūn robes of his own.[115]

We should also note here that in 888 Odo, the self-styled king of west Francia, removed goods from the monastery of St-Denis, among which were several impressive robes:

> Cappam ex diaspro cum auiculis auro paratam I.
> Pallium cocetineum cum elephantis I.
> Pallium purpureum cum grifis I.
> Pallium dio[prasium] cum pauonibus I.[116]

That is, one white cloak with small birds in gold; one scarlet pallium with elephants; one purple pallium with griffins; and one brilliant green pallium with peacocks. Although a pallium might be a liturgical gown, both Einhard and Notker used the word to describe royal cloaks or long gowns.[117] Charles the Bald and his father had given the monastery some of the objects Odo alienated, but doubtless not all.[118] Still it is not necessary for us to suppose that any of these coverings descended from Charlemagne, but we cannot ignore that these animal cloaks belonged to a conception of an earthly paradise of animals that was special to a line of self-styled animal kings. Otto III wrapping Charlemagne in cloth decked out with elephants reflected the largeness of the same vestimentary claim. For a king to clothe himself in decorative royal animals was to announce to all that he was truly the king of beasts and master of both the natural and human worlds and he possessed the power to sprinkle his animal cloths like a gentle rain on the church.

The cloaks are an example of the relics of a king-of-beasts legend that was passed to the Middle Ages, but they were not alone. Charlemagne's wax tablets were said to have been made from his elephant's tusks as, perhaps, were some of the legendary horns of Roland.[119] These were the debris, as it were, of the animal park of the mind that Charlemagne had begun making in the 790s. And Abul Abaz quickly became the central symbol of Charlemagne's animal farm, long remembered by Einhard and his fellow courtiers. The Irishman Dicuil in the 820s still recalled that "everyone in the kingdom of the Franks saw an elephant in the time of the emperor Charles."[120]

But gardens can be dangerous places. For just as Satan had stalked Eve in Eden and the old men had stalked Susanna in hers (Dan. 13),[121] there was a worm in the earthly paradise of both Charlemagne and Louis. The dark presence that haunted the lush garden of Carolingian civilization was evil or its apprehension. Walahfrid sensed that evil in the great, brooding equestrian statue of Theoderic, which Charlemagne had removed from Ravenna to set up in his courtyard at Aachen. For the monk the statue blackened the good purposes of the collective mission to Christianize and civilize the Carolingian world. Agnellus may have been pained by the loss of Ravenna's statue and therefore, have exaggerated its monumental majesty (being so large that birds built nests in the nostrils of the immense bronze horse), but Walahfrid felt instead the pain of Theoderic's dark presence as a raging lion who marched alone through pitch-black hell, his statue now casting a shadow over the fragile garden of an orthodox kingdom.[122] Theoderic bestrode his horse nude, burnished as a sign of his unquenchable greed and pride. In Walahfrid's poem we stroll in our imaginations through leafy, verdant Aachen, pass the gloomy statue, and then return safely to Louis's exotic garden paradise.

Charlemagne himself knew that there were problems in the paradise of social and economic relations he set down in the *De uillis*. Inside it he thought that all would be well if his stewards were obedient, reliable, and responsible, but he knew that they were not. Moreover, he saw that the evils of temptation, malfeasance, and malefaction were forever present in the paradise of his estate and he worried about his own people hiding grain from him and about poachers in his woods.[123] Inner evil may have troubled him most, but outer evil required resisting as well.

Outside the good garden of Carolingian civilization and always threatening to invade its estates and to steal and destroy what belonged to the king was the wolf. Charlemagne waged a never-ending war against wolves at the same time that he was fighting the Lombards, Avars, and Saxons. The battle against wolves had been waged for centuries in early medieval society and the Burgundian Law Code outlined the compensation owed to those who had been injured by accidentally springing the wolf trap of a neighbor.[124]

But, like almost everything else he touched, Charlemagne made a systematic and concerted effort to win the war against the one predacious beast that refused to submit to his authority. In the *De uillis*, in a chapter called *de lupis*, the king stipulated that he was to be told how many wolves had been captured and their skins were to be delivered to him. In May his men, with poison and hooks or pits and dogs, were to seek out and seize wolf cubs.[125] His agents were to have wolf hounds (*luparii*) and were ordered to turn over their wolf skins to the king *ad nostrum opus*, though what use he put them to is not known.[126] Perhaps, the pelts were just to serve as evidence that the animals had been freshly killed.

He was still enforcing his campaign against wolves late in life and it extended to his episcopal appointees. In 813, Frotharius, the newly promoted bishop of Toul, wrote to the emperor to thank him for committing into his hands a flock of the holy church so that he might defend it against the teeth of ravening wolves, whom he would suppress and kill if he could. Though talk of sheep and wolves was most often designed to be metaphorical in the mouths of clerics,[127] Frotharius meant it literally here.

> For after you entrusted that episcopal see to me, I killed two hundred and forty wolves in your forests; I say "I killed" because they were taken on my orders and personal command.[128]

The fragment of this report ends there, but had it continued Frotharius would probably have informed the emperor that the two hundred and forty wolf hides were being sent to Aachen.

Wolves were a problem in the Carolingian world. Like other opportunistic agents (including the Northmen), they prospered during times of disruption and took advantage of Carolingian disorder. After the Battle of Fontenoy in 841, wolves were seen scavenging among the dead bodies.[129] They preyed on Carolingian domestic animals, particularly the domesticated pigs sent into the forest during the summer months. One wonders if Carolingian estates were surrounded by walls and guarded by dogs in order to insulate them from marauding wolves, thus carving out islands of civilization in a wider, wilder natural sea. And the stories of wolf depredations are chilling. In one heartrending case a Carolingian mother watched helplessly as a wolf carried off her child.[130]

Frotharius himself later wrote a letter to two abbots about a widespread set of natural disasters (including a plague of wolves) that had recently beset their region.[131] A possible date for this letter is 846 when the *Annals of St-Bertin* reported that during that hard winter wolves had attacked the people of western Gaul with impunity and in Aquitaine armies of them, as large as three hundred in number, had taken boldly to the main roads and went wheresoever they pleased.[132] Frotharius sympathized with the abbots, whose people were suffering from this foul infestation of wolves, which had already killed many. Supposing that sin lay behind this disaster, he ordered prayer, fasts, and penance by his monks in joined voice as the necessary remedy.

The appeal to the divine was in keeping with the general Carolingian reaction to catastrophe, especially to problems that seemed to have no easy solutions and troubled the minds of all; and wolves worried everyone. If there were real wolves out there in the Carolingian countryside, there was also the haunting fear of them striking at will, raiding resources, eating people alive. The Bible had long predisposed Christians to rank hatred of wolves, for the Israelites were a people who raised sheep and guarded them against wolves. Even its metaphors feature rapacious wolves and vulnerable flocks. The biblical peoples longed for a time when the wolf would graze with sheep and the leopard lie down with the kid (Isa. 11:6, 65:25). Saint Paul was thought to have transformed himself from a wolf persecuting Christians into a lamb ready to stand up to the wolf in defense of his flock. In the First Bible atop the opening of the Letter to the Romans we see a wolf cowering before an erect lamb, a before-and-after drawing of the divine transformation of Saul into Paul.[133]

Biblical and early medieval peoples thought of the wolf as extraordinarily greedy; he was the *rapax lupus*, greedy, ravenous, and always on the hunt for innocent prey.[134] Stories of wolves eating people limb by limb expressed the worst fears of the early Middle Ages, the farmer's fear of becoming food. The father of Abbot Maiol of Cluny caught one such Alpha monster out of whom poured the whole limbs of people when it was gutted.[135] So medieval men and women, at least within ecclesiastical circles, were quick to call their enemies, be they rebellious peoples or fallen bishops, wolves who would sink their teeth into the righteous.[136] When an emperor like Louis saved a sinner or baptized a pagan, he was deemed a good and gentle pastor: "What you make part of God, you snatch from the mouth of the wolf."[137]

Yet the wolf was a puzzling animal and medieval men and women often told stories about them and watched with amazement as wolves did strange things such as entering churches during Mass or ringing church bells.[138] The wolf was also a stock character in medieval animal tales: Julian of Toldeo a century earlier was already warning poets about the dangers of popular songs such as the one that began "Lupus dum ambularet uiam, incontrauit asinum," "While a wolf was walking down a road, he encountered an ass."[139] And Alcuin wrote a poem called "The Cock and the Wolf" in which a proud rooster, seized by a lurking wolf, immediately began to flatter him: it was not so much that he minded being eaten by such a marvelous mouth, he said, but he deeply regretted that he would not live long enough to hear him sing since he had heard stories about his amazing voice. Predictably enough, when the wolf opened its mouth to sing, the cock flew off into a tree, and chided the wolf for having valued false praise and empty words over the immediate needs of its stomach.[140] Dungal, an Irish monk of St-Denis, in the prologue to a letter he sent to Charlemagne said he hoped he would not be struck dumb like the wolf of the popular proverb.[141] Alcuin also used the wolf as a figure in an arithmetical brainteaser for his students: how best with but one boat to transport across a river a wolf, a ram, and a small bundle of fodder without damage to any of them.[142]

The wolf was, as Theodulf and others portrayed him, Satan or his stand-in. In Alcuin's animal allegory letter, which as we saw dealt with the scandalous attack on Pope Leo, the wolf represents the devil who would steal the rooster's voice lest he sing the truth.[143] And Alcuin warned Charlemagne to guard his own flock against the ravening wolf during the same scandal.[144] Elsewhere Alcuin called Charlemagne the true pastor of his flock;[145] he was the shepherd forever on guard against the wolf-devil and his many tricks.

But the fear of the wild wolf lay close to home and may already have crept inside the image of Charlemagne's domesticated paradise. In a famous vision the dying Wetti saw Charlemagne on an illumined plane with an animal gnawing at his genitals.[146] Though the monk did not name the animal, it is hard not to suspect that a wolf was meant, for it was the chief paragon of animal greed and imbued with true and unreformed animal wildness. Wolves and Northmen were viewed as agents of God's divine punishment for a sinful people.[147]

If that was the common understanding, of the ravening wolf, what are we to make of the bronze wolf that stood inside the very door of Charlemagne's own chapel in Aachen? From it came the name for the great door at the west end of the cathedral, long known as the Wolf's Door. The bronze wolf brought to Aachen from Italy is now thought to represent a she-bear and may once have served as a late antique, Roman water spout.[148] An ursine water pipe may not sound all that imposing to us, but at Charlemagne's court the piece was probably always taken as a wolf. Fixed and immobile, it stood as a guarding and feral presence at the door of the church at Aachen as parishioners passed under Charlemagne's tribunal balcony. Now submissive (as suggested by its sitting form) and subject to Charlemagne's will, the wolf of Aachen had been invited inside his church. If Charlemagne took importunate charge over the real wolves of his realm, the statue at St-Mary's suggested that even wolves could be brought inside his civilized dominion, just as the peacock and the elephant had been.

They were all part of the animal world now tamed and under the king's sure control. And that was as it should be: "For every nature of beasts, of birds, and of serpents, and of the rest is tamed and has been tamed by the nature of humans (James 3:7)." And Christ had granted his favored few the power to trample upon wild beasts: "Behold I have given you the power to tread upon serpents and scorpions and upon the full force of the enemy and nothing will harm you (Luke 10:19)."[149] So too Charlemagne, as had Pepin, needed to be seen exercising his authority over both the wild and the domesticated. His very horse, said a poet, rejoiced to receive the weight of his magnificence.[150] So should all animals. The so-called bronze Throne of Dagobert, which was deposited at St-Denis, has four legs in the shape of panthers—a fitting royal seat for these masters of beasts.[151] Lothar I is shown sitting on just such an animal throne in one of his manuscripts (figure 1.18).

For Alcuin the entire world, all its people, birds, and beasts sang out to King Charles, "Valeto, pater," "Go well, father." They all belonged to his great paternal commonwealth and sang his praises.[152] But if Charlemagne confidently exercised his authority over the animal world, his men could do so only by acts of extreme imitation and cruelty. Notker tells the story of a rabid retainer by the name of Eishere who spitted pagan enemies on a spear as though they were small birds and tadpoles and bore them around shrieking in their incomprehensible tongues. He degraded his enemies as mere worms, not human beings.[153] In battles at court, it was customary to insult an enemy by likening him to an animal: Theodulf called the little Scot he hated a wild, furious, and shameful creature.[154] But it mattered what animal you were likened to in this game of animal associations, since the poet also thought of Charlemagne as lighter than a bird, stronger than a lion.[155]

For his courtiers one of Charlemagne's special gifts was his power to transform the natural world. An unknown poet (supposed by some to be the Anglo-Saxon Lull),[156] writing in 777, thought of the rebellious Saxons as savage beasts whom Charlemagne had come to conquer. In mastering them, Charlemagne had transformed those wild wolves into gentle lambs, black and noisy crows into white doves, wing-footed griffins and flying monsters into peaceful birds, and fearsome hounds into furry deer. He even safely placed vicious tigers and yellow-maned lions among his herds of cattle.[157] This too was part of the paradisiacal ambition of Charlemagne; to turn a wild and untamed frontier into a lush and peaceful gamepark of people and animals.

Gottschalk later said that Christ could even transform the soul of a beast into that of a human being;[158] Christ-like Charlemagne would settle for the less ambitious goal of transforming Saxon wolves into Christian lambs. His son's poet thought that just as all the animals of the forest, bears, boars, and quavering rabbits, wolves and stags, feared the hunter Louis, so too in time would hostile peoples, Bulgars, Saracens, and Bretons, Danes and Moors, lay down their necks before his imperial might.[159]

Yet Charlemagne's enemies were thought to wish to unsettle the peaceful animal kingdom he was making. When, in 810, the cattle of his kingdom began to die off from disease, a rumor spread that Grimoald IV of Benevento had sent agents to the north to spread a poisonous dust over his fields. Charlemagne himself did not believe that his enemy was the cause of the epizootic, but he did call on his people to pray and fast. In the countryside, however, some believed the rumor of chemical warfare and executed a number of the alleged dust-spreaders.[160] In 810, too, Charlemagne himself fell from his horse as a meteor flashed overhead while he was on his last campaign.[161]

Carolingian artists were particularly good at depicting horses and their riders falling, which they took as a sign of punishment for the sin of pride.[162] The twentieth-century Italian sculptor, Marino Marini, would in an extraordinary sequence of equestrian statues use the same image to express the modern alienation of humans from the natural world, the pain of the horse in revolt beneath its burden, and the rider's inability any longer to master animal or world.[163] The Carolingians understood something of the same, for if all the natural world was in harmony when a good and great ruler was at his peak, it might also reflect the disturbance of that concord caused by a willful people in revolt against God's authority: birds at war, rampaging wolves, and a skittish horse mirrored a world unhinged by God's growing anger at a Christian world now adrift.

But that was the disturbed world at the end of Charlemagne's reign, when troubles were already spreading and the animal world and sky began to reflect a breakdown in political order. In the golden light of the late eighth century, when there was an ordered understanding between man and beast, and Charlemagne was lord of all, few such disturbances were recorded. Charlemagne bestrode all creatures and even brought the elephant and wolf in from the wild. He collected, disciplined, domesticated, ordered, and cherished—all animals were subject to his will. The wolf that would gnaw at his genitals and the suppurating epizootic lay in the future. In the golden age of his animal park, all creatures, as in Eriugena's notion of the Return, would return to God through Charlemagne as part of his grand scheme of world order.

For finally Charlemagne as imagined by his court and perhaps by himself was both an active force for and a symbol of the domestication of the wild world, one that had turned from hunting and gathering to farming, from the ferocious to the peaceful, from the uncouth to the civilized, from Merovingian murder to Carolingian Christianity, and from untamed nature to a lush garden filled with the birds and beasts of paradise.

This idea of the transformation of the natural world animates Carolingian images of progress and power, and Charlemagne, as king of men and beasts, lorded it over all. The image of his omnipotence, of which the mastery of animals was but a subset, was a powerfully reassuring antidote to the deep-seated worry that instability was the norm and disaster an onrushing inevitability of a corruptible and often compromised age. For a time at least Charlemagne had been the king of beasts and his world had glimpsed, however briefly, a new paradise, one filled with peacocks, elephants, and domesticated wolves and the sweet promise of an unending harmony with nature, and so with God.

CHAPTER 3

KAROLVS MAGNVS SCRIPTOR

Every so often we should roast an old chestnut, open it up, and see if something mushy and edible lies inside or if everything has turned hard and dry. And to my mind one of the hoariest nuts around is whether Charlemagne could write. Down the years the story of the illiteracy of Europe's first great educational reformer has been repeated over and over again, accepted baldly by some, devoutly doubted by others.[1] Students never quite know what to make of an emperor who ruled the vast expanse of nascent Europe, but could not reportedly master a simple skill they take for granted.[2] Familiar though the issue of Charlemagne as a writer might be, there are matters here to ponder and questions to pursue.

The inquiry is not an entirely idle one, for if Charlemagne was illiterate as some have claimed then Carolingian high culture might be thought a great lie inasmuch as it was not in essence what it pretended to be, and this splendid fraud would have been perpetrated by the learned men gathered around an illiterate king. In that grim construction a wise sovereign would only have been imagined sitting at the center of a learned court that passed him intricate Latin poems and flattered his humanist learning; for his part the great unlettered one would not in reality have been able or inclined to provoke debate about such esoteric topics as the substantiality of darkness and nothingness and all his high-minded educational reforms would have been but the enlightened schemes of others.

And there's our rub, for if Charlemagne was profoundly illiterate and knew little Latin, he could not have participated to any significant degree in the Latinate culture he was supposed to have established and to have lovingly cultivated at his court. What a very bizarre world that would have been, all play acting and pretend, wrapped in an elaborate covering of written words that the king himself could not penetrate or comprehend. Were that true, we would be left to rewrite the educational history of Europe.

Of course, that is to frame the problem too simply. For literacy or its lack is not to be defined exclusively in terms of whether someone can write or not, but rather in terms of a wider set of linguistic skills of which writing may be the most difficult to master.[3] In both Latin and English, 'writing' is a multilevel and expansive term that encompasses both the manual skill of handwriting and the composition of works of both an ordinary (as in 'he wrote out a shopping list') and extraordinary kind (as in 'James Joyce wrote *Ulysses*'). Hence, 'writing' as a term often remains opaque, eluding immediate and unqualified understanding. Moreover, it is a word that may not have kept pace with our changing world or, at least, it has long been losing its tangible connection with its manual and instrumental past, that is, with hand, pen, and ink. At the moment I was writing this sentence no pen touched paper and my manual involvement was limited to five fingers moving clumsily over a keyboard (three on one hand, two on the other). In the not too distant future I shall be able to speak straight to print and that would still be a form of 'writing.' For most of my colleagues at the university 'good writing,' when applied to each other and to their students, means, I suspect, 'the clear and correct written expression of estimable, organized thought' and not just a solid command of the language and its grammatical constraints, and certainly not the ability to produce a script pleasant to the eye. Despite that narrowing of meaning, the manual and compositional both belong to 'writing' or, at least, they did so in the Middle Ages.

In Charlemagne's case, the place to start (and end, for that matter) is with Einhard whose historical reliability and usefulness for the study of Charlemagne and his career were recently dismissed by Roger Collins.[4] In the twenty-fifth chapter of the *Life of Charlemagne*, Einhard does supply us with a famous, if frustratingly oblique account of Charlemagne as a writer:

> He also attempted to write and, for this reason, used to place both wax-tablets and notebooks under the pillows on his bed, so that, if he had any free time, he might accustom his hand to forming letters. But his effort came too late in life and achieved little success.[5]

That comment falls at the end of Einhard's quick and cautious survey of the state of Charlemagne's learning and for all its unforgettable charm fails to tell us things we should like to know.

But it is the actual meaning of what he does tell us that eludes easy explanation. Edward Gibbon, always so sure of himself, had no doubt: "in his mature age, the emperor strove to acquire the practice of writing, which every peasant now learns in his infancy."[6] Gibbon ridiculed those who tried to elicit anything but a straightforward reading of Einhard's state-ment,[7] but that is just what I would propose to attempt here. Scholars of Charlemagne have for the most part been led by Einhard to believe that Charlemagne never mastered handwriting. F.L. Ganshof simply said of Charlemagne's writing that, "despite the exercises he forced himself to practice when he could not sleep, he never fully mastered [it]."[8] Friedrich Heer printed a plate of a charter of Charlemagne from 774 and said of its KAROLVS monogram that the king "only made the strokes in the centre as he could write very little."[9]

If Charlemagne did not learn to write that would represent an area in which his family had fallen short of the achievements of some of its Frankish predecessors in the Merovingian house that Einhard caricatured as utterly spent.[10] Ian Wood noted that the autograph signatures of five Merovingian kings survive,[11] and we know from Gregory of Tours that not only did King Chilperic I write poetry, but he also played like Claudius of old at inserting new characters into the Latin alphabet.[12] Gundovald, the pretender to the royal inheritance of Chlothar I, could apparently both read and write since Gregory of Tours described him as "litteris eruditus."[13] One may be skeptical about the depth of royal learning or writing profi-ciency in the Merovingian age, but, given the slender evidence, Wood's conclusion that "members of the royal family were able to read and write throughout the seventh and early eighth centuries" seems sound enough on the surface.[14]

The state of official learning may well have declined in the first half of the eighth century and the Pippinid mayors of the palace may have put little effort into being even minimally educated themselves, but we do know that Charles Martel and his son Pepin the Short promoted modest cultural revivals at their courts, ones fed in particular by the monasteries of St-Denis in Neustria under Fulrad and Fulda in Austrasia under Boniface.[15] Still a patron might preside over a literary revival without being literate himself, a thing Jonathan Swift thought of positive advantage to writers:

> For patrons never pay so well,
> As when they scarce have learn'd to spell.[16]

The evidence seems lacking one way or the other to support the pro-position that Charles Martel wrote,[17] but he saw to it that his sons were educated. He apparently sent his son Pepin to St-Denis to be educated,[18] Carloman later became a famous and doubtless literate monk, and another son named Jerome seems to have copied out a Latin text when he was only nine years old.[19]

But what of Pepin's sons Charlemagne and Carloman? Sadly we know little about where or how they were educated in their formative years.[20]

Their cousin Adalhard, later abbot of Corbie, was about ten years younger than Charlemagne, but his biographer claimed that he had been trained by masters alongside prince Charlemagne and the other young warriors of the palace (*inter palatii tirocinia*).[21] Adalhard's training at court was probably martial in nature and his advanced learning in letters may have been acquired at the monastery of Corbie to which he moved in a huff when he was twenty years old.[22] One may also suspect that Benedict of Aniane chiefly received military instruction at court. His father sent him to the court of Pepin and his queen "to be educated among its students,"[23] but his biographer immediately followed that comment with praise of Benedict's accomplishments as a young soldier.[24] Some celebrated scholars were associated with Pepin's court, including Chrodegang of Metz and Virgil of Salzburg, and perhaps Ambrosius Autpertus,[25] but we do not know if those learned men ever taught there.

Einhard said that Charlemagne had been reared from infancy in the Christian religion, which should suggest some degree of formative instruction even if that early education largely consisted of the memorization of Latin prayers and the fundamentals of the Catholic faith. But he disclaimed any knowledge of Charlemagne's early life;[26] this is but one of Einhard's many biographical black holes, a few pointed out by the biographer, most left dark and unseen. He did, however, say that Charles: "believed that his children, both his daughters and his sons, should be educated first in the Liberal Arts, which he himself had studied."[27] In the general letter that Charlemagne sent out between 786 and 800, he noted, "by our example we urge those whom we can to take up the study of the Liberal Arts."[28]

By his own testimony, then, Charlemagne claimed training in the Liberal Arts, but the critical question is when was he so educated. Einhard informs us that Charlemagne received instruction in (Latin) grammar from Peter of Pisa and in the other Liberal Arts from Alcuin, but the former came to Charlemagne's court some time after 773–74 and had returned to Italy before 796 and Alcuin arrived in 782 after meeting Charlemagne the previous year in Parma and he took up the abbacy of St-Martin's of Tours in 796.[29] In 782 Charlemagne was forty years old and his personal interest in astronomy and arithmetic was encouraged by Alcuin, as Einhard reported and the evidence confirms.[30] In the 780s a number of Charlemagne's children were already entering their second decade.[31] Are we then to suppose that the king advised his sons and daughters to take up the Liberal Arts as he himself was first receiving instruction in them or should we wonder if he had begun his education as a boy or young man at court or some monastery and then returned to it in the 780s and early 790s?

Einhard rapidly and elliptically surveys the educational accomplishments of the king. He reports that Charlemagne was such an able and gifted speaker that at times he seemed garrulous (*dicaculus*)[32] and he attempted to learn foreign languages. He spoke (and, therefore, understood or, perhaps, just prayed in)[33] Latin as well as he spoke his native German. Donald Bullough supposed that he would have pronounced Latin with a " 'soft' Italian pronunciation and not the 'hard' Northern one discernible in Alcuin's poetry."[34]

He understood (spoken) Greek better than he could speak it himself.[35] This report-card like remark might be taken as no more affirmative in claim than Ben Jonson's assertion that Shakespeare had but small Latin and less Greek. Given the scanty knowledge of Greek in northern Europe during Charlemagne's time,[36] we would have been surprised had Einhard, let alone Charlemagne, been expert in Greek. Nor does Einhard claim much for his king here, but one is left wondering why he mentioned it all. One possible explanation would be that he was following Suetonius's scheme for treating the literary and educational capacities of the Julio-Claudian emperors and among the topics that fell within his categorical approach to the emperors was their command of both Latin and Greek. Among the Caesars, Augustus comes closest to being the model for Einhard's imperial linguist, since he was never as proficient in Greek as he was in Latin and never spoke it with real fluency.[37] If Einhard's source of inspiration here was Suetonius, as seems likely, then his surprising comment should alert us that, with respect to Charlemagne's learning, he may not always have been sizing things up on their own terms, but was instead examining his king's literacy through a Suetonian filter.

There is still another possible explanation for Charlemagne's so-called knowledge of Greek since it is not impossible that he did know a few words of Greek, which he could have picked up from his courtiers and the Byzantine ambassadors who passed through his own and his father's royal courts. It would have been pleasing for him to say a few words to those visitors in their own language.[38]

Charlemagne's basic understanding of Latin cannot, I think, be seriously doubted.[39] The literary and bureaucratic language of his court was Latin[40] and even the capitularies Charlemagne issued verbally were sent out in Latin, even if they are sprinkled with German technical terms such as *herisliz* (for desertion) and *herribannum* (for the payment of the host). Moreover, numerous Latin poems were written for him.[41] What could have been the point of courtiers flattering the king in a language he did not understand at all? That would have defeated the very purpose of panegyric. Even before he moved to Francia, Alcuin advised a fellow poet to take himself to Charles's court and there at the feet of the king to set out his verses,[42] which were written in Latin, of course. And the Acts of the Second Council of Nicaea (787), after they had been translated into Latin, reached Francia in 790 and were read out in Charlemagne's presence and he disapproved of much that he heard.[43] Moreover, Charlemagne liked, according to Einhard, to listen to Augustine's *City of God* read out at dinner.[44] Surely, unless Einhard was engaged in outright fabrication here or Peter of Pisa's grammatical lessons had been utterly wasted, Charlemagne listened to this work in Latin rather than some translation of it into German, for which there is no surviving evidence, no extant ninth-century *Gottesstaat*. German would not be developed as a fuller literary language for at least a generation or two.[45]

That he could speak Latin may also be indicated by the *Opus Karoli*, commonly known as the *Libri Carolini*, the Frankish court's response to Byzantine iconodulism, for the court copy of that unpublished work survives in Vatican City, Vat. Lat. 7207.[46] In its margins, as minutely studied by Ann Freeman, are one and two word comments on the text; these were originally written in Latin in Caroline minuscule, but were later erased and replaced with Tironian notes. One hypothesis of a string of scholars has been that Charlemagne listened to the Latin text prepared by Theodulf of Orléans and his court scholars and made comments such as "bene," "recte," and "prudenter."[47] To tie these comments directly or exclusively to Charlemagne may be to overreach, but one cannot but associate the book itself, the *Opus Karoli* or Charles's work, with the king and his immediate circle: the text itself was a closely guarded one, received no circulation, and was officially discussed at the Synod of Frankfurt in 794.[48] We need to understand that some verb such as "said," "put," or "expressed" is implied by these adverbs of approbation; hence, "that is **well** said," "that is **rightly** put," "that is **wisely** expressed," and so on. Later (though how much later is not clear) some scribe replaced those comments written in minuscule with less obtrusive Tironian notes, probably in preparation for the copying of the corrected text. The worry may have been that scribes would incorporate the marginal comments into the finished text where they did not belong.[49] Still the notes were deemed important enough to preserve. The comments, albeit brief and mostly banal, do convey an official sanction, though whether they were the judgment of the assembly or of Charlemagne himself may be impossible to determine. Still, since Charlemagne was a participant in the deliberation and the draft work was nominally his, the Vatican manuscript would seem to strengthen the probability that Charlemagne had a working knowledge of spoken Latin even if it does not prove it. But it would strain credibility to believe that the Latin text was orally translated into German for him, so precise and careful is its language, or to imagine that he commented on it in German and that those comments were then translated by a scribe into Latin and only then inscribed in the margins.[50] In short, much suggests that Charlemagne could understand and speak Latin, as Einhard claimed; that is to say nothing about how completely he had mastered the language.

Could he read? Here the evidence is elusive and the resolution of the question less certain. One is reminded of some wit's observation that one could argue that Sherlock Holmes was unable to read since on many occasions when the detective received a letter in one of Arthur Conan Doyle's stories he handed it over to Watson to read aloud. In Charlemagne's case the lack of direct evidence wants explaining.

'Reading' is almost as variable and expansive a term as 'writing' and may also disguise a variety of reading abilities and situations from the accomplished to the halting. It is striking that Einhard made no comment on Charlemagne as a reader, which could be taken as an indication that he assumed that he could (as Suetonius supposed Roman emperors could) or the opposite, that he did not wish to draw attention to a glaring inadequacy of the great king.

On this point we should consider very seriously Asser's *Life of King Alfred*, which is, on one level, the story of the king's progress as a reader. Of course, the importance of reading was as much Asser's preoccupation as Alfred's, for reading underlay their relationship and cemented Asser's special cultural connection to the king.[51] Alfred had remained utterly ignorant of letters until he was eleven, but paid close attention as old English poems were recited.[52] Even into his thirties, he still could not read, yet he ensured that his youngest son Æthelweard was instructed in reading and writing both English and Latin, and that he also studied the Liberal Arts. Alfred's inability to read weighed heavily on his mind and he continued to listen, almost enviously, as others read to him.[53] Finally, Asser says, on the same day the king both learned to read [Latin] and to translate [from Latin into Anglo-Saxon] and after that he liked to read out loud to himself.[54] The king also asked Asser to copy out some material for inclusion in the enchiridion or commonplace book he carried around with him. Nowhere does Asser state that Alfred could also write with his own hand and the king's request that Asser copy out a relatively small portion of text suggests that he probably could not; his efforts were instead directed toward reading and translating.[55]

In Charlemagne's case the evidence for his ability to read is circumstantial and inferential at best. It matters not at all for purposes of resolving the matter that Charlemagne received books dedicated to him,[56] that he may have ordered a wider collection of books,[57] or that he possessed a library and disposed of it for sale in his last testament.[58] Nor, in general, does the overblown praise of his courtiers clarify the matter; rather, the opposite: it wantonly obscures it. The poet of the epic poem *Karolus Magnus et Leo Papa* praised him as a brilliant teacher of grammar and dialectic, outstripping all others in culture.[59] The Saxon Poet, who generally depended for particulars on Einhard, said independently of him in this instance that Charlemagne constantly read the Bible and the Fathers,[60] but his was a distant and uninformed assumption, though a revealing one.

For the most part Charlemagne would have listened to material read out to him. One bishop said of one of the letters he sent to him: "This is the letter which we sent for the ears of the lord emperor."[61] Leidrad of Lyons also assumed that Charlemagne would listen to the letter he sent him (*audiatis* and *auribus uestris*).[62] Our richest source is the correspondence of Alcuin and he too, in most cases, assumed that Charlemagne would listen to his letters. He was, for instance, asked by the king to prepare a short account of the life of Saint Richarius that would be suitable for Charlemagne's ears.[63]

Most remarkable of all Alcuin wrote to the king in 799:

> We give thanks to your venerable and pious nature that you ordered that little book, which was sent to you as you ordered, read out (*recitari*) to the ears of your wise nature and that you ordered a collection of its errors and that you returned [the work to me] for correction.[64]

Alcuin doubted that Charlemagne's scholars had caught all the errors in the recited text, but the reception of his text fit within a court pattern. It was apparently Charlemagne's custom, as with the Acts of Nicaea II and the *Opus Karoli*, to have difficult texts read out loud and in committee, and so Alcuin's reference to the recitation of his work does not resolve the issue of Charlemagne's personal ability to read. A powerful and prosperous ruler of Charlemagne's sort would chiefly have had others read to him, but then so had Augustus and so would Alfred, even once he had learned to read.[65]

Charlemagne lived in a world in which silent and even private reading was relatively rare, so that we should not expect to find a description of the busy king nestled in a castle corner or camp tent quietly reading the works of Augustine.[66] And yet the Carolingian court and its wide network of officials, ecclesiastics, and lay people was replete with readers, some of them royal.[67] Alcuin noted in a letter that his copy of Bede's work on the Epistles was out on loan to Charlemagne's sister, the nun Gisela, and on another occasion he sent Gisela and one of Charlemagne's daughters a collection of texts by Bede for them to copy and return.[68] Dhuoda would conceive of books and reading as central to the life of her son William, who was at court in the early 840s, and she sent her manual to him there.[69] Eriugena, the philosopher and sometime poet, saw Charles the Bald's queen, Ermintrude, "often reading books."[70]

Pierre Riché assumed that all the Carolingian princes after Charlemagne were fully literate and he may be right,[71] but the hard evidence is almost as thin as it is for Charlemagne. Yet Thegan did draw special attention to Louis the Pious's constant devotion to psalmody and reading "in which he was not a beginner."[72] Thegan, a careful reader of Einhard, may here have been contrasting his literate Louis with Einhard's less than fully literate Charlemagne, for he may have known or just suspected that one read, while the other did not. Still, if royal reading was common in the following generations it would make Charlemagne's particular difficulties all that much more perplexing.

In Alcuin's intriguing letter of 799 looked at above, there is a suggestion of something closer to an individual and private reading of documents by Charlemagne. Alcuin said:

> I have sent to your excellency certain forms of expressions made clear by illustrations and verses drawn from [the writings of] that venerable father [Peter of Pisa]. [I have also enclosed] on the blank [piece of] charter you sent me some drawings of arithmetical problems for your amusement. May you now find dressed what came to me bare and think it appropriate that the [charter] that came to me dignified by your mark is [now] covered by my writing. And if those forms [of expressions] should have too few illustrations, Bezaleel [the nickname for Einhard], your, no, rather, our close assistant, will be able to supply you with more [illustrations] of that father's verses. He is also able to understand the meaning of the figures in that little book of arithmetical learning.[73]

There are matters of interest here: first, that Charlemagne sent Alcuin a piece of parchment that the abbot filled (or ordered filled) with writing; that the miscellany of materials sent was one of personal interest to Charlemagne and continued the education in grammar and arithmetic that Alcuin and Peter had begun with him; that the materials were not formal and meant for a wide readership at court, but for the king's personal instruction and amusement; that if Charlemagne wanted more selections of Peter's Latin, he could turn to Einhard; and if stuck on the arithmetic, he could also seek out Einhard's help. This passage suggests that Alcuin had written out (at least on the charter) material of a fairly rudimentary nature for the king, his mature student, to study himself, but Einhard was close at hand to help him if he got into trouble. Moreover, he described the material he placed on the parchment as "drawings" (*figurae*) and one has to wonder if Charlemagne might have warmed to arithmetic and astronomy because they were less word-bound and if the setting in which he felt most comfortable was an oral rather than literary one; hence Einhard's presence.[74]

Still if Charlemagne could not read at all, why would Alcuin have sent him a complex acrostic poem that was not meant to be listened to, but looked at?[75] Even here an explanation is possible. Perhaps Alcuin imagined that such a poem could still be read aloud and, better yet, that its delightful visual intricacies could be best shown and explained by the poet himself. The poet's personal attendance on the king, the singular audience for such a poem, would then have been all that much more necessary, which would go some way toward explaining the early popularity of such poetry at court. Acrostic could have been an eye-pleasing form of literature for the semiliterate and an interpreter-intensive class of poetry for the poet. Even the learned knew that acrostic verses were difficult and needed explaining to the less lettered.[76] Still, the *carmina figurata* or figure poetry of the ninth century, with its lines and letters manipulated to create pictures on the page and a sculpted effect, surely appealed to the eyes of the less literate.[77]

Theodulf assumed that some of his court poems would circulate hand to hand throughout the palace before finally reaching Charlemagne, but what happened to these *Zirkulardichtungen* once they reached their destination is a different matter.[78] They may just, once again, have been read out loud to the king.

With many members of Charlemagne's family able to read or, at least, deeply interested in books, it is difficult at first to believe that he could not read, but there is, in fact, almost no evidence that he could and the problems encountered by King Alfred on his way to learning to read are cautionary to say the least. By concentrating so much attention on how hard it had been for Alfred to learn to read and the great importance of his eventual breakthrough, Asser forces us to notice Einhard's absolute silence on Charlemagne's ability to read. But Asser, for his part, also knew the virtue of quiet disguise and declined to discuss his king's inability to write with his own hand.

Could Charlemagne write? Writer is a term, as Bullough pointed out, that "necessarily embraces both *dictator* and scribe."[79] In the ordinary sense, then, of basic composition, the issuing of laws and decrees would seem to suggest that Charlemagne was primarily a dictator of texts. The evidence of Alcuin requesting the correction of his treatises, the response to Nicaea II, and the putative *Opus Karoli* marginalia would all seem to suggest that the king, working in committee or through his wise men, commented on written texts even if they were read out loud to him. It is into this category that we should probably place Thegan's comment that in his last days Charlemagne devoted his time "to correcting books." He says that with the help of Greeks and Syrians he corrected the four Gospels.[80] Once again then we encounter a report of Charlemagne at work upon books in the presence of assistants who could both read and write. We should note here

that Thegan in describing Louis the Pious's educational accomplishments depended directly upon the model of Einhard's description of
Charlemagne's abilities in Greek and Latin, but carefully avoided applying
to Louis Einhard's words about Charlemagne's fledgling attempt to write.[81]
Instead, several times he emphasizes that Louis could write with his own
hand; it was almost as though he were once again drawing a firm distinction between his learned Louis and the less learned Charlemagne, particularly for the benefit of those who knew of Einhard's crafty portrayal of his
king's literacy.[82] Thegan knew the real story, he seems to imply.

Yet the literate act of 'writing' can also be confined to and can surely
count composition as one of its several aspects. Einhard had been led by
Suetonius to expect that emperors would compose works and so in the
twenty-ninth chapter of the *Life of Charlemagne*, he reported that the king
had ordered the writing down of the [Germanic] songs of the deeds of
ancient kings, had begun a grammar of German,[83] and had named in
German the months and winds. Einhard preserved this last list, which,
however slight and totemic, is indisputably a composition. So, although the
evidence is thin, Charlemagne was thought by one contemporary, at least,
to have worked at composition and he supplied one actual work as proof.
Yet we need to note that the emperor's literary work, as presented by
Einhard, was all in German.

Alcuin went further. In the dedicatory poem to the *De rhetorica*,
he wrote:

> Scripserat haec inter curas rex Karulus aulae
> Albinusque simul: hic dedit, ille probat.

> [King Charles amidst the cares of the court wrote these things
> And Alcuin at once [responded]: this famous man put
> [questions], that one explored [them].][84]

And he presented the work as one of collaboration—*unum opus amborum*.
Charlemagne did not, of course, write the *De rhetorica*,[85] but is it all
Alcuin's? Is it beyond the bounds of possibility that Charlemagne, who had
been instructed in rhetoric and who attempted, according to Einhard, to
compose his own grammar, had put questions to his teacher that formed
some part of Alcuin's systematic presentation. After all, we do see Alcuin in
his letters attempting to answer Charlemagne's questions about the stars
and Scripture.[86] In one of those letters, Alcuin praised the layman who had
asked a question about the swords in Scripture, which Charlemagne had
then passed along to Alcuin:

> I know that by your wise questioning you want to rouse us from lethargy
> and to teach more than to learn things you are unacquainted with, for we

found written under your authority on that page that to question wisely is
to teach. . .[87]

Here Alcuin acknowledged that the letter he had received was sent out
under Charlemagne's name, but others, he knew, had written it.

Alcuin thus leads us to the important issue of Charlemagne's nominal
composition of written works. What issued from the court under his name,
even the letter to his wife Fastrada while he was on summer campaign,[88]
should be regarded as the polished products of court scholars and secretaries, but we need not think that these letters were invented completely
independent of the king for he may well have dictated some of them or
parts of them. For this reason Alcuin insisted that Charlemagne collect
about himself able scholars who could fix up his prose and present it in the
best light:

> Your authority should instruct the *pueri* [in this instance, his scholars or
> secretaries] of the palace so that they record most elegantly whatever that
> most lucid eloquence of your mind will have dictated. In this way wherever
> a document bearing your name circulates it will reveal the excellence of your
> royal wisdom.[89]

One possible interpretation of Alcuin's comment would be that he thought
that Charlemagne normally spoke a rough version of a Latin text that
should then be polished and perfected by accomplished secretaries.

But Alcuin also realized that some texts came from court in the king's
name that he had not actually composed. Scholars writing to Charlemagne
at court were also faced with a dilemma, since they realized that their letters would be read aloud to the king. It may not have been possible to send
him anything that was meant for his eyes only, that is, a strictly personal
message. Moreover, answers were also 'public' and were spoken to or composed by and certainly written out by the chancellor and his men though
they were sent out as though they came directly from the king.

In one case, Alcuin blew the whistle on this game of pretending that a
letter from Charlemagne was actually his.[90] He apparently did not like this
royal letter and acknowledged that he probably deserved the beating he had
received from the king's servants (the *pueri*) or scholars[91] and that one of
them had landed a mighty blow. He dressed up his prickly response in
Virgilian allusions, but he was seeking to address the real writers behind the
king's letter and to direct his resistance toward them and not his lord.

But the question with which we began now needs answering on its own
terms. Could Charlemagne take pen or stylus in hand and write? There are,
as already seen, examples of individuals such as King Alfred who could read

and even compose Latin, but who were not able to write with their own hand.[92] In Charlemagne's case, the issue of the monograms on his charters, despite the importance it has often been given, would seem to be largely immaterial. Even today a busy and powerful person might only mark or initial a document prepared for him or her.[93] No one should assume that kings, prime ministers, and presidents could not write, because what survives are their initials; and no one should assume that they could write because they signed their names, since signatures can be learned and may not denote accomplished literacy. The absence of signed charters as we move from the Merovingian into the Carolingian age may primarily represent a change in notarial practices. Whereas a few Merovingian kings had signed charters, the notaries of Pepin the Short and his son Carloman employed the formula "Signum † [nominis] gloriosissimi regis" with variations.[94] On Charlemagne's charters his officials substituted the KAROLVS monogram for the cross. Theodor Sickel long ago proposed that Charlemagne and Louis the Pious denoted their approval of a charter by making marks within their monograms, specifically by making a smaller square or lozenge within the central square of the monogram.[95] The difference between monograms with and without these added marks is noted in the MGH edition of Charlemagne's charters as MF (F standing for "firmauit" or "he confirmed") and M (for monogram).[96] But since it has generally been assumed that Louis the Pious could both read and write, the very fact that he too employed the same system of denoted monograms rather than a signature should suggest that the lack of royal signatures on charters tells us next to nothing about royal literacy, though it does make one wonder why Thegan fussed so over Louis's hands-on treatment of his charters.[97]

Had Einhard not left us his puzzling comment on Charlemagne's efforts to learn how to write, the working assumption of most scholars might have been that Charlemagne could write with his own hand as they assume in the case of Louis and his sons. But Einhard did leave us with that report, even though he must have known that it was inconsistent with the general reputation of the learned Charlemagne disseminated by his court and poets. It would be well for us to examine his statement more closely:

> Temptabat et scribere tabulasque et codicellos ad hoc in lecto sub ceruicalibus circumferre solebat, ut, cum uacuum tempus esset, manum litteris effigiendis adsuesceret, sed parum successit labor praeposterus ac sero inchoatus.[98]

Temptabat et scribere: that is, he also attempted to write. The "et" should be taken as "also" and refers back to the preceding list of Charlemagne's linguistic achievements in Latin, Greek, and his study of the Liberal Arts, particularly arithmetic and astronomy. Writing with his own hand was part of a sequence of achievements and the biographer's placement of it last carries the recognition that Charlemagne had failed to master this one skill after his other accomplishments.[99] Einhard presents the king's linguistic achievements in roughly descending order of expertise and accomplishment,[100] leading from the *dicaculus* king of oral culture to the *labor inchoatus* of the written. The "et" may also contain a small element of surprise, that is, that in the midst of all his other busyness, Charlemagne had also added the challenge of learning to write, which Einhard may have considered an unusual skill for a layman (though he was one himself) and, strictly speaking, an unnecessary one for a king to possess.

Tabulasque et codicellos: Einhard here identifies the two different writing surfaces the king stored under the pillows of his bed. The use of the enclitic "-que" along with "et," meaning "both. . .and," also suggests that the author wished to distinguish two different surfaces. The first one, wax tablets, was the standard writing surface in daily use by students, scholars, and officials.[101] Although even Gibbon may have been tempted to regard tablets as childish instruments, in the ninth century they were the chief, albeit temporary, writing surface of all and the head of Charlemagne's own chancery, Ercenbald, wore double tablets, a diptych, on his belt and was ever ready to take down words.[102]

The easiest understanding of the second surface, the *codicelli*, would be that these were small parchment books, though there are several other possible interpretations: one that they too were tablets,[103] another that these were unattached scraps of parchment, or still another, as found frequently in Suetonius, that they were imperial documents written by the emperor's own hand and thus closer to the modern meaning of codicil.[104] Unless some distinction can be drawn between different kinds of wax tablets, it seems unlikely that Einhard meant to say that Charlemagne had two sets of wax tablets in his bedroom and more likely that he wanted to distinguish between different kinds of writing surfaces. Dhuoda specifically called the parchment volume she sent to her son William a *codicillum* or little book[105] and the Saxon poet in his crib of Einhard transformed *codicellos* into *cum paruis codicibus*,[106] literally that he had little codices. Hence it may be most reasonable to associate, as the Carolingians themselves did, Charlemagne's *codicelli* with parchment in some small book form.

When wax tablets and parchment are found together as here it may also indicate different stages of writing either in terms of learning to write or composing. These surfaces, of course, required different writing instruments, but Einhard does not tell us that Charlemagne had either a *stylus* or *penna* in hand, so we cannot immediately tell which surface he was actually writing on. Moreover, writing with ink on parchment was a more advanced skill and required more implements: pen, ink, and pumice for erasure for a start.[107]

Einhard's story of Charlemagne and his wax tablets achieved an interesting afterlife, since not only did the Saxon poet repeat it,[108] but the later ninth-century *Vision of Charlemagne*, feeding off of Einhard's passage, reported how the king awoke one night after a dream and wrote down on his bedside tablets the German words he had seen on a dream-sword.[109] The writer of the account, thus, assumed that Charlemagne could both read and write (in this case, German).

Hincmar of Rheims assumed the same. At the end of an exasperatingly long and controversial career, the archbishop was still harping on the need for kings to heed their advisors, but in 881 he had a new king, young Louis III, to train and so he organized a council at St-Macra of Fimes and published the results. In the final chapter he addressed the king directly. He told him that he had known men who had worked under Charlemagne and that the great one had chosen to surround himself with wise and distinguished advisors.

> And at the head of his bed he possessed wax tablets with a stylus and what[ever] he pondered day or night concerning the good of the holy church or the progress and stability of the kingdom, he noted down on those tablets. When he was with the advisors who were in attendance he went over those things. And when he came to the assembly he revealed everything, which had already been subtly considered, to the full gathering of his advisors and sought to achieve those things through common consent.[110]

The "wax tablets" placed at the head of the king's bed lead us directly to the report in Einhard's *Life of Charlemagne* and not to Einhard himself or to some other oral witness. Rheims did possess a copy of Einhard's biography during the archbishop's time.[111] Hincmar too interpreted Einhard's elliptical passage, eliminating the *codicellos* and supplying the stylus (*graphium*) necessary for working in wax. For him, Charlemagne was not learning to write, but was skillfully writing out *agenda* for he and his advisors to consider before proceeding to an assembly. In advising a young king to take advice, Hincmar's concern was to emphasize that Charlemagne wrote for purposes of good governance, not in pursuit of his personal education.

Ekkehard IV of St-Gall reported that Charlemagne's two large ivory tablets, made from his elephant, ended up at his monastery.[112] It has been claimed that these very tablets survive today as the covers of St-Gall cod. 60.[113] All of these accounts serve as reminders, relics, as it were, of the powerful impression left by Einhard's account of *Karolus Magnus scriptor*, Charlemagne the writer.

Ad hoc in lecto: that is, [he had these instruments] for this reason. . .on his bed. Medieval men, women, and monks did occasionally read in bed and one Carolingian capitulary said that if monks wanted to read after sext (when most apparently wanted to take a siesta) they should do so either in church or in their beds.[114] Of course, given the darkness of those rooms at night, candles were necessary for night reading, but also dangerous.[115] Abbot Maiol of Cluny fell asleep one night while reading *The Celestial Hierarchy* of the Pseudo-Dionysius by candlelight and awoke to find his room in flames.[116]

Sub ceruicalibus circumferre solebat: that is, that he used to place his writing surfaces under his pillows. The Saxon Poet, however, in his recreation of the scene spoke of Charlemagne carrying his tablets and little books around with him wherever he went,[117] which, as I shall shortly show, is the exact opposite of Einhard's telling image of the emperor storing the tablets and notebooks under the pillows on his bed. Here the meaning of *circumferre* is less to carry around, than to spread around under his pillows, though the image does conjure up thoughts of an uncomfortably lumpy pillow and Hans Christian Andersen's fairy tale of the princess and the pea. Still it was better than the snake that crawled out from under the young Nero's pillows, leaving its old skin behind.[118]

Vt, cum uacuum tempus esset, manum litteris effigiendis adsuesceret: that is, so that, if he had any free time, he might accustom his hand to forming letters. Thus Einhard has told his readers where Charlemagne wrote (in his bedroom) and when (during his spare time). The next phrase is especially important, for Einhard now tells us that Charlemagne was training his hand to shape characters; that is, that he was not so much writing as learning to write. *Effigio* is a relatively rare word taken from *effigies* or copy, which was itself derived from *effingo*, and the manuscript tradition of the *Life* contains many manuscripts that preferred to employ *effingendis*,[119] but the meaning would change only marginally if we chose one reading over the other, for both suggest shaping by pressing. This "shaping" also connotes "molding," from which we can now infer that Einhard thought Charlemagne was working in wax and not on parchment.[120] It is also necessary to note here that the Saxon Poet dropped this sequence entirely, for his Charlemagne attempted to write and carried books and tablets around with him at all times and all places.

Sed parum successit labor praeposterus ac sero inchoatus: that is, that his effort came too late in life and achieved little success. Einhard does not, unfortunately, define success. Did it mean simple knowledge of the characters, basic manual ability, or calligraphic and compositional excellence? But, however he measured success, he was sure that Charlemagne had achieved little of it. What is particularly interesting here is that Einhard twice supplies the same reason for Charlemagne's failure; his effort was out of season (*praeposterus*)[121] and begun too late (*sero inchoatus*). In this repetition we sense Einhard's customary reluctance to criticize Charlemagne or, at least, his habit of supplying excuses for his few failings. But he also supplies a critical fact, that Charlemagne took up writing late in life and his report of it and its personal features (the bedroom, pillows, wax tablets, and failure) suggest that this effort probably occurred while Einhard was at court and was something he personally observed—it may have been one of those things about which he was not sure anyone else could report.[122] Here too we need to remember that Alcuin had testified that Einhard was Charlemagne's assistant on the path to greater learning after 796.

What was Charlemagne writing in bed? It strikes me that there are two answers to this question: one, that at some early stage of his training he would most likely have been copying the alphabet or some short text, and, another, that he was attempting to learn how to write Caroline minuscule letters.[123] As to the first, since we know that he was writing in wax on tablets (*litteris effigiendis*), then the *codicelli*, whether they were parchment notebooks or small books, probably contained the texts he was copying. Numerous alphabets are to be found in Carolingian manuscripts and some of these doubtless served beginners as exemplars or were themselves the products of such exercises. Lupus of Ferrières asked Einhard for a copy of the scheme of uncial or capital letters that the royal scribe Bertcaud possessed; a copy of which may still survive.[124] And, indeed, as a boy Charlemagne's son Hugh asked for a copy of the alphabet to be written on a small piece of parchment so that he could begin learning it.[125] In the *Admonitio generalis* Charlemagne even seems to call for the correction of the *notas*, which might or might not be the model alphabets that boys first tried to imitate when learning to write.[126] The *codicelli*, however, may suggest a longer text and not just a single scrap of parchment with an alphabet on it.

As to the second, since Einhard informs us that Charlemagne took up writing late in life he would almost certainly have been trying to write and learn Caroline minuscule letters. Whether the existence of the new script was the very reason he took up writing is another question. By the 780s this script had begun, surprisingly quickly, to displace a variety of older scripts.[127] We know that the new script was at court by 781–83 since it was used to write the poem of dedication to King Charles in the so-called Godescalc Evangelistary.[128] And the court copy of the *Opus Karoli* from 793 (Vatican City, Vat. Lat. 7207) was written in Caroline minuscule along with its now erased original marginal notes.[129] Thus, when Einhard himself arrived at Charlemagne's court in the years 791–92 that new or reformed script had already taken hold.

Caroline minuscule is a script characterized by regularity and restraint, by fairly upright and uniform letter forms, by a standardized set of character shapes with little gross variation, by forms with few flourishes, by the spare use of ligatures to join letters, by the employment of a few common abbreviations, by a small but discrete space between letters, and by word division.[130] Charlemagne does not seem to have commanded the creation of Caroline minuscule, which was inchoate at monasteries such as Lorsch and Tours, but he and his court were committed by the late 770s to achieving an educational reform that stressed the correction and regularization of ecclesiastical texts and an improved script suited those purposes.

Not just the famous letter known as the *De litteris colendis*,[131] which called for higher standards of literacy, but even the *Admonitio generalis* stated the same goals and the latter specified that texts should be well written by men of mature age, that is, by trained scribes in their adult years.[132] Charlemagne himself or those writing on his behalf had already begun to fuss over punctuation (the question mark being one of their new signs)[133] and were especially attentive to details of legibility, standardization, and correctness. Charles and his court began to promote the spread of the new script. David Ganz observed that the monastery of Regensburg may have adopted Caroline minuscule after Charlemagne and his court visited in 792.[134]

Between 750 and 780 Charlemagne himself would have been exposed to pre-Caroline and a host of other scripts (uncial, half-uncial, and cursive) in a variety of local forms. The scripts of his youth and, indeed, any time before the 790s were varied, often ornate, irregular, and frequently cursive in appearance. The charters placed before the young king's eyes would have seemed a daunting forest of letters with elongated ascenders, pseudo-ligatures, and elaborately curved serifs. It was almost as if those Merovingian and early Carolingian scribes had labored to enhance the mystery of their art and hence their own indispensability by writing inscrutable and calligraphically complex scripts. Moreover, book scripts varied substantially from monastery to monastery and if Charlemagne wrote anything in his youth, his script would have reflected the style of the court or some specific place such as St-Denis.

If Charlemagne had studied as a youngster, he would have worked on wax tablets. Jerome's letter about the education of Paula recommended that she first be given a set of play letters made of boxwood and described how her fingers were to be guided as she first traced those letters in wax.[135] The wood models he recommended would have been best suited to the relatively straight lines of Rustic Capital letters and not Roman cursive. We do not know that Charlemagne ever received such rudimentary training in his younger years.

So, whatever scripts he had seen before he took office and whatever script he may have tried to copy as a boy (and it is hard to imagine that he never held a stylus in his hand even as a plaything), these were out of fashion at his court (and later the kingdom) by the 780s. They were surpassed by Caroline minuscule, which was adopted and promoted by his own court. But these were also years of intense activity and constant warfare for Charlemagne and he may not have applied himself to learning the new script or any script in a concentrated way for many years, for Einhard tells us that Charlemagne was old when he began practicing writing letters or, to be more precise, Caroline minuscule letters.

In 792 when Einhard appeared at court Charlemagne would have been about fifty years old, but those were years in which the war against the Saxons and others continued, the court chapel was being built in Aachen, the great project of building a waterway between the Danube and Rhine rivers was undertaken, and there were stirrings of grander international engagements. It may be that Einhard's observations about Charlemagne the writer refer to an even later period around 800 when his life had settled down somewhat. It was around this time that Alcuin told Charlemagne that Einhard could assist him with his studies. The king cannot have found it easy to learn Caroline minuscule. As David Ganz remarked, "To learn this new script was a difficult process, for the technique of using a quill requires precision and some training in reading and forming the strokes of the letters."[136]

Not just that, for Charlemagne's hands were old and the fine motor skills of hand-and-eye coordination necessary for employing a stylus or pen may have made reproducing the regularities and rigorous economy of Caroline minuscule difficult for him. The new script demanded that he close the upper loop of the letter *a*, constrain the length of ascending and descending strokes, not run letters together, and all in all restrain his hand. If he had learned another script some forty or more years earlier, he would have been engaged not just in learning a new script, but also in unlearning the techniques and characteristics of writing an older one. Einhard along with Alcuin seems to have shared the notion that one learned best when young, which may in neurological terms, at least when it comes to physical activities demanding precision, be true.[137] One court scholar advised his students:

> Boys, learn now! The time for training passes quickly. . .
> While your minds are quick and strong, dear fellows,
> Don't resist learning. . .[138]

Hrabanus knew from Vegetius that if warriors did not learn how to mount and ride horses early, they would never learn that skill well later in life.[139]

Twice in one sentence, as we saw, Einhard insisted that Charlemagne had taken up writing too late to achieve success.

In any event, according to Einhard, who should have known, Charlemagne never mastered fashioning letters. If that referred just to learning Caroline minuscule letters, why did he not say exactly that? One explanation might be that Einhard lacked the technical vocabulary to express himself clearly on the point,[140] that is, that the Carolingians themselves lacked a special or, at least, distinctive nomenclature for separating styles of script and seem not to have had a special word for Caroline minuscule.[141] It may be that the diminutive *litterulae* was occasionally used to signify Caroline minuscule as in Alcuin's description of Ercenbald:

litterulis, cartis miseris solatia praestat.[142]

[with small letters (and) charters he assists the needy.]

But *litterulae* was a word commonly used to describe an unpretentious epistle, thus invoking a *topos* of humility, and may never have been a specific name for minuscule script of which there were, after all, many kinds. It is striking how often in the Middle Ages great advances went unrecorded or, rather, the specifics of the transformation remain unexplained in the written record. The new plow technology of the early Middle Ages is an example as is, and more famously, the invention of Gothic architecture. The perfection of Caroline minuscule remains something of a mystery: no one quite tells us how it was initially conceived or officially promoted.

Thus, if the answer to what Charlemagne was writing in bed is an alphabet or short text written in Caroline minuscule, and the answer to when he was writing in bed is late in life during what little spare time was available to him, the answer to why he was writing in bed may be the most intriguing question of all. The short answer, I suspect, is that he did not want anyone to watch him write or watch him fail. His bedroom was a private realm protected by guards at the door and with officials and petitioners kept at bay.[143]

In public, where the king spent most of his time, he had no need to write since he was waited on by scribes such as Ercenbald who were always ready to take down his words. The court was filled with accomplished scribes, the *turba scriptorum* or crowd of scribes Alcuin described hanging on Ercenbald.[144] Moreover, Charlemagne with Alcuin's active urging had insisted upon correct texts, proper punctuation, and elegant expression.[145] What lay behind Charles's preoccupation with textual purity, of course, was the theological fear, so evident in the *De litteris colendis*, of offending God through clumsy and insulting speech, which was often caused by poorly written texts. Alcuin's preoccupation with excellent and exact scribal work surfaces in several of his poems[146] and Charlemagne's own capitularies evinced the same concern. Not only was the *De litteris colendis* concerned with correct copies and, therefore, careful writing, but the *Admonitio generalis* specified that religious texts must be copied scrupulously by expert scribes.[147] In one capitulary it was summarily stated "Concerning scribes: they should not write badly."[148]

Charlemagne's own fussiness on the matter was legendary. In a decidedly strange poem a certain Fiducia told Bishop Angilramnus of Metz, who died in 791, that while he had been at court (apparently at work writing out a text) he had on one occasion caught the attention of the king, but:

> Me tetigit Carulus dominus de cuspide pinnae:
> Errore confectus scriptio nostra fuit.[149]

> [Lord Charles struck me with the point of a pen:
> Our writing were ruined by an error.]

How serious or, indeed, physical the rebuke actually was is open to question, especially since Fiducia made pointed fun of his supposed ignorance by deliberately mangling both the meter and syntax of the last line of his poem.[150]

The real physical and mental abuse of scribes was not unknown. Some of the early medieval *probationes pennae* that Bernhard Bischoff printed and that were jotted down by scribes themselves as they tested their pens are startling:

> —If you don't write well, you [will] receive harsh blows.
> —If you don't write well, you will receive whacks on your back.
> —Learn to write, boy, lest someone mock you.
> —[If] I don't know how to write, I will be but an ass.[151]

These catchphrases are chilling precisely because they were probably learned by these scribes when they were schoolboys and still came to mind years later. Charlemagne himself was, to be sure, one of the architects of a scribal culture that disapproved of and actually punished the incompetent.

To read Notker's *Deeds of Charlemagne* is to encounter a Charlemagne who was given to the physical enforcement of correct standards; this was the demanding taskmaster Fiducia encountered. Charlemagne himself refused to reproach a choirmaster who threatened to hit a reluctant cleric with a small stick unless he sang for the emperor.[152] Charlemagne himself did not carry a small stick (*peniculus*) but a very large one, a veritable rod (*baculus*) of hard and knotted applewood, which served as a powerful weapon.[153] And he was quick to anger both at noble boys who were lazy in their studies and at a bishop who mocked a young man's singing, for he turned on him with blazing eyes and knocked him to the ground.[154] When supervising public readings he would indicate who should read by pointing his finger or his rod at the selected one. Still Notker doubted that most of these readers actually understood what they read out loud, for theirs was not true reading, but mere memorization, he reckoned.[155]

In all of this we cannot help but sense Charlemagne's lack of confidence in his own literary abilities. Said Einhard, a closer source by far than Notker on matters of the king's learning:

> He very carefully corrected the way in which the lessons were read and the psalms sung, for he was quite skilled at both. But he himself never read publicly and would only sing quietly with the rest of the congregation.[156]

This bashful and reticent public singer is the one who also withdrew to his apartment to practice writing in private. Even there he was secretive, for he did not leave his tablets lying about but placed them under his pillows. Did he lack the proper furniture to store them on or was he hiding the evidence of his rudimentary efforts from the few officials who might enter his private quarters? In the case of his public singing, what Einhard presents as an indication of the great one's humility may instead suggest a king who lacked public confidence in his learning and his command of proper Latin.

And so in the matter of his singing he kept relatively quiet in public and in the matter of his writing he withdrew from the public's gaze. In his bedchamber he could escape the eyes of those who could write and thus avoid the frowns of those who had achieved the standards of perfection he himself had sanctioned. In his world, where charges of hypocrisy were common and kings were warned to be on guard against it,[157] and public shame was the order of the day, Charlemagne may not have wished to humiliate himself in public with a clumsy stylus and the appearance of ineptitude. Nor would he have welcomed the image of himself as a mere schoolboy. A Stoic critic of Marcus Aurelius had once poked fun at the sight of an old ruler still attending school: "Oh Zeus, the aging emperor of the Romans is hanging tablets around his neck in order to go to school, while my King Alexander died at the age of thirty-two."[158] The emperor Charlemagne would not, it is safe to say, have found such mockery pleasant.

His retreat, however, may have seriously hampered his faltering attempts to learn how to write, since busy public figure that he was he can never have found the time or support for regular practice that learning to write requires; and he probably did not ask for help in mastering basic handwriting. Writing in a bed, moreover, cannot have been the best place to learn. When Hrabanus Maurus fell ill, he found it far from convenient to lie in a bed rather than to sit in order to read and write.[159] Einhard may have been one of the very few who actually knew of Charlemagne's private exercises in writing.

If, as the evidence seems to suggest, Charlemagne never mastered reading, then his difficulties in learning how to write would have been severely compounded. Indeed, an inability to read would have been the most serious impediment of all, and the example of King Alfred shows just how much could be accomplished by one who could read. Since, despite all his progress in reading, Alfred did not apparently learn how to write with his own hand, the challenge facing Charlemagne would have been that much more formidable.

To return to the problem set out at the start: Carolingian court culture was not a fraud, but neither was it quite what it pretended to be, at least not at its core, for its energetic and pulsating heart was a sovereign who was not fully literate and yet around him gathered a phalanx of client-scholars who carefully constructed an image of a learned, wise, eloquent, and all-knowing king. They adorned him with elevated epithets and paid obeisance to his intellectual accomplishments, but their compliments about his learning are, if examined closely, weak at the edges and their hyperbole suspicious, for exaggeration not only does not describe but often works to signal an actual weakness. No one ever stepped forward to specify in hard and convincing fashion that Charlemagne could read or write with his own hand and Einhard, who as always was too clever by half, told us only enough to leave some matters ambiguous (as, for instance, on the king's ability to read) and others excused.

In his ambiguity Einhard strangely demonstrates an instance of his relative and revealing reliability, for he said what he thought he could say about Charlemagne's learning without speaking untruths or belittling the accomplishments of his patron. If by his excessive caution and prudence of expression he misled uncareful readers and those prone to praise Charlemagne such as the Saxon Poet into believing in the king's full literacy, so be it. In managing the light and shadows in his portrait Einhard would probably not have been displeased if some seers failed to negotiate those areas that fell into greater shade. But, to be fair, we need to remember that he could have said nothing at all in which case Charlemagne's reputation as a *litteratus* would have been relatively secure. Perhaps a Suetonian imperative led him to cover off subject categories he would otherwise have preferred to leave aside.

The image of the wise Charlemagne, his persona as a learned ruler, was nonetheless one of the great creations of the Carolingian court and should be appreciated as such. How could this new David not be a writer when the first David had composed psalms; metaphors demand consistency and paintings perfection. The real man was able to speak and understand Latin, but probably did not read or read with any ease, and yet he bravely tried to learn how to write.

It cannot have been easy being Charlemagne. In a Latin culture that strove for perfection and mocked imperfection, he struggled and the mask of learning that his courtiers fitted awkwardly to his face must have weighed heavily. In the midst of a thriving literary culture he was forced to seek out the private realm of his bedroom where he could try to write a new script, sweet "Caroline,"[160] on his wax tablets. For a variety of reasons it did not come easily and he never took up regular writing. But it was admirable that he tried at all. He was, after all, not expected to be able to write; kings had no need to write, since so many could do it so well and so professionally at their bidding. Still we should acknowledge that the desire and the expectation for kings to be learned existed: Alfred himself wanted to be able to read and compose; Procopius mocked the emperor Justin who did not know his ABCs and could not even sign his own name;[161] and Charlemagne wanted to try his hand at writing. His Old Testament models, David and Josiah, as learned and law-bearing kings,[162] may have led him to aspire to greater intellectual heights.

In a certain light, Charlemagne's failure might be viewed as the most human indication of how deeply he sought to live up to the ideals that he and his court had set, for literacy lay at the heart of the educational reform of the court that he had so assiduously promoted. The court culture that was in its infancy in the 770s as he slowly began to collect scholars and set new standards of Latin literacy had swiftly outpaced him. It left him behind, never quite able to catch up to its rapid development. Perhaps, to cast his deficiency in a positive light, Charlemagne's relative lack of literacy actually allowed his literary and Latinate court culture to flourish, since it gave his courtiers a useful role and an area in which the king did not dominate and choke off or overdetermine development.

As for Charlemagne himself as *scriptor*, too much was against him: his age, a demanding new script, his isolation, and his pride. But it may have been that not being able to read or read well was the real weakness that doomed his efforts to learn how to write.

It took some courage for Einhard to tell us of his hero's failure to achieve complete literacy and some candor to document a weakness in the one whom he held in greatest awe. And imagine my surprise too, dear reader, for I began my study convinced that Charlemagne could write and set about collecting the evidence, but ended by wondering if he could even read. Things are, indeed, not always as they seem to be or as we would wish them to be, but then the destruction of our own assumptions is one of the historian's highest callings.

CHAPTER 4

OF CAROLINGIAN KINGS AND THEIR STARS

To study the historical sky or, rather, the sky in history may not be an entirely empty exercise, not if that sky spoke to the past and its actors, not if it became a focal point for their historical attention, and not if it was invested with meanings that weighed heavily on the earth-bound. This exploratory study moves from a consideration of Charlemagne and his stars to the divinatory and historical meaning of stars in the Carolingian age, and finally ends by examining the place of kings in the stars and as stars.

I

Let us begin on an oblique angle and with Alcuin, which often amounts to the same thing. Not long after becoming the abbot of St-Martin's of Tours he wrote to Charlemagne:

> Following your direction and high purpose, I, your Flaccus, am busy serving some at St-Martin's the honey of Sacred Scripture; others I attempt to intoxicate on the aged wine of ancient studies; others I am beginning to feed the fruit of the fine points of grammar; [and] some I am overjoyed to enlighten on the arrangement of the stars as if painted on high in some great man's house. I have become many things to many people in order to teach many for the benefit of God's holy church and for the glory of your imperial kingdom, lest the grace of almighty God be wanting in me and lest the generosity of your goodness cease.[1]

This letter, as with so many he sent to the king, is a rhetorical feast behind which lies the inescapable fact that one of them was an all-powerful patron and the other his needy client. Since as *magister* Alcuin fed his charges the honey of Scripture and the food and drink of the Liberal Arts, he pleaded in this begging letter for Charlemagne's help in acquiring some of the rare books he had once known at York. Alcuin would be dead within seven years, but in 797 his posting to Tours had energized him and here we find him in golden form, crafting sentences to seduce a king.

What strikes me most of all is the nugget buried in the middle of that mound of words, the one that suggests a pedagogy of the stars. This good client had a charming and manipulative manner (what good beggar does not?) and he was playing to his king's fascination with the resplendent heavens. The arresting image of the stars painted on the *culmen* or ceiling[2] of a great man's house may seem simple enough, but behind it lies a complex cosmology that courses in sinuous if oft broken line back to antiquity and to the opening passages of the Bible.[3]

The modern physics of creation may still confound most of us still with its postulation of an inconceivably immense and sudden cosmic excrescence in one violent moment crudely and sarcastically called the Big Bang; but the sequence presented by Genesis, being more poetry than physics, is more satisfying as literature and more comforting still as an account of divinely directed and ordered creation, for it describes a controlled and purposeful division of cosmic goods. Yet it does give one pause to realize that according to Genesis God made light and named day and night on the first day of creation, but did not create the assumed sources of that light—the sun, moon, and stars—in the dome of the sky until the fourth day in order to mark the passage of time and to shed pleasing light on the earth (Gen. 1 : 3–19). What that first light was we are never told. Early medieval readers of the Bible, particularly the poets, might be forgiven for thinking of the stars not just as timepieces, the star stuff of the *computus* and the calculation of paschal dates,[4] but as ornaments fixed on the hard dome of the world. Alcuin, the ever-clever riddler, tickled the king's son with an image of the stars as the *pictura culminis, nautorum gubernatores, noctis decor*, the painting on the ceiling [of the world], guides for sailors, the adornment of the night.[5]

A half century later Sedulius Scottus, one of those Irish *peregrini* who wandered from afar to wait on royal and episcopal pleasure, would speak of "the painted sphere of the heavens shimmering with the gift of light."[6] And he longed (as only those who forever lack such luxuries can) for a ceiling that glistened and shone as did his bishop's, for a shimmering ceiling served as a metaphor for the heavens that he trusted would one day welcome him and his patron, Hartgar.[7] His fellow Irishman, Eriugena, knew from Pliny that the very etymology of the word *caelum* (the heavens) derived from the picture of the stars as though etched on some engraving (*caelatum*).[8] The firmament was thus artful, firm, and made for humans to see.

Alcuin worked with the same image in mind when he wrote to Charlemagne, for the painted roof of the great man's house was the pale earthly image, a simulacrum, of the great painted dome of the heavens.

And if God was the greatest one, Charlemagne was certainly a great one, and by the late 790s he had a magnificent *domus* of his own, the palatine chapel of St-Mary's at Aachen, and in its soaring cupola was an image of the Lord. Our confidence in the original design of that mosaic may no longer be as settled and sure as it once was, but it still seems likely that an image or symbol of Christ in a star-studded sky surrounded by the Elders of the Apocalypse once lofted above the great royal octagon.[9] The magnificent Codex Aureus of St-Emmeram seems to capture in its first opening (figure 4.1: fols. 5v–6r) his grandson gazing up into that vaulted heaven of the end of time and around the Lamb of God shine brilliant stars.[10]

My suspicion is that Charlemagne may have been somewhat impatient with the static picture of the painted heavens Alcuin conjured up for him, for what caught his attention when he gazed into night's dark pool of scattered light was change and motion, not the fixed stars but the moving ones: planets, comets, and meteors. In another letter Alcuin realized that what Charlemagne wanted him to do was to separate out the constellations from the wandering lights in the sky.[11] Einhard noted the king's special enthusiasm for the study of astronomy, for "with deep purpose and great curiosity [he] investigated the movement of the stars."[12] It was not just the stars then, but their dynamic motion that fascinated him.

The most beautiful and precious of the three silver tables Charlemagne possessed depicted in delicately engraved lines the universe in three linked circles.[13] This table alone Louis the Pious kept back for himself from the prearranged distribution of his father's goods. Thegan described its cosmic circles as shield-like.[14] In the midst of the civil war of the next generation, Lothar removed the table from Aachen, chopped it up, and paid off his vacillating supporters with his pieces of silver.[15] The table showed, if we may trust the annalist, the world, its stars, the movement of the planets, and the principal constellations.[16] Again the stars Charlemagne pondered in the sky and on his table were in flux.

Seneca once mildly complained that the heavens may bore us by their familiarity, but should some new wonder flash across the sky we all stand staring in amazement and perplexity.[17] That was Charlemagne, but many of us have also shared in the same elemental amazements. We stood transfixed in 1997 as the comet Hale-Bopp passed softly through the night sky. But too seldom do we look at the sky these days and when we do we do not see what the Carolingians saw, for theirs was a pregnant sky and it was that older awareness of the power of the heavens themselves of which Peter Brown reminded us:

> Living as we do in a bleakly submonotheistic age, we tend to look up into the sky and to find it empty. We no longer see there a *mundus*, a physical

4.1 Charles the Bald gazes up at the Lamb of God in the Codex Aureus of St-Emmeram (Munich, Bayerische Staatsbibliothek, Clm. 14000, fols. 5v–6r).

universe as heavy as a swollen cloud (for good or ill) with the presence of invisible beings.[18]

The flatlanders of the late ancient world knew that above them in that swollen sky so full of powers and potentialities flitted the *daemones*, both the good (*calodaemones*) and bad (*cacodaemones*) spirits.[19] And the early Middle Ages came to think that angels, those ministers of divine pronouncement, spilled down from on high like a cascading waterfall of divinity in nine easy steps. Such beings may have been unseen, but they were far from unimagined. In the Sacramentary of Metz, a gorgeous but unfinished manuscript, one page is crammed full of the various ranks of angels, most prominently a Seraph with its six wings covered with eyes as though to keep constant watch over the world below.[20]

Beyond the angels were the twinkling stars, the consorts of God. If we are to understand earlier ages more fully and subtly, events and attitudes, both the ordinary and extraordinary, we need to examine what may not strike us as immediately important to our world, but which may have been critically important to theirs. If the Carolingian worldview depended to some degree on a sky alive with power and the promise of divinization, we as historians need at least to attempt to engage their conviction if we are ever to understand ninth-century actors and their too often unstated assumptions about how they thought their world worked.

We might first want to consider just when Charlemagne's interest in the stars tilted from curiosity into something more intense, into something almost imperial. The Charlemagne Einhard knew in the late 790s was one who was intensely interested in unusual events in the heavens, but there is no evidence that when younger the king had much cared about the stars. Stargazing may have been a late life interest of his and its opening moment may fall very near the writing of Alcuin's letter. There his own sometime teacher set out his mission at St-Martin's to train students in Scripture, grammar, ancient learning, and astronomy, all for the benefit of the church and to supply educated men for Charlemagne's *imperiale regnum*, his imperial kingdom, which is Alcuin's own intriguing phrase.

One cannot but notice that the *Royal Frankish Annals* in its original form contained no references to stars prior to 798, which would make of the period since Pepin the Short's rise a starless half century, at least in historiographical terms.[21] The reviser of the annals added a small notice of a solar eclipse to the entry for 764 and beginning with the entry for 807 the astronomical information in the annals multiplies dramatically.[22] There would be no compelling reason for us to associate the original annalist's astral attention in 798 with the king were it not for its correlation to Charlemagne's own growing interest in the stars and the remarkable set of letters he exchanged with Alcuin.[23]

In early November 797 Alcuin wrote the king about the nineteen-year cycle of the moon, a letter that may have provoked a debate at court since at the end of the following March he responded to two letters that had come to him in the king's name. "O wisest researcher into natural things and most devoted investigator into the meaning of each and every cause [of things], my Lord David," was the sticky praise Alcuin spooned out, but he was worried that in his absence the king had surrounded himself with pseudo-Egyptians, the *pueri Aegyptiaci*, who wanted to alter the very calendar and to begin the year in September.[24]

In July Charlemagne sent the abbot four gifts, which Alcuin interpreted as symbols of the first four days of creation. The candles or oil he associated with the creation of light on the first day; vestments with the covering of the firmament on the second; gold with the third day since it came from the earth; and finally an intricately designed dish reminded him of the endless roundness of the sun and the moon's passage through the constellations. On the dish, then, Alcuin saw an image of the creation of the sun and stars on the fourth day. Its circularities suggested the roundness of the universe itself, the same sort of curved design Charlemagne encountered when he gazed upon his engraved silver table, his *caelum caelatum*, his engraved heavens.[25]

The king's messenger not only brought gifts to the abbot, he also conveyed a request: Charlemagne wanted to know more about the moon and its phases. Before answering, which he did at length, Alcuin once again praised the king's natural astronomical instincts, for only Charlemagne could "easily understand the sun, moon, and stars."[26] God had given him the clearest knowledge of divine law and the most satisfying understanding of natural things.[27] And the king stood in exalted company, for Abraham himself had shown the way. The patriarch had understood and venerated the creator because he had studied the stars and in so doing had become an *amicus dei* ever fortified in his faith.[28] What Alcuin recommended to his king was an astronomy that would draw him closer to the numbers imbedded in the stars and in Scripture and to an appreciation of God's deeper sidereal design.

The poet of *Karolus Magnus et Leo Papa* also extolled Charlemagne's privileged penetration of natural mysteries, for God had revealed to him the universe's development from its earliest beginnings.[29] Special insight into the stars became, at least in panegyric, an assumed imperial virtue. It also contained the promise of angelic elevation as Sedulius Scottus later suggested to some noble:

Felicibus et uisis
Superna specularis:
Ex sopho m<i a>latus
Nunc angelus clarescis.[30]

[You observe the heavens
For fortunate signs;
From being a wise man to us
You now begin to shine as a winged angel.]

This was the wise man's way up and out, even if in the here and now it conflated observation and aspiration. Alcuin hoped that through astronomy his new Abraham would become a true friend of God and in the end a resident of the resplendent heavens.

Here a gnawing, but practical doubt surfaces: was that what Charlemagne was searching for when he scanned the sky or was he seeking a more immediate and practical understanding of the unfolding heavens? The summer of 798 found the king campaigning in Saxony. He asked his aged abbot to compose a soothing song that would calm his men amidst the raucous noise of war,[31] but it may have been the broken music of the spheres that worried him most of all. Both he and Alcuin had noticed that the planet Mars had disappeared, and they had looked for it for a long time (*diu quaesiuimus*).[32] It had been absent from the sky, according to the royal annalist, for an entire year.[33] In his reply Alcuin remarked on its sudden reappearance and tried to explain the phenomenon in both mythological and astronomical terms.[34] One is left wondering if, despite the learned character of Alcuin's answer, Charlemagne's concern with the missing planet may have been more martial than astronomical, for the sky-god of war had disappeared and only returned when the king was himself on the Saxon front and at war. His thoughts, then, were both on the clatter of war and the surprise of a strange sky that had until late lacked its familiar red wanderer.

There was, of course, no cult of Mars at Charlemagne's Christian court, but there was an endless interest in war at the palace of the great *belliger*, the bringer of war. The exiled poet Ermold the Black would later assert that anyone who knew the Frankish tongue should know that Hludowicus, the name of Charlemagne's son Louis the Pious, meant "illustrious Mars."[35] But then he was a poet with Virgilian tastes and, in describing the paintings in the palace at Ingelheim, he betrays his poetical and political schooling. For him Charles Martel was the first Carolingian master of Mars and his son Pepin had conquered the Aquitainians through the favor of Mars.[36] No matter the verse formulas at work, now stripped of their deeper paganism, this poetical shorthand still manifests an older vocabulary of divine relationships.

By September the king had returned from summer campaign and he sent a messenger in haste to Alcuin to ask him to scrutinize the sky again.[37] He wanted him to expound further on the subject of the wandering stars, a request that followed hard on the disquieting disappearance and reappearance of Mars. Alcuin once again turned to explain the movements of the planets.[38] That Charlemagne might understand the matter better, he even drew up a chart, a *figura*.[39] Alcuin, though claiming to lack the necessary books, cited Pliny and Bede in trying to address the king's question. But the important issue for Charlemagne, we may suspect, was to have his schoolmaster explain the implications of the puzzling astronomical event they had both witnessed.

The next spring found the two of them still wrestling with things astronomical. The king sent Alcuin charts of the moon's circuit and his master sent back still other materials,[40] for he believed that it was his duty to dig up little particles of gold from the earth and that it was the king's to wear on high a royal diadem shimmering with the gems of wisdom.[41] These royal crowns were themselves in symbolical terms star-studded and radiant suns.[42]

In Charlemagne's circle, stargazing was something of a royal function and it may be that, as much as anything, that drove Carolingian intellectuals to pursue their study of the stars. Not astronomy as natural science, then, but as political and theological hermeneutic may lie at the center of the Carolingian patronage of astronomy. Theirs was, after all, a court culture and a king's interests might dictate the beginnings and rough directions of intellectual inquiry. And what interested Charlemagne soon spread to those around him.[43]

In the same letter of July 798 Alcuin also addressed questions put to him about the moon by a woman whom he called *filia mea, famula uestra fidelissima*. Since Charlemagne was on campaign at the time, Ernst Dümmler suspected that this woman, whom Alcuin called his daughter and the king's most faithful servant, was Liutgard, Charlemagne's wife, who may well have traveled with him that summer two years before her death.[44] It is probably Liutgard too whom Alcuin described in a court poem a few years earlier:[45]

Noctibus inspiciat caeli mea filia stellas,
Adsuescatque deum semper laudare potentem,
Qui caelum stellis ornauit, gramine terras,
Omnia qui uerbo mundi miracula fecit.[46]

[At night let my daughter look upon the stars in the heavens
And become used to praising at all hours [our] powerful God,
Who adorned the sky with stars, the earth with grass,
[And], through his Word, worked all the world's miracles.]

If this woman was in fact the queen, then it might be thought that she and the king shared an intimate interest in what transpired in the heavens, perhaps because their real interests were personal and dynastic.

The connection had been laid down for them by God: "His dynasty will continue forever, his throne, like the sun before me. Like the moon, it will stand eternal, forever firm like the sky" (Ps. 88:37–38). Or again in a prayer for King Solomon: "May he live as long as the sun endures, like the moon, through all the generations" (Ps. 71:5–6). But what if God decided to stop the sun or darken the moon, and the Carolingians were for the most part convinced that he could? Star scanning was a function and responsibility of the king's special place in the divine scheme of things; King David had been a stargazer too. And it extended down the generations. One poet said of a grandson of Charlemagne that his august mind was able to understand the very law of the stars, "composed with numbers and various signs."[47]

Alcuin's praise of Charlemagne's special ability to discern the workings and profound meaning of the stars should be set somewhere along that faint borderline that lay between the exultation of panegyric and a quieter confidence in the specialness of the royal person. Throughout the late 790s Charlemagne and his court also had their eyes on the imperial prize,[48] and it may not be extravagant to wonder if, at that critical juncture, they were on the lookout for any signs of divine pleasure or displeasure that God might deign to send their way in the sky. There was too an old idea formulated by Eusebius and Jerome that the world's allotted time might run out in the year 800, at the end of the sixth age, but no Carolingian seems to have explicitly expressed much worry over the matter.[49] Still the late 790s was a time when it seemed important to study what God was up to in the skies overhead.

Charlemagne's scrutiny of the heavens did not cease after his imperial coronation in late 800 or Alcuin's death in 804, but remained intently focused on the unusual. The royal Frankish annalist, who mirrored the emperor's interests in ways we have not always sufficiently appreciated, reported that between September 806 and September 807 there had been one solar and three lunar eclipses, that Mercury had been observed as a dark spot above the sun (or perhaps it was a sun spot), and on 26 February after an eclipse of the moon immense battle lines had appeared in the sky.[50] Charlemagne may well have asked one of his scholars what these events signified, but no record of such an inquiry now survives; our one indication of royal interest being his house history.

But in 810 when the sun and moon experienced two eclipses each he wrote to the abbot of St-Denis, seeking his opinion on the surprising occurrence of two solar eclipses in one year.[51] The letter passed into the hands of the Irishman Dungal, a monk of St-Denis, who researched the matter, as Bruce Eastwood has shown in rich detail, by consulting Pliny and Macrobius, and he wrote a learned response to the emperor's perplexity.[52] The monk was reassuring, for he found nothing particularly shocking in the two eclipses and he in essence told Charlemagne not to worry, that all was right with the world and Christ's appointment of its moving parts.

Still Charlemagne may have felt that the stars were against him in 810. On his last campaign against the Danish king, Godefrid, he had set out from camp before dawn one summer morning when a meteor flashed across the sky from right to left. "As everyone pondered what this sign meant,"[53] Charlemagne's horse collapsed under him like some medieval version of a Marino Marini sculpture of a horse buckling under its rider. Only Einhard tells us this story, but it is detailed and believable.

The account belongs to that remarkable penultimate chapter of the *Life of Charlemagne* in which Einhard, impressed by Suetonius's habit of amassing signs of approaching imperial deaths, collected and shaped his own set for his own Caesar. The first portents he presents are all astronomical and there again we seem to meet the extraordinary eclipses of 810, a dark spot on the sun (which may memorialize and make more mysterious the 807 report of Mercury's supposed darkening of the sun), and the account of the meteor that felled Charlemagne. The other portents—the bridge over the Rhine that burned down, earthquakes, a lightning bolt knocking off the golden apple from the peak of St-Mary's, and fading inscriptions—complete a picture of the collapses, destruction, and obliteration that preceded the emperor's death according to Einhard's categorical construction.[54]

Here, however, the biographer says in the space of one short chapter, two contradictory things: that Charlemagne himself knew from these signs that his death was drawing near and that he rejected all these incidents or acted as if they had nothing to do with himself. It is not impossible that both statements are true, one a reflection of the personal, the other the public posture Charlemagne was forced to assume. In the case of the eclipses we know that it was Charlemagne himself who wanted answers about their significance and that, since 797, he had been pressing his wise men for a close reading of the stars.[55] Alcuin and Dungal had answered with the best and most comforting science they had at hand, but Einhard's interests may have been closer to the king's. What did it all mean, as his retainers had asked when they saw that sudden meteor?

II

Carolingian kings wanted the sky read, wanted their scholars to weigh the pressing intersection of divine messages and temporal prospects, and wanted, most of all, peace of mind. Hibernicus Exul, one of the king's poets, promised that those who carefully studied the stars would obtain presages of things to come.[56] And later Sedulius Scottus hoped not only that Lothar I, clothed in purple, might always triumph, but also "that

neither the sun nor the moon might do him harm."[57] Since the sun and
moon are not normally lethal, Sedulius's protective prayer surely takes the
sun and moon as signs in the sky ever on the verge of revealing God's hidden plan for the emperor. These worries were grounded in Old Testament
intimations of the meaningfulness and powerful presence of divine signs:
Et misit signa et prodigia in medio tui (Ps. 134:9).[58]

This Carolingian watchfulness should probably not be classified as "the
reemergence of astrology" in the West, as Stephen McCluskey has,[59] since
the fundamental point is that learned Carolingians were not so much
actively prognosticating as reading what they thought had been forced on
them, and there is an important difference. To isolate irregular and unpredictable happenings in the heavens was to doubt astrology and instead to
affirm God's power to do in the sky whatever he wished, to communicate
howsoever and whensoever he chose. Divine signs, especially importunate
ones, demanded attention. Would it not be a demonstration of the sin of
pride to spurn God's own pointed warnings? The ninth century would
produce gorgeous manuscripts of astrological signs such as we encounter in
the Leiden *Aratea*,[60] but virtually no horoscopes and no sophisticated
mathematical reckonings of human fortune.[61]

Still the line between astronomy and astrology was often lightly drawn in
the Middle Ages.[62] ASTROLOGIA and ASTRONOMIA were even interchange-
able figures in depictions of the quadrivium.[63] But the critical point on
which the two sciences turned was whether active divination was pursued
or not. Hrabanus Maurus in his little, Isidore and Augustine-fed treatise on
magic condemned *astrologi, genethliaci* (who based their divinations on the
day of birth), and *mathematici* and *horoscopi* who calculate the future based on
the stars.[64] But these were ancient professions, not Carolingian ones, and
Hrabanus's investigation was more antiquarian than contemporary.

What generally worried the Carolingian ruling classes was the threatening resurgence or, perhaps, just the traditional persistence of a paganism
that compromised the plenitude of God's power by diffusing it.[65] Strange
ideas, both novel and traditional, about the workings of the universe
percolated up and down. Boniface had complained to the pope that Virgil,
the bishop of Salzburg, taught that below this world there was another
world and also another sun and another moon.[66] Beliefs that ate away at
divine omnipotence or called into question an assumed cosmology that was
its reflection worried men like Boniface, especially since out there in the
Carolingian countryside there were other ideas still at work and they were
often more ancient and accepted. There a set of popular notions about the
stars long predated Christianity's appearance on the scene and mixed with
it when it arrived. Four of the items in the eighth-century *Indiculus
superstitionum* concern the stars.[67]

The most striking (and innocent) report of popular astral beliefs is supplied by Hrabanus himself and the critical core of the incident does not
concern divination, but old and popular techniques for coping with the
astronomically unexpected. One night the bishop heard a racket outside his
room and soon learned that the moon was in eclipse and that his parishioners thought that if they shouted they might ease its struggle and return
it to vibrant life once again. Some visitors told him that on other occasions
(and presumably elsewhere) they had heard horns blowing and the grunt-
ing of pigs, and had seen men hurling arrows and spears toward an eclipsed
moon. These people apparently believed that the moon was being eaten or
attacked by some monster whom they might scare off. Others believed that
to appease these moon-sucking demons they should destroy hedgerows
and break dishes. Good pastor that he was, Hrabanus tried to explain to his
flock that natural forces could account for the moon's eclipse and that it
was not an omen.[68] Having watched as the fragments of the comet
Shoemaker-Levy 9 fractured into pieces and collided with Jupiter in 1994,
some of us may be reluctant to make light of an earlier age's concern over
dramatic events that occur in an unknown night sky.[69]

For Hrabanus divination was an active and malicious attempt to discover
and manipulate the future by magical means. But even Hrabanus would not
have doubted that God controlled the heavens or that when he made signs
in the sky an orthodox king should ignore them. In 837 when a sad and
foreboding comet, which we now know was Halley's Comet,[70] appeared
in the sky for twenty-five days Louis the Pious immediately called on one
of his courtiers, the one popularly known to us as the Astronomer since, as
he said of himself, he was reputed to know the stars.[71] The Astronomer
tried to buy time, as even Louis realized, for a more cautious reading of the
comet lest he rush to announce something precipitous and unfortunate.
But Louis would not be put off and so sent the Astronomer into an adjoin-
ing room (effectively then, an observatory) to study the star that very night.
The two of them had had such conversations before. "But I know," said the
emperor (presumably, of the tail of Halley's), "that this is a sign of comets
about which we have spoken before. Tell me what you think it portends!"[72]
Not what the comet was, but what would follow from it was Louis's true
concern.

Comets, and not just the appearance of Halley's, were evidently much
on Louis's mind. But just as Dungal had ignored Charlemagne's real question, which was 'what does this astronomical event mean for me and
mine?', so did the Astronomer his son's, for he too tried to hold fast to the
learned and rational. But the emperor quickly came to the cold heart of
the atter, which he realized the Astronomer had been avoiding. Everyone
knew, Louis insisted, that such an event announced a change in the fortunes

of the kingdom or the death of a prince.[73] Even Hrabanus allowed as much.[74] The Astronomer wisely assured the emperor that, according to Scripture, he should not be dismayed by those signs in the sky that make nations shudder.[75]

Louis agreed that it was all up to God, who had made both the stars and humans, but he was firmly convinced that the stars conveyed divine messages:

> We can never wonder at or praise enough the mercy of one who deigns by such important signs to admonish our ignorance, since we are sinners and not penitent. Since, therefore, this showing concerns both me and everyone, let all of us according to our ability and understanding hurry to improvement, lest our lack of penitence obstruct the mercy already extended by God and we are found unworthy.[76]

The Astronomer was later informed that after their meeting Louis had drunk a little wine (stronger than he usually drank) with his men, sent them home, observed a personal vigil, and toward dawn prayed and praised God. In the morning he ordered generous alms to be given to the poor and to priests, monks, and canons, and special masses were celebrated. Then Louis went hunting in the Ardennes forest; and the hunt was a particularly bountiful one, surely a sign that his alert reading of the comet had been both accurate and timely and his actions the wanted balm.

Lupus of Ferrières may also have seen the passing of Halley's Comet. A letter reached him on 29 April, sent by a fellow monk who likely saw the comet when it first appeared, so that Lupus himself may not have caught sight of the "faint star" (if it was Halley) until late in its journey past earth. In his letter the monk asked Lupus a series of questions about syllables, pronunciation, orthography, and finally comets.[77] "Concerning the comets which have been seen, it would seem that there is more to dread than discuss," Lupus replied.[78] He observed that the Bible did not mention comets at all, but he was prepared to turn to pagan authorities for their fearful reports of the pestilence, famine, and war announced by them. Virgil had observed that comets signaled the onset of civil war and Caesar's murder and Lupus noted that Jerusalem's destruction had been preceded by a sword-shaped star. Still, not all stars brought about disaster since Mithridates's greatness had been foretold by the appearance of an impressive comet. But the comet of 837 struck him as faint and unimpressive, all in all a transitory disturbance of the heavens over which he did not long linger.

If Lupus preferred philology to astronomy, his old friend Einhard read a great deal into the new comet. He shared Louis's penitential concerns and wrote a lugubrious letter of alarm to the emperor. But by 837 Einhard had become decidedly morose, for he was feeling aged and infirm, had still not fully recovered from the shock of his wife's death, and remained dismayed by the revolts and searing political disruptions of the previous years. The common opinion of the ancients, he said, was that comets marked the onset of sad times. In all of the Bible, he observed only the appearance of the star announcing Christ's birth (Matt. 2:2) had foretold something good. The appearance of this new comet, then, was an indication that the Franks deserved the punishment heading their way. It mattered not at all whether humans were warned of God's anger by a human, an angel, or a star. The warning itself was everything:

> Only this is necessary: to understand that the appearance of the star was not without meaning, but warned humans that by being penitent and calling upon the mercy of God they may work toward avoiding his future anger.[79]

Then he outlined cases in the Bible in which penitent peoples had been spared God's wrath, but he suspected that a recent attack by the Northmen on the kingdom had been only a partial payment for God's anger.[80] A much heavier punishment was about to fall.

Had Einhard's opinion been solicited? My suspicion is that it had not, for Louis had his own expert and accommodating astronomer close at hand. But his old courtier could not leave well enough alone. He may have been worried that Louis and his court scholars would miss the real point of the phenomenon, soon forget the comet, or that they might just rationalize it away, the careful court approach the Astronomer had in fact taken. For Einhard there was no mistaking what the comet meant: for by it God was warning the Franks that a major catastrophe, well beyond the local damage the Northmen had recently done, would descend on them if they did not mend their ways. That sharp-edged complaint had been around since the 820s and much of Einhard's writing betrays a trace of it,[81] but the letter of 837 was a *cri de coeur*, however resigned and baleful, for the king to pay closer attention to the dire state of the emergency announced by the comet. The shrillness of Einhard's letter is startling, but it was also a fair reflection of the mood of someone who now lived on the margins of royal power and was despondent over how Louis's calamitous decade had played out in spite of all the manifest warnings he had received from angels, saints, and humans.[82]

To return to the Astronomer: he had cleverly avoided the emperor's direct question as best he could, but he was in fact convinced that comets and eclipses do foretell death and disaster. In their face-to-face encounter Louis may have forced him to commit to a benign or, at least, neutral reading of the comet, but Louis himself seems to have been unsure of the conclusion he had coerced. Instead he acted on the divine warning he thought he had received. Not only did he reassure his men and send them home to look after their own, he also ordered the distribution of charity, the performance of prayer, and the holding of special masses. He also planned a trip to Rome, often the overt response of a penitent ruler seeking to assuage God's displeasure.[83]

Louis had proceeded in much the same way in 823 after a series of strange events struck: an earthquake at Aachen, strange sounds in the night, a girl who abstained from food for over a year, lightning, hail and stones dropping from the sky, and plague. Then he had concluded, "by these prodigies a great disaster in the future was most certainly portended for the human race."[84] That time too he had ordered the appeasement of an angry God by fasts, prayers, and the distribution of alms.

As to the Astronomer, Halley's Comet is virtually the only astronomical event in his biography not accompanied by the death of a great person or some related disaster. In February 817, he observed, an eclipse of the moon was followed by an unnatural collection of comets, whereupon Pope Stephen V died. Not much later a building in Aachen collapsed on the emperor and his followers.[85] In 818 Louis's wife, Ermengard, died, and the Astronomer was quick to note that an eclipse of the sun had preceded her death.[86] Ten years later two of Louis's counts were campaigning in Spain and suffered a stunning defeat: "At night terrible battle lines [in the sky], glowing red like human blood and blazing with a shockingly fiery color, had preceded this calamity."[87] Late in 828, the Astronomer reported, a set of strange events including two lunar eclipses occurred and, of course, the rebellion of 830 followed not long afterward. In 838 he reported the appearance of another comet:[88] "The death of Pepin [Louis's son] followed not long after [it showed] its frightening face."[89]

Finally, of course, a biographer so impressed by a portentous sky could not let Louis himself leave the stage without a light show and that happened on 5 May 840 when a "preternatural" and total solar eclipse took place:

> Although this portent should be ascribed to nature, nevertheless it was completed by a woeful departure. For it was portended by this that the greatest light of mortals, the light that shone for all upon the candelabrum set up in God's house, our emperor of pious memory, would soon be taken from us and that the world would be left in darkness and distress upon his leaving.[90]

The Astronomer moved in a world of light and shadows where even a solar eclipse six weeks prior to the emperor's death found its real referent in his passing. For him eclipses were all at once natural and preternatural events, and almost always connectible and meaningful.[91] Hrabanus Maurus, depending on Isidore, maintained that though portents seem to run against nature and our expectations, they actually belong within divinely created nature.[92] The portentous was purposeful because God was its ultimate author, and so the Astronomer and others watched and waited.

Carolingian historians as a group might almost be plotted on a graph demonstrating which ones read and wrote historical significance into natural portents and which did not. The Astronomer's fellow biographer Thegan, for instance, entirely ignored the stars as did Hincmar of Rheims when, in 861, he took over the composition of the *Annals of St-Bertin*. Their disinclination to factor in the stars was a conscious and complex decision about the intersection of narrative, historiography, and cosmology. Thegan and Hincmar may have decided that God did not speak through the stars or, at least, not in a way that pertained to the story they were telling. Or they may have decided that it was not for them to read God's mind or that Christ had already warned them not to expect these light shows as demonstrations of his cosmic power (Matt. 16:1–4). Even there in the Gospel, however, the message was equivocal, since Christ rejected the challenge from the Pharisees and Sadducees to work a wonder in the heavens, but revealed that he too knew something of reading signs in the sky; a red sky in the evening meant fair weather the next day, our 'sailors' delight'.[93]

Among the many Carolingian historians who did think the stars played an important part in historical narrative, most worked by a kind of parataxis, that is, they tended to isolate astronomical and natural portents, making them stand alone in separate sentences without a close grammatical or causal connection to the sentences and events around them. Hence these historians worked by association, setting down a portentous eclipse beside the death of a prince without directly linking the two events. On our imaginary chart, these writers would fall somewhere toward the middle and upper half of the graph, for they constructed and associated but refused to connect and explain. Einhard and the Astronomer should be placed toward the top, for not only did they collect examples of the sky's strange phenomena, they also attached them to important events in the sodden earth below.

In his elegant history of the civil war, Nithard reported that a comet in February 842 coincided with the conference that led to the famous pact of Louis and Charles at Strasbourg; when they were finished with their meeting it vanished.[94] He does not in this case, except by parataxis, treat the comet as anything other than a temporal coincidence, yet he took the trouble to report it. He also witnessed a solar eclipse while working on his book; here his use of the astronomical was somewhat heavy-handed for he inserted the account as an aside four months out of chronological (though not authorial) sequence near the end of the second book on the exact eve of the bloody Battle of Fonetnoy.[95] Unless we are to believe that the solar eclipse occurred at the very moment he finished writing the sentence, "Quae quidem Lodharius solito more insolenter spreuit et uisuros se quid agere deberet respondit," at six o'clock on the morning of 18 October 841, then we are allowed to suspect that he set the out-of-place eclipse down where he did in his narrative account of the evening of 24 June as a divine comment on the sad story of the fratricidal battle of 25 June that he had next to relate. With this solar eclipse now narratively portentous, he was able to fuse historical and authorial time and bring the wheeling heavens into meaningful conjunction on parchment and in narration with the disastrous battle yet to unfold.

Thus Nithard, even though more subtle than other narrators, also assumed that the stars and history were linked, just as Louis himself had when he challenged the Astronomer to voice his own unspoken assumption. Nithard likely supposed that his reader, Charles the Bald, shared his thinking about the stars and could be counted on to make the connections he laid out for him. But the final chapter of his fourth and final book, which Janet Nelson has characterized as a personal history unlike the royally commissioned books that preceded it,[96] broke through mere implication and ends with a delicate weaving together of pessimistic signs of the world's ruin. God had turned the very elements against the mad sinners of Francia:

> Once [during the time of Charlemagne] the elements themselves were in our favor, but now they are hostile to all everywhere. As Scripture, which was given to us as a divine gift, says: "And the world shall wage war against the mad" (Wisd. 5:21). At the same time on March 20, an eclipse of the moon occurred. On top of that a great deal of snow fell that same night and, by the just judgment of God, it inspired sadness in all. I bother to mention this because pillage and crime broke out everywhere and that foul weather took away all hope of good [to come].[97]

Not only do the heavens and the climate serve as the final passage of Nithard's history, but they are shown here to contain a chilling expression of God's disappointment over the Carolingian world's turn toward sin and outright madness.

Florus of Lyons in his rueful poem on the division of the empire in the civil war was equally gloomy and also looked to the sky, for he thought the elements and stars reflected in their acting out the rending of Francia. The heavens had foretold the evil event through bloody battle lines of fire and an eclipse that blocked out the sun and allowed the stars to shine during the day.

> Quod monstrum scimus bellum ferale secutum. . .[98]
> [We know that a savage war followed that portent. . .]

The second annalist of the St-Bertin annals, Prudentius of Troyes, failed to report the visit of Halley's Comet, though he would certainly have done so had Louis the Pious died, for he too was convinced that the stars spoke of and to kings. Thus he reported that Pepin had died eight days after a lunar eclipse, that after a solar eclipse Louis the Pious died, that in 855 two comets were seen in the sky, which he associated with the deaths of Pope Leo IV and the emperor Lothar, and that in 859 battle lines and bloody columns were seen in the night sky at the time of a new Danish assault on the kingdom.[99] It is somewhat unsettling to move from an annal so stuffed with stars and one in which the natural and human worlds so intimately intersect to Hincmar's starless continuation.

The various annalists of the *Annals of Fulda* would also fall somewhere on the upper half of our imagined graph, since they regularly treated astronomical and natural phenomena, but often without connecting them explicitly to historical events.[100] Still, on two occasions these annalists, though carefully avoiding making too close a connection by practicing a kind of compromised parataxis, drew a tighter bond between the astronomical and historical. In June 875, the annalist reported, a brilliant comet had appeared "foretelling by its appearance the amazing, no rather the lamentable event that quickly followed, although we should worry that because of our manifest sins it portended even more serious [disasters] to come."[101] The first disaster was a sudden flood that wiped out a village in eastern Franica and killed eighty-eight of its inhabitants, but the more serious event, the report of which immediately follows in the annal, was the death of the emperor Louis II. In 882, another entry noted that a comet with a particularly long tail filled the sky, "foretelling by its appearance the unfortunate event that quickly followed," for King Louis the Younger's illness grew worse and two days later he died.[102]

But if the eastern annalists were relatively sparing in their use of the stars, Gerward, the supposed author of much of the *Annals of Xanten*, littered his brief entries with sky dust.[103] He too worked paratactically, but his entries are so sparse that the reader cannot avoid connecting the dots. Gerward and his contemporaries assumed the existence of a parallelism between the events of the heavens and earth, which reflected each other in reality even if not in exact chronology. An annalist working with separable and plausibly unconnected materials had the singular advantage of ordering the separated bits on parchment. In Gerward's annals the entries are often so thin that the importance of the stars looms even larger. In 817, for instance, he reported that Lothar was made emperor; fiery battle lines were observed in the sky; and Bernard of Italy revolted.[104] In 832 he reported a lunar eclipse (it was actually a complete solar eclipse)[105] after which one of Louis's sons approached the emperor in a rebellious mood.[106] And so on:

835: lunar eclipse; pagans attack.

836: battle lines in the evening sky; pagans attack Christians.

837: immense winds and comet; pagans attack.

838: earthquakes and fire in the form of a dragon in the sky; heresy breaks out.

839: severe flooding; sailors see fire in the sky; battle lines in the sky.

840: battle lines in the sky on two nights; eclipse of the sun; Emperor Louis the Pious died.

841: three rings appear in the sky; civil war between Louis's three sons.[107]

842: comet; the civil war continues.

Part of the problem with the *Annals of Xanten* is that it was later taken over and edited by a continuator at Cologne and some of Gerward's later entries were radically shortened and edited almost to the point of meaninglessness. But there is no avoiding Gerward's fusion of the heavens and the historical earth, particularly in the earlier synchronic portion of the annals in which he felt most free to line up events and starry signifiers in a connected, if still paratactical pattern. His continuator would imitate his lead and even find his own rings in the sky.[108] This continuator said that the significance of strange events in the world was known to God alone, but he was careful to record them, for they might in the end prove to be significant.[109]

The desire not to encroach on God's mind and so avoid the sins of pride and presumption was certainly at work, but some ninth-century observers also recognized, as Lupus had, that comets were equivocal phenomena. One clever cleric said that it all depended upon where the comet had come from (and here we should remember Einhard's precision in noting that the meteor that felled Charlemagne had cut across the sky from left to right), for if it came from the direction of Jupiter or Venus, it signified good things; if from Mercury, since he was the minister of gods, it signified either prosperity or adversity.[110] Despite the hesitation of some, many of the annalists and historians were convinced that they knew, for God was speaking to them through the sky; the stars were *opera digitorum tuorum*, the works of his fingers (Ps. 8:4). Even the doubters worked with a map of heaven and earth fixed in their minds, and their refusal to cite and interpret comets and eclipses should not be taken as an indication of doubt, but rather as a ceding to God what was properly his to know and dispose.

III

Almost the most overlooked aspect of Charlemagne's death has been what we can only suspect was Einhard's first memorialization of the great man (unless of course it was he who actually wrote the epic poem *Karolus Magnus et Leo Papa*). Long before he composed the emperor's biography, as the keeper of public works at Aachen, he may have supervised the construction of a first tomb for Charlemagne:[111] "and a gilded arch with an image and inscription was erected above the tomb."[112] Since the inscription sounds like Einhard's,[113] it is not impossible that the tomb itself was of his design and the memorial subtly evokes an assumed cosmology, for the gilded arch represented not just the triumphal arch imagery that Einhard was later to explore on his now lost silver reliquary,[114] but the very vault of the heavens that the emperor's image (if that is what it was) now surmounted and where Charlemage was now *receptus sideribus*, taken back by the stars. According to Eusebius, after Constantine's death the people of Rome had honored him by dedicating a portrait that showed him resting above the vault of the heavens in an ethereal realm.[115] Einhard's may have been a similar evocation.

Two schemes of the other world may seem to have been competing in the Carolingian imagination, but when looked at closely they may not have been at odds at all. The horizontal landscape we encounter in the Utrecht Psalter with its walled cities, riders, churches, unfolding battles, and a Lord and psalmist who stroll about as though through some human garden, also has infernal pits into which sinners are dragged by demons with fiendishly delicate hooks. This was the imagined world that many of the visionaries entered in their dreams as they walked from place to place led by a guide; it was a relatively horizontal landscape that would not have been unfamiliar to the people of late antiquity.

But this relatively flat terrestrial world is not the high heaven that we meet in other Carolingian manuscripts. The illustrators of the Utrecht Psalter knew this and so employed a special convention when they wanted to indicate the higher celestial realm, for they drew a circle surrounded by the constellations showing Christ and his cross just piercing its celestial boundaries (fol. 36r). The Carolingians knew, as the Psalm said (Ps. 106:26), that some would ascend into the heavens, while others would fall into the abyss. Perhaps it was for that reason that earthquakes, though they too were carefully recorded portents, were of less far-reaching interest to the Carolingians; they belong to a complete profile of the portentous, but they came from below, from the underworld of the pit, and it may have occurred to some that they spoke less clearly and divinely than did the high Thunderer, *Tonans* being, for the poets, another word for God.

On the *Majestas Domini* pages of Carolingian gospel books and bibles, Christ, who is offset by a lozenge-shaped mandorla, sits upon the globe of the world. In the Stuttgart Gospels (fol. 1v), produced at Tours in the 830s, Christ sits upon a blue globe while his feet rest upon a smaller green globe: "The heaven is my seat and the earth my footstool" (Isa. 66:1). The heavens around him are star-filled and cloudy.

> Hic mundi caelique sedet
> Rex summus et auctor.[116]
>
> [Here sits the highest king and creator
> Of the world and the heavens.]

Christ surmounts the world and, as it were, the very vaults of heaven.

In the first painting of the Gospels of St-Médard of Soissons (figure 4.2: fol. 1v), a book that was made by Charlemagne's court school, we encounter everything but the stars.[117] Four columns wrapped in a red curtain rise up in front of a building and support an architrave with depictions in medallions of the symbols of the four evangelists; their symbols are set against still more architecture, this time evoking the heavenly city of Jerusalem. But then, in one of those surprising moments that greet students of Carolingian art, which has a constant capacity to startle us with its invention and attention to detail, our eyes settle on the Sea of Glass (Rev. 4:6). For on top of the long panel rests a greenish horizontal band containing tiny fish, birds, fishers, and an angel in flight. Above it three bands, the final one painted a cloudless blue, represent the realm beyond the crystalline heavens and the Lamb of God is set above even that confinement in a medallion and casts rays of light down upon the Elders of the Apocalypse and the evangelists and the gospel books they hold.

But if the St-Médard Gospels mapped the heavens, the *Majestas Agni* of the Codex Aureus restored its stars (figure 4.1). Charles the Bald gazes up into the circular heavens from his throne on the facing page. He sees a layered sky dotted with stars: two occupy the corners above the vault of the crystalline heavens, four flank the Lamb, a large eight-pointed sun hovers below him, and a shrouded moon lurks between the parted Elders.[118] Personifications of the Earth and Sea are set outside and below the sacred circle in which the Elders of the Apocalypse adore the Lamb of God and offer him golden crowns. Again we see three or more vaults in the upper heavens, including the Sea of Glass, and the Lamb of God resting upon a green globe.

The important aspect of these illuminations for us is that in Carolingian cosmology Christ was thought to inhabit the realm above the heavens; his throne was set beyond the stars (Isa. 14:13), which lay under his feet: "God

4.2 Adoration of the Lamb in the Gospels of St-Médard of Soissons (Paris, Bibliothèque Nationale, ms. lat. 8850, fol. 1v).

walks upon the vaults of heaven" (Job 22:14). No wonder, given this mar-riage of verticality and blessedness, that Carolingian thinkers occasionally dreamt of flying. Walahfrid Strabo wrote a poem about a certain Polachar who dreamed one night when the stars were twinkling in the sky of being carried heavenward by the eagle of Jupiter. But, weighed down by his earthly heaviness as they soared, he became sick and soiled himself.[119] The heavens, we may suppose Walahfrid to have been saying, are not easy to reach by the earthbound. Eriugena in his sublime philosophical homily, the *Vox spiritualis*, imagined the evangelist John, the eagle, flying high, not over the material air and ether, but in contemplation, and descending from the high mountain of theology to fly in majestic flight over the valley of human history far below.[120] And Theodulf assumed that, since the soul's origin lay in heaven, the human spirit would eventually shuck off the weight of its corporality and soar to the stars.[121]

In the First Bible of Charles the Bald, which was most likely made in the summer of 845, there is an elaborately illuminated initial D that begins Jerome's letter to Paul (figure 4.3). Inside the rim of the letter the painters of St-Martin's of Tours placed ten signs of the Zodiac.[122] In the trough of the D they painted the sun driving his chariot, while Pisces intersects the

4.3   Zodiacal 'D' in the First Bible of Charles the Bald (Paris, Bibliothèque Nationale, ms. lat. 1, fol. 8r).

circle of the sun, and below them is a female figure of the moon with a sliver of the moon on her head; she drives an oxen cart.[123]

At first the presence of this Zodiacal D in a Bible may strike us as strange, but it belongs. The sun, moon, and constellations remind us of the fourth day of creation and so it served as an appropriate illustration for the story of Genesis shortly to begin. Jerome's letter was, however, the specific inspiration for the elaborate initial, since in it he mentions the state of learning, teachers, and the Liberal Arts including astronomy. But, more to the point, Jerome pointed out that Daniel himself had "said that the just shine like the stars and the wise, that is, the learned, resemble the firmament."[124] And in the Hebrew tradition he had discovered another reading: "those who were learned will shine like the splendor of the sky and those who have instructed many in justice will shine like the stars for all time."[125] This is the text that the Turonian artists adorned with the Zodiacal D. The promise of perpetual star-likeness was the right beginning for a king's book and it was the initial letter of the word Dominus or lord that the painters chose to fill with constellations.

Not only did God speak through the stars and the elements, which was the very thing that Charlemagne and his heirs wanted to understand, but he had reserved a place for good kings in the high heavens. Their royal destiny and that of the blessed lay in journeying to the stars, soaring beyond the ethereal choirs and the vaults of heaven. Paschasius Radbertus imagined his hero Adalhard of Corbie so elevated in death that, with his feet on the high plain of heaven, he stood in snowy dress and looked down upon the clouds and stars below him.[126] He was with Christ.

The visionary and self-styled prophet, Audradus Modicus, never soared quite so high, but in his elevating dreams he met Christ and his saints at the border that ran between ether and air,[127] where Paul had said Christ would descend at the end of time (1 Thess. 4:16–17). And his God worked eclipses as his calling card and purposefully played with the elements; he could even stop the sun for three straight days at critical moments in human history.[128] To send messages to humans, many were convinced, God had once and could again, if he so chose, change the very course of the sun, the moon, and the heavenly bodies.[129]

The ancients had believed that some humans might, in the fullness of time, become stars, for all of us were thought to contain in our souls particles of the divine fire, a spark that made us one with the stars.[130] *Itur ad astra*, the passage to the stars, was the longing for the heaven of immortality and the promise of pacific wisdom that cut across all classes in the ancient world and found variable and touching expression on countless ancient epitaphs. "Mother, do not weep for me. What is the use? You ought rather to reverence me, for I have become an evening star among the gods."[131] Pliny the Elder thought that to enroll men such as the emperor Vespasian among the starry gods was fitting payment for all that they had done in the wide world.[132] Caesar, as celebrated by Virgil and Ovid, became a star, the *Caesaris astrum*, and Hadrian cherished the dead Antinous as a new star in the heavens.[133] This astral longing did not fade away with the slow and somber passing of the pagan world, but persisted on early Christian gravestones and was ultimately to be subsumed and Christianized in Carolingian cosmology.

But what were the mechanics of this heavenly ascent? Here too the tradition was rich and there were witnesses, people who had gone before.[134] Plutarch's Thespesius had seen the stars up close and had watched as the souls of the blessed dead became fiery bubbles in the sky.[135] Claudian imagined Theodosius the Great entering the stars on a trail of light.[136] Most familiar to the Middle Ages would have been Cicero's account of *The Dream of Scipio* in which Scipio the Elder transports his grandson to the celestial spheres, showing him the ordered majesty of the cosmos, its nine spheres, the planets, and the sun, moon, and earth. Despite the overwrought reading of that short text by Macrobius and his medieval readers, Cicero's point, as so often, was simple and straightforwardly political, for Scipio, the grandfather, informed the younger Scipio that if he labored on behalf of the Republic he would be transported to the Milky Way, there to become a star.

The Carolingians were the natural inheritors of the astral aspirations of the ancient world; it was their rediscovery of that tradition in the texts they read that fueled the romanization of their astronomy, giving it a contour and richness that had dimmed in previous centuries.[137] Adding that tradition to their own Christian convictions confirmed their belief that God ruled the skies, that Christ kept his abode above them, and that their own spirits would fly heavenward. It was an awesome place and the journey to it divinizing. Boniface described how the monk of Wenlock in his transporting vision had been carried by angels on high and had seen the earth encircled by a blazing fire, its flames throbbing in and out as though breathing, engulfing the entire fabric of the world.[138]

The heavens waited for great kings to join Christ's starry company. Even Charlemagne's fame had preceded him there. The poet of the verses of the Godescalc Evangelistary said that Charlemagne, *heros* and *triumphator*, was already "known above the heavens," that is, to Christ.[139] The poet of *Karolus Magnus et Leo Papa* wrote that even while the king lived his name had vaulted to the stars.[140] More than just an excess of panegyric, these claims deepened the understanding of Charlemagne's name for KAROLVS was KARA LVX or precious light according to his poets.[141] Not only was he a lighthouse overshining all living souls, but (and here the panegyric does overreach, if that is possible for panegyric) he even outshone the sun, for while the sun was gone for half the day and was often covered in clouds, Charlemagne always blazed forth. He was an everlasting star.[142]

Of course, Christ himself was the first sun; hence the large sun immediately below the Lamb of God in the Codex Aureus is a Christological symbol of the first order (figure 4.1). On those facing pages parallelism reigns as the image of the enthroned Charles the Bald was positioned directly across from the large eight-pointed sun and his head and the glowing sun exactly meet when the pages of the book are closed.[143] This solar imagery of kingship was both embracing and out-reaching. Ermold said that a king's *aduentus*, his arrival, was just like Phoebus illuminating the whole world with his rays.[144] The metaphor of the king as a sun also wrapped around his family and kingdom, bathing them in the warmth of his light. Charlemagne was said to tower over his family, just as the sun does at its peak in the sky.[145]

Even before Charlemagne's death, his poets were already anticipating his journey to palaces in the sky, his elevation to the stars.[146] The concluding line of the Irish Exile's epitaph for Charlemagne is both an acclamation and a resounding prayer:"May the soul of Charles obtain the star-bearing vault [of heaven]."[147] After Charlemagne died Ermoldus and others spoke of how his fame had penetrated the stars and beyond, by which they meant that it had reached Christ's seat beyond the ethereal choirs.[148] The poem *De exordio gentis Francorum* said of him:

Nomen habens astris liquit memorabile terris[149]

[Possessing an unforgettable name in the stars he left the earth behind.]

Gerward wished that Louis the Pious's distinguished name too might be lifted to the stars[150] and Walahfrid, in an acrostic poem, hoped the same for Louis's eldest son, the ever imperial Lothar.[151]

Some of these sun-struck courtiers went even further, for they claimed that not only did the spirits of their kings seek the heavens,[152] where they wished they might live forever in *arce poli*,[153] but that they actually arrived. The souls of their dead kings reached the stars and took up residence. Louis the Pious:

Transiit ad Christum, uitamque remisit in astra[154]

[Crossed over to Christ and sent his life back to the stars.]

For Sedulius Scottus, Charlemagne, the famous son of Pepin, now ruled new kingdoms in the starry heavens.[155] Another poet hoped that a heavenly band of angels might help Charles's son to rise high into the ethereal heavens.[156] A poem on the Frankish princes said that after Louis the Pious died, *penetrauit sidera caeli*, he entered the very constellations of the heavens;[157] another that he had traveled *aetheris ad fabricam*, to the abode of the heavens.[158] Thus the longing for the heavens, the spreading astral repute of the king, and his *aduentus* among the stars and beyond the ethereal choirs constituted the disparate stages of a Christianized Carolingian apotheosis.

The Irish on the continent were the most exuberant of all Carolingian panegyrists and the effusive Sedulius Scottus the quickest to invoke the stars. His poetry is shot through with starlight.[159] In his list of the seven most beautiful things in all of God's creation, he placed a generous peace-loving king alongside the brilliance of the sun and the fullness of the moon.[160] God's creations all! His kings were 'stars': Louis the Pious was now a shining star above;[161] Louis II of Italy was a noble star;[162] and Louis the German was an outstanding star, a new star of heaven, a brilliant star, and an imperial star.[163] Lothar I was a glittering star sent from the heavens, though now lying under the heavens,[164] and, after conquering the Northmen, he was the morning star of the Franks with a fame reaching beyond the heavens.[165]

Of Charles the Bald, he said that "a golden hope" and "noble star" had now come to bathe the earth in his splendor.[166] In yet another poem he spoke of Charles as a new star with a radiant visage shining on the peoples of the western lands, illuminating them with Charlemagne's image and splendor: "this star has a countenance like that of the angels."[167]

For Sedulius, the astral radiance of Carolingian kings extended to those around them, particularly to their families. A newborn son of Lothar I was extravagantly described as a new star, the glory of the world, the hope of Rome, and the light of Europe.[168] Another king descended from two emperors shone as a royal star.[169] And Charles the Bald and Louis the German were twin stars and only their father Louis could have raised two such sons under the star-filled heavens.[170] Queens gave birth to stars[171] and even the daughter of Ermengard and Lothar I lit up the heavens like a brilliant star herself, for she was a star of surpassing beauty.[172] "May they [the emperor and empress] adorn the heavens with descendants created as if from the noble line of Abraham," said Sedulius of these imperial parents and their families of stars in the making.[173]

But Sedulius did not restrict his star talk to the royal family only, for he seems to have thought, following Daniel (Dan. 12:3) and Jerome, that all just men would shine in the sky like stars and wise men would cleave to the heavenly firmament.[174] Thus, even nobles could hope in the fullness of time to ascend to the city of the sun and become citizens in the citadel of the star-filled heavens.[175] Count Eberhard of Friuli was a glittering star on earth,[176] while his dead son had already reached the summit of the starry heavens to shine brightly among the innocents and his new son was destined to be a paragon on earth and a brilliant star in heaven.[177]

If nobles could be likened to the stars, so too could churchmen. Saint Boniface was already a "brilliant star" and Sedulius longed to gaze upon this star now shining upon the earth.[178] He imagined his own bishop, Hartgar, on his return trip from Rome as a star driving away the gloom[179] and the poet anxiously scanned the sky (and not the road) for his return.[180] When his bishop died, the other stars were cast into darkness and even the sun sullenly hid its face.[181] The poet praised other bishops with this ornate starry language: Franco was a brilliant star and the golden light of the cosmos,[182] "a golden star radiant with piety,"[183] and he wished that Tado, the archbishop of Milan, might ascend to the heights of the starry heavens, led to paradise by a band of angels.[184]

Sedulius went still further, fusing the stars and the fates of kingdoms in *On Christian Rulers*, a work that throbs to the Boethian rhythm of alternating pieces of poetry and prose. For a state should glow like the morning star[185] and the king should imitate God, the father of light, the creator of the sun and moon, and the entire cosmos, and shine radiant thoughts and wisdom's light on his land.[186] The obverse of this cosmological coin was that the rise and decline of kingdoms were like the phases of the moon, waxing and waning, until in the end the moon turned to darkness and the summit of the state collapsed as did the tower of Siloam when no one rose up to support it.[187]

Eriugena, more comfortable in his position at the court of Charles the Bald than was the ever-striving Sedulius, had no need to praise so many patrons to the sky, but he did need to flatter his main patron, Charles of the *astrea stemmata*, his starry pedigree and crown.[188] In the preface to his ambitious retranslation of the works of the Pseudo-Dionysius the Irishman called on his king to participate in an ongoing celestial conversation, the heavenly whisper with the above.[189]

Although there is some restraint in his Latin panegyric, his few Greek lines of praise tend to be excessive. In one poem written entirely in Greek, he threw off all reserve and praised his king as handsome, well-formed, and radiant, and compared him to Mercury in the heavens, a star in a diadem, a brilliant sun, the evening star, and the white goddess (Venus).[190] Thus Charles the Bald took his place in the poeticized heavens as the equal of the other shining stars even while he lived. Charles liked Greek things and, if he understood Eriugena's astral exaggeration, he would not, I suspect, have been offended. The Irish philosopher may have had a Byzantine model for his poem, since around the millennium the disgruntled Liutprand of Cremona was shocked in Constantinople to hear the Greeks praise the emperor Nicephorus II as though he were a living god and one of the stars of heaven.[191] Eriugena may not have gone quite so far, but he did, in Greek, call on Christ to lead Charles above the stars and to help him find a place in the heavenly choir.[192] Indeed, he wished that all the peoples beset by the pirates from the North would be transported to the heavenly choirs beyond the stars.[193]

Eriugena's theme all along was that the mind would set beleaguered Carolingians free, especially his king:

Si uis OYPANIAC sursum uolitare per auras
EMΠYPIOCque polos mentis sulcare meatu,
OMMATE glauciuido lustrabis templa sophiae,
Quorum summa tegit condensa nube caligo,
Omnes quae superat sensus NOEPOCque ΛOΓOCque.[194]

[If you wish to soar through the celestial realms above
And to plow the fiery heavens with the dynamism of [your] mind,
You will, with sparkling eyes, scan the temples of wisdom,
Whose heights are covered by a mist thickened by cloud,
Which overwhelms all sense, intellect, and reason.]

For Eriugena and his king to fly to the heavens was to think their way there, to enter the mist enshrouded temple of reason and truth, and then to soar above the confusion of the compromised world below.

His magnificent poem, the *Aulae Sidereae*, on the starry court of the heavens, was also written for Charles the Bald.[195] There he begins by synchronizing the clock of the constellations and the moments of Christ's human history, for the rhythms of the universe and Christ's cosmic nature perfectly intersected.[196] The last quarter of the poem turns to consider Charles the Bald, whom the heavens praise, for he was building a splendid church. Sitting on a heavenly throne, he gazed down upon all. By conjuring up the starry court of the heavens at the start of his poem and by ending with his all-seeing king seated upon a *thronus celsus*, a heavenly throne, Eriugena had completed a circle that would bring Charles back to the *caelestis gaudia regni*, the joys of the celestial kingdom.

Eriugena also wrote a poem about a state robe that Empress Judith made for her husband Louis the Pious, "So that the enrobed hero might shine upon his people."[197] Many of these royal gowns were studded with jewels, as was the one Eriugena said Ermintrude made for Charles the Bald.[198] The point once again was to wrap a king in stars as a token of both his nature and his destiny. Later Notker would picture Charlemagne standing before a window; he was decked out in gold and jewels, glittering like the rising sun, while around him stood his three sons like the heavenly host.[199] To look closely at some of the robes covering Charles the Bald in his paintings is to see that they are dotted with stars. On both his Psalter and the Codex Aureus portraits the king wears a dark sky-blue tunic covered with golden stars, which on the Psalter are large and on the Codex small and plentiful (figures 1.19 and 4.1).[200] Charles's mantle in the *Codex* is also fringed with shining jewels. In 888 Odo of West Francia visited St-Denis, which had become a special site of Charles's benefaction after he became its lay-abbot, and removed some of its treasures: "He took one purple cloak covered with golden stars and beautifully made in a round shape."[201] This cloak was quite likely once Charles the Bald's own starry mantle.

That cloak does not survive, but the celebrated Starry Mantle of Henry II does. On it, against a dark blue background, are sewn personifications of the constellations and other heavenly figures embroidered in golden thread.[202] Despite all the evidence that the mantle was made for Henry in the early eleventh century, I have always been tempted to connect its design or, at least, the impulse behind its creation in some way to Charles the Bald and the Carolingian preoccupation with royal stars. The connection is not impossible since so many of Charles's treasures, including some of the objects and precious manuscripts Odo removed from St-Denis did end up in Henry's imperial city of Bamberg. The Mantle's imagery and thinking are to my eyes more Carolingian than Byzantine.[203] In any event, it was hard for Carolingian poets not to think of their emperors as surrounded by stars even before they died. When poor Charles the Fat, soon to squander his empire, arrived outside besieged Paris in November 886, he was encircled by arms and soldiers and looked for all the world like the very heavens adorned with twinkling stars (*caelum ueluti splendoribus astreis*).[204] Starry decoration and imperial titles worked to separate even woefully situated emperors such as Charles the Fat from the harsh realities of their own creeping impotence and the growing empowerment of the lesser local men around them.

In many ways the most enigmatic starry object of the Carolingian age is the Cathedra Petri.[205] Its very association with Charles the Bald was not confirmed until 1968 when it was extracted from Bernini's monumental sculpture in St-Peter's where it had rested for centuries and now rests once again. It is a throne, but a throne such as the Middle Ages and subsequent ages have hardly ever seen. For wordlessly it expresses the culmination of Carolingian thought about their kings and their exalted place not just in the stars, but at the joint between the worlds.

Let us make our own ascent from the bottom to the top of this wood and ivory throne (see the schematization, figure 4.4). We should begin in the bottom register, which holds a series of ivory plaques that were once topically inlaid with gold or jewels. We begin there, as it were, in the mud and muck at the bottom end of creation with strange sea and land monsters—here a deformed elephant-worm, a scorpion, a weird rabbit, and a conch-creature just emerging from his shell. Eriugena would have

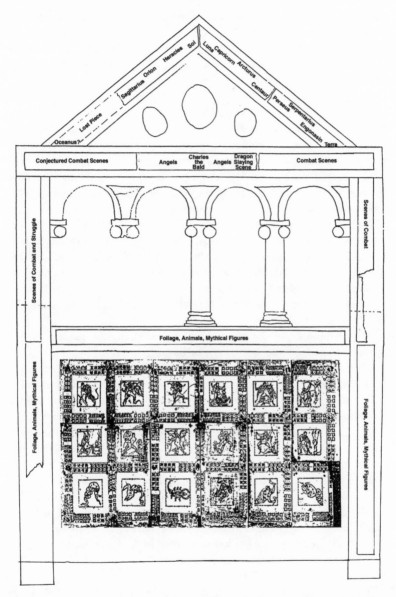

4.4   Schematization of the front face of the Cathedra Petri (St. Peter's Basilica, Vatican City).

understood and may even have suggested the imagery at work here, for the material world is filled with the deformed and things scarcely comprehensible. These irrationalities, he thought, were properly called beasts, since they were in continual revolt against the discipline of reason and constantly worked to disturb the natural motions.[206]

Above that layer of material irrationality lie two registers of ivory plaques depicting the labors of Hercules.[207] In the *Periphyseon*, Eriugena had spoken of human nature as the hydra of Hercules, for "who but Hercules (for this [name] signifies virtue), can see through the hydra, a many-sided source of infinite depth."[208] If Eriugena is our guide, as he was Charles's, then, we begin in the lowest portions of the Cathedra Petri as if in some sensible world at war, where virtue first begins to exercise its raw resistance to the dark forces at work in the world.

So also the carved panels along the sides of the lower half of the throne frame that natural world with foliage, animals, and mythical creatures. It is bracketed on top of the rectangular field by the same. When seated on the throne, Charles the Bald had the lower world under him as Christ does on his *Majestas Domini* pages, his weight pressing down on it as though to keep it in place and under control. Let the king overcome his sensual urges, said Sedulius.[209]

But at the level of the king's stomach and chest, the site and source of martial virtue,[210] the side panels of the throne back contain scenes of combat and struggle as soldiers fight their way up some Jack-in-the-Beanstalk–like foliage shooting arrows and hurling javelins at their enemies as they climb. This layer of human conflict spills over onto the horizontal panel on the back of the throne. But at the center of that panel Charles the Bald himself is shown in half-form, bearing a scepter, while angels separate him from the violence and tumult of the world around him and offer him crowns of glory (figure 1.22). These guardian angels serve as brackets of holiness for like Christ the king was located in this corrupted world, but not entirely of it; he was an in-between being, human and yet informed by the divine. But then Hercules too was an in-between being and Sedulius urged his king, who could (like Hercules) wrestle lions, to overpower pride.[211] The angel to Charles's left is captured in the act of slaying a dragon just as the archangel Michael did, signifying the destruction of the world's evil by the forces of holiness.

The king's head when he was actually seated on the throne would have risen above the pinnacle of the triangular summit of the throne, as though its supreme and ascendant point.[212] On the enthronement page of the Codex Aureus the throne lacks a pediment precisely because there was no need for one when the heavens opened to the king's left and Charles's head served as the earthy peak of his painted throne. But on the ivory panels of the Cathedra, which rise up along the gable, our eyes traverse the heavens. Personifications of Sea (now lost) and Earth root the bottom of the panels on each side as we ascend and then are followed by personifications of the constellations: Sagittarius, Orion, Heracles on the damaged left side and Engonasin, Serpentarius, Perseus, Centaur, Arcturus, and Capricorn on our right. The two rising ivory panels end at the peak with the sun and moon. The three large oval spaces in the center of the pediment may once have held religious scenes, perhaps carved in clear crystal.[213]

Thus, when Charles the Bald sat on his throne, his very body was, in Platonic terms, in relative harmony with Carolingian cosmology, his lower parts a swirling cauldron of the animalistic and irrational against which virtue as represented by Hercules strove mightily to resist; here Hercules was both a hero waging war against the dark forces of the world and a lower being trapped in a realm of unending and irrational conflict. Charles's breast, filled with the invigorating *spiritus* of war, was positioned on the throne so as to fight bravely against the wicked and war-like. But his head rose above the stars, the fixed constellations, for Charles's enthronement was also an act of Christian apotheosis and the culmination of the Carolingian dream of rising from this world into and beyond the stars where Christ had gathered together his celestial court.

★ ★ ★

Time, I would suggest, for us to pay more attention to what the archaeoastronomers might call the cultural astronomy of Charlemagne and his family.[214] The Carolingian interest in the stars should not surprise us, and indeed may seem to some merely another historical commonplace. The Egyptians, Greeks, and Romans had looked upward first, fashioned a vocabulary, and set down the symbolism that lay at the core of a belief in the heavenly state of the stars. Nor should it surprise us to find the same imagery, now subtly adapted to their own Christian, cosmological, and panegyrical needs, being used by the Carolingians. Rather that was the point, for to channel the stars was to participate in the agreed upon contours of the high heavens and to stabilize an unstable present by focusing on the enduring permanence of the stars. Yet the uneasiness of the Carolingians and their kings is palpable; it is no accident that the constellations, the fixed and guiding stars, surrounded and surmounted Charles the Bald on his wood and ivory throne, for they were both an enduring heavenly home and an invitation.

Nor should it be surprising that Charlemagne, on the very edge of the drama that was to lead him to Rome and to his final imperial destiny, should have been alert to unexpected movements in the heavens. He and his court imagined the sky to be a deep and mysterious reflection of God's judgments, a God who too often and in dire emergencies seemed distant and ineffable. The seductive promise of the sky was that, if only the stars could be read right, kings and their wise men might understand God's mind and advance information was as critical then as it is now. Comets and eclipses, however unhappily, opened a jagged window on the mind of an angry God who did shake kingdoms, did carry off kings, and did unsettle sinful peoples.

But the uncertainty of reading the stars did not make of these kings and their courtiers despairing fatalists; instead it kept them guessing, eyes fixed on the sky, always inclined to wait for the hard evidence of the outcome the stars had intimated. That was the delicate and dangerous game the historians and annalists played. Charlemagne may have publicly scoffed at the signs of his imminent end and Louis the Pious may have forced the Astronomer to supply a favorable dismissal of Halley's Comet, but for all their public posturing they still believed that the stars were speaking to them.

Under the protective and enveloping shade of Charlemagne's personal interest in the stars (or, at least, Abraham's), his scholars began to work at the science of the stars. Rational scientific inquiry may well have been the happy by-product of a less than scientific interest in divine messages written in the sky, but it was the unwavering conviction of all parties that God was the writer of cosmic messages that mattered. It was this assumption that drove forward both the king and a proto-scientist such as Dungal. Throughout the ninth century, stargazing became a royal and imperial function, and one of its effects was that Carolingian poets transformed their kings into stars and painters painted cosmological scenes of an end time into which their kings could comfortably fit themselves.

It would be wrong of us to dismiss this Carolingian interest in the stars just because at points it may seem familiar, unhistorical, and unscientific, and much better for us to approach it as another cluster of a complicated Carolingian culture. These were not just the idle praises of poets, then, and not just the worries of kings and their historians about the intertwining of historical disasters and astronomical oddities, but beliefs that belonged to an accepted understanding of the universe itself. Beneath them may have moved the deeper drive of an anxious age to find its true place in God's creation and a fitting seat for its kings and saints in the almost everlasting cosmos. For these Carolingians, as noisy as ever, to write their history not just in annals and biographies, but also in the stars, was to convince themselves that they belonged, that the long shadow of usurpation had lifted, and that even the dark clouds of civil war and invasion could not obliterate their place in the cosmos. That was the underlying theme of Eriugena's sweeping synthesis in the *Periphyseon*. Where, after all, did Carolingian kings go when they died? They journeyed, as Romans had a thousand years earlier, to the stars and beyond the stars to the ethereal choirs where they were awaited by Christ and his saints, blessedly free at long last from the grim doings of the disordered and sinful world below. The Cathedra Petri imagines that very entanglement in an irrational world at war and a king's elevation beyond it into the stars.

To hold on to the stars was to gain some purchase on the slippery ledge of divine immortality in a human world that was too rapidly transforming all around. If the Roman world had moved at a monumental pace up and down for a millennium, the Carolingian world moved with blinding speed, generation by generation, because its achievements were so recent and its power structures so thinly laid down. No wonder that the stars like the imperial title seemed to offer so much more; these were hedges against the fragilities and wearying worries that ran through and threatened to destroy their small start. The stars offered a way up and out and so it should not surprise us in the end that Alcuin directed Charlemagne to lift up his eyes to see the stars painted on high in his great man's house or that Eriugena wanted Charles the Bald to enter into that celestial conversation that would once and for all abnegate a transitory and tortured present and instead affirm the imperishable life of the stars that awaited all wise and righteous kings.

CHAPTER 5

WHISPERING SECRETS TO A DARK AGE

To my ear one of the most beautiful of all Latin words is the onomatopoeic *susurrus*, whispering, which evokes in me a measure of regret over the loss of so many medieval mutterings and airy thoughts that would, had they survived, have promised (though that too, I realize, is an illusion) to complete us and make what we do whole. Or is history like the courtroom where hearsay should be dismissed as untestable evidence by responsible weighers of fact?

Still, if we listen carefully, we can almost hear the faint whispering of the early medieval court, almost see two powerful courtiers draw close to a window outside the emperor's bedchamber in the palace at Aachen to talk quietly about stolen saints' bones.[1] They spoke in hushed tones, but then one of them was an overt and the other a covert thief, and neither of them dared to disturb the emperor.[2] Years later at another palace window the powerful archbishop of Rheims could be overseen deep in quiet conversation about the fate of his nephew, the brash bishop of Laon. Over the next twenty-four hours, he met and spoke *secretissime* with other bishops, covertly received documents, and hid them in his gown; all in an attempt to straighten out a crooked bishop.[3]

Early medieval courts were full of such scenes: of powerful individuals slipping away to private places to talk in lowered tones, of private meetings and dinners where business was done[4] and conspiracies hatched, of meaningful glances and penetrating eyes, of nods, winks, and special signs. To look at the famous Presentation Miniature of the First Bible of Charles the Bald is to gaze from the outside upon a world rich in gesture, declarative dress, and the grand sweep of processional motion that animated Carolingian court society (see figure 1.14).[5]

Historians probably think too little about the degree to which, because of their fixation upon the written record, they have allowed their inquiries to be shaped by the inscribed noise of the past rather than its quiet opposite, the whisper that wants not to be heard. Those matters that the actors of an age attempt to hide from one another may be the most important ones of all or, perhaps, the very act of trying to hide them has only worked to heighten their seeming importance, and that too is part of the point of keeping secrets. For to create and hold a secret is to define and, more importantly, to delimit an audience, privileging and empowering a select few by virtue of their access to and protection of the 'hidden', but excluding all others who are automatically cast outside the secret's circle. Secrets thus shape identities and define membership within a group. Those on the outside want in and their drive to uncover the hidden tends to grant advantage to the secret's holders, who can trade on their special knowledge and reinforce the superiority of their situation.

Keeping secrets is a dynamic social and political activity that wants investigation, but how does one go about looking for the hidden, for what is not supposed to be present in the received record? While it may be impossible to recover things successfully covered, by testing the seeming silence and examining those moments when secrecy failed, we may come closer to history's great *tabula obscura*, to the hiders and the hidden.[6]

The court societies that formed around kings, counts, and bishops in the early Middle Ages were particularly susceptible to intrigue and gossip, for theirs was a world crafted out of personal contacts and oral contracts in which literacy rarely held the upper hand and the spoken word was almost always more important than the written.[7] Their common sign for silence is one familiar to us over a thousand years later: "put a finger to your mouth," advised Alcuin.[8] But the whisper almost always won. At Mersen in 851 three royal brothers, who had fought a desperate war against each other a decade earlier, agreed that they would now act openly and honestly toward each other and would not "willingly listen to the manufactured lies and slanders [reported to them] by secretive and whispering men."[9]

In theory there were no secrets in the early Middle Ages that could or should be hidden to God or to his chief representatives on earth, clerics and kings.[10] Three of the Gospels contain Christ's warning that "Nothing is concealed that will not be revealed, no secret that will not be known."[11] Or as Auden said of the unkeepability of secrets:

> At last the secret is out, as it always must come in the end.
> The delicious story is ripe to tell to the intimate friend.[12]

But for the early Middle Ages God was no intimate friend; he was instead a scrutinizing and fearsome omnipresence. Among his many names was *inspector secretorum*; he was the examiner of secrets and revealer of hypocrisy.[13] Job had invoked him as the *custos hominum*, as much the watcher of humans

and their secret lives as their guardian (Job 7:20). Even Carolingian murderers could not hope to conceal themselves from God, "to whom all
secrets are known."[14]

And God himself sanctioned spying of a very earthly sort. He had commanded Moses to send men into Canaan to search it out (*ad considerandam
terram*) before the Israelites invaded and Moses as God's spymaster sent his
spies (*exploratores*) to discover if that alien land was rich or poor, what its
cities were like, and whether the people who lived there were strong or
weak (Num. 13). Since God knew all, he here counseled his earthly representatives to use their human ingenuity to collect by clandestine means all
the information they required for righteous ends.

Spying of the right sort was divinely sanctioned and kings, priests, and
monks in the Middle Ages did not just search out sin, but wanted strategi-
cally valuable information about the wider world that Christians inhabited
and the hidden designs of their own people.[15] They were thought to possess a faint portion of God's ability to see all, both outwardly and inwardly.
Christ could read men's minds (Matt. 12:25). Gregory the Great reported
in his *Dialogues* that nothing could be kept secret from Abbot Benedict of
Nursia, "on whose ears fell even the sounds of the unspoken thoughts"
of others.[16] The Carolingian abbot, Wala of Corbie, who was likened to
another famous monk, Arsenius, by his hagiographer, was supposed to have
possessed the same finely tuned inner ear and searching eye. He laid bare
the hidden sins of others and by clever conjecture could catch out both
monks and kings in their concealed crimes.[17]

We should not suppose that early medieval monasteries ever achieved
their goal of shutting off the noise of the external world, smothering it in
soft blankets of perpetual prayer and monastic silence, for they teemed with
secrets, with gossip, and with novel forms of nonverbal communication.[18]
The *Rule of Saint Benedict* tried to legislate against secrecy, stipulating that
the fifth degree of humility was for the monk not to hide his evil thoughts
or secret sins from his abbot.[19] It should not surprise us to realize that there
was nothing quite as leaky in the early Middle Ages as the supposedly silent
monastery out of which poured secrets, sometimes in a flood. Paschasius's
dialogue, the *Epitaphium Arsenii*, is small evidence of the chattiness of
the Carolingian monastery, and of the dark hue that colored so much
monastic chatter. And Gottschalk of Orbais, though he had been declared
a heretic for his belief in double predestination and imprisoned in the
monastery of Hautvillers, was able to slip his writings out of the monastery,
send sympathetic monks on a mission to the pope, and plot his own
escape.[20]

But this was an acutely watchful world. Hincmar of Rheims cited
the Pseudo-Cyprian's observation that the very word 'bishop' meant

'watchman' (*speculator*) and he concluded from this that the bishop's job was to watch over the life and morals of those committed to his care.[21] It was this ongoing visitation of the believer's soul that came to be institutionalized in confession. The Carolingians, with their drive to regularize and formalize Christian life, were to take up the codification of confession with a certain zeal.

Charlemagne himself was styled a great watcher. He was widely viewed as a paragon of vigilance and this was presented as one of his central royal capacities.[22] Notker the Stammerer, late in the century, when Charlemagne's reputation had assumed legendary dimensions, would call him *uigilantissimus*, that most watchful of men.[23] He was supposed to have had his chapel at Aachen constructed in such a way that he would be able to peer down upon parishioners and subjects from above. The theocratic symbolism here is striking and the image of Christ that filled the cupola of the chapel and rose above the enthroned emperor reinforced the verticality of a watchful world overseen by superior scrutiny. As an all-seeing ruler, Charlemagne peered into the personal lives of his courtiers and family, just as God did. He missed nothing.

A celebrated Lorsch legend captures the theme perfectly. A courtier was supposed to have crept into the palace one night to make love to one of the emperor's daughters. The lovers awoke and discovered to their dismay that it had snowed during the night and realized that, come morning, Charlemagne would surely detect a man's footprints in the snow trailing away from the palace. So the couple hit upon the idea of having Bertha carry Angilbert upon her back as a way of disguising his tracks. But the ever vigilant Charlemagne, who rarely slept through the night, awoke and peered out the palace window and saw his daughter lumbering across the snowy palace courtyard with her lover on her back.[24]

At the domestic level the story expressed a lingering memory of Charlemagne's intense scrutiny, but the same theme was also at work in politics, for, according to Notker, even the king's magnates "could not hide themselves from the eyes of the ever watchful Charles."[25] His grandsons too were thought to have possessed a portion of the same ability to foresee and suppress the plots of their enemies.[26] The vigilance of powerful kings and their trusted courtiers made the Carolingian court and, perhaps, all courts claustrophobic and edgy places in which to live and work, for kings and their close advisors were always on the lookout for secretive and deceitful nobles and advisors.[27] Even the presence of Einhard, that most prudent of courtiers, and Theodulf, the lazy wolf, might induce a chilling effect on court conversation.[28] In the tense world of Charlemagne's beleaguered heir, Louis the Pious, the highly politicized monk Paschasius lamented that he now had no "friend to whom I might risk revealing all my secrets, for even he might betray them to [my] enemies."[29]

Kings and courtiers employed spies in the early Middle Ages, though an enemy's spies and being spied upon (as opposed to one's own active and necessary spying) were widely held in low regard. To call someone a spy or informer (*delator*), for instance, without having proof, brought a relatively stiff penalty for defamation in Salic Law.[30] Though spying was not a profession in the ninth century, spies were a necessary part of learning about one's enemies and a constant worry for kings. When Louis the German invaded western Francia in 858, for instance, he sent some men he thought loyal to his cause "to spy (*ad explorandos*) and report to him" on his brother's activities, but they betrayed him and went over to the other side.[31] In 839 his father suspected that some Swedes, for whom the eastern emperor vouched and sought free passage through Francia, were in fact spies (*exploratores*).[32] And in the great crisis of 830, when resistance to a hated imperial chamberlain was growing, Abbot Wala made sure that he had reliable men of his own in the palace who could surreptitiously investigate what transpired and, as soon as something secretive was said, to find it out, determine its truth, and report back to him.[33] Sometimes 'spies' were detected and paid a heavy price. In 823 two high papal officials were blinded and then decapitated in the Lateran palace because it was believed they were working for the emperor Lothar I and not the pope.[34]

In a world of decentralized and highly personalized government with slow and irregular communication, kings and their rivals craved information and could obtain it best through reliable and well-placed spies. Thus, even great kings, who were thought to have the divine gift of gazing into the hearts and minds of their subjects, promoted the process of information gathering in practical ways.

They were also allowed, like God and unlike their subjects, to keep secrets from everyone else. God's secrets may have been the profound truth of the creation that occurred somewhere deep "in his secret hiddenness" (*suo arcano mysterio*),[35] in the *arcana* of nature,[36] and in the great unknowns of the unfolding of history (both individual and universal), but the king's were more immediately important. The keeping of secrets was for the most part a one-sided affair. Subjects were not supposed to keep things concealed from the king, but he could and should from them.[37] In fact, in Charlemagne's General Capitulary for the Missi of early 802, by the terms of which subjects were supposed to swear a new oath of allegiance to Charlemagne now that he was emperor, it was stipulated that they were not to bring any enemies who had hostile designs into the kingdom and they were not to remain silent about anyone's infidelity toward the king.[38]

Indeed, when strangers came to court, the king had the privilege of grilling them about any and all information they might have.[39]

But kings themselves were advised by their courtiers not to divulge information. Said one:

> But just as the most salutary plans and precepts of the almighty God should be divulged, so sometimes the plans of wise rulers should be kept hidden from their enemies. For indeed there are no better plans in a state than those which an adversary does not know; and truly a journey will be a safe one if one's enemies do not suspect that it is about to occur.[40]

In this division into God's good news, which was to be spread outward, and the king's sensitive business of state, which was to be kept in (see Tob. 12:7), we see the interlocking pattern and complementarity of the Carolingian informational world. But the impetus behind both the spreading and retention of intelligence depended upon the king and his own wisdom, and it was a heavy burden.

Lupus of Ferrières went so far as to supply young King Charles the Bald with a set of authorities on the importance of a king keeping his mouth shut:

> Think many things, but do not speak all of them, since, according to Sacred Scripture, "He that guards his mouth, keeps his soul from trouble" (Prov. 21:23) or, according to secular letters, "tell no one what you wish to keep secret, since you cannot expect silence from another when you do not observe it yourself" and "a word spoken cannot be taken back."[41]

As so often, this specimen of a Prince's Mirror was designed to shape a young prince, in this instance recommending to him the practical virtue of silence in a listening world that would waylay and ruin him if his tongue should slip.

At court it was imperative to guard the secrets of a king. Lupus recommended that the king surround himself, as had the Roman Senate, with men who would hold fast on every side as a mighty wall of silence.[42] Among many courtly virtues, "wisdom" and "prudence" were considered paramount and, indeed, often synonymous terms for early medieval men and women. When Walahfrid Strabo praised Einhard's wisdom and prudence, what he partly meant was that Charlemagne had been able to trust Einhard "with his many secrets."[43] Hincmar late in the ninth century put a special priority upon the king selecting wise men as his officers, men who were wise, as he said:

> not in some clever or deceitful way, nor according only to the wisdom of this world, which is hostile to God. They were instead to understand that

wisdom and intelligence by which they might overcome those who rely on human trickery and, by means of their own just and right wisdom, over-throw completely their very basis of support.[44]

Courtiers had to agree that whatever they had discussed "in confidence," whether it concerned individuals or high politics, could never be mentioned to a servant or anyone without the general consent of all.[45] Hincmar pointed out, as one hears university department heads tell their tenure and promotion committees even today, what a ruination would follow from breaking confidentiality: an individual, a family, or a whole province might become bitter and bent on revenge, when the individual "would have done nothing if he had not known of that conversation."[46]

The Carolingian court had the protection of secrets built into its very operation. Hincmar claimed that the archchancellor's very title was A SECRETIS (the master of secrets), and that his job was to employ wise, intelligent, and faithful men who would record imperial commands and "faithfully guard the secrets of the [king]."[47] The king took counsel with his chief men prior to the annual general assembly, but whatever decisions were reached were to be kept strictly secret and hidden to all others. This was done in part to protect decisions from those who might undermine them.[48] The deliberations and determinations of the king and his chief magnates were to be concealed from the wider court for a variety of reasons; and so was sensitive information. In 793 Charlemagne concealed the magnitude of a military defeat to the Saxons, one might suppose, in order not to demoralize the Franks.[49] And when Louis the Pious decided to redistribute part of Francia, taking territory away from his three older sons in order to give it to his youngest, he did not officially proclaim it and his immediate courtiers were compelled to keep the plan a secret,[50] with good reason too, for rebellion waited on that decision.

It is in the matter of conspiracies that we see the Carolingians at their most secretive and most anxious. The Double Capitulary of Thionville of 802 stipulated that those who entered into a conspiracy and sealed it with an oath were to be put to death if the conspiracy was harmful.[51] Those who assisted the plotters were to flog each other and to cut off each other's noses. If no harm had been done, they were to flog each other and cut off each other's hair. If the conspiracy was sealed not with an oath, but by clasping hands, the conspirators needed to swear that their actions had had no evil intention. Carolingian kings worried constantly about nobles assembling without their approval. In 838 Louis the Pious could be found worrying about a private meeting of his sons Lothar and Louis the German;[52] in 874 it was Louis the German who was now worried when one of his sons met secretly with some of his nobles. The aged king, who knew too well the clever art of filial deception, immediately set out to intercept his own duplicitous son.[53]

Kings who imagined that the oaths taken by their nobles would protect them from conspiracies were frequently to be disappointed, since they lived in an age of multiple, overlapping, and frangible oaths that were often insincere at their very taking. Tassilo, the duke of Bavaria, confessed that when he conspired against Charlemagne in 788 he had encouraged his men to swear falsely. When swearing their oaths to Charlemagne, he urged them to "think otherwise in their minds and swear deceitfully."[54] This may remind us of children who even today when they unwillingly make a promise they have no intention of keeping cross their fingers behind their backs. But oaths in a world weak in legal accountability lay at the very core of social and political stability so that their willful perversion seemed a worrisome phenomenon to the powerful. Dishonest swearing threatened to rend the very tissue of expectations on which Carolingian order rested.

Yet, in the competitive world of the early Middle Ages, noble conspiracy was almost always in the air. The most well documented of these plots were the two occasions on which Louis the Pious was overthrown by his sons. After the emperor decided to give his youngest son a portion of the Frankish realm, his oldest son, "Lothar plotted not openly, but secretly to destroy what his father had arranged."[55] But Louis was aware of these schemes against him, for, according to one of his biographers:

> he discovered that the clandestine machinations of those whom he had spared were slowly spreading like a crab and were inciting the minds of many by means of secret devices; he decided to erect a tower, as it were, against them.[56]

His defensive tower against these cancerous plots was Bernard of Septimania, whom he appointed chamberlain in 829.[57] But the fire in the bellies of these disgruntled nobles only fed on the fresh fuel of this new imperial insult. The supporters of Louis's older sons waged a successful underground campaign against the changed conditions of Louis's court. They convinced the young kings that they had been insulted by their father; that Bernard was arrogant and despised them and their interests; and that Bernard and the empress, their stepmother, had committed adultery.[58] Paschasius Radbertus in his broadside against Bernard went so far as to claim that the chamberlain's secret goal was to slay the emperor and his sons in order to steal the empire.[59] The effect of the underground campaigns of 830 and 833 was, said the Astronomer, like water beating steadily upon even the hardest of rocks, for it finally brought about a yawning fissure and forced Louis's sons into an open break with their father. Evil talk had finally, he said, corrupted good manners.[60] We know about these secret conspiracies precisely because they were widespread and led to revolt, and because Louis eventually overcame them and penetrated the codes of silence in which they had been cloaked.

We can easily imagine the incentives for conspiracy,[61] but how were plots sealed and concealed? The lack of incriminating written evidence suggests that early medieval plots of this sort were not literary affairs, that is, conspirators did not generally conspire by letter or sign on a ruled line and make written pacts. Rather, we may surmise that they schemed their intrigues in face to face discussion, swore whispered oaths to each other, and clasped hands. Of course, such plotting was best suited to the most confident, calculating, and daring of men.

Legend had it that Pepin the Hunchback lacked the necessary nerve when he plotted against his father Charlemagne in 779. He and some nobles were supposed to have discussed their plan to murder Charlemagne in a church, but "after the meeting, [Pepin], fearing his complete safety, ordered a search to see if anyone was hiding anywhere in the corners or below the altars [of the church]."[62] And, in fact, a cleric was discovered hiding beneath an altar, but he swore that he would not betray them. Despite his promise, he immediately hurried to Charlemagne to inform on the conspirators. He encountered, however, a slight problem gaining access to the king. Palace government was such a tightly controlled operation that the two chief officers, the archchaplain and count of the palace, arranged all appearances before the king so that he would not be bothered by trivial petitions. In this strange case, Charlemagne himself wanted to know who was banging on his bedchamber door and, over the protests of his women, he answered the door and suppressed the conspiracy. In general if a secret matter such as a rumor of conspiracy was to be brought to the king's attention, the informer still needed to go through proper channels, though he might be allowed the privilege of revealing the secret to the king alone.[63] Court protocol and the complex structures of palace government protected kings from danger and nuisance, but they might also leave them cut off from immediately helpful news.

Still conspiracies seem to have been relatively hard to keep secret, at least during the reigns of strong kings. To be successful they had to involve a large number of nobles and even members of the royal family, but those very conditions worked to produce premature disclosure.[64] A duke of Moravia, for instance, learned from a conspirator that his uncle planned to have him strangled at a banquet in his honor,[65] the very set-up Theoderic the Great had employed to assassinate his rival, Odovacar. Early medieval men and women may also not have been as skilled as Roman senators or Renaissance courtiers at studied deception or hiding their feelings.

Said Notker of one young cleric in the presence of Charlemagne: he was "not able to contain within his chest the heat of his mind," and so blurted out his criticism of a corrupt bishop.[66] Both his facial expression and words betrayed the passion of the cleric, but he was not alone in breaking forth in a moment of high anxiety. Pepin the Hunchback, as we saw, was supposed to have feared the very shadows as he conspired to overthrow his father. And Charles the Fat, another royal son caught up in conspiracy against his father, broke down in public.[67] As well, conspirators needed the support of other nobles, but noble loyalties were complex, many-sided, and shifting in the ninth century.[68]

There were rewards for informers (Fardulf, the Italian cleric who had revealed Pepin the Hunchback's conspiracy, was made abbot of St-Denis)[69] and dreadful consequences for conspirators. Pepin's fellow-plotters were executed by sword or hung, while he himself was tonsured and placed in a monastery.[70] The Romans who were rumored to have plotted against the life of Pope Leo III were rounded up and butchered on the pope's command.[71] Once plots were uncovered, extraordinary measures were taken to discover their full dimensions. The nobles who had supported Bernard of Italy in his resistance to his uncle Louis the Pious in 817 quickly revealed who was involved and what they had hoped to accomplish.[72] Torture was practiced, even on the command of popes, it was charged, when examining conspirators.[73]

The real problem for conspirators in the early Middle Ages was how to keep a conspiracy secret. An Italian magnate had cheated a widow out of her property, whereupon she appealed to the emperor for justice. As the case turned against the lord, he arranged for three of his men to murder the woman, but he began to worry that he would not be able to keep the conspiracy secret with three others in on it and so he ordered one of the men to kill the other two,[74] thus anticipating Benjamin Franklin's aphorism that three men can keep a secret if two of them are dead.[75]

Sometimes, even reducing the number of conspirators was not enough. Paul the Deacon in his *History of the Lombards* tells a fanciful story of how King Cunicpert had conferred in secret with his stable-master about how to kill two nobles. While going over the details of the assassination a large fly landed on the windowsill and disturbed the king, whereupon he struck it with his dagger and managed to sever one of the fly's legs before it flew off. Later when the two nobles were approaching the palace, they encountered a one-legged man who told them the details of the king's plot against them. Cunicpert went to some trouble to ascertain the source of the leak, at first suspecting his stable-master, before finally realizing the role played by the informative—or rather transformative—fly on the wall.[76] Paul's exemplary story confirmed his world's belief that conspiracies, no matter how carefully contrived and concealed, could not be kept secret, for God saw all and despised treachery. A world away Dante, with a certain grim pleasure, would deposit all his famous and not so famous traitors in the lowest circle of hell, Roland's betrayer among them.

Of course, the identification of an act as treacherous depended like so much else on the particular perspective of the claimant. We need only look at Einhard's account of his acquisition of the relics of the martyrs Marcellinus and Peter to see how slippery perspective could be in the ninth century. His story is one of a theft or, rather, of a theft within a theft. For he sent his man Ratleig to Rome to retrieve relics from the unctuous and untrustworthy relics merchant, Deusdona. When the deal fell apart, his men cased a cemetery, tested its monuments to see if they could be violated, sneaked back at night to pilfer bones, hid the stolen relics in special cases, lay low in Rome, split up with the booty, and sought to avoid the authorities as they escaped.[77]

In reporting these events, Einhard cannot have been unaware that others would deem them criminal acts,[78] but he had his reasons for publicizing them. Not only was he committed to celebrating the powers of his saints, he also wanted to let all know that an agent of Hilduin, the powerful abbot of St-Médard of Soissons, had stolen a portion of the relics on the return journey, which he had now reclaimed. In this way he could proclaim to the Carolingian world that he had finally reunited the disunited bodies of his saints and put a stop to rumors of their separation. The justification for *furta sacra*, that the saint was a powerful agent in his own right and fully present in his surviving bones, and could not be stolen against his will, was for Einhard unidirectional; the saints would go where they wished to when they wished to and no human could resist them.[79] And they apparently wanted to be with him and not Hilduin, and their miracles burst forth like a summer rose bush as a sign of their renewed pleasure.

The intrigue-filled first book of the history of the translation of the saints may seem to the modern reader merely to describe a common theft, but it is a most uncommon account of medieval secrecy in action, of a covert conspiracy to grave-rob, and of the ends aimed at and means used. What remains surprising to the modern reader is Einhard's almost barefaced description of the conspiracy to commit a crime, which was a hidden operation at the time of its commission, but a publicly celebrated one once the bones had passed the Italian frontier into the safe land of Francia. It may have been left to God to judge, but the saints had already spoken. Their miracles seemed to justify what Einhard and his grave robbers had done.

Despite Einhard's subsequent celebration and manifest justification, the crimes themselves belonged to the Carolingian world of whispers and clandestine action. We are lucky to know anything about the theft at all. What the early Middle Ages lacked, for the most part, in all its plots were secure or, at least, novel instruments of deception, though it may be that we are simply unaware of techniques that were successful. The methods reported by the ancients were dangerously familiar. Both Herodotus and Aulus Gellius had, for instance, described how a message could be cut into the wood of a wax tablet before the wax was laid down on it.[80] Gundovald, the pretender to the Merovingian throne, tried to send a message to his supporters in just this fashion, but his emissary, the abbot of Cahors, was intercepted and the message uncovered, whereupon the abbot was savagely beaten and thrown into prison.[81]

Wax tablets remained the most common writing surface of the early Middle Ages. The poet Theodulf described the chancellor Ercenbald wearing wax tablets on his belt, ever ready to take down words and render them without sound.[82] One of the great virtues of the wax tablet was that it could not be easily read, since it had to be held up to the light at a particular angle, and could be easily defaced.[83] It is unlikely that many of the secret messages of that highly erasable medium were ever transferred to parchment.

Everyone knew that letters were not safe from hostile eyes, though sometimes they learned that lesson the hard way. The Merovingian queen mother, Brunhild, sought to kill the mayor of the palace and to this end sent a secret letter to one of her supporters at court. He read the letter and then tore it up, throwing the bits onto the ground. One of the mayor's men found the fragments and was able to reconstruct the letter on a wax tablet. Once the mayor had learned of the plot against him, he and his king immediately arranged the assassination of the queen.[84] They had poor Brunhild executed in brutal fashion, even by Merovingian standards—she was first tortured, then strapped to a camel and paraded before the troops, and was finally tied to an unbroken horse by her hair, one arm, and one leg and dragged to her death;[85] all because a letter was cut up rather than burnt.

In a later, more literate and cautious age, courtiers were careful not to be caught out in their correspondence.[86] Alcuin reported to his correspondent Arno, the archbishop of Salzburg, that:

> The previous letter, which came to me in your name—containing certain complaints about the habits of the pope and your [state of] danger there on account of the Romans—was brought to me by Baldricus, whom I assume to be a cleric of yours. He also brought a cloak sewn in Roman fashion, a garment of linen and wool. But since I did not wish that letter to fall into the hands of another, Candidus and I were the only ones to read it. Then it was cast into the fire, so that no scandal could arise through the carelessness of the one storing my written materials.[87]

Paranoia or, perhaps, just extreme prudence permeates this passage. Alcuin assumed that the letters he received, even confidential ones, might be overseen by others and that his secretary could not be relied on to protect his sensitive documents. Moreover, one is even tempted to wonder whether the incriminating letter containing Arno's dangerously candid comments about the scandals of the pope had been sewn into the cloak Baldricus brought. Why else would Alcuin have mentioned the cloak in the middle of the passage, sandwiched between his discussion of his handling of the damning letter? Was this to wink cleverly at Arno?

The chief problem with letters on parchment, aside from their durability (that is, as Alcuin saw it, their capacity to survive, implicate, and embarrass), was that they had to be carried by third parties over great distances and lengths of time. It is necessary to distinguish, as the Carolingians themselves often did, between the carriers of written letters and messengers whose job it was to speak a memorized message. Letters written on parchment were always in danger of falling into the wrong hands, especially if the carrier was waylaid or untrustworthy. Sometimes letters simply did not arrive: Lupus of Ferrières complained to one correspondent that the letter he had sent three years earlier had never arrived, either "through deceit or neglect."[88]

Carolingian letter-writers often spoke disparagingly of their letter-carriers. Alcuin doubted their reliability and was anxious not to entrust his carriers with sensitive correspondence, if he could help it.[89] Still he preferred, if possible, to write to his friends rather than to rely on the weak memories of his messengers.[90] But some matters were just too sensitive to trust to writing. Hence, he told Arno in early 800, in the midst of the Roman scandal, that "There are many matters I want to discuss with you which I do not wish to put in a letter because of the unreliability of the carriers."[91]

Lupus supplies an example of the simple weaknesses of his carriers. He informed Odo of Corbie that, as well as the letter he was reading, he had also sent along some peaches. He feared that the courier would, however, have eaten them along the way. In that case, he told Odo to make sure he handed over the seeds, unless he had eaten those too or claimed that they had been stolen.[92] We may surmise that in this case the letter itself was sealed and that the courier was illiterate.

Although Carolingian letters do not seem to have been forged as often as charters were, letter-writers clearly thought they could be and went to some trouble to verify and validate their letters.[93] Alcuin closed one letter by saying: "So that you might know that this is my letter, I have sealed it below with my seal."[94] Einhard knew the tricks of those who could copy signatures on charters, but he thought that they would make some mistake in dating or detail.[95] All kings had signet rings, ecclesiastics possessed seals, and Carolingian writers sought to individualize their signatures with epithets and paraphs.[96] Still one has to wonder how many false letters still pass as genuine in Carolingian letter collections?[97] In the Merovingian period, bishops were quick to condemn as false letters that got them into trouble with hostile kings, though most of those letters seem to have been genuine.[98]

Despite the risks people did send letters and there must have been a few trustworthy carriers. Even here, we should probably distinguish between different classes of letter-carriers, that is, between simple couriers, oath-bound vassals acting on their lord's behalf, and, best of all, friends traveling from place to place who might pass along letters.

Still Einhard, the ever prudent one, preferred in sensitive matters to send trusted messengers rather than dangerous documents. He told one of his correspondents:

> In fact, I think that it is better to trust a loyal man than a written document, since if a document or piece of parchment falls [out of the hands] of its bearer, every secret it holds is revealed, but a loyal messenger, [even if] tortured, does not betray the message entrusted to him. Therefore, everything that I wished to say to you, had you been present, I have told your loyal man. . .[99]

What Einhard's statement suggests is the extent to which sensitive correspondence was conducted orally;[100] written letters were often just formal and uninformative exercises, excuses for a messenger to travel from one place to another, there to speak the real message. The written message was often, then, merely an introduction and validation of the more important one that was to be delivered *uiua uoce*. One of Bishop Frotharius's letters is of this kind, a written introduction of a *missus* who would speak the message.[101] In 751 as the usurpation of the Merovingian line unfolded and Boniface was seeking permission to establish the monastery of Fulda, he informed the pope in writing that his emissary had secret messages meant for him alone; some were contained in writing, but others would only be conveyed orally.[102] Thus, while the letter itself dealt with important matters, it also served to introduce and certify a messenger who would speak of even more delicate matters.

Lupus too employed the same technique, which allowed him to send messages without committing to anything very definite in writing. To one of his correspondents he achieved near opacity: "God regards favorably, I suspect, the matter you indicated to me in secret and [the whole business] will be faithfully explained to you by the one who brought [me] this message."[103] For the sender of a confidential message, there was more safety, more wriggle room, in speaking rather than writing down something controversial. If a messenger betrayed a master's oral missive, it would still be difficult to prove that he was not simply inventing or misrepresenting his master's message.

But messengers too were suspect and early medieval men and women often remained reluctant to convey secrets orally through them. Alcuin had no great confidence in the feeble powers of recall possessed by his messengers and peasant couriers.[104] Similarly, Lupus asked another courtier to send him a personal letter about the king's schedule, since he did not trust messages brought by messengers; they were just too often garbled.[105] Frotharius went one step further and asked, as it were, for duplicate copies (one written, one spoken) of the time of a future meeting.[106]

In matters of great import it was deemed best to arrange face-to-face meetings at which dangerous secrets could be whispered to each other. Lupus wrote to one of his correspondents:

> I have learned of certain news that should be passed along with such caution that I do not think it safe to put it in a letter, yet it is so necessary [for you] to know it that you should come, as quickly as possible, to discuss it with me, but on the pretext of some other business.[107]

In this case he must have felt that he could not transmit even the oral message via his messenger. That had also been the point of Alcuin's message to Arno, that it was better to talk privately than to risk writing publicly and permanently. Even when a correspondent had asked a pointed question about some sensitive matter, Carolingian letter-writers often preferred to duck the question and postpone passing inscribed information, preferring to speak rather than write down their secret thoughts and sensitive news or to send them orally through an intermediary.

The slipperiness and allusiveness of many Carolingian letters has not always been sufficiently appreciated by modern readers, but their elusiveness and indirection were the direct products of the dangers of court politics and the insecurity of correspondence. Einhard was a particularly guarded correspondent. Listen to him here:

> with respect to those matters about which [your relative and man Eburo] believed he would bring some definite news to you, I can inform you of nothing definite [in writing] and cannot indicate [anything orally] through him, since the changing nature of things that has recently occurred in this kingdom [in 830] has shaken me to such an extent that I am almost entirely unsure what I should do. . . .[108]

That is a lot of words to say little except that there was little he could say.

What did Carolingian writers mean by "secret letters," which is a phrase that recurs? Perhaps, in the main, they meant a "private" or "personal" letter. The Carolingian world, after all, had fewer private moments and private places than the modern world affords us. After dinner one night the relics merchant Deusdona slipped Einhard a document, which he asked him to read in private.[109] Was this what early medieval men and women thought of as "secret correspondence," meant for the eyes of one person only? Certainly some of Louis the Pious's correspondence with cities in Spain was "secret" in a different way. The letter he sent to Merida was, for instance, clearly subversive: he spoke about the harshness of the city's Muslim rulers and urged the city's [Christian] residents to send a message to his army in the Spanish march should they wish the Franks to come to their aid.[110] And Pope Leo, after he had been attacked in Rome, sent news in secret to the eastern emperor about what had befallen him.[111] We may suspect, then, that what was generally meant by a "secret letter" was not one in code, but one that was sent from the sender to the receivers alone, for their eyes only, and that few people were to be informed of the letter's existence or conveyance.[112]

It remains somewhat surprising that the Carolingians were not sophisticated cryptographers, since theirs was a precocious literary age in which they rediscovered numerous ancient literary forms.[113] Moreover, they enjoyed wordplay of precisely the kind out of which a cryptographic imagination is born. They wrote riddles, hermeneutical treatises, and palindromes. Hrabanus Maurus composed an elaborate acrostic poem *On the Praises of the Holy Cross* in which the verses are to be read in various complex and interlocking patterns (figure 1.15).[114]

Some of these word games were certainly political in intention. Paschasius Radbertus, for instance, in his defense of the oft disgraced Wala, abbot of Corbie, wrote one of the strangest hagiographies of the Middle Ages. He cast the *Epitaphium Arsenii* or *Life of Wala* as a dialogue between monks who refer to political personages under suggestive, if oblique pseudonyms.[115] Acrostic poetry could also serve as a way for sending hidden messages. A monk of Reichenau named Wetti had a vision in 824 in which he saw the dead emperor Charlemagne on a purgatorial plain with an animal gnawing at his genitals. In this monastic dream Charlemagne was made to pay for his infamous lust and lecheries. When the young monk, Walahfrid Strabo, who had been at Wetti's bedside, came to render the *Vision of Wetti* into verse he chose to hide the names of the accused in acrostics. Thus, in the passage describing the emperor's fate, the initial letters of the lines vertically spelled out KAROLVS IMPERATOR.[116] In this way, one listening to the poem or reading it out loud might miss its specific target, but a careful reader could not.[117] Still Walahfrid's cleverness seems a literary trick and not an attempt to deceive deeply.

Letter writers had techniques for sending messages in code. Alcuin put one salutation in a number code: "The first letter to the first and the fifteenth to the sixth. . .," that is to say the 1st = A [Alcuin] to the 1st = A [Adalhard] and the 15th = P [Pater] to the 6th = F [Filius]. The same letter contains, as Jan Ziolkowski said, "a bewildering cryptogram of animals names substituted for the names of real people."[118] Moreover, a special kind of letter of recommendation or introduction called an *epistola formata* could begin or end with a numerical puzzle designed to allow the receiver to verify and validate the letter's authenticity. These puzzles were formed with Greek letters, which were not widely and consistently known in the ninth century, so that they must have caused not a few Carolingians to scratch their heads. But the intent to conceal was often undercut by a key in the letter itself that would assist in the decoding.[119]

The Carolingians knew some rudimentary forms of encryption and may have been inspired by what they knew of ancient techniques such as Caesar's wheel.[120] A ninth-century text, the *De inuentione litterarum*, on the discovery of letters, contains two different techniques for hiding messages. Hrabanus, its supposed author, asserts that Saint Boniface, an Anglo-Saxon, showed his predecessors (at Fulda) a technique for replacing vowels with dots and he supplies a chart of the equivalencies: A = two dots, E = three; I = one; O = four; and V = five. He noted that Boniface had not invented the scheme, but had learned it from the ancients.[121] Immediately following this scheme there is a second one in which the consonants B, F, K, P, X replace the vowels A, E, I, O, V.[122] Yet another early medieval system substituted the first few letters of the first five numbers for the vowels. Thus *pri* for "primus" stood for 'a', and so on.[123]

These early medieval systems of substitution were fairly primitive and would not have fooled a clever Carolingian code-breaker for long. But they also seem not to have been put to diplomatic purposes; instead they existed as intellectual puzzles for learned monks and literate priests.[124] Indeed, we have one delightful example of monastic code-breaking of just this sort. An Irish monk living in Carolingian Francia in the first half of the ninth century sent a cryptographic test to his fellow countrymen resident at the court of a Welsh king. The report we have says that Dubthach "believed himself the best of all the Irish and Britons and thought that neither the learned Irishmen nor the Britons in the circle of King Mermin could expertly read and understand that message."[125] But the four Irishmen who were presented with the task of solving Dubthach's cryptogram not only figured out that he had employed a system that substituted Greek numerals for Latin letters, they even pointed out a mistake in Dubthach's encryption and answered with a cryptogram of their own.

But if encryption was unsophisticated and letters were insecure, how were secrets kept and conveyed? Perhaps it was simply, as we have seen, that secrets in the early Middle Ages were chiefly confined to the whispered word. At the heart of a text known as *The Vision of the Poor Woman of Laon*, which criticizes Louis the Pious for the murder of his rebellious nephew, Bernard of Italy, lies the revelation of a secret conversation the emperor and his wife were supposed to have had outside in an enclosed space or orchard (*pomerium*), away from prying eyes and erect ears. Their dark secret, we may suspect, was that Queen Ermengard had counseled the emperor to displace Bernard in favor of her own three sons, thus driving him into revolt and toward the awful punishment that awaited him.[126] Whispered secrets, of course, belonged not just to the high court, but to the common countryside, where there was often a great deal to conceal from official scrutiny. Charlemagne knew that peasants hid grain from his tax collectors, and he charged his stewards with discovering the buried grain.[127] Agobard of Lyons, a reforming bishop, found that he could never track down the storm-makers who worked their magic in northern Europe.[128] People who still engaged in pagan practices must have quickly learned to hide their beliefs from priests with their penitentials and Carolingian judges with their capitularies. We possess lists of what those officials thought people might have believed,[129] but we lack inquisitorial records of the sort found for later ages. Since the early medieval church lacked rigorous investigative procedures, we may suspect that it was not particularly good at unearthing the secrets of the countryside of northern Europe. That close and invasive investigation of Christian souls would wait until the later Middle Ages and Reformation.

There was, as well, in the ninth century a world of gesture that we can scarcely recreate today, though it would be rash to assume that it was any more developed or systematic than Carolingian cryptography. When Louis the Pious was held captive by his son Lothar in 834, another one of his sons sent legates to his father at Aachen:

> Lothar agreed to allow them to see his father in the presence of his spies (*insidiatores*), one of whom one was called Bishop Otgar [of Mainz], [while] the other was the treacherous Righard. The legates, coming within sight of Louis, prostrated themselves humbly at his feet. After that they greeted him on behalf of his namesake son [Louis the German]. They did not wish to speak secret words to him because of the spies who were present, but by certain gestures of signals they made him understand that his namesake son had not consented to this punishment of his father.[130]

In this case the legates could have used either secret words or secret signs depending upon the situation in which they found themselves.

There is also the issue of the disguises that early medieval men and women used to avoid detection. In a world where dress was a surer indication of status than it is today, 'dressing down' as a worthless slave, monk, pilgrim, or priest, often seems to have fooled those who would intercept couriers, messengers, and those in flight. When Lothar, for instance, tried to stop some Italian bishops from sending a message to his father, the emperor, they responded by sending a messenger disguised as a beggar who safely made his way north.[131] Hincmar reports that he had sent sensitive letters to Rome "by means of his clerics dressed as pilgrims in order to avoid the traps of his enemies."[132]

Deception was often more a matter of feigned mission than misleading dress. In the early Middle Ages politicized churchmen were perfectly placed to act as double agents, since they always had two masters and could claim to be serving one, while in fact serving the other. After Louis the Pious's overthrow in 830, he secretly sent a trusted monk to two of his sons to seek his restoration. Guntbald traveled "on the pretext of religious business," but offered the usurpatious sons land if they would restore their father.[133]

But the Carolingians never cease to surprise me, so I am reluctant to conclude that they lacked sophisticated strategies for deception, including written ones. Although there were centers whose falsification of documents was detected and rejected even at the time,[134] there were some large secretive enterprises that were successfully hidden. A group of clever clerics working somewhere in northwest Francia put together the so-called Pseudo-Isidorian or False Decretals in four separate collections. The Pseudo-Isidorian Decretals proper, which is the fourth collection in the series, reworked portions of thousands of genuine papal pronouncements in order to concoct new and unauthoritative papal legislation and precedents.[135] To this day, no one is quite sure who did this or even what their exact intentions were. Surely this was a secret operation of the highest order and it succeeded brilliantly, at least as an exercise in deception. And, of course, it took seven centuries for the papally produced Donation of Constantine from the mid-eighth century to be proved false.

It is striking that we are still not sure what some of these 'fraudulent' documents mean. Perhaps the real problem is that we expect early medieval men and women to have hidden things in the way that we do, that is, by scrambling a clear message that can be unscrambled at the receiving end. What if, as a result of the lack of secure means for sending sensitive messages, the goal was more often to send an oblique or ambiguous communication that required interpretation rather than decoding at the receiving end. The onus would then have been placed on the receiver to understand the message, not on the sender to make it perfectly clear. Or, as a Rwandan proverb would have it, "A message is given to many, but those who are meant to understand understand."[136] What was wanted, then, was a sympathetic reader, a shared set of circumstances, and a common body of knowledge. Indirect communication of this sort lies close to conversational culture, where with the slightest grimace, shrug, or upraised eyebrow, we can overlay our speech with a directed meaning, pointing our listeners and seers in more definite directions than the spoken or written word alone might lead them.

It was with an expectation of just such informed and insightful interpretation at the receiving end that a Carolingian bishop, probably from Cambrai, sent a set of biblical quotations to the emperor Lothar I in the midst of his civil war with his brothers (for the text, see appendix 2).[137] James Westfall Thompson and Samuel Padover speculated that the citations concealed a confidential message sent "in the guise of a collection of quotations from the Bible and canons."[138] If that were true it would open up the rather daunting prospect that deep within the millions of words written by Carolingian authors on the Bible secret messages lie buried. The Bible then would truly become the Great Code of the Dark Ages, and the hermeneutical drive of the age would finally intersect with the profoundly theocratic character of its politics.

But it is not necessary to think that this particular collection of biblical quotations contains some secret message, at least not as we would normally regard one, for its meaning is relatively clear and constitutes a running commentary, an editorial as it were, on recent events encased in the Bible's safe authority.[139] We postmoderns lack the ability medieval men and women had to speak through the Bible and the Fathers, Virgil and the poets, that is, to communicate by speaking in ancient catchphrases. By such acts of ventriloquism or, to be more precise, textloquism, quotational cultures can use safe and authoritative blocks of text to say what could not otherwise be said, at times practicing a very public sedition cloaked in a once removed voice. If the ancient *cento* or patchwork of lines and phrases of poetry extracted from writers such as Virgil and Lucan had been employed to make fun of the high literary style, the Christian version in the hands of the Carolingians would be more authoritative and, indeed, deadly serious. Lothar's bishop exploited the plasticity of the Bible and its sea of words to communicate his partisanship while documenting its divine authority at the same time.[140] His was an interpretable message with the divine sanction built into its very structure as if it were a communiqué from God. The trick was to let the quotations do all the work, take all the risk.

Thus, with his excerpts the bishop invited the emperor to reflect on God's anger at the rise in an evil time of vain and upstart princes, of child kings (like Charles the Bald), and of wicked and lying brothers (such as Louis the German and Charles). The passage from Ecclesiastes that "Blessed is the land whose king is noble, and whose princes eat in due season," which is repeated, serves as a refrain and was meant to confirm Lothar in the rightness of his position as an elder and divinely sanctioned ruler whose brothers were not ready to rule. It was not yet their time. The last ten citations seem meant to move the emperor to the restoration of justice, that justice that had been perverted and overthrown by his bad brothers and their greed (as laid out in the third citation). Those citations also encouraged Lothar to think forward to that day when he would rightfully sit in judgment on his rebellious brothers and the crimes of bribery, theft, murder, and adultery they had encouraged. By following a damning sequence of biblical passages, the bishop had said everything and nothing, had pointedly condemned young princes and reassured their noble older brother, and had still not named anyone. Only one trained in the delicate art of whispering early medieval secrets and speaking indirectly could have produced such a thunderously quiet document. There was an art to this, one learned in the war of whispers that curved through corridors of power in the early Middle Ages.

But obliquity and cleverness of creation came with a price for so much depended on the goodwill, cooperation, and intelligence of the receiver. And in 830 Einhard had a problem. As the first rebellion against Louis the Pious broke out, he had written to Gerward, one of the emperor's officials, to plead illness as an excuse for his nonappearance at court and he alluded cryptically in a postscript to his saints' revelations, which had foretold all of the sad events then unfolding in the kingdom.[141] Gerward seems not to have seen the point, and Einhard wrote back in frustration:

> It is not clear to me what I should think about you, whether, that is, you did not understand my letter or did not care about my peril. But I am led more easily to [the former] interpretation, for I would rather think that as a result of certain preoccupations my letter was not carefully read and understood by you than to believe that your Kindness had no concern for the danger threatening me. . . .I now ask you and stubbornly beg you to reread again and understand the letter I sent you.[142]

What Gerward may have overlooked or purposely discounted was Einhard's subtle suggestion that only his martyrs, if properly cared for and invoked by their chosen custodian, could save the kingdom from utter collapse and the emperor and his wife from sure ruin. Communication by indirection, understatement, and allusion may have been a refined art in the ninth century, yet on occasion it failed, sometimes undone by its own cleverness, sometimes by feigned obtuseness at the receiving end. When it did fail, as here, it reveals how much power this subtle form of communication had transferred to the receivers of elliptical messages, for these readers became small gods of determination, deciding what to understand, what to neglect, and what to bend.

Finally, I conclude this inquiry with a worry. If one of the characteristics of court cultures in general is their secretiveness, how confident can we be of our understanding of those worlds if we have not understood either their secret codes or their ways of keeping secrets hidden from each other, have not been able to penetrate their systems of signing through gesture and spoken word, and have not entered into the state of mind of someone like Einhard who kept his mouth shut, his letters oblique, and his ears open? If we cannot penetrate the secret whispers of a court culture shaped and shaded by the presence of dangerous powers and a palpable climate of fear, can we ever be sure how much we truly know and what things truly meant? Our fate as historians might then be the one imagined by Robert Frost:

> We dance round in a ring and suppose,
> But the Secret sits in the middle and knows.[143]

CHAPTER 6

A WORLD GROWN OLD WITH
POETS AND KINGS

A king at his peak may be a plenitude,[1] but what is he in his decline as the parts begin to fall away? King Lear's senescence consumed his world, sapping the vigor and perverting the actions of those around him like some gaseous and volatile Jupiter swallowing small orbiting moons. The all too human disaster of his failing strength and judgment spread outward, destabilizing not just a kingdom, but the smaller domestic governments within his reach.

One of those small worlds housed Gloucester and his sons. By issue and envy Edmund may always have been waiting to waylay his father and right-born brother, but it was Lear's *coup de vieux* that unsettled the kingdom and gave him the chance to work his mischief. And yet Edmund understood his privileged brother's situation perfectly, the dilemma of a rightful heir forever waiting to inherit. In the false letter he composed and foisted on his father, Edmund presented what should have been Edgar's own understandable complaint:

> This policy and reverence of age makes the world bitter to the best of our times, keeps our fortunes from us till our oldness cannot relish them. I begin to find an idle and fond bondage in the oppression of aged tyranny, who sways not as it hath power but as it is suffered.[2]

Gloucester could so easily believe this misleading message because it rang true; it expressed the universal plaint of all aggrieved and impatient heirs.

Shakespeare knew of the unsettlements that royal old age brings on and in *King Lear* gives us both an end-king pecked at by pelican daughters as he confronts the conjoined horrors of the loss of judgment and power and the bastard Edmund's overthrow of a legitimate brother and an aged and easily fooled father; two separate dilemmas, both defined by the problem of succession. In one a sonless father is all legitimacy, but unhinged by age; in the other, an adulterous father and legitimate son are usurped by illegitimate and resentful issue. Yet it is Lear's aged errancy that encompasses and infects the body politic and shades his world with the old.

The *topos* of political senescence was not, of course, Shakespeare's invention, but a much older literary reflection of the historical tensions that surface as royal societies slip under the end reigns of aged kings. The problem was, at times, a particularly sharp one for the Carolingians and the *topos* that appears in their poems and in their historical narratives paralleled and at times mirrored historical hotpoints in the transition of power; it was not, then, just the abstract shadow of some literary tradition spilling downward from distant descent since the theme of historical senescence may have its home, on occasion, in the actual.

The great architect of our awareness of the surface contours of literary commonplaces, E.R. Curtius, observed that historians often fail to recognize the *topos* of senescence when they encounter it and instead unwittingly take such statements as 'the world is in grey old age' as self-expressions of the Middle Ages.[3] Just as often, one suspects, historians have knowingly employed the larger *topos* of aging as a structuring principle on which to construct grand historical edifices; Oswald Spengler's work would be a case to consider. *Topoi* and clichés can be and, perhaps, always are cultural tools used lever-like to move small worlds.

On a day-to-day basis, historians of the Middle Ages are likely to dismiss outright such commonplace configurations as irrelevant to the reconstruction of the knowable past, but that may be to miss the point for the sources they read have sometimes been shaped by the *topoi* they too quickly dismiss. Even Curtius, despite his encyclopedic treatment of the commonplace, seldom stopped to wonder what might lie behind the use of a given figure in a given time. Historians of cultures and ideas want more: to understand images and ideas in their moment and to restore the surrounding historical specifics to specific expressions, returning the passively commonplace to the actively expressed. For the *topos* used is always a chosen one, selected from thousands at hand because of its particular or seeming appropriateness. And students of a time need to study the competing and prevailing (or, at least, group) subjectivities that lie behind both choice and use. The Carolingian world may not have been in gray old age, but it may have felt as if it were to some contemporaries and to understand them we need to understand their own unsettlements and special convictions. The topical theme of political senescence in the ninth century bears examination, then, not just as a recurring rhetorical type, but as another cultural cluster of a greater historical moment.[4]

Senescence is a special *topos*, since it is a subset of the organic metaphor, the metaphor most frequently applied to the state.[5] Whenever we find the state compared to a diseased body, a poisoned body, or a body naturally growing old, we are in the presence of this metaphor, and it is one that imposes a situational model on its user.[6] If, for instance, the state is said to be declining into old age, the implication can be drastic, since a body once youthful and full of energy and now thought to be old and decrepit must eventually die. There can be some prolongation of life, but no reversals. If, however, the state is compared to a diseased body, the underlying intention of the author may be to urge someone to effect a cure. Historians, however, need occasionally to remind themselves that the state is not a body, and that they are not 'country doctors' capable of diagnosing an amorphous historical corpse.[7]

Carolingian historiography has not been free of the organic metaphor.[8] Heinrich Fichtenau, in particular, argued that the Carolingian empire, itself a late manifestation of the *regnum Francorum*, seemed to have entered the period of its old age during Charlemagne's later years.[9] Indeed, an organic conception of Carolingian history underlies the work of many modern historians. In the reign of Pepin the Short and his unroyalized predecessors some seem to see the youthful period of the Carolingian historical experience, in Charlemagne its maturity, and in Louis the Pious and his successors its old age and decline—a beginning, middle, and end; juvenile, middle, and old age. Fichtenau and F.L. Ganshof only tinkered with the model when they observed that the first signs of decline had really appeared during the last period of Charlemagne's reign.[10] The received pattern of ninth-century history, therefore, has often been one of progressive senescence.

I say 'received' because the pattern is not the invention of any modern historian, but is imbedded in the Carolingian sources themselves. Charlemagne himself apparently thought of his kingdom as a body that needed ministering, at least according to the Astronomer.[11] And in the so-called *Visio Karoli Magni* Charlemagne as his own dream-interpreter divides Carolingian history into three descending ages and foresees its inevitable decline and cessation.[12] Lurking in the background too was an apparently low-grade apocalyptic anxiety about the end of the sixth and final age of world history in 800, the six thousandth year since creation according to early Christian chroniclers.[13]

Senescence is a particular historiographical theme of the ninth century, one that first came into prominence around the start of the century, and its seed bed lay in a specific instance of group aging. The late writings of Alcuin belong to the particular emotive and experiential realm of the old. Read in that light, they seem a mournful song on the subject of his own advancing age. He was already over sixty and in poor health when he came to St-Martin's of Tours in 796 as its abbot. To Charlemagne he wrote that in the morning of his life and at the height of his powers he had worked in Britain, but now, in the evening of his life, he labored on in Francia.[14]

His body, he told the king, was broken, and he implored him to study one of Jerome's letters on the failure of the body and the strengthening of the mind in old age.[15] To a friend he complained that he was beset by the double burden of infirmity and old age.[16] Along with most Carolingians Alcuin tended to link sickness and old age as though these two conditions properly belonged together.[17] Infirm old men and women and phrases such as *debilitata senectus*, "crippled old age," appear so frequently in the sources as to make (for the reader, at least) the Carolingian conception of senescence seem at times to have been primarily pathological.[18]

The linking of old age and infirmity did, however, have some utility. Like others, Alcuin used the double burden of agedness and illness as an excuse for not attending to the king's demands upon him.[19] His invocation of the theme of senescence, even by way of excuse, was also not without literary sophistication. He likened himself to an old Entellus fending off the assaults of a young Dares, who would harass his old age.[20] He called upon the king and his friends to defend their old poet.[21] In letters to friends he aped Ovid, complaining that now "tired old age enters my room on quiet foot."[22] Theodulf, full of bitter fun, seems to have grown tired of the excuses of the whining dotard of Tours: let old Flaccus answer for himself, says Theodulf on the matter of Alcuin's nonappearance at court, "he has the time"; time, in other words, before he dies.[23]

Alcuin did not, however, restrict the *topos* of senescence to the purely personal and literary, but projected it onto the world around him. We should never forget that the historical pessimism we encounter in writers such as Alcuin and Einhard (and for that matter Spengler) was not the product of some objective sizing up of their worlds, but of a highly attenuated and personalized view of the outside often driven by events on the inside. For both of them the personal, physical, and psychological became by projection a fact of the world and separable from self. For some of them, to be old was to see oldness all around them.

Alcuin's formulaic response to the events he witnessed at the end of his life was *tempora sunt periculosa*, these "times are dangerous ones."[24] Everywhere he saw the good fortune of his age sliding into misfortune. In his long poem on the sack of the monastery of Lindisfarne, he linked the fall of the four ancient kingdoms (of Babylon, Persia, Greece, and Rome) and his own world overrun by pagans (in Africa, Asia, Spain, and even Rome) with the example of a single aging man, whose body had begun to fail him:

Quid iam plura canam? Marcescit tota iuuentus,
    Iam perit atque cadit corporis omne decus,

Et pellis tantum uacua uix ossibus haeret,
Nec cognoscit homo propria membra senex.[25]

[What more can I sing of now? All youth grows feeble,
And all beauty of the body now passes and fails.
Slack skin just barely clings to the bones,
The old do not even recognize their own bodies.]

So too an aged Alcuin feigned not to recognize the broken and failing world around him. In an awful and impermanent age, comfort could only be found in that singular point of permanence, God, on whom all attention must be fixed. He seemed to think that if he alerted the brothers of Lindisfarne to the sadness of all times, the worst of which was their own, the blow of their recent sack at the hands of the Northmen would somehow be more bearable.[26]

If Alcuin's belief in the mutability and decline of things reflected and was shaped by his personal senescence, it still belonged to a larger group reading of the Carolingian world. His was a powerful and well-placed voice able to persuade others that their world was growing old and, in addition, many in his audience of friends both at court and throughout the kingdom were themselves reaching old age alongside their aged poet and king. These courtiers had once been part of a world of intimate court camaraderie that was breaking up just before the turn of the century. Earlier there had been a certain youthfulness and joy among the poets gathered around Charlemagne, itself another extension of the personal upon the political, the internal upon the external. One thinks of their poems of pomp and play, and of the charming nicknames the men fashioning the Carolingian renaissance gave to each other.

After 796, however, many of these scholars had begun to go their own separate ways: Paul the Deacon, Peter of Pisa, and Paulinus of Aquileia returned to Italy, Alcuin exchanged Aachen for Tours, and Angilbert spent most of his time at St-Riquier. A sense of separation and loss pervades the post-796 poems of some of those men, who increasingly styled themselves *senes uates*, "the old poets."[27] Together they came to share an awareness of agedness as a common condition and a way of viewing the exterior world.[28]

In his poem *O mea cella*, Alcuin laments the silencing of the poets at Aachen, the absence of Alcuin and Angilbert from court, and the stilling of the singing boys. He personalized the decline of his times, reducing all to a single specimen of aging:

Qua campis ceruos agitabat sacra iuuentus,
    Incumbit fessus nunc baculo senior.[29]

[The precious youth who hunted deer in the fields is now
    A tired old man leaning on his walking stick.]

Peter Godman observed that the "ponderous spondaic movement" of that last line even imitates "the old man's weary step."[30]

Theodulf of Orléans, who had remained behind after the other poets had departed, also coupled the theme of senescence and an awareness of changed times. In one of his later poems, written after he had been sent into exile in 818, he too contemplated the evident end and ruin of all things. The old world was failing, and the embittered Theodulf was convinced that now "nothing stands fixed as it did before."[31] In a letter of Cyprian to Demetrian that described in dramatic fashion the physical exhaustion of his world Theodulf found a kindred pessimism.[32] Everywhere the exile thought he saw the utter defeat of what had once been young:

> Non uiget, ut uiguit dudum, uegetata iuuenta,
>   Cuncta senectus atrox ore nigrante uorat.[33]
>
> [Lively youth no longer flourishes as it once did,
>   Dreadful old age now devours all in its black maw.]

This in Theodulf's own decline and disgrace.

The *topos* of senescence may have assumed historiographical force in the early ninth century because Charlemagne's poets projected their own personal aging and changed circumstances onto the times in which they lived. Or, perhaps, their aging just made them more receptive to the ever-present shadows of anomie always waiting to be detected. In either case, these men did not go gently into their old age, they went complaining and would take their world down with them. *Tempora sunt periculosa*, indeed, when the old believe the whole world to be in decline with them.

The theme of senescence also colors some of the important histories of Charlemagne's reign. We need to remember that these historians were primarily witnesses of Charlemagne's later years. Einhard was only in his early twenties when he arrived at the court of Charlemagne, who was already fifty. But his biography of the emperor was not written until years later, when as an older man himself he looked back on his younger days at court in the presence of the great one. The *Life of Charlemagne*, thus, presents the nostalgic memories of an aged writer writing in a new time of troubles. Evidence for Einhard's myopia is not hard to find: he admitted, for instance, that almost nothing was now known about the early period of Charlemagne's life.[34] Instead he leaves us with a portrait of an aged ruler, who loved to soak in hot springs, who wept over the deaths of his friends and children, and who took up writing too late in life to become proficient.[35] Of the physical traits mentioned by Einhard, the most striking is the king's glorious head of gray hair.[36] The later medieval and epic image of Charlemagne as an old and holy emperor with a flowing white beard derives, in part, from Einhard's biography. The *Song of Roland* with its two-hundred-year-old king anxiously stroking his beard was an indirect heir of Einhard's memory of the old Charlemagne. Louis the Pious's historians (the Astronomer, Thegan, Ermold, and even Nithard) all remembered a Charlemagne who was, as they said, "full of days in his fine old age."[37]

In Ermold the Black's poem in praise of Louis, Charlemagne is made to speak directly to the issue of his old age. He reminds his gathered nobles in 813 that when his body had been young and vigorous he had taken up arms and every enemy of the Franks had feared him. But now his blood had grown sluggish and cold, harsh old age made him listless, and flowing gray hair covered his white neck. His warlike right hand, once famous throughout the world, now trembled. His children had died before him, except Louis, whom he now embraced as his co-emperor.[38]

Like so much else about ninth-century kingship, the great length of Charlemagne's life and reign became an influential model for his successors. In his prince's mirror, Sedulius Scottus contrasted the brief and unhappy days allowed to the reprobate with the many and happy years given to just and holy rulers.[39] In the major annals one can discern the same underlying pattern: bad kings die disastrous, sad, and premature deaths, while good kings die in peaceful old age.

In the extraordinary thirty-second chapter of the *Life of Charlemagne*, Einhard weaves together a winding-sheet of portents in which to wrap the dying Charlemagne: eclipses, the collapse of buildings, the fiery destruction of a great bridge, a meteor that caused him to be thrown from his horse, earthquakes, lightning striking the cathedral in Aachen, and the fading of an inscription that memorialized the king.[40] Today we tend to read this collection of portents the wrong way around. We look back to Einhard at work, with his Suetonian model at hand, creating and constructing an intended effect. But his contemporaries surely read him forward. For them the natural world was God's ongoing creation and not only reflected, but signaled the passing of a great king and it matched that approaching rupture with its own. Nature itself fell out of joint as Charlemagne began to die, for the great king had encompassed his world.

Before reading that singular chapter we would do well to turn to Einhard's preface and Walahfrid Strabo's prologue to the biography, even though both were written after the biography. Einhard's introduction (which was written for an unnamed friend) is a melancholy one, dwelling on his worry over the spreading forgetfulness and oblivion of the post-Charlemagne world, and Walahfrid marvels that in a new age of mist and blindness and amidst the great disturbance of Louis the Pious's reign Einhard should have held so firm.[41] It was as if the calamitous signs of

Charlemagne's death, those natural mirrorings of his aging, served as the historical prologue to the sufferings of the late 820s and 830s for it was the world itself that had begun to groan and creak in sympathy as the first emperor began dying. Louis inherited a world that was already broken, already out of joint. Thus Charlemagne's aging spread to the wider world and to the future and, though he was no Lear in thundering caprice and confusion, he still shaded it with the problem of his senescence.

The *topos* of senescence, then, assumed an important place in ninth-century historiography because of the conjunction of Charlemagne's own aging and that of his highly vocal and aging courtiers. In poetry and histories, senescence became a theme of historical conviction, a conclusion that both described and explained. The remembered Charlemagne was old and his later years were characterized as a period of spreading senescence. The Carolingian interest in the theme did not end with Charlemagne, but continued to color ninth-century history as a whole and the aging of his heirs.

It would, however, be wrong to dismiss as mere coincidence the aging of rulers and the recurrence of the theme of senescence. The *topos* itself may be clothed in age-old figures[42] that obscure the direct description of the world outside, but its very invocation was still the particular product of a particular history. There may, in other words, have been specific reasons why the time of an aged ruler was a progressively disturbed one. Aged Carolingian rulers were beset by special political and familial problems that were, in fact, brought about by their advanced age. And the historical *topos* of senescence may have existed as a parallel structure beside that history, reflecting through a rhetoric of perceived disorder an indirect, yet deeper impression left by the time or, at least, the subjective awareness of it. Beside the ancient and borrowed guise of the *topos* of senescence,[43] then, we need to set the actual activities of aged Carolingian rulers.

Perhaps we should, in general, turn away from overmuch examination of attitudes toward the aged and move to a consideration of the activities of aged medieval men and women in their social and group settings. For even when we lack a plentiful set of direct observations on old age, as we do for the ninth century, we still possess examples of the lives of aged men and women.

To begin with, if we can overcome our general reluctance to employ statistical evidence for an upper class (the only group for which we have sufficient information of this kind), I believe that we can calculate with some rough accuracy the average life expectancies of members of the royal family (for the specific figures, see appendix 3). For the thirty-eight males born between Charlemagne in 742 and Louis the Child in 893 for whom we possess fairly good birth and death dates (the possible series is forty-nine) we obtain a life expectancy at birth of 33.5 years. If we remove six infant deaths from the calculations, the average normal life expectancy of a male Carolingian rises to 39.6 years. These figures do not seem all that unreasonable when we remember that Charlemagne's brother Carloman died at nineteen and his own two vigorous sons Charles and Carloman (renamed Pepin) died at thirty-nine and thirty-three respectively.[44] Moreover, royal males seem generally to have died from natural causes, and rarely from wounds sustained in battle or from assassination.[45]

Unfortunately we have firm birth and death dates for only three Carolingian queens, and the average of their lives is thirty-four years. Carolingian queens seem to have married young and died young. Although Hildegard, "the mother of kings" as Paul the Deacon described her,[46] bore Charlemagne nine children, she had married him at twelve and died at twenty-five. Indeed, few first wives outlived their royal husbands, though Emma, the wife of Louis the German, reigned for thirty-nine years and only died a few months before her husband in 876. When a queen did survive her husband, she often assumed an important matriarchal position in the house of her son the king. Bertrada, Charlemagne's mother, pursued a policy of reconciling her two antagonistic sons and even managed to lead Charlemagne into a marriage of political convenience with a Lombard princess.[47] After Carloman died in 771, however, Charlemagne repudiated this wife and relegated his mother to a subordinate position within his household.

More common was the situation described by Hrabanus Maurus: Ermengard, the wife of Lothar I, had just passed from her juvenile years to a mature age when she died.[48] During the same period one can obtain sure dates for ten women born within the royal family (from a possible series of forty-one); these women had an average life expectancy at birth of 32.6 years and a normal life expectancy past infancy of 40.5 years.

These figures suggest that the average Carolingian male or female from the royal family could expect to live somewhere between thirty-five and forty years. While the average life expectancy figures at birth are doubtless somewhat high, perhaps not fully incorporating infant deaths, the normal life expectancy figures for individuals who survived the childhood years would seem fairly close to the mark and are consistent with other pre-industrial peoples of Europe.[49] The length of life of members of the royal family should no doubt be counted the upper limit for a group within society as a whole.[50] Paleodemographers have suggested, on the basis of early medieval skeletons that reveal approximate ages at death, a much lower figure for the life expectancy of common people.[51]

It may even have been the case that a few Carolingians who lived into their thirties felt that they had already attained old age. Still maximum life span could, in rare cases, reach eighty or slightly more.[52] We may hear less talk about agedness in the ninth century because fewer people lived out lives that reached into old age and, instead, often died, as Hrabanus said of Ermengard, in their mature years. But here we enter the realm of subjective age classifications. How old was 'old' for the Carolingians?[53] We should guard against equating the Carolingian use of *senex* with modern notions about the elderly. For the one was an informal type of social stratification based on an estimation of outward appearance, health, and social position in which one was labeled old by individuals who had few objective standards by which to call one old, while the other is a formal means of classification instituted by the state and its legislative programs according to a determination of one's documented age. In the ninth century, a thirty-five-year-old poor woman with gray hair, poor health, and a walking stick would have been labeled an old woman (*anus*); today the same woman would simply be thirty odd years away from collecting an old-age pension.

Following Isidore, Hrabanus said that the period of *grauitas* began at fifty and lasted until seventy, and then was followed by *senectus*, which lasted until death.[54] But little suggests that Isidore's six-fold classification of ages gained currency during the ninth century.[55] Working Carolingian authors from annalists to hagiographers tended, instead, to reduce the ages to three: *puer, iuuenis*, and *senex*.[56] Since we rarely meet *iuuenes* over forty in the sources,[57] *senectus* might apply to some members of society over forty, but perhaps not all.

In the case of kings and princes, the line that marked the passage into old age was never clearly drawn, in part because ninth-century writers seldom spoke of a king as old while he still lived and was healthy. They had no need, moreover, to identify a king by age, since he was already well known and in need of little identification. Princes, on the other hand, were sometimes characterized as young; age labels served to distinguish the numerous Charleses, Carlomans, Louises, and Pepins of the Carolingian line from each other. As well, what marked off the royal boy from the royal man was an initiation rite in which boys coming of age at puberty were invested with sword, shield, and horse by their fathers.[58] The act of accepting a boy into the ranks of adulthood and manhood (which may not be the same thing) also had the effect of impressing upon him his subordination in terms of age and authority to his father.

But no formal moment or rite of passage marked the aging of a king. Perhaps he only became aware of his agedness with the passing of his cohort, the onset of illness, and the consequent diminishment of his peripatetic capacity to travel into the far-flung parts of his kingdom in order to execute his commands in person. The deaths of old and trusted friends also reminded Carolingian kings of their own advancing age. By 805 Charlemagne had surely noticed the dying off of both his own and the subsequent generation; his son Louis suffered the same fate in 836–37 as his contemporaries began to die and the sinews of the state were snapped, or so said the Astronomer.[59]

The most famous Carolingian rulers lived relatively long lives: Charlemagne died at seventy-one, Louis the German at seventy, Louis the Pious at sixty-two, Lothar I at sixty, and Charles the Bald at fifty-four. They may be the most famous Carolingian kings precisely because they lived long enough to accumulate extensive power, for political advantage tended to accrue to long-reigning kings. No Alexander the Great of towering youthful triumph would ever appear among the Carolingians. Power and territorial control tended to fall to those who outlived their relatives. Thus, Charlemagne gained undisputed control of Francia upon the timely death of his brother Carloman late in 771. The historian Thegan, exploiting a biblical theme, began his biography of Louis the Pious with the argument that the youngest son is often the best of sons,[60] but Louis was only the best of Charlemagne's sons in one way: he outlived his more dynamic brothers and so inherited the entire empire on his father's death in 814. Charles the Bald quickly seized the opportunities presented by the deaths of his nephew Lothar II in 869 and his brother Louis the German in 876 to invade their kingdoms. Even the imperial title fell to him after the death of his nephew Louis II in 875.[61] This was the waiting game of Carolingian kingship.

It cannot have been easy for kings to grow old. If they lived long lives, Carolingian rulers faced particular problems that arose from the very joining of agedness and title, which they could not have easily anticipated when younger. Since Carolingian kingship was largely personal, anything that affected a ruler personally affected his governance of the kingdom, and age and health were chief among those things. Efficient government depended more on the king's willingness, energy, and ability to respond to outbreaks of trouble than it did on any administrative agencies within the kingdom. Old age impaired the peripatetic function of Carolingian kings. Charlemagne, for instance, made Aachen his principal palace during the last twenty years of his life and only infrequently left it after 808. The relentlessly mobile Charlemagne of the *Song of Roland* is a figment of epic need. The *Royal Frankish Annals* instead reflects the king's newfound sedentary life after 800, as he haunted Aachen, received foreign ambassadors and legations, convoked councils, and there made law.[62]

The last of these does seem to have been an activity of the final third of his life. We seem to see, if we may judge by the volume and tenor of his capitularies, the transformation of Charlemagne from warrior into lawmaker, settler of disputes, and statesman, though that too may be an effect of the *topos* of historical senescence. And Einhard issued a qualified complaint that after Charlemagne took up the imperial title he had not done as much as he might have or even as he wished to set the kingdom's laws in order.[63] Charlemagne's later juridical activity, as his biographer seems to have seen it, was an imperial function. It was also (and he did not note this) a product of his new settledness as an old ruler, for it reflected an attempt to control from a distance and by means of traveling judges, the *missi dominici*, an empire he could no longer administer in person. The weakness of central royal power in the early Middle Ages was never as evident as when an aged king decided to settle down. Thus, the *missi* may be regarded either as a sign of the growing sophistication of Carolingian government or the opposite, as a telling sign of its feebleness, for it was not working as it should when a king needed to depend on corruptible judges (at least that was Theodulf's view of the available temptations) in the field.[64]

The palace administration, which was not sophisticated enough to handle the large numbers of petitioners attracted by Charlemagne's fixed residence, often suffered from confusing congestion. Moreover, even if Charlemagne was increasingly concerned with obedience to his laws, he could not be sure that they were being obeyed unless he was constantly on the move and could judge for himself the nature of local situations or had good people who would do the same on his behalf. But the *missi dominici*, who were supposed to oversee the implementation of law in the provinces and to correct local abuses, were themselves often the instigators of trouble, especially if they remained in office or in one place for too long. We should remember that Louis the Pious began his reign with the stated intention of reforming the abuses of justice that had gone unchecked during Charlemagne's last decade. One of his first acts was to send out hand-picked *missi* to investigate; they reported back that they had found many people who had been deprived of their hereditary lands or their freedom under Charlemagne.[65]

Even more significant, it seems that old Carolingian rulers were reluctant to initiate wars of conquest, though those wars might, in the long run, have checked future invasions and suppressed incipient aggression. Charlemagne's last campaign was the one against the Danish king Godefred in 810, but it was only in response to a threatened invasion. When Carolingian kings began in the ninth century merely to respond to incursions instead of anticipating them and cutting them off at their source, as Charlemagne had done with the Saxons and Avars, they played a dangerous game of catch-up they could never quite win; they were always two steps behind the many enemies who gathered at the edges of their vast territory. It is no coincidence that aged Carolingian rulers experienced military difficulties: one thinks of the threats posed by the Danish in the north and the Saracens in the south during Charlemagne's last years, Louis the Pious's problems with the raids of the Northmen, Charles the Bald and the Saracen assault on Italy in 877, and Charles the Fat's utter inability to rise effectively against the Northmen in the 880s.

It was not so much that these were especially dangerous attacks (indeed, most of them were sporadic raids) as it was that aged rulers were unable to mount vigorous and foresighted campaigns: the potential for invasion of the huge empire was always there threatening, but, as Ermold put it, the warlike right hand of the Carolingian king trembled in old age. In all fairness, it must not have been a happy prospect for an old king to set out personally for war. During his last military operation, when already sixty-eight years old, Charlemagne fell from his horse, much to the shock of his assembled troops.[66]

One way around the problem was for the aged ruler to employ his sons to carry out his military campaigns. Both Charlemagne and Louis the Pious did just that. Perhaps the most famous of these wars was the one that Charlemagne's son Pepin waged against the Avars in 796. In a poem celebrating his victory, an anonymous poet asked not only for long life for Pepin but also for his father Charlemagne to continue to reign, to grow old, and to beget sons who would maintain his palaces during his life and after his death.[67]

In fact, it was exceedingly difficult for a ruler to grow old peacefully if he had sons, and somewhat bizarre to suppose that a living son of Charlemagne should have welcomed newborn brothers. Germanic tradition extended a privileged place in law to fathers: a son ought not to oust his father while he was still strong and able to perform his duties, Bavarian law said.[68] But in the wake of Louis the Pious's troubles with his rebellious sons, Lupus of Ferrières would prudently advise Charles the Bald not to give power to his sons during his lifetime; better that they should beg favors from him than the reverse.[69] If only Lear had known.

Carolingian sons frequently rebelled against their old fathers. Charlemagne was fifty when his son Pepin the Hunchback led a revolt against him in 792; Louis the Pious was fifty-two when his elder sons first rebelled in 830; Louis the German suffered the first of a series of rebellious machinations by his sons in 860 when he was fifty-four; and Charles the Bald's son Carloman revolted in 871 when his father was forty-eight.

The reasons for these revolts are complex. In part they were bred by the royal policy of setting up young sons in specific regions of the kingdom. This had the double effect of distancing the young princes from their fathers and at the same time subjecting them to the pressures of regional politics and local aristocracies with their own wants. These princely kings often ended up establishing regional power bases from which to resist their fathers. Although Charlemagne too followed the practice of establishing his sons in their own kingdoms, he was saved from open revolt by the deaths of two of his contending sons and by his clever policy of keeping his sons engaged in wars of expansion.

Louis the Pious and Louis the German were not, however, to be as lucky. Indeed, throughout his last years, Louis the Pious constantly attempted to assert his paternal and royal authority over his older sons, Lothar and Louis the German, never with any lasting success. In 840 he chased the rebellious Louis from Thuringia into Bavaria, where he belonged, but ill health forced the beleaguered father to give up the campaign. He died a short distance from his favorite palace of Ingelheim on an island in the Rhine. On his deathbed Louis forgave his recalcitrant son, but wanted him to know that it was he who had led his gray-haired father to his death.[70] Ironically, late in life Louis the German himself was to suffer repeated revolts by his own sons. The fact of the matter is that a Carolingian ruler who lived a long life and had many middle-aged sons simply could not satisfy their natural desire to exercise independent power. Gloucester's unseating was Shakespeare's variation on the theme of the rebel son.

There is another issue, a moral one, about Charlemagne's life after 800, that needs to be framed in terms of the policies of an aged ruler. I will let the good Anglican Edward Gibbon present the charge in his best dudgeon:

> Without injustice to his fame, I may discern some blemishes in the sanctity and greatness of the restorer of the Western empire. Of his moral virtues, chastity is not the most conspicuous: but the public happiness could not be materially injured by his nine wives or concubines, the various indulgence of meaner or more transient amours, the multitude of his bastards whom he bestowed on the church, and the long celibacy and licentious manners of his daughters, whom the father was suspected of loving with too fond a passion.[71]

Indeed, ten years after the emperor's death Wetti, a monk of Reichenau, was supposed to have had a vision in which he saw an animal gnawing at the genitals of Charlemagne. When the shocked visionary asked his angelic guide how such a man, who had been almost alone in the modern age in defense of the church, could suffer so, the angel answered that, although he had done many remarkable things that had pleased God, he had given himself up to the delight of debauchery and had wished to end the great length of his life in the sin of lust.[72] Thus, some of his monastic critics thought that Charlemagne's lechery was a product of his senescence, for after a life of good deeds and serial monogamy he lost control of his libido and morals late in life with the weakening of his will.

Nothing could be further from the truth. What the critics of Charlemagne's personal life did not fully appreciate was that they were witnessing the deliberate policy of an aged ruler and it was one also reflected in the handling of his daughters, and not for the salacious reasons that Gibbon wickedly implied. Statecraft and not lust governed the king's domestic arrangements. Charlemagne was reluctant to marry off his daughters because he feared that the offspring of such legitimate marriages would threaten his dynastic line: his immediate family long remembered that his bitter enemy Tassilo, the would-be king, had been the product of just such a lateral marriage by one of Charles Martel's daughters.[73]

In his own case, I suspect that Charlemagne did not marry again after Queen Liutgard's death in 800 in order not to sire any more legitimate sons and by such a birth complicate his succession. At that time he still had three living legitimate heirs, and that must have seemed enough. By the terms of the *Diuisio regnorum* of 806 the emperor had divided his kingdom into three parts in the manner in which it had been divided earlier between himself and his brother Carloman.[74]

The *Diuisio* is a detailed document, anticipating every eventuality but one: what should happen if a new legitimate heir were to be born to Charlemagne. That was deliberate. Of course, he could have made a new division of territories if the need arose, but it seems more likely that Charlemagne intended to remain unwed in order not to confuse the question of his succession. The three sons he sired after 800, one in 807 when he was sixty-five, were all illegitimate. Charlemagne, the defender of the church and Christian morality, was prepared to endure ecclesiastical criticism (though it was mostly driven underground while he lived)[75] several times during his reign, always in the greater interests of his dynasty. Thus he summarily divorced a legitimate wife, kept his 'naughty daughters' at home and unmarried, and took concubines late in life. Einhard claimed or feigned ignorance about the reasons for these domestic embarrassments.[76]

Unfortunately Louis the Pious did not pay close attention to the example of his father or his piety would not allow him to subvert his Christian mores in favor of the interests of his house.[77] Louis already had three legitimate heirs by 817 when, perhaps aware of his own mortality after a near-fatal accident, he divided his territories into three in the *Ordinatio imperii*.[78] Ignoring the older Frankish form of strict patrimonial partition, Louis decided that the empire (though not the kingdom) should pass undivided (as it was not possible to divide the unitary thing that an empire was) to his son Lothar. Again there was no provision made for the birth of another legitimate heir, but that is just what happened. When Queen Ermengard died in 818, Louis at first seems to have thought of not marrying again, which would have preserved his succession as set out in 817. Under pressure from some of his nobles, however, Louis eventually married Judith, who bore him Charles the Bald in 823.[79] At the urging of his new queen, he attempted to alter the terms of the previous agreement with his sons, in order to make room in the kingdom for his new son. When his elder sons revolted in 830, they justified their action on the grounds that they only wanted to restore their father to his proper position in his house, for Louis was widely reputed to be a cuckold: Judith was said to have committed adultery with the chamberlain, Bernard of Septimania.[80] Agobard of Lyons wrote works in which he demonstrated, by way of biblical examples, the danger of a young wife for an old king.[81] On his side Louis and his supporters attempted to invoke the positive commandment that children ought to honor and obey their parents.[82] A good deal of this debate centered specifically on the respect due to an aged parent, an issue that became highly politicized during the last decade of Louis's life.[83]

Finally, as Carolingian kings succumbed to old age, they were subjected to the pressure of suitors attempting to jockey for position around them. Einhard and the imperial party at court pressured Charlemagne into accepting Louis as co-emperor in 813. And Judith and her advisors, in their turn, badgered Louis late in life to guarantee protection for Charles the Bald after his death. Even if old age was a natural time of transition in the passage of Carolingian power from one generation to the next, for the aged ruler himself it was a time backloaded with woes. If he was not fending off ambitious sons, he was often faced with the opposite: a dearth of heirs. That was, in particular, the heartfelt fate of Lothar II and Charles the Fat. No wonder then that many of them thought of retiring in their final days to monasteries in imitation of Pepin the Short's brother Carloman.[84] Even Charlemagne left open the possibility in the testamentary statement recorded by Einhard that he might withdraw from worldly affairs.[85] Louis the Pious constantly raised the possibility of his retreat, and Lothar I did end his days as a monk at the monastery of Prüm. One can hardly blame these troubled rulers for wishing to find relief in monastic retirement from their particular condition as aged Carolingian rulers.[86]

In conclusion, I wonder if it is not now possible to see some of the reasons for the occurrence and importance of the *topos* of senescence in the ninth century. On the one hand, at the level of events, aged Carolingian rulers faced a special set of political and familial problems that made their later years a turbulent time for the kingdom as a whole. Lear's condition was one that swallowed up his world and his time, forcing all to work through it; the Carolingians suffered similarly, both in deed and word, from crises of historical succession and senescence. The concentration of divinely sanctioned power in the hands of but one individual until his death made senescence a natural and largely unavoidable weak point in royal rule.

Some of Charlemagne's poets, who were themselves aged, felt the world-ending nature of the problem of the senescence of their time, perhaps Alcuin and Theodulf most dramatically and personally of all.

The world around them, they thought, was groaning with age and debility. Even if that aging world was an immediate product of their own perception and experience, it was still keenly felt as external and real. Their language of senescence may have been borrowed, but the problem was their own and Charlemagne's aging may have provided the background conditions and cause of their unease. At a deep-seated and personal level, then, the royal poets and historians of the ninth century picked up on and reflected the mood that embraced both court and kingdom when it was in the "quavering grip" of an old king. Conscious of their art, if not of the underlying reasons for their anxiety, they transformed a historical given into its poetical correlative. They were growing old with their king and they made their world grow old with them.

CHAPTER 7

THUNDER AND HAIL OVER THE
CAROLINGIAN COUNTRYSIDE

What farmers thought, how they imagined their world to work, and what strategies they consciously adopted to confront a capricious natural world are matters that rarely surface in the records of the Middle Ages. No writer in the ninth century spent much time pondering the thoughts of those who worked and managed the land, probably because it was assumed that those thoughts were unremarkable. Yet what could be more central to a fuller appreciation of an age like the Carolingian, in which countryside and agricultural concerns dominated, than to acknowledge the importance and, indeed, intelligibility of popular thought?

What most worried Carolingian farmers before their crops were harvested was the weather and what most pressed them afterwards were the claims made upon a portion of that harvest by demanding lords. The common Carolingian dread of destructive thunder and hail storms not only tells us something about the nature of the rural economy of the period,[1] but also about the way in which people responded to calamity and, on occasion, turned it to their advantage.

One day in 815 or 816 Agobard, the bishop of Lyons, encountered a crowd about to stone to death three men and a woman bound in chains.[2] The bishop learned that the people of his diocese believed that ships traveled in clouds from a region called Magonia in order to retrieve the produce that had been cut down by hail or been lost in storms. The people explained to Agobard that the four captives were aerial sailors who had fallen out of one of those cloud-ships.[3] After reasoning with the captors, the bishop believed that he had finally uncovered the truth behind the story and, with the captors in a state of confusion, the matter was apparently resolved.

Unfortunately, Agobard neglected to tell us what specific and revealing truth he uncovered. What he did do was write a fascinating tract "Against the Absurd Belief of the People Concerning Hail and Thunder."[4] In it he supplies us with a scattering of information about the notion held by the people of his diocese that some people could manipulate the weather. The main thrust of his piece, however, was to demonstrate that God controls the weather, not humans. Perhaps we shall never know what conspiracy Agobard discovered that day near Lyons, but we can attempt to work our way back into the meaningful world that he and his flock inhabited.

In the treatise Agobard tells us that in the regions around Lyons virtually everyone believed that hail and thunder could be brought about by the will of humans. By "virtually everyone," he explained that he meant nobles and common people, city folk and country folk, old and young.[5] As soon as these people heard thunder and saw lightning, they would at once summarily declare that it was a "raised storm."[6] When asked why they described it so, they explained that the storm was raised by the incantations of people called stormmakers (tempestarii).[7] Occasionally, when they heard thunder or felt a light puff of wind, people would utter a curse against the stormmaker in which they asked for the evil-speaking tongue that caused the storm to become parched and silent.[8]

Many people believed that the stormmakers had struck a deal with the aerial sailors in which the sailors gave the stormmakers money and received in return grain and other produce, which they carried back to Magonia in their ships.[9] Agobard heard incredible accounts of the prowess of the stormmakers, that they could, for instance, control hail so precisely that they could make it fall, if they wished, upon a river and a useless forest or upon a single tub under which one of them hid.[10] On at least one occasion, Agobard heard of someone who had been an eyewitness to one of these events, and he soon tracked him down. Under persistent questioning, however, the man admitted that he had not been personally present when the stormmaker worked, but he resolutely maintained the truth of his account and named the stormmaker, the time, and the place of the deed.[11] Agobard learned that in many places men claimed that they did not know how to send storms, but, nevertheless, knew how to defend the inhabitants of a place against storms. The people reached an understanding with these defenders about what percentage of their crop they should pay in return for protection, and they called this regular tribute the canonicus. Agobard lamented that people who never willingly gave tithes to the church or charitably supported widows, orphans, and the poor, freely paid tribute to those who offered to protect them from storms.[12]

In what amounts to an appendix to his tract, Agobard supplies another example of what he thought of as popular foolishness.[13] A few years before his campaign against the stormmakers, when a great number of cattle in the kingdom were struck by disease and died (that was in 810), a story circulated that Grimoald IV, the duke of the Beneventans, had sent some of his people to spread a special dust on the fields, mountains, meadows, and springs of northern Europe in order to kill the cattle of his enemy, the emperor Charlemagne. Agobard claims that he both heard and saw that many people were apprehended and some were killed because of their alleged crime. They were tied to pieces of wood and cast into rivers where they drowned. It amazed Agobard to learn that many of the accused had actually confessed that they had possessed the poisonous dust and had scattered it, and that neither torture nor the threat of death had deterred them from giving false witness against themselves.

Agobard's reaction to these popular beliefs was self-consciously rational and Christian. In the case of the dust-spreaders, for instance, he thought that the people had not stopped to consider how such dust could selectively kill cattle and not other animals, how it could be spread over so wide a territory, and whether, in fact, there were enough Beneventan men, women, and children to carry out such an immense undertaking. It saddened him to think that in his time such great foolishness overwhelmed the wretched world and that such absurdities were believed by Christians. He was not alone, at least not among the powerful and the learned.[14]

The bishop similarly thought that the belief in the power of the storm-makers to control the weather was another example of popular foolishness that he could rationally undermine and disprove. When the land was too parched to sow, he wondered why people did not call upon the services of the stormmakers to wet their fields?[15] Why, in fact, should crops ever fail, if the stormmakers controlled the weather?[16] Why do they not kill their enemies at will with sudden hailstorms, if they have the power?[17] For Agobard, only God could control the weather and not the evil stormmakers.[18] He devoted most of his treatise to the consideration of Old Testament citations that demonstrate the divine origin of weather. If even Job could not unlock God's treasure trove of hail (Job 38:22–30), then how could these storm-makers? For these men:

> by whom they say violent winds, crashing thunder, and raised storms can be made, show themselves to be puny men, devoid of holiness, righteousness, and wisdom, lacking in faith and truth, and hateful even to their neighbors.[19]

As grateful as we should be for Agobard's fascinating account, we should not for a minute fall into the trap of thinking that his is an anthropological description of a set of popular beliefs in the environs around Lyons in the early ninth century. The bishop never fully describes the belief in weather-making, in part because his point was to refute and not to explain that belief and, in part, because the believers seem to have resisted talking to him. He admitted that he had had great difficulty in locating eyewitnesses and at least one of these recanted that he had seen such an event, but held fast to the truthfulness of his story. One suspects that Agobard never got inside local belief systems, but operated from the outside as their official critic.

His rationalism seems to have met some of the same dead ends that Dr. Livingstone encountered in southern Africa in 1853 as he sought to disprove the local belief in rainmaking.[20] When Livingstone asked the rainmaker if he could make it rain on a specific spot, the rainmaker, apparently puzzled, answered that it had never occurred to him to do so, since all should enjoy the blessings of plentiful rain. In frustration at the rational and persistent questioning of his beliefs, the rainmaker finally said to Livingstone: "your talk is just like that of all who talk on subjects they do not understand. Perhaps you are talking, perhaps not. To me you appear to be perfectly silent."[21] For both Agobard and Dr. Livingstone the belief that humans can control the weather was an important barrier to the Christianization of a rural population.

What we also need to remember about Agobard was that he belonged to the reform movement that was sweeping through the ruling circles of the Carolingian empire after Charlemagne's death. In 814–17 Louis the Pious cleansed his father's 'unwholesome' palace by casting out his 'naughty' sisters, ordered the *missi* to restore justice in the kingdom to those who had been arbitrarily mistreated, and introduced a wide-ranging reform of monasticism.[22] During these years Agobard was the country bishop or suffragan of Lyons and apparently aspired to attract the attention of the reformers.[23] His early writing, which was dominated by works devoted to reform, may well have begun with the treatise against the belief in weather-making. Moreover, as a transplanted Spaniard, Agobard may have brought with him to Francia the deeply ingrained conviction of the higher clergy of Visigothic Spain that weather-making was evil and should be sharply suppressed.[24]

In the battle against perceived paganism Agobard also put on the old and venerable mantle once worn by the likes of Martin of Tours and Caesarius of Arles, great foes of paganism in Gaul. The tradition had been continued in the Carolingian kingdom by the missionary Boniface and restated by Alcuin, who had urged Arno, the bishop of Salzburg, to imitate Christ by preaching against superstition wherever he found it, be it in castles or countryside.[25] These men were convinced, as one historian put it, that "there was a barbarian not far below the skin of every Frank. . . ."[26]

But Agobard was hardly the first Carolingian to be concerned about the belief in storm-raising, since we find numerous condemnations of both the belief and practice in official sources. The *Indiculus*, an eighth-century list of popular paganisms, includes a reference to a superstition concerning storms and around 775 Cathwulf, an Anglo-Saxon admirer and advisor of Charlemagne, called on him as an agent of God to correct, judge, and damn stormmakers and other evil-doers (*maleficii*).[27] In the famous capitulary, the *Admonitio generalis* from 789, whose chapters were to be repeated so often in other legislation, Charlemagne acted on that counsel and added to the list of Biblical injunctions against augury and incantation one against stormmakers.[28] Cathwulf had advised the king to suppress the stormmakers and other evil-doers lest he lose his *honor* here and now or in the future.[29] Even if the *honor* referred to was the king's good standing with God and his duty to protect Christians from pagan and diabolical beliefs, another meaning of *honor* is high public office and in Charlemagne's case his religious and royal natures were fused: "you are in all these matters a minister of God and an avenger."[30] Cathwulf's concern and Charlemagne's own laws should alert us to the possibility that storm-raising was considered to be a real and contemporary problem in the eighth and ninth centuries, one that worried the king himself for it threatened to ruin and unhinge not just the church, but his own religious and royal mandate.

In the most important legislative reference to weather-making, one of Charlemagne's church councils ordered that those who make storms and do other evil things by incantation, augury, and divination should be captured and turned over to the chief priest of the diocese where they were found. Under his supervision they were to undergo a careful examination to determine whether they would confess to the evil things they had done. Nevertheless, the examination was not to be so harsh that they died as a result; rather stormmakers were to be incarcerated until, with God's help, they promised to reform. But there was a concern that these people, once caught, might escape a strict examination because of rewards given by counts or their subordinates. Hence, it was stipulated that the chief priests should not hide news of comital interference from their bishops who, under such circumstances, should personally take charge of the accused individuals.[31]

At the Council of Paris in 829, convened under the auspices of Louis the Pious and Lothar I, there was a pointed condemnation of storm-making among the other pernicious remnants of paganism:

> For some say that by their evil deeds they can stir up the air and send down hail, predict the future, and take away the produce and milk of some and give it to others. And countless other things are said to be done by such people.[32]

The Council commanded that, if any men or women were found guilty of practicing storm-making, they were to be severely punished by the lay ruler, since they had openly dared to serve the devil.[33]

Penitentials from the eighth century forward were equally concerned to curtail the belief in storm-making. Earlier penitentials such as the one ascribed to Bede and the so-called Burgundian Penitential imposed pennances of seven years, three of those on bread and water, for the sin.[34] The Carolingian penitentials treat the senders of storms (*immissores tempestatum*) as practitioners of magic, and Hrabanus Maurus in his work *On the Magical Arts* classed weather divination as a species of magic.[35] The stormmaker, working by means of incantations, was classed by Agobard and the capitularies as a *maleficus*, a word that sometimes simply means evil-doer, but sometimes means wizard.[36] The enchanter (*incantator*) was also a *maleficus* and was the pagan worker most closely connected with the enchanting stormmaker by Carolingian sources. Indeed, Agobard's geographical term Magonia might be translated as Magic Land (from *magus* or magician), and, therefore, might be his own satirical coinage.[37] For Regino of Prüm, those evil-doers, enchanters, and senders of storms, who cloud the minds of men through the invocation of demons, should be harshly punished.[38] Burchard of Worms in his tenth-century manual for confessors, the *Corrector*, urged priests to ask their parishioners if they either believed in or had partaken of the perfidy that enchanters and those who call themselves the senders of storms could, through demonic incantations, provoke storms or change the minds of people.[39]

Both Hrabanus and Agobard were anxious to eliminate the popular support for pagan middlemen like the stormmakers and diviners who stood between the church and its people. Agobard rigorously attacked the stormmakers, not to win them over, since he never seems to have personally met one, but to discredit their claim to power over the elements. His goal was to destroy the popular belief in the power of the stormmaker. Agobard treated those who believed that the weather could be controlled by men as deluded and superstitious, while the penitentials prescribed the means by which the wayward could be reincorporated into Christian society.

Charlemagne and his family may have felt uneasy about the popular belief in storm-making for a complementary set of reasons. From at least the time of Boniface, the Carolingian family had tied its own fortunes to the church and a process of Christianizing Francia. For them, stormmakers posed a perceived threat to their power since they seemed to belong to the decentralizing face of paganism. What Charlemagne really worried about, if we may judge by the council, was that local priests, counts, and comital agents might conspire to protect the stormmakers. Perhaps he suspected that local counts would or always had established regional power bases by forming strong bonds with pagan priests. This was not unlike the stubborn problem Charlemagne had encountered in Saxony; paganism, in short, was a political as well as religious offense, since it had proved to be a powerful agent of resistance to central authority, both religious and royal.[40] And the case of the dust-spreaders is a fascinating example, however opaque, of the perceived mixing of pagan and political interests; it seemed to at least one element of the Carolingian population to concern a ducal enemy of Charlemagne and magic. Moreover, since the Carolingian family had sanctioned one priesthood with a powerful institutional structure, it could ill afford to countenance the presence of another, or rather a diffusion of others, within the kingdom. Charlemagne and his successor were troubled by the enervating effect that popular paganism might have on their control of the Carolingian countryside and, indeed, of the Christian foundations of their broader undertaking.

But if the official attitude toward the belief in stormmakers and their claims was critical, rational, and Christian, it was also external. What we would want to recover (were it possible) is the internal attitude, to discover what the people around Lyons actually believed about the stormmakers. Since those individuals Agobard encountered left no record of their own, we shall have to settle for a tentative reconstruction of what they might have believed, why they believed it, and what advantages those beliefs brought them.

The first thing that needs to be said is that the popular belief in weathermakers was a very old and, indeed, traditional belief, one that might almost be called western Indo-European, since one can find versions of it among the Greeks, Romans, Germans, and Scandinavians.[41] Seneca made fun of the people of Clenia who appointed hail-officers, and he added that "An older uneducated time used to believe that rains were brought on or driven away by incantations."[42] Six hundred years after Agobard's death, Dr. Hartlieb, who possessed that particularly Renaissance fascination with magic, confronted a confessed hailmaker in Bavaria. When the woman, lying in her cell with one leg in irons, refused to teach the doctor her art unless he spurned Mary and invoked three devils, he turned her over to the inquisitor who had her burned alive.[43] From antiquity until at least the sixteenth century, it would seem, Europeans had believed in stormmakers. In view of this it is more likely that rigorous orthodoxy was the newcomer to the countryside of Carolingian Europe, not the popular belief in stormmaking. Here, as in so much else, Agobard and an intrusive Carolingian clergy, supported by a centralizing monarchy, were attempting to impose universal standards of belief and conduct. It was that very process of pressing Carolingian, Christian conformity upon the countryside and cities of Francia, after all, that brought the belief in storm-making to the attention and scrutiny of officials such as Agobard and that led to the production of the written record over which we linger.

Of the actual practices of the stormmakers in Carolingian Europe we can say little. All sources agree that they performed their weather magic by incantation, but the words and the actions associated with them are never recorded. The popular curse against the tongue of the stormmaker suggests that people may have thought that the power lay in a secret magical formula spoken by a special and self-proclaimed agent of superhuman forces. The story reported by Agobard that the stormmakers claimed that they could make it hail upon a single tub (*cupa*) under which they would hide is striking since later accounts often described the stormmaker as pouring out hail from a tub.[44] As to the sex of the stormmakers, we should note that the church officials at the Council of Paris in 829 thought that a stormmaker might be either male or female. But in the Carolingian sources the words used to describe the stormmakers—*tempestarii*, *immissores*, and *defensores*—are masculine in gender.[45]

Stormmakers seem not to have simply specialized in weather magic, but to have delved into other matters related to the rural economy such as the enchantment of crops and foodstuffs and predictions about the farming year. Agobard identified two types of weather-makers, defenders, who prevented storms and received a regular tribute, and the so-called stormmakers, who raised the wind to destroy crops and received a price for them from the sky sailors from Magonia. From Agobard's account we can see that the people seem to have thought of these as two faces of the same coin, the benign and malevolent manipulation of the weather respectively. To both of these types we shall return later, but for the moment it is important to think about the popular conception of weather-makers. They were not gods, but the agents of one or of forces that remain unmentioned in the relevant Carolingian literature. In the eleventh century, Adam of Bremen, when writing about Scandinavian religion, said " 'Thor,' they maintain, 'presides over the sky; it is he who rules thunder and lightning, wind and rains, fine weather and crops.' "[46] Though Agobard and the Carolingian penitentials characterized human weather-making as the work of the devil and his agents, the stormmakers themselves may have appealed to some lingering form of that Germanic thunder-god whose name we still honor on Thursday.

Though our knowledge of the actual practices of the stormmakers is bound to remain scanty and speculative, we can still ask why people clung fast to their belief in them and what advantages that belief brought them in their daily lives. The touchstone in both the incidents related by Agobard is the rural economy or, more to the point, crops and cattle. Northern Europe was still covered in the eighth and ninth centuries by old and obstructive forests,[47] so that human habitation clung of necessity to the natural land clearings and easy transport provided by river valleys. But this also made Carolingian villages and small cities particularly vulnerable to storms, to flooding, and to raids by the Northmen. The Carolingian economy had also developed a particular reliance on cereals and cattle, but the former could be severely damaged by hailstones and the latter by murrain. Carolingian annals are filled with stories of the destructive power of storms, the ravages of wet weather, and tales of dying cattle. These things mattered to the usually laconic annalists because in a subsistence economy they affected a community's very chances for survival. The royal Frankish annalist noted that in 820 constant rain had produced disastrous economic results, setting off a chain reaction of crop failures, outbreaks of disease among men and cattle, and delayed planting of the next season's crops.[48] In another year in Frisia two thousand four hundred and thirty-seven people were killed in a flash flood,[49] further demonstrating the vulnerability of Carolingian villages to excessive and unpredictable rainfall. As the poet put it colorfully when he prayed for good weather:

> Ecce nunc aquosus aer imbre rura perluit,
> Vberes agros, uides, ut uber unda dissipet.[50]
>
> [Look this wet weather now pelts the countryside with violent rain,
> So that an immense wave of water washes away our fertile fields.]

With its low crop yields, theirs was an economy that had a small margin of success even in good years, and could hardly cope with ruinous weather in bad ones.[51]

Some climatologists and historians believe that the climate of Europe deteriorated slightly in the ninth century, becoming marginally colder, wetter, and stormier.[52] Our evidence, however, may be skewed, since a slowly expanding or, at least, concentrated population certainly complained more vociferously about the weather because its economic success was so vulnerable to certain kinds of weather conditions.

In fact, today the area around Lyons remains one of the regions in France most susceptible to violent thunder and hailstorms, generally in the months between May and August.[53] At the end of June 1545 Benvenuto Cellini was caught in just such a hailstorm outside Lyons. He claimed that hailstones the size of walnuts and lemons had pummeled his band of travelers, toppled their horses, and broken tree branches. A mile further on they found fallen trees, the bodies of animals, and dead shepherds.[54] Even if we allow for some measure of exaggeration (which, it must be admitted, abounds in Cellini's autobiography), the storm he suffered through is not all that unusual.

A Carolingian annalist reported that on 21 July 882 while Charles the Fat was laying siege to the camps of the Northmen near the Rhine a great thunderstorm arose followed by "such immense hail that no human being could claim to have seen such before." These hailstones were not round and smooth as usual, but spiked (*cornuta*), uneven, and rough; and they were huge. These hailstones could scarcely be encircled by a thumb and middle finger (thus, perhaps, being about 15 cm. along the perimeter, approximately the size of a lime). Not surprisingly horses broke loose and buildings in the enemy fortification collapsed.[55]

Hailstorms frequently last from fifteen to sixty minutes, are generally the product of severe thunderstorms, and most often occur in the summer, often late in the day. Moreover, the size of the hailstones described by Cellini and the Frankish annalist fall within the norm, and there are frequent reports from India today of both cattle and people dying from hail.[56]

If Cellini's storm was destructive enough to bring down tree branches, sheep, and shepherds, we can imagine what it would have done to fields of standing wheat. Hailstorms tend to drop their stones in a moving swath that may measure 100×20 km.,[57] so that the amount of damage they can do may be extensive, if local. Moreover, even today wheat is the crop most vulnerable to severe damage by hailstorms,[58] though vineyards and orchards may also suffer. The amount of economic damage done by hailstorms, it stands to reason, should relate proportionally to the amount of land under cultivation and to the vulnerability of the crops grown. The Carolingian popular anxiety about hailstorms was grounded in an economy that had become heavily committed to and dependent upon cereal crops. In the earlier Middle Ages in northern Europe (and despite Cellini's dead shepherds) pastoralists would have been somewhat less worried about the possibility of hailstorms and even floods. In the ninth century, however, a coincidence of grain crops and violent storms led to understandable concern and complaint.

The timing of the hailstorms in the area around Lyons likely seemed to contemporaries to be most unfortunate, designed in fact to do the maximum amount of damage. If one struck in April or May, it would level the unharvested spring wheat so necessary to survival in this subsistence economy after winter reserves of food had run low or been exhausted. Charlemagne called May *Winnemanoth* or the "month of joy" because the spring wheat had been harvested and fodder for the horses and cattle had returned.[59] In the famous Labors of the Months illumination made during Agobard's lifetime (figure 7.1: Vienna, Osterreichische Nationalbibliothek Cod. 387, fol. 90v) a man representing April's work holds a sheaf of spring wheat (see the first panel of the second register).[60] The king called June and July *Brachmanoth* and *Heuuimanoth* or "plowing month" and "hay month," which are depicted as such in the Labors illumination (second register, panel three and third register, panel one). If a hailstorm struck in those months, it might damage the hay needed to support cattle and horses later in the year. Worse still, even a small hailstorm in late spring or early summer

7.1 Labors of the Months (ca. 820) (Vienna, Österreichische Nationalbibliothek Cod. 387, fol. 90v: Bildarchiv d. ÖNB Wien).

could utterly destroy a field of juvenile wheat before it had had a chance to form ears. The summer would have seemed very long to farmers who had lost their wheat crop in June. If a hailstorm struck in August— Charlemagne's *Aranmanoth* or the "month of the ears" when the heads of cereal plants fully form, again shown in the Labors by a farmer harvesting the ripe wheat (third register, second panel)—then mature fields of grain could be felled. Violent thunder storms have been known on rare occasions to deposit up to half a meter of hailstones, thus effectively burying a crop. Fields that escaped substantial accumulations would still suffer damage, but some portion of the flattened crop lying on the ground might be collected before it rotted. Even then much of the grain would have been irretrievably scattered by the storm, the hailstones, and the accompanying winds.

Carolingian annalists most often linked hailstorms to the damage done to crops and subsequent human suffering. The royal Frankish annalist noted that in 823 in many regions devastating hail had destroyed crops and lightning storms had done much damage. After that, disease had raged furiously in the kingdom and had killed people of both sexes and all ages.[61] The so-called Ratisbonne continuator of the *Annals of Fulda* succinctly stated that, in 889, "The crops having been destroyed by hail, human beings are suffering wretchedly from want of produce."[62] Both the annalist of Xanten and the annalist of Fulda complained in independent entries that 872 had experienced a particularly calamitous summer of thunderstorms in which hail had destroyed crops and done much harm to people.[63] And Frotharius, the bishop of Toul, connected a year of dire want with a drought and damage done by hail.[64] The reason why people in the ninth century were so troubled by thunderstorms and hail, therefore, was because they threatened the chief product of their agricultural economy.

The loss of much winter or summer wheat to hailstorms could so unbalance local and even regional economies that it might lead to famine. Moreover, the people of the ninth century had come to depend upon bread as their staple food and apparently ate inordinate amounts of it.[65] When wheat was wanting in Charlemagne's world people soon went hungry, or worse. After widespread frost and damage to the harvest in 762, said one chronicler, in the following year "many men died from lack of bread."[66] In 845 when parts of Gaul were occupied by invaders, people were so desperate for bread that they were said to have eaten loaves made of dirt and a meager amount of flour.[67]

Given the importance of cereal crops and the inevitability of hailstorms in the Carolingian countryside, what were farmers and a society dependent upon cereals to do? There was, it should be said, a tendency at all levels of this society to assign responsibility for the weather to higher powers and to see it in terms of retribution and reward. To the ninth century mind such events could not, after all, be neutral, mere accidents. Scripture itself confirmed that God sent punishing lightning-like arrows from his bow and that he cast down hail from his stony anger (Wisd. 5:22–23). Thus, the annalist of Fulda understood God's judgment to be at work when, during a terrible storm in September 857, an enormous bolt of lightning shaped like a dragon burst into the church of Saint Peter at Cologne and struck three men standing at different points in the congregation.[68] In 875 another annalist said that after the appearance of a comet, which gave clear proof of men's sins, a frightening flash flood had destroyed a village and its eighty-eight inhabitants.[69] God could occasionally direct his retribution against the enemy as in 847 when he was thought to have whipped up a storm to destroy the Saracens who had pillaged St-Peter's in Rome.[70] Carolingian iconography, though dependent on older models, reinforces the same view of the weather. In the Utrecht Psalter (figure 7.2: fol. 16r) disembodied heads poke through from a cloud to blow up a violent hail-filled storm over flooding waters and to smash trees, breaking them into pieces; these heads are personifications of the angry words of God (Ps. 28:3–10). In another scene angels in a cloudy sky cast lances that become dread bolts of lightning as they approach the earth (Ps. 139:11; figure 7.3: fol. 78v).[71]

Agobard's intention was not to argue for a natural explanation of the weather,[72] but to assign real responsibility for it to God, who might be appealed to by special, intercessory agents. Thus, when frightened by thunder and lightning, he said, the faithful should beseech the intercession of the holy prophet Samuel who had once prayed to God for rain and received it (1 Kings 12:16–25). His own half-faithful people, on the other hand, foolishly looked to the trickery of the stormmakers.[73] Since the days of Caesarius of Arles and Pope Gregory the Great, the church had sometimes sought to replace paganism by assuming its functions. When the people of the Carolingian countryside turned to the local priest and asked

7.2   Hailstorm in the Utrecht Psalter, Ps. 28:3–10 (Utrecht, Cat. Cod. ms. Bibl. Rhenotraiectinae ms. 32, fol. 16r).

7.3   Angels cast lightning-bolt lances in the Utrecht Psalter, Ps. 139:11 (Utrecht, Cat. Cod. ms. Bibl. Rhenotraiectinae ms. 32, fol. 78v).

for rain, they found that he had a special prayer designed specifically for the purpose.[74] In the Gregorian Sacramentary used by the Carolingian clergy there were also special masses for driving off thunderstorms.[75]

In the account of the life of the eighth-century abbess Leoba of Bischofsheim written by Rudolf of Fulda in the 830s, we can glimpse the general reaction of a rural population to thunderstorms, and the church's intercessory response. An awful storm was said to have risen in the area around Mainz. Its lightning bolts and thunder claps struck dread into the hearts of all, even the bravest, and the sky suddenly turned dark. First the people drove their cattle into their houses, lest they perish in the storm, and then fled themselves—men, women, and children—to Leoba's church. These people probably thought that a stone building was a safer refuge in a thunderstorm than their wooden and thatched houses. But the storm even rattled the church, and whimpering families huddled together as the thunder rolled and lightning flashes cast a strange light through the windows of the darkened church. When all implored Leoba to save them, she cast off her cloak and threw open the doors of the church. She made the sign of the cross into the face of the fury of the storm and called on Christ to protect his people. The storm immediately abated, the clouds passed over head, and the sun shone once again.[76]

In Sweden an even more dramatic or, at least, perilous use of Christian weather-making occurred in the middle of the ninth century. The Christian convert Herigar found himself at a public assembly at which various hostile pagans began to praise their own gods, the ones who had brought them great prosperity, and they condemned him for religiously separating himself off from all of them and for persisting in his own (new and) useless belief. In a bold move Herigar challenged them to test the power of their many gods against his one. Since a storm was then threatening, he suggested that they call upon the names of their gods to prevent the rain from falling on them and he would implore Christ to stop even a single drop of rain from touching him. The two sides began their imprecations, whereupon (as in all good holy stories) the rains came, the pagans were drenched, and Herigar and his assistant remained bone dry.[77] If a millennium later David Livingstone could without great cost discount the efficacy of native weather magic, a Christian believer in Sweden in the ninth century had fewer options. Still he did not just take up the challenge, he suggested the very test to be used, for by it he could engage the religious beliefs of the pagans in the natural world they all shared, calling forth a manifest miracle of the one against the many and the demonstrably dry against the suddenly wet. By testing the utility and success of their religion on one small point, Herigar may have hoped to avoid impenetrable theological differences and cut instead straight to the superior power of his God and to cast in a clear light his own privileged access to the divine. Agobard, I suspect, would not have been greatly disappointed by Herigar's demonstration, since what he denied to the stormmakers, he permitted to the omnipotence of his own God and deserving holy men with their mouths full of pious prayers.

But, though the church might attribute divine power over the natural world exclusively to God, the people of the Carolingian countryside were never sure that that was their only option. They were prepared to shop around for solutions to their vexing problems. Einhard, for instance, tells us of a woman from Niedgau who had dislocated her jaw one morning while yawning. In great pain and with her face locked in a horrible grimace, she first sought out some local women who tried to treat her with herbs and incantations. When that failed, relatives took her on horseback to the church in Seligenstadt where Einhard had newly installed the relics of the saints Marcellinus and Peter who were believed to be able to effect cures. When the woman looked up at the bell tower of the church, her jaw snapped back into place and credit was given to the saints.[78] The point of the incident, for our purposes, is that the suffering woman had been prepared to seek out a variety of cures successively and, perhaps, saw no contradiction between them. Like most people of the age, her attitude toward the mysteries of the natural world was more open and flexible than Agobard would allow. Hers was a strategy born of sharp necessity; she sought the efficacious, trying whatever might help and perhaps only believing in it when it did work or when a treatment was coincident with a cure.

When a violent thunderstorm struck, people may also have thought it just as reasonable to look to human agents who, in the name of a deity such as Thor, claimed to possess some special control over the elements. Both the church and people shared an essential conviction that someone controlled the weather, but the farmer's immediate problem was not to determine correct cosmology; it was to cope with bad weather or the prospect of it. As Evans-Pritchard long ago discerned among the Azande in Africa, one of the functions of the belief in rainmaking and magic is to allow people to explain experience, especially unfortunate events.[79] Such beliefs do more to account for events after they have happened than they do to explain the causes of things before they occur. Notice, in fact, how well the description given to Agobard about the cloud-ships fits the physical nature of a hailstorm. Thunderstorms in the summer often assume the shape of a dark anvil or ship as the updraft of a towering cumulonimbus cloud fashions a frontal projection while hailstones are being formed deep within the storm (see figure 7.4).[80] Moreover, after a field of wheat had been thoroughly scattered by a violent hailstorm like the one endured by Benvenuto Cellini or Charles the Fat's troops, it might have seemed as if the crop had been stolen by the departing cloud, since so little of the cereal would have remained behind. In this light, then, the belief in weather-making could be viewed as a way for people to account for events that were beyond their control.[81]

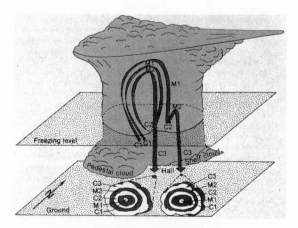

7.4   Profile of hailstorm. After Joe R. Eagleman, *Meteorology: The Atmosphere in Action* (New York: Van Nostrand, 1980).

Or we might argue that the belief in stormmakers allowed Carolingian farmers to achieve some small measure of control over their relations with the divine in matters meteorological. For to believe in the stormmakers was also to assign responsibility. The farmer's gamble was a good one, for to his mind if the weather magic worked, he received a safe harvest; if it did not, he knew whom to blame. He could accuse the malevolent, delinquent, or simply impotent agents of a sky-god for the damage done to his crops. Agobard observed that the stormmakers were "hateful even to their neighbours,"[82] and he recorded the curse against them people uttered when a storm was brewing.[83]

Moreover, there is that matter of the four aerial sailors who were chained and about to be stoned. Whatever Agobard thought was going on, those people had been publicly blamed for cooperating in the raising of a recent storm and the destruction or disappearance of crops. One wonders whether not a few medieval stormmakers might have suffered the fate of the Uganda rainmaker who in 1987, as reported by Reuters, was beaten to death in the district of Kabale by villagers who blamed him for causing the hailstorms and torrential rains that had recently devastated their crops and homes. The unfortunate man had unwisely warned the villagers that if they did not show him more respect, he would summon up hailstorms to remind them of his power.[84] The people of the Carolingian countryside seem to have been ready, too, to level blame of this sort for natural disasters. When cattle began dying in 810, the story soon spread that they had been poisoned by outsiders; some people, whether strangers or not, were soon executed despite Charlemagne's explicit disapproval.

If the Carolingian farmer paid a small tribute to the stormmaker for protection against bad weather, perhaps he thought that it was worth the price, since it was the only kind of crop insurance available to him. Keith Thomas argued that one of the factors that led to the decline of magic in the early-modern world was the introduction of insurance.[85] In the ninth century, however, without any protection from the utter devastation of a total crop loss, villages may have found in the stormmaker someone who seemed to offer some small measure of control over potential calamity. But the farmer also knew whom to blame if the violent storm struck anyway, for the stormmakers in some regions had been paid to prevent storms, while in others they were assumed to be the bringers of bad weather.

But Agobard thought that he had uncovered something else, not a religious or social reason for the belief in weather-making, but a simple conspiracy, a case of fraud. He suspected that at its base the belief in weather-making was promoted by greedy people for personal gain. Hence, those who claimed only to protect people from storms charged for their service. Agobard lamented, in this case, that the deluded population would willingly surrender tribute to a weather-maker while withholding tithes from the church and charity from widows and orphans.[86] But the belief in the existence of the stormmakers may have given some people a certain economic leverage in a world in which they lacked many such advantages.

What we need to bear in mind is that from the farmer's perspective not only storms 'robbed' crops, but also lords, both lay and ecclesiastical. To the farmer in the ninth century, formal and informal taxation may have been more predictable than hailstorms, but it was hardly more appreciated. To give but one example, Hincmar of Rheims relates that in Remigius's day, during a time of scarcity, the men and women of one of the saint's villages had become drunk and rebellious. They decided to burn the heaps of grain collected for the bishop rather than surrender them. Saint Remigius responded by calling upon God to curse the men with hernias and the women with goiters.[87] One has to wonder, in view of the popular resentment of and occasional resistance to taxation, if the tribute paid to the weather-makers was not effectively an anti-tithe, the means precisely for a peasant to avoid paying his tithes. Agobard characterizes the *canonicus* as the rival and replacement of the tithes owed by Christians to the church where they received the sacraments.[88] Perhaps farmers occasionally argued that they could not pay their tithes since there was not enough left of their harvest once their defenders had been paid. Agobard's parish priests, if they heard this excuse, probably wondered—as we might today—whether a weather tribute had been paid at all or whether this was just another strategy used by farmers to fend off demands upon their grain in a world of subsistence agriculture.

What are we to make of the story of the four aerial sailors whom the crowd was about to stone to death? Perhaps—to attempt a natural explanation first—the unfortunate four were strangers who had been captured in a field of devastated wheat, attempting to steal its scattered remains, and who had been blamed by villagers for the hailstorm itself. The word Magonia may refer, then, not to a Magic Land, but to a Land of Unscrupulous Dealers (from *mango* or *magono*) in stolen crops.[89] In this light, the people around Lyons would once again have been engaged in assigning blame for crops that had suddenly disappeared.

Agobard's accusation, however, fell not on the four prisoners, but on "those who had produced them in public."[90] After persistent questioning those people became, says Agobard quoting Jeremiah 2:26, "as confounded as a thief when he is captured." What scam might these people have concocted? Again it is hard not to think that we might be distant witnesses to a scheme to hide grain from the scrutiny of those who would tax it. We should not underestimate the ingenuity of those who worked and managed the land, nor underrate their ability to deal with demanding lords.

Charlemagne, for instance, had commanded his own royal stewards to be alert that:

> depraved men in no way conceal our seed either under the ground or in other places and, in this way, make the harvest seem scarcer. Likewise let the stewards watch those people for other evil deeds, lest on occasion they be in a position to make mischief.[91]

If Charlemagne's own people buried their grain in order to avoid paying their assigned dues, attempts to hide grain may have been fairly common in the Carolingian countryside. One suspects that what Agobard learned that day in his diocese was that a group of people had seized the opportunity of a recent storm to hide some ripe wheat from the rest of the village and their lord and to blame its disappearance on a storm and four outsiders. The association of these individuals with the cloud-ships from Magonia would have made some sense to the people around Lyons, because the legend of how storms stole crops was familiar and widely accepted.

Thus, the belief in stormmakers survived and persisted because it was traditional, because it was useful in explaining natural phenomena and in assigning blame, and because it supplied some with the means to gain an economic advantage over others. Survival in the Carolingian world demanded different and flexible strategies for coping. In a subsistence economy one wanted to avoid, if possible, the exacting demands made by lords and church upon the small surplus of a recent harvest. If the widespread belief in stormmakers and the theft of crops by clouds could be turned to advantage, why would some farmers not do so? Like the land, lords and ecclesiastical landholders needed to be cleverly managed. But storms that threatened a community's very chances for survival, that could bring about hunger and deprivation, were ultimately unavoidable. The Carolingian peoples, however, had a weak sense of purely accidental phenomena; they were convinced that a cause could be found for everything and responsibility could be properly allocated. Stormmakers may have had some prestige in the Carolingian countryside, but they seem never to have achieved the central place in their world that African rainmakers did in theirs. They were relegated to the peripheries of power, to the countryside and beleaguered paganism, where they may mostly have been popular tricksters tipping over tubs to make hail and performing magical acts. Their neighbors, however, had another use for them: they could blame them for disastrous weather, they could revile them, and they could curse them. But they also needed such people or, rather, they held fast to the belief in what they represented as agents of intercession who had a special way with the dynamic powers that filled the swirling sky. In a world where men and women were almost completely dependent upon the success of their cereal crops for simple survival and where hail and severe thunderstorms threatened even that, the belief that some human being played a role in controlling the weather may have seemed both reasonable and reassuring.

Could Agobard have offered them more or just more of the same? Perhaps, competing priesthoods and a variety of religious beliefs allowed people in the Carolingian countryside to pick and choose how best to manage their lives and cope with the serious aggravations and sudden catastrophes that dogged their days. There was a wisdom and a necessity to that that we may not always have appreciated.

APPENDIX 1

THE NAME OF THE ELEPHANT

stat elephantus prisco nomine . . .

The elephant arrived with an Arabic name that Charlemagne and his courtiers chose not to change. Nor did Einhard report that name, only the Royal Frankish annalist, who, in the entry for 802, named him as Abul Abaz or, rather, some manuscripts of the annals do. Others furnished such Latinate confusions as "ambulabat," "abulabat," and "ambulabaz."[1] These scribes seem to have had some difficulty resolving the elephant's foreign name, but then so have we.

Yet the elephant's name may not be without some importance, however thin the evidence, since it is one of the very few tantalizing indications of cross-cultural contact between Europe and Islam in Charlemagne's time. The elephant traveled with its name, so that both the beast and its name were foreign cultural products adopted by the Carolingians. But what did the name mean to Harun and his court or to Charlemagne and his, and why did the Carolingians retain it? Indeed was it customary for the Carolingians to give their animals personal names?

The Arabic form of the name was most likely some form of Abu al-ʿAbbas or Abuʾl-ʿAbbas. Abu is a patronymic meaning "father of." Though some have speculated that Abul Abaz was a name derived from the name of the Prophet's uncle, the experts I consulted thought that association extremely unlikely.

My colleague Derryl MacLean observed that the common Arabic patronymic Abu is frequently used "to preface the proper names of animals and to describe attributes." He went on to say that "if the name should be read as Abu al-ʿAbbas (or some form of these roots), and there are doubts (simply consider the Sanskrit *ibha* for elephant or the Arabic *Abraha*, the Yamani famous for marching with elephants on Mecca in the year of Muhammad's birth or, even, al-Ahbash, Ethiopians), then there are two obvious explanations. First, the term is used for this royal elephant because it was associated with the ʿAbbasids as gifters. In this case, it would simply mean 'the Abbasid elephant'. Second, it could be related to a different vocalization of the same root, ʿabasa which is used in variant forms three times in the Qurʾan to signify frowning. If this is the case, then the *kunya* Abu al-ʿAbbas could be rendered something like 'father of frowns' or 'wrinkles' and be applied to the elephant's overall wrinkled appearance or dour demeanor."

In surah 105, called "The Elephant," Muhammad recorded that God had stopped the person of the elephant who had marched on the Ka'aba in Mecca in 570. And Paul Cobb of Notre Dame went on to point out to me that the famous elephant who refused to proceed against the holy site was thought to be named Mahmud and that the twelfth-century Arabic commentator Zamakhshari in his *Rabi' al-abrar wa-nusus al-akhbar* noted that the patronymic of this 'first' elephant was Abu`l-`Abbas. Whether a source dating from three centuries after the time of Hārūn and Charlemagne can identify the `Abbasid meaning of the name I leave to Islamicists to resolve.[2]

If the patronymic Abu`l-`Abbas traveled with the elephant and served effectively as its surname one might wonder if the elephant also had another name. The name Abul Abaz may simply have served as a generic, Arabic name for elephant. Charlemagne's elephant was a creature of wrinkles, but he may also have been named after that famous Islamic war elephant who had devoutly obeyed God at a critical moment in history. Whether Charlemagne or his court understood any of this or read significance into it is not known, but it would be fascinating to know more. Even old names may mean and transform into something strange in a new setting.

APPENDIX 2

THE COLLECTION OF BIBLICAL CITATIONS SENT TO EMPEROR LOTHAR I DURING THE CIVIL WAR WITH HIS BROTHERS, CA. 842–43[1]

1. (Gen. 6:5–6)
   In Genesis we read that: "And God seeing that the wickedness of men was great on the earth and that all the thought of their heart was bent upon evil at all times, and it repented him that he had made man on the earth."
2. (Dan. 12:1–4)
   In the 78th chapter of Daniel we read that: "But at that time shall Michael rise up, the great prince, who standeth for the children of thy people: and a time shall come such as never was from the time that nations began even until that time. And at that time shall thy people be saved, every one that shall be found written in the book.

   And many of those that sleep in the dust of the earth shall awake: some unto life everlasting, and others unto reproach, to see it always.

   But they that are learned shall shine as the brightness of the firmament and they that instruct many to justice, as stars for all eternity.

   But thou, O Daniel, shut up the words, and seal the book, even to the time appointed: many shall pass over, and knowledge shall be manifold."
3. (Amos 5:12–14)
   In Amos [we read that]: "Because I know your manifold crimes, and your grievous sins: enemies of the just, taking bribes, and oppressing the poor in the gate.

   Therefore the prudent shall keep silence at that time; for it is an evil time.

   Seek good, and not evil, that you may live: and the Lord, the God of hosts, will be with you. . ."
4. (An adaptation of Job 12:24–25)
   In the 78th chapter of Daniel [we read] that: "He may let go the heart of the princes of the earth and deceiveth them that they walk in vain where there is no way.

   They shall grope as in the dark and not in the light, and he shall make them stagger like men that are drunk."

5. (Eccles. 10:16–17)

"Woe to thee, O land, when thy king is a child, and thy princes eat in the morning!

Blessed is the land whose king is noble, and whose princes eat in due season. . ."

6. (An adaptation of 1 Thess. 2:16)

Whence now the present "anger of God" comes upon us and the future anger of God will be even greater: let us say it will be greater if we do not correct ourselves.

7. (Dan. 12:1)

For Scripture says: "and a time shall come," that is now, "such as never was from the time that nations began even until that time."

8. (Jer. 9:4–5)

"Let every man take heed" now "of his neighbor, and let him not trust in any brother of his: for every brother will utterly supplant, and every friend will walk deceitfully.

And a man shall mock his brother, and they will not speak the truth: for they have taught their tongue to speak lies, they have labored to commit iniquity."

9. (Jer. 9:8)

"with his mouth one speaketh peace with his friend, and secretly he lieth in wait for him."

10. (Hos. 4:1–3)

"there is no truth, and there is no mercy, and there is no knowledge of God in the land.

Cursing, and lying, and killing, and theft, and adultery, have overflowed, and blood hath touched blood.

Therefore shall the land mourn, and every one that dwelleth in it shall languish, with the beasts of the field, and with the fowls of air; yea, the fishes of the sea shall also be gathered together."

11. (see 6 earlier)

"And" on account of this "the anger of God will" now "come upon us."

Indeed we ought to beware not to receive from men the rewards of such an age.

12. (Ps. 126:2)

And in the Psalm [we read that]: "It is vain for you to rise before light, to sit up late, you that eat the bread of sorrow."

13. (Exod. 20:17)

Where is it that divine Scripture speaks against this? "Thou shalt not covet thy neighbor's things."

14. (Eccles. 10:16–17)

And in Ecclesiastes [we read that]: "Woe to thee, O land, when thy king is a child, and thy princes eat in the morning!

Blessed is the land whose king is noble, and whose princes eat in due season. . ."

15. (Isidore, *Sententiae* 3.52; PL 83:5B)

"For when wicked judges judge they will weigh not issues, but gifts."

16. (Isidore, *Sententiae* 3.54; PL 83:6B)
    "He who judges rightly but expects a gift of money perpetrates a fraud against God because by accepting money he sells justice which he ought to bestow freely."
17. (Zach. 8:19)
    "The all-powerful Lord tells us to love peace and truth."
18. (Wisd. 1:1)
    Wisdom says: "Love justice, you that are judges of the earth."
19. (Is. 1:17)
    "Learn to do well; seek judgment, relieve the oppressed. . ."
20. (1 Cor. 4:5)
    "Therefore judge not before the time. . ."
21. (*Proverbia aliqua S. Patricii*, PL 53:828B)[2]
    "Do not judge hastily. . ."
22. (Ecclus. 20:7)
    Solomon said: "A wise man shall hold his peace till he see the opportunity."
23. (1 Thess. 5:21)
    The Apostle Paul says: "Investigate all things."
24. (Isidore, *Synonyma*, 2.85; PL 83:864B11–12))
    "First investigate and then judge."

APPENDIX 3

CAROLINGIAN ROYAL LIFE SPANS

The dates for the Carolingian royal family are taken from Siegfried Rösch, *Caroli Magni progenies* 1, Genealogie und Landesgeschichte, 30 (Neustadt an der Aisch, 1977). The dates used here are based on the direct male line including illegitimate children, though not the children of illegitimate royal males or legitimate princesses. This may at first seem arbitrary, but when the series of all Carolingian offspring is studied as a whole it becomes apparent that the greater the distance from the direct male line, the vaguer and more unreliable the dates of the offspring become.

The following are the royal males, listed in reverse order of longevity, who were considered in the calculation. The ages of individuals have been estimated in cases where precise dates for either birth or death are lacking. The greatest variation can never be greater than three years, and this in only a few cases. Eleven individuals for whom dates were unreliable were omitted.

The total of estimated years lived by these individuals is 1272.6, thus producing an average life expectancy at birth of 33.5 years. Disregarding the first six individuals who died in infancy, a total of 1,266 years was lived by thirty-two individuals, thus producing an average life expectancy past infancy of 39.6 years.

Name	Birthdate	Deathdate	Life span (in years)
Infant son of Charles the Bald	875 Mar. 23	875 Apr.	0.1
Charles, son of Charles the Bald	876 Oct. 10	877 Apr. 7	0.5
Pepin, son of Charles the Bald	872–73	873–74	1
Drogo, son of Charles the Bald	872–73	873–74	1
Louis, son of Louis III of Bavaria	877	879 Nov.	2
Lothar, son of Charlemagne	778 Apr. 16	779–80	2
Lothar, son of Louis the Stammerer	866	884 Dec. 12	17
Louis IV, the Child	893	911 Nov. 24	18
Charles jr., son of Charles the Bald	847–48	866 Sept. 29	18
Louis III, son of Louis the Stammerer	863–65	882 Aug. 5	18
Charles, son of Lothar I	845	863 Jan. 24	18

Name	Birthdate	Deathdate	Life span (in years)
Carloman, brother of Charlemagne	751	771 Dec. 4	19
Bernard, son of Carloman (a.k.a. Pepin)	797	818 Apr. 17	21
Hugo, son of Louis III of Bavaria	855–860	880 Feb.	22
Zwentibold, son of Arnulf of Carinthia	870–71	900 Aug. 13	29
Louis the Stammerer, son of Charles the Bald	846 Nov. 1	879 Apr. 10	32
Carloman (renamed Pepin), son of Charlemagne	777	810 July 8	33
Lothar II, son of Lothar I	835	869 Aug. 8	34
Charles, son of Pepin I of Aquitaine	825–30	863 June 4	36
Hugo, son of Lothar II of Lotharingia	855–60	895	38
Charles jr., son of Charlemagne	772–73	811 Dec. 4	39
Hugo, son of Charlemagne	802–806	844 June 16	40
Pepin I, son of Louis the Pious	797	838 Dec. 13	41
Pepin II, son of Pepin I of Aquitaine	823	864	41
Pepin the Hunchback, son of Charlemagne	770	811	41
Louis III, son of Louis the German	835	881 Jan. 20	46
Arnulf, son of Louis the Pious	794	841 Mar.	47
Charles the Fat, son of Louis the German	839	888 Jan. 13	48
Arnulf of Carinthia, son of Carloman of Bavaria	850	899 Dec. 8	49
Charles the Simple, son of Louis the Stammerer	879 Sept. 17	929 Oct. 7	50
Carloman, son of Louis the German	830	880 Sept. 29	50
Louis II, son of Lothar I	825	875 Aug. 12	50
Charles the Bald, son of Louis the Pious	823 June 13	877 Oct. 6	54
Drogo, son of Charlemagne	801 June 17	855 Dec. 8	54
Lothar I, son of Louis the Pious	795	855 Sept. 29	60
Louis the Pious, son of Charlemagne	778 Apr. 16	840 June 20	62
Louis the German, son of Louis the Pious	806	876 Aug. 28	70
Charlemagne	742 Apr. 2	814 Jan. 28	71

The following graph indicates the percentage of mortality of the series of thirty-eight royal males distributed according to decades. Notice that the distribution of morality in decennial groups is remarkably even until the seventh decade. Even if infant mortality is too low because of underreporting, the distribution as a whole is quite different from a graph of modern mortality rates, which would reveal a steady rise in the sixth and seventh decades and much lower percentages during the earlier decades. The graph supports what we know from the sources: illness at any

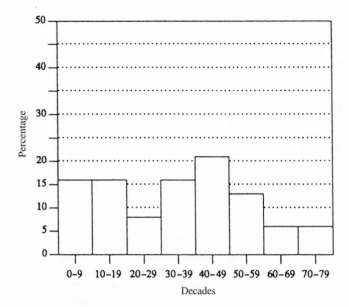

age could be and often was fatal. Old age itself contributed less to overall mortality than it would in modern society.

Reliable dates for both the births and deaths of Carolingian queens are rare. Although their deaths and the lengths of their reigns are often recorded, their birthdates are mostly unrecorded. In fact, only three queens can be safely dated:

Name	Birthdate	Deathdate	Life span (in years)
Hildegard, wife of Charlemagne	758	783 Apr. 30	25
Judith, wife of Louis the Pious	805	843 Apr. 19	38
Ermintrude, wife of Charles the Bald	830 Sept. 27	869 Oct. 6	39

It is virtually impossible to draw a conclusion from these three examples, though the average life of these three persons was 34 years.

For the female offspring of the Carolingian line, our information is also of a particular kind. Whereas for the queens few birthdates are available, for the female offspring birthdates are often available but deathdates are scarcer. Again this specific reporting reflects proximity to the royal house: queens were born outside of it and, therefore, their births occasioned little interest. They died, however, in contact with the royal court, and, thus, their death dates and the ends of their reigns were of great interest to the annalists. The princesses, however, were born in royal circumstance, and their births were frequently noted as important events; but when they left the

royal house, either to marry or to take up religious life, historians connected with
the court lost track of them.

Reliable dates are obtained for ten princesses:

Name	Birthdate	Deathdate	Life span (in years)
Hildegard, daughter of Charlemagne	782 June 8	783 July 8	1
Adalhaid, daughter of Charlemagne	773–74	774 July–Aug.	1
Gisela, daughter of Louis III	852–55	868 Apr. 28	14
Hildegard, daughter of Louis the German	828	856 Dec. 23	28
Rotrud, daughter of Charlemagne	775	810 June 6	35
Hiltrud, daughter of Lothar I	826	865–66	40
Ermengard, daughter of Louis III	852–55	896	43
Gisela, daughter of Louis II	860–65	907	45
Rothilde, daughter of Charles the Bald	871	928–29	57
Bertha, daughter of Lothar II	863	925	62

The average of 326 years lived by these ten individuals is 32.6. Again, one suspects
that infant mortality is greatly underreported. If one subtracts the two infants from
the calculations, the life expectancy of the remainder rises to 40.5 years. The possible series of royal females is forty-one individuals, thus making the ten available sets
of dates open to serious qualification.

ABBREVIATIONS

Full references can be found in the first citation of a work in each chapter. Classical authors have been cited according to the standard subdivisions of their works and all of these, unless otherwise cited, can be located in the Loeb Classical Library. Square brackets indicate the entire page length of an article. Line references, particularly for poetry, follow a period after the page reference; hence p. 29.11 refers the reader to line 11 found on page 29. The following abbreviations are found in the notes:

CCCM   *Corpus Christianorum: Continuatio Mediaevalis* (Turnhout, 1971–)

CCSL   *Corpus Christianorum: Series Latina* (Turnhout, 1953–)

CSEL   *Corpus Scriptorm Ecclesiasticorum Latinorum* (Vienna, 1866–)

MGH   *Monumenta Germaniae Historica* (Hanover and Berlin, 1826–)

       Cap.   *Capitularia regum Francorum*

       Con.   *Concilia*

       Ep.   *Epistolae*

       PLAC   *Poetae Latini Aevi Carolini*

       Schriften   *Schriften der Monumenta Germaniae Historica*

       SRGUS   *Scriptores rerum Germanicarum in usum Scholarum*

       SRM   *Scriptores rerum Merovingicarum*

       SRG n.s.   *Scriptores rerum Germanicarum. Nova Series*

       SRL   *Scriptores rerum Langobardicarum et Italicarum, saec. VI–IX*

       SS   *Scriptores*

PL   *Patrologia Latina*, ser. ed. J.P. Migne (Paris, 1841–64)

NOTES

Chapter 1   Charlemagne's Mustache

1. See Conrad Leyser, "Long-haired Kings and Short-haired Nuns: Power and Gender in Merovingian Gaul," *Medieval World*, March/April (1992): 37–42; William Sayers, "Early Irish Attitudes toward Hair and Beards, Baldness and Tonsure," *Zeitschrift für Celtische Philologie*, 44 (1991): 154–89; Edward James, "Bede and the Tonsure Question, *Peritia*, 3 (1948): 85–98.

2. See E.R. Leach, "Magical Hair," *Journal of the Royal Anthropological Institute of Great Britain and Ireland*, 88 (1958): 147–64; C.R. Hallpike, "Social Hair," *Man: The Journal of the Royal Anthropological Institute*, 4 (1969): 256–64; Wendy Cooper, *Hair: Sex, Society, Symbolism* (London, 1971); Raymond Firth, *Symbols: Public and Private* (London, 1973), pp. 243–98; Gananath Obeyesekere, *Medusa's Hair: An Essay on Personal Symbols and Religious Experience* (Chicago, 1981); Grant McCracken, *Big Hair: A Journey into the Transformation of Self* (Toronto, 1995); Allan Peterkin, *One Thousand Beards: A Cultural History of Facial Hair* (Vancouver, 2001).

3. Petronius, *Satyricon* 58.8.5: "qui de nobis longe uenio, late uenio? solue me." There are a number of possible answers to this old riddle, but Petronius's character chose an obscene one.

4. Aulus Gellius, *Noctes Atticae* 17.9.18–27.

5. But see H. Platelle, "Le problème du scandale: les nouvelles modes masculines aux XIe et XIIe siècles," *Revue belge de philologie et d'histoire*, 53 (1975): 1071–1096; Giles Constable, "Introduction," to Burchard of Bellevaux, *Apologia de barbis*, ed. R.B.C. Huygens, *Apologiae duae*, in Corpus Christianorum: Continuatio Mediaevalis, 62 (Turnhout, 1985), pp. 47–130; Robert Bartlett, "Symbolic Meanings of Hair in the Middle Ages," (5 March 1993), *Transactions of the Royal Historical Society*, 6th ser. 4 (London, 1994), pp. 43–60; Simon Coates, "Scissors or Sword? The Symbolism of a Medieval Haircut," *History Today*, 49.5 (May 1999): 7–13.

6. But for a very useful survey of the evidence for Late Antiquity, see Walter Pohl, "Telling the Difference: Signs of Ethnic Identity," in *Strategies of Distinction: The Construction of Ethnic Communities, 300–800*, ed. Walter Pohl and Helmut Reimitz, in The Transformation of the Roman World, ed. Ian Wood, vol. 2 (Leiden, 1998), pp. 51–55 [17–69].

7. Paul the Deacon, *Historia Langobardorum* 1.9, ed. L. Bethmann and G. Waitz, MGH: Scriptores rerum Langobardicarum et Italicarum, saec. VI-IX

(Hanover, 1878), p. 52. At *Historia Langobardorum* 4.22, ed. Bethmann and Waitz, p. 124, Paul describes the appearance of the hair of the Lombards on the painted walls of a palace at Monza. See also Pohl, "Telling the Difference," in *Strategies of Distinction*, pp. 56–59.

8. See Michael McCormick, *Eternal Victory: Triumphal Rulership in Late Antiquity, Byzantium and the Early Medieval West* (Cambridge, 1986), pp. 289–93 and fig. 12.

9. See Percy Ernst Schramm, *Herrschaftszeichen und Staatssymbolik: Beiträge zu ihrer Geschichte vom dritten bis zum sechzehnten Jahrhundert*, Schriften der Monumenta Germaniae Historica, 13.1 (Stuttgart, 1954), pp. 219–22 and plate 18c. For a color photograph of the same, see Magnus Backes and Regine Dölling, *Art of the Dark Ages*, trans. Francisca Garvie (New York, 1969), p. 15. On Germanic and Ostrogothic hair styles, see Patrick Amory, *People and Identity in Ostrogothic Italy, 489–554* (Cambridge, 1997), pp. 338–41.

10. Tacitus, *Germania* 31.2.

11. See Pohl, "Telling the Difference," in *Strategies of Distinction*, pp. 51–54.

12. See Juvenal, *Satire* 13.164–65: "flavam caesariem"; Claudian, *In Eutropium* 1.380: "flauis. . .Suebis"; *Panegyricus de quarto consulatu Honorii Augusti* 446–47: "flauam. . .Sygambri/caesariem"; *De consulatu Stilichonis* 1.203: "crinigero flauentes uertice reges"; Sidonius Apollinaris, *carmen* 5.220: "flauo. . .marito." See also Pohl, "Telling the Difference," in *Strategies of Distinction*, pp. 53–54.

13. Tacitus, *Germania* 4.2; Isidore, *Etymologiae* 19.23.7, ed. W.M. Lindsay, in *Isidori Hispalensis episcopi Etymologiarum sive originum libri XX*, 2 vols. (Oxford: Clarendon, 1911): "[cirros] granos et cinnibar"; and see Pohl, "Telling the Difference," in *Strategies of Distinction*, p. 51.

14. Tacitus, *Historiae* 4.12–37.

15. Tacitus, *Historiae* 4.61. For a similar oath, this time by the Saxons, see Paul the Deacon, *Historia Langobardorum* 3.7, ed. Bethmann and Waitz, p. 95.

16. Ammianus Marcellinus, *Res gestae* 27.2.2, and see Pohl, "Telling the Difference," in *Strategies of Distinction*, p. 54.

17. Tacitus, *Germania* 38.3.

18. Tacitus, *Germania* 38.3–4.

19. Claudian, *Panegyricus de quarto consulatu Honorii Augusti* 655, for instance, simply spoke of the "crinitus Suebus." See also Claudian, *De consulatu Stilichonis* 1.203: "crinigero flauentes uertice reges." On this issue, see Jean Hoyoux, "*Reges criniti*: chevelures, tonsures et scalps chez les Mérovingiens," *Revue Belge de philologie et d'histoire*, 26 (1948): 479–508; Ekkehard Kaufmann, "Über das Scheren abgesetzter Merowingerkönige," *Zeitschrift der Savigny-Stiftung für Rechtsgeschichte: Germanistische Abteilung*, 85 (1955): 177–85.

20. Amory, *People and Identity in Ostrogothic Italy*, pp. 340–41.

21. See also Peter Brown, *Society and Holy in Late Antiquity* (Berkeley, 1982), pp. 83–84. Eriugena in the 850s glossed the word long-haired as "CRINITA quia omnes philosophi criniti erant." See *Iohannis Scotti Annotationes in*

Marcianum 57.15, ed. Cora E. Lutz, Medieval Academy of America, publication no. 34 (Cambridge, Mass., 1939), p. 64.

22. Sidonius Apollinaris, *carmen* 12.1–7 and trans. Helen Waddell, *More Latin Lyrics from Virgil to Milton*, ed. Felicitas Corrigan (New York, 1977), p. 87.

23. *Codex Theodosianus* (XIIII.x.4) from 12 December 416, ed. T. Mommsen and Paul M. Meyer, in *Theodosiani libri XVI cum constitutionibus Sirmondianis et Leges Novellae ad Theodosianum pertinentes*, 1.2 (Berlin, 1905; repr. 1962), p. 788.

24. Claudian, *In Eutropium* 1.383–84: "nostris detonsa Sygambria signis"; *Panegyricus de quarto consulatu Honorii Augusti* 446–47: "ante ducem nostrum flauam sparsere Sygambri/ caesariem. . . ."

25. See McCormick, *Eternal Victory*, p. 313.

26. See *Liber Pontificalis*, Hadrianus 32–33, ed. L. Duchesne, *Le Liber Pontificalis: texte, introduction, et commentaire* (Paris, 1886; repr. Paris, 1955–57, 1981), p. 496. And see *Lives of the Eighth-Century Popes (Liber pontificalis): The Ancient Biographies of Nine Popes from AD 715 to AD 817*, trans. Raymond Davis, in Translated Texts for Historians, 13 (Liverpool, 1992), p. 137; T.F.X. Noble, *The Republic of St. Peter: The Birth of the Papal State, 680–825* (Philadelphia, 1984), p. 134. Paul Fouracre and John Contreni kindly pointed me to this incident.

27. Notker, *Gesta Karoli Magni* 1.32, ed. Hans F. Haefele, MGH: Scriptores rerum Germanicarum, Nova Series, 12 (Berlin, 1959), p. 44. On the image of the carpenter at work at his wood with compass and plane, see Isa. 44:13 on which Notker drew.

28. See J.M. Wallace-Hadrill, *The Long-Haired Kings and Other Studies in Frankish History* (London, 1962) and repr. as *The Long-Haired Kings* (Toronto, 1982), pp. 156–57, 232–33, 245–46.

29. See Sidonius Apollinaris, *carmen* 5.238–240; Gregory of Tours, *Historiae* 6.24, ed. Bruno Krusch and Wilhelm Levison, MGH: Scriptores rerum Merovingicarum, 1 (Hanover, 1951), p. 291. And see Averil Cameron, "How did the Merovingian Kings Wear Their Hair?" *Revue Belge de philosophie et d'histoire*, 43 (1965): 1203–216; Pohl, "Telling the Difference," in *Strategies of Distinction*, pp. 54–55; Schramm, *Herrschaftszeichen und Staatssymbolik*, 1, pp. 213–217 and plate 13.

30. Gregory of Tours, *Historiae* 2.9, ed. Krusch and Levison, p. 57.

31. Agathias, *Historiae* 1.3.4, ed. R. Keydell, *Agathiae Myrinaei Historiarum libri quinque*, Corpus Fontium Historiae Byzantinae, 2 (Berlin, 1967), p. 13; trans. Joseph D. Frendo, *Agathias, The Histories*, Corpus Fontium Historiae Byzantinae, 2A (Berlin, 1975), p. 11. On this passage, see Cameron, "How did the Merovingian Kings Wear Their Hair?" pp. 1208–214.

32. On this issue, see Cameron, "How did the Merovingian Kings Wear Their Hair?" pp. 1203–216.

33. *Leges Burgundionum: Liber constitutionum siue Lex Gundobada*, 6.4, ed. L.R. de Salis, MGH: Leges Nationum Germanicarum, 2.1 (Hanover, 1892), p. 47.

34. See *Leges Burgundionum: Liber constitutionum siue Lex Gundobada*, 33.1–4, ed. de Salis, p. 67; 92.1–4, p. 111; *Pactus Legis Salicae* 24.1–4, ed. K.A. Eckhardt,

MGH: Leges Nationum Germanicarum, 4.1 (Hanover, 1962), pp. 89–90;
97.1–2, p. 255; *septem causas* 3.1, p. 270; 8.4, p. 273; *Lex Salica* 35 (34), ed.
'K.A. Eckhardt, MGH: Leges Nationum Germanicarum, 4.2 (Hanover,
1969), pp. 74–75; *Lex Salica Karolina* 33.1–4, ed. K.A. Eckhardt, in MGH:
Leges Nationum Germanicarum, 4.2, p. 213.

35. Gregory of Tours, *Historiae* 8.10, ed. Krusch and Levison, pp. 376–77.

36. Sidonius Apollinaris, *epistola* 3.3.7.

37. Gregory, *Historiae* 7.31, ed. Krusch and Levison, p. 350. And see Cameron,
"How did the Merovingian Kings Wear Their Hair?" pp. 1213–214.

38. Gregory of Tours, *Historiae* 2.41, ed. Krusch and Levison, p. 91.

39. See Simon Schama, *Landscape and Memory* (New York, 1995), pp. 81–120.
On the imagery of trees and royal lines, see also Notker, *Gesta Karoli Magni*
2.14, ed. Haefele, p. 78.

40. Gregory of Tours, *Historiae* 5.14, ed. Krusch and Levison, p. 207.

41. *Passio Leudegarii* 6, ed. Bruno Krusch, MGH:SRM 5 (Hanover, 1910), p. 288
[282–322]. An English translation of the *Passio* is available in Paul Fouracre
and Richard A. Gerberding, *Late Merovingian France: History and Hagiography,
640–720* (Manchester, 1996), pp. 215–53.

42. While the *Regula Magistri* associated tonsure with the taking of the monastic habit, the *Rule* of Saint Benedict failed to mention it: see *RB 1980: The
Rule of St. Benedict in English and Latin with Notes*, ed. Timothy Fry (Collegeville, Minn., 1981), pp. 442, 456. Nonetheless, the weight of tradition
led even Benedictine monks in the Middle Ages to be tonsured: see Benedict of Aniane, *Concordia regularum* 62.10, 65.29, ed. J.P. Migne, Patrologia
Latina 103, cols. 1244B, 1298B–C.

43. Apuleius, *Metamorphoses* 2.8–10.

44. Apuleius, *Metamorphoses* 11.3–30.

45. Avitus, *epistola*, in *Epistolae ad diuersos*, 46, ed. Rudolf Peiper, MGH: Auctores
Antiquissimi 6.2 (Berlin, 1883), p. 75.

46. Gregory of Tours, *Historiae* 3.18, ed. Krusch and Levison, p. 118.

47. Gregory of Tours, *Historiae* 3.18, ed. Krusch and Levison, p. 119.

48. *Gesta Dagoberti I regis Francorum* 3.9, ed. Bruno Krusch, MGH:SRM 2,
p. 517; and see Clare Stancliffe, "Kings who Opted Out," in *Ideal and Reality in Frankish and Anglo-Saxon Society: Studies Presented to J.M. Wallace-
Hadrill*, ed. Patrick Wormald with Donald Bullough and Roger Collins
(Oxford, 1983), pp. 154–76.

49. Gregory of Tours, *Historiae* 9.38, ed. Krusch and Levison, p. 459: "incisis
capillis et auribus." It is not impossible that the two cuttings were applied as
separate punishments for different crimes.

50. See Hoyoux, "*Reges criniti*," pp. 507–508.

51. See *Liber historiae Francorum* 43, ed. Bruno Krusch, MGH:SRM 2,
pp. 315–316 [215–328]. For a translation of this text, see Fouracre and
Gerberding, *Late Merovingian France*, p. 88. On the incident itself, see Ian
Wood, *The Merovingian Kingdoms, 450–751* (Harlow, 1994), pp. 222–24.

52. See *Liber historiae Francorum* 45, ed. Krusch, pp. 317–318.

53. See Wilhelm Levison, *England and the Continent in the Eighth Century: The Ford Lectures Delivered in the University of Oxford in the Hilary Term, 1943* (Oxford, 1946), pp. 115–21.

54. Einhard, *Vita Karoli Magni* 1, ed. G. Waitz after G.H. Pertz, 6th ed. overseen by O. Holder-Egger [hereafter ed. Waitz], MGH: Scriptores rerum Germanicarum in usum scholarum (Hanover, 1911), pp. 2–3; trans. Paul Edward Dutton, in *Charlemagne's Courtier: The Complete Einhard*, Readings in Medieval Civilizations and Cultures, 3 (Peterborough, Ont., 1998), p. 16.

55. See the examination of this fable by Henri Pirenne, "Le char à boeufs des derniers Mérovingiens, note sur un passage d'Eginhard," in *Mélanges Paul Thomas. Recueil de mémoires concernant la philologie classique* (Bruges, 1930), pp. 555–60.

56. Pepin was born ca. 714.

57. Paul the Deacon, *Historia Langobardorum* 6.53, ed. Bethmann, p. 183. See also Pierre Riché, "Le renouveau culturel à la cour de Pépin III," *Francia*, 2 (1974): 62 [59–70] and repr. in Riché, *Instruction et vie religieuse dans le Haut Moyen Age*, Variorum Reprints, CS 139 (London, 1981), item XI. On the relations of Liutprand and Charles Martel, see Jan T. Hallenbeck, *Pavia and Rome: The Lombard Monarchy and the Papacy in the Eighth Century*, Transactions of the American Philosophical Society, 72.4 (Philadelphia, 1982), pp. 34–35.

58. See Yitzhak Hen, *Culture and Religion in Merovingian Gaul, A.D. 481–751*, Culture, Beliefs, and Traditions, 1 (Leiden, 1995), p. 139.

59. See Joseph H. Lynch, *Godparents and Kinship in Early Medieval Europe* (Princeton, 1986), p. 180.

60. Fredegar, *Chronica* 2.58, ed. Bruno Krusch, MGH:SRM 2, p. 82.

61. *Gesta Theoderici regis* 15, ed. Bruno Krusch, MGH:SRM 2, p. 207.

62. Paul the Deacon, *Historia Langobardorum* 4.38, ed. Waitz, pp. 132–33.

63. See particularly Hen, *Culture and Religion in Merovingian Gaul*, pp. 137–43; Pierre Riché, *Education and Culture in the Barbarian West: Sixth through Eighth Centuries*, trans. John J. Contreni (Columbia, S.C., 1976), pp. 232–34.

64. *Ex Adrevaldi Floriacensis Miraculis S. Benedicti* 14, ed. O. Holder-Egger, MGH: Scriptores 15.1 (Hanover, 1887), p. 483.40–42.

65. Riché, *Education*, pp. 233–34 and Hen, *Culture and Religion in Merovingian Gaul*, pp. 142–43. And see also Régine Le Jan, "Frankish Giving of Arms and Rituals of Power: Continuity and Change in the Carolingian Period," in *Rituals of Power from Late Antiquity to the Early Middle Ages*, ed. Frans Theuws and Janet L. Nelson (Leiden, 2000), p. 285 [281–309].

66. See Cameron, "How did the Merovingian Kings Wear Their Hair?" pp. 1214–215.

67. *Vita sanctae Geretrudis* 2, ed. Bruno Krusch, MGH:SRM 2, p. 456.

68. *Annales regni Francorum* 745–46, ed. F. Kurze after the edition of G.H. Pertz [hereafter ed. Kurze], MGH:SRGUS (Hanover, 1895), pp. 4–7. The annalist's dates for Carloman's journey to Rome and into monastic life are wrong. It should also be noted that the reviser, in describing Carloman's

conversion, replaced the original entry's "se totondit" with "dimissa saeculari gloria habitum mutauit."

69. See *Ex Adrevaldi Floriacensis Miraculis S. Benedicti*, ed. Holder-Egger, p. 84 and Paul Edward Dutton, *The Politics of Dreaming in the Carolingian Empire*, Regents Studies in Medieval Culture, ed. Eugene Vance (Lincoln, Neb., 1994), pp. 174–75.

70. Einhard, *Vita Karoli Magni* 2, ed. Waitz, p. 4; trans. Dutton, *Charlemagne's Courtier*, p. 17.

71. Notker, *Gesta Karoli Magni* 2.12, ed. Haefele, p. 72.

72. Notker, *Gesta Karoli Magni* 2.15, ed. Haefele, pp. 78–80.

73. See McCormick, *Eternal Victory*, p. 290 n. 142.

74. The Bible presents many different attitudes on hair and baldness. Samson in Judges 16, of course, had his locks cut off. In Jer. 7:29, God ordered the mourner to cut off his hair and throw it away. Absalom shaved his head once a year: see 2 Kings 14:25–26. Mich. 1:16 praises baldness and Paul, in 1 Cor. 11:6, commanded women to keep their heads, with their glorious hair, covered when in the temple. And see Paulinus of Nola, *epistola* 23.10–34, ed. W. Hartel, CSEL 29 (Vienna, 1894), pp. 168–96.

75. Alcuin, *epistola* 16, ed. Ernst Dümmler, MGH: Epistolae 4 (Hanover, 1895; repr. 1974), p. 43.

76. See Neil Stratford, *The Lewis Chessmen and the Enigma of the Hoard* (London, 1997), p. 14 and plates 10–11, which show the backs of six of the king pieces, but one of these (Cat. 81) is intriguingly short-haired, perhaps for the western European market.

77. Theodulf, *carmen* 25, ed. Ernst Dümmler, MGH: Poetae Latini Aevi Carolini 1 (Berlin, 1881; repr. 1964), p. 484.37–47. See also Peter Godman, *Poetry of the Carolingian Renaissance* (Norman, Okla., 1985), pp. 152–53.

78. Judges 16:17–19; Virgil, *Georgics* 1.404–409.

79. Hrabanus Maurus, *Commentaria in librum Iudicum* 2.19, PL 108:1196C10–11 and for the entire passage on the meaning of hair, see 1196A–D.

80. See Karl F. Morrison with Henry Grunthal, *Carolingian Coinage*, Numismatic Notes and Monographs, 158 (New York, 1967), p. 124 and fig. 319. See also Bernd Kluge, "Nomen imperatoris und Christiana Religio: das Kaisertum Karls des Großen und Ludwigs des Frommen im Licht der numismatischen Quellen," in *799: Kunst und Kultur der Karolingerzeit. Karl der Große und Papst Leo III. in Paderborn*, Beiträge zum Katalog der Austellung, Paderborn 1999, ed. Christoph Stiegemann and Matthias Wemhoff (Mainz, 1999), pp. 82–90.

81. A point confirmed for me by Bryan Ward-Perkins.

82. Simon Coupland arrived at the important conclusion that Carolingian artists, even when depending on older models, introduced contemporary details into their work: see Simon Coupland, "Carolingian Arms and Armor in the Ninth Century," *Viator: Medieval and Renaissance Studies*, 21 (1990): 50 [29–50].

83. For a depiction and analysis, see Hubert Mordek, "Von Paderborn nach Rom—der Weg zur Kaiserkrönung," in *799: Kunst und Kultur der Karolingerzeit*, Beiträge zum Katalog, p. 52 [47–54] and also Donald

Bullough, "Roman Books and Carolingian *Renovatio*," in Bullough, *Carolingian Renewal: Sources and Heritage* (Manchester, 1991), p. 1 and n. 2 [1–38] and Bullough, "*Imagines regum* and Their Siginificance in the Early Medieval West," in *Carolingian Renewal*, pp. 60–61 [39–96]. The most faithful drawing of the now largely illegible bull, the one presented here, comes from François Le Blanc, *Dissertation historique de Charlemagne frappés dans Rome* (Paris, 1689–90), title page and p. 24.

84. See Morrison with Grunthal, *Carolingian Coinage*, p. 159 and fig. 515; *799: Kunst und Kultur der Karolingerzeit. Karl der Große und Papst Leo III. in Paderborn*, vol. 1: Katalog der Austellung, Paderborn 1999, ed. Christoph Stiegemann and Matthias Wemhoff (Mainz, 1999), p. 71, fig. II.32 and p. 73, fig. II.36; Ildar H. Garipzanov, "The Image of Authority in Carolingian Coinage: The *Image* of a Ruler and Roman Imperial Tradition," *Early Medieval Europe*, 8 (1999): 211 [197–218]; Genevra Kornbluth, *Engraved Gems of the Carolingian Empire* (University Park, Penn., 1995), pp. 23–24 and fig. 40. And see the seals of Louis the Pious, Lothar I, Charles the Bald, and Charles the Fat shown in Jacques Boussard, *The Civilization of Charlemagne*, trans. Frances Partridge (London, 1968), pp. 200–201.

85. J. Grimaldi, the papal librarian's comment, from *De aula Lateranensi* (1617): trans. C. Davis-Weyer, *Early Medieval Art, 300–1150* (Eaglewood Cliffs, N.J., 1971; repr. Toronto, 1986), p. 92 and repr. in Paul Edward Dutton, *Carolingian Civilization: A Reader*, 2nd ed. (Peterborough, Ont., 2004), pp. 59–60 and on p. 61 a reproduction of one of the drawings of the mosaic.

86. See Schramm, *Herrschaftszeichen und Staatssymbolik*, 1, pp. 219–22 and plates 18–20.

87. Sidonius Apollinaris, *epistola* (To Agricola) 1.2.2.

88. Sidonius Apollinaris, *carmen* 5.241–42: "uultibus undique rasis/ pro barba tenues perarantur pectine cristae" has been taken to refer to the clean-shaven Franks having thin mustaches which they combed. But "crista" refers to a crest or tuft and not necessarily to a mustache, though that may be the most reasonable inference. Still, "crista" never caught on as a word for mustache.

89. See Agnellus, *Liber Pontificalis ecclesiae Ravennatis* 94, ed. O. Holder-Egger, MGH: SRL, p. 338; and trans. in Dutton, *Carolingian Civilization*, p. 56; and Walahfrid Strabo, *De imagine Tetrici*, ed. Dümmler, MGH:PLAC 2, pp. 370–78.

90. See Hartmut Hoffmann, "Die Aachener Theoderichstatue," in *Das Erste Jahrtausend: Kultur und Kunst im werdenden Abendland an Rhein und Ruhr*, Textbande, vol. 1, ed. Victor H. Elbern (Düsseldorf, 1962), pp. 318–35. One hypothesis is that the statue represented the emperor Zeno.

91. See Peter Lasko, *Ars Sacra, 800–1200*, 2nd ed. (New Haven, 1994), p. 13. See also Bullough, "*Imagines regum*," in Bullough, *Carolingian Renewal*, pp. 61–62 on the issue.

92. Alcuin, *Disputatio Pippini cum Albino* 22, ed. Lloyd William Daly and Walter Suchier, in *Altercatio Hadriani Augusti et Epicteti philosophi* (Urbana, 1939), p. 138.

93. Einhard, *Vita Karoli Magni* 22, ed. Waitz, p. 26.

94. Theodulf, *carmen* 25, ed. Dümmler, MGH:PLAC 1, p. 485.71–72.

95. For a color plate of the fresco, see J. Hubert, J. Porcher, and W.F. Volbach, *The Carolingian Renaissance*, trans. James Emmons, Stuart Gilbert, and Robert Allen (New York, 1970), plate 18, p. 22.

96. *Erchemperti Historia Langobardorum Beneventanorum* 4, ed. G.H. Pertz and G. Waitz, MGH:SRL, p. 236. And see the case of Liutprand, the Lombard king, who according to a passage in the *Liber Pontificalis* forced the Romans of Campania to be shaved and dressed in the Lombard fashion: *Liber Pontificalis* 92.15 Gregorius III, ed. Duchesne, p. 420.

97. *Annales regni Francorum* 792 (revised version), ed. Kurze, pp. 91, 93; Einhard, *Vita Karoli Magni* 20, ed. Waitz, p. 25; Notker, *Gesta* 2.12, ed. Haefele, pp. 71–74.

98. Nithard, *Historiae* 1.2, ed. P. Lauer, *Nithard, Histoire des fils de Louis le Pieux*, in Les classiques de l'histoire de France au Moyen Age, 7 (Paris, 1964), p. 8.

99. Astronomer, *Vita Hludowici imperatoris* 44, ed. Ernst Tremp, in MGH: Scriptores rerum Germanicarum in usum scholarum separatim editi, 64 (Hanover, 1995), pp. 454, 456. Also trans. Allen Cabaniss, *Son of Charlemagne: A Contemporary Life of Louis the Pious* (Syracuse, 1961).

100. *Annales Bertiniani* 852, ed. Félix Grat, Jeanne Vielliard, and Suzanne Clémencet, in *Annales de Saint-Bertin* (Paris, 1964), pp. 64–65; *Annales Fuldenses siue Annales regni Francorum orientalis* 851, ed. F. Kurze after G.H. Pertz [hereafter ed. Kurze], MGH:SRGUS (Hanover, 1891), p. 41.

101. *Annales de St-Bertin* 854, ed. Grat et al., p. 70.

102. *Annales regni Francorum* 818, ed. Kurze, p. 148; Nithard, *Historiae* 1.2, ed. Lauer, pp. 6, 8. See also the case of Herbert in Nithard, *Historiae* 1.3, p. 10.

103. *Annales de St-Bertin* 873, ed. Grat et al., p. 190.

104. See Elizabeth Sears, "Louis the Pious as *Miles Christi*: The Dedicatory Image in Hrabanus Maurus's *De laudibus sanctae crucis*," in *Charlemagne's Heir: New Perspectives on the Reign of Louis the Pious (814–840)*, ed. Peter Godman and Roger Collins (Oxford, 1990), pp. 605–628.

105. For a color plate, see Hubert, Porcher, and Volbach, *Carolingian Renaissance*, plate 140, p. 152. On the various identifications of the figure, see Nikolaus Staubach, *Rex Christianus: Hofkultur und Herrschaftspropaganda im Reich Karls des Kahlen*, vol. 2: Die Grundlegung der 'religion royale,' Pictura et Poesis, 2.2 (Cologne, 1993), pp. 225–227.

106. See Paul Edward Dutton and Herbert L. Kessler, *The Poetry and Paintings of the First Bible of Charles the Bald*, in Recentiores: Later Latin Texts and Contexts, ed. James J. O'Donnell (Ann Arbor, 1997). There is, however, one apparent exception to the rule. The portrait of Charles the Bald in his Prayerbook (Munich, Schatzkammer der Residenz, for. 38v) lacks a mustache. On this manuscript, see Robert Deshman, "The Exalted Servant: The Ruler Theology of the Prayerbook of Charles the Bald," *Viator: Medieval and Renaissance Studies*, 11 (1980): 387–417. The KAROLVS REX FRANCO<RUM> medallion figure of fol.lv of the First Bible of Charles the Bald also lacks a mustache.

107. See Paul Edward Dutton and Édouard Jeauneau, "The Verses of the *Codex Aureus* of Saint-Emmeram," *Studi Medievali*, 3rd ser. (1983): 75–120 and repr. in Jeauneau, *Études Érigéniennes* (Paris, 1987), pp. 593–638.

108. See Percy Ernst Schramm and Florentine Mütherich, *Denkmale der deutschen Könige und Kaiser: ein Beitrag zur Herrschergeschichte von Karl dem Großen bis Friedrich II, 768–1250*, Veröffentlichungen des Zentralinstituts für Kunstgeschichte in München, 2 (Munich, 1962), p. 137 and fig. 58; Wolfgang Braunfels, "Karls des Grossen Bronzewerkstatt," in *Karl der Grosse: Lebenswerk und Nachleben*, vol. 3: Karolingische Kunst, ed. Wolfgang Braunfels and Hermann Schnitzler (Düsseldorf, 1965), pp. 168–202; Florentine Mütherich, "Die Reiterstatuette aus der Metzer Kathedrale," in *Studien zur Geschichte der europäischen Plastik. Festschrift für T. Müller* (Munich, 1975), pp. 9–15; Lasko, *Ars Sacra*, pp. 12–13; Robert Melzak, "Antiquarianism in the Time of Louis the Pious and Its Influence on the Art of Metz," in *Charlemagne's Heir*, pp. 629–40; Bullough, "*Imagines regum*," in Bullough, *Carolingian Renewal*, p. 62; Michael McCormick, "Paderborn 799: Königliche Repräsentation—Visualierung eines Herrschaftskonzepts," in *799: Kunst und Kultur der Karolingerzeit*, Beiträge zum Katalog, pp. 71–81; Danielle Gaborit-Chopin, *La statuette équestre de Charlemagne*, Collection solo, 13 (Paris, 1999).

109. See *La Cattedra lignea di S. Pietro in Vaticano*, Memories, 10: Atti della Pontificia accademia Romana di archeologia, ser. 3 (Vatican City, 1971) and Lawrence Nees, *A Tainted Mantle: Hercules and the Classical Tradition at the Carolingian Court* (Philadelphia, 1991), and plate 2.

110. Anne Robbins first kindly pointed this out to me and in July 2002 I was able to confirm this in the Louvre for myself.

111. Janet L. Nelson, *Charles the Bald* (London, 1992), p. 13.

112. *Genealogia regum Francorum*, ed. G. Waitz, MGH: Scriptores 13 (Hanover, 1881), p. 247. See Kurt-Ultich Jäschke, "Die Karolingergenealogien aus Metz und Paulus Diaconus: mit einem Exkurs über Karl 'den Kahlen,'" *Rheinische Vierteljahrsblätter* 34 (1970): 190–217.

113. Hucbald, *Ecloga de caluis*, ed. Paul von Winterfeld, MGH:PLAC 4 (Berlin, 1899), pp. 267–71. Thomas Klein's brave attempt in his translation of the poem to approximate the alliteration of the poem by using *b*-lines and *c*-lines demonstrates the difficulty of achieving Hucbald's effect in English: see Thomas Klein, "*In Praise of Bald Men*: A Translation of Hucbald's *Ecloga de caluis*," *Comitatus*, 26 (1995): 1–9.

114. Richard E. Sullivan, "The Context of Cultural Activity in the Carolingian Age," in *The Gentle Voices of Teachers: Aspects of Learning in the Carolingian Age*, ed. Richard E. Sullivan (Columbus, Ohio, 1995), p. 81.

115. See Herbert L. Kessler, "An Apostle in Armor and the Mission of Carolingian Art," in *Arte Medievale*, 11 (1990): 17–41.

116. *Synesii Cyrenaei Calvitii Encomium*, ed. J.G. Krabinger (Stuttgart, 1834) and Synesius of Cyrene, *In Praise of Baldness*, trans. George H. Kendal (Vancouver, 1985).

117. Burchard of Bellevaux, *Apologia de barbis*, ed. R.B.C. Huygens, *Apologiae duae*, CCCM 62, pp. 151–214.

Chapter 2   Charlemagne, King of Beasts

1. Or so we may surmise, since this Byzantine fabric was moved in the twelfth century to Charlemagne's shrine and survives today in Aachen. See Percy Ernst Schramm and Florentine Mütherich, *Denkmale der deutschen Könige und Kaiser: Ein Beitrag zur Herrschergeschichte von Karl dem Großen bis Friedrich II, 768–1250* (Munich, 1962), p. 154 and plate 104. On the details of Otto's repairs, see *Chronicon Novaliciense* 3.32, ed. C. Bethmann, MGH: Scriptores 7 (Hanover, 1846; repr. 1925), p. 106.

2. Alcuin, *epistola* 181, ed. E. Dümmler, MGH: Epistolae 4 (Hanover, 1895), p. 299.8–9.

3. For background reading, see Keith Thomas, *Man and the Natural World: Changing Attitudes in England, 1500–1800* (London, 1983), particularly pp. 92–191; Erica Fudge, *Perceiving Animals: Humans and Beasts in Early Modern English Culture* (London, 2000); Steve Barker, *Picturing the Beast: Animals, Identity, and Representation* (Manchester, 1993); Rod Preece, *Animals and Nature: Cultural Myths, Cultural Realities* (Vancouver, 1999); Nigel Rothfels, ed., *Representing Animals*, Theories of Contemporary Culture, 26 (Bloomington, 2002).

4. For studies of animals in the Middle Ages and perceptions and representations, see *Beasts and Birds of the Middle Ages*, ed. Willene B. Clark and Meredith T. McMunn (Philadelphia, 1989); L.A.J.R. Houwe, *Animals and the Symbolic in Medieval Art and Literature* (Groningen, 1997); Joyce E. Salisbury, *The Beast Within: Animals in the Middle Ages* (New York, 1994); Francis Klingender, *Animals in Art and Thought at the End of the Middle Ages* (London, 1971), esp. pp. 95–336; Kenneth Clark, *Animals and Men: Their Relationship as Reflected in Western Art from Prehistory to the Present Day* (London, 1977); and the as yet unseen, *Il mondo Animale: The World of Animals*, in Micrologus: Nature, Sciences and Medieval Societies (Rivista della Società internazionale per lo studio del Medio Evo latino), vol. 8 (2000); David Salter, *Holy and Noble Beasts: Encounters with Animals in Medieval Literature* (Woodbridge, Suffolk, 2001).

5. On the art, see especially the essays of Stephen O. Glosecki, "Movable Beasts: The Manifold Implications of Early Germanic Animal Imagery," in *Animals in the Middle Ages: A Book of Essays*, ed. Nona C. Flores (New York, 1996), pp. 3–23; "Men among the Monsters: Germanic Animal Art as Evidence of Oral Literature," *The Mankind Quarterly*, 27.2 (1986): 207–214; and "Wolf Dancers and Whispering Beasts: Shamanic Motifs from Sutton Hoo?" *The Mankind Quarterly*, 26.3–4 (1986): 305–319. See also George Speake, *Anglo-Saxon Art and Its Germanic Background* (Oxford, 1980), pp. 77–92. For the depiction of a dragon-prowed boat in ninth-century art, see the Utrecht Psalter, fol. 27v, in E.T. De Wald, *The Illustrations of the Utrecht Psalter* (Princeton, 1932), plate 44. For the dragon banner, see Florentine Mütherich and Joachim Gaehde, *Carolingian Painting* (New York, 1976), p. 122, plate 46.

6. *Annals of St-Bertin* 846, ed. Félix Grat, Jeanne Vielliard, and Suzanne Clémencet (Paris, 1964), p. 52; *The Annals of St-Bertin*, Ninth-Century Histories, 1, trans. Janet L. Nelson (Manchester, 1991), p. 63.

7. See also the general prohibitions against bestiality at Lev. 18:23 and Deut. 27:21.
8. Dicuili Liber de mensura orbis terrae 7.52, ed. J.J. Tierney, Scriptores Latini Hiberniae, 6 (Dublin, 1967), p. 88. See also Caroline Walker Bynum, Metamorphosis and Identity (New York, 2001).
9. Dicuili Liber de mensura orbis terrae 6.31, 6.34, 6.30, ed. Tierney, pp. 66–67.
10. See Ratramnus, epistola, ed. E. Dümmler, MGH:Ep. 6 (Berlin, 1925; repr. 1974), p. 157; and trans. Paul Edward Dutton, in Dutton, Carolingian Civilization: A Reader, 2nd ed. (Peterborough, Ont., 2004), pp. 452–55. See also John Block Friedman, The Monstrous Races in Medieval Art and Thought (Cambridge, Mass., 1981), pp. 188–96; Dudley Wilson, Signs and Portents: Monstrous Births from the Middle Ages to the Enlightenment (London, 1993), particularly pp. 3–29, which strangely despite the title has almost nothing to say on the Middle Ages; and Robert Olsen and Karen Olsen, "Introduction: On the Embodiment of Monstrosity in Northwestern Medieval Europe," in Monsters and the Monstrous in Medieval Northwest Europe, ed. K.E. Olsen and L.A.J.R. Houwen, Mediaevalia Groningana, New Series, 3 (Leuven, 2001), pp. 1–23.
11. Ratramnus, epistola, ed. Dümmler, MGH:Ep. 6, p. 156.27–29.
12. Ratramnus, epistola ed. Dümmler, MGH:Ep. 6, pp. 155–57. The Areobindus Diptych shows a pair of cynocephali, one male, one female, on its third register. See n. 92 below.
13. Augustine, De ciuitate dei 16.8, ed. Bernard Dombart and Alphonse Kalb, in Corpus Christianorum: Series Latina, 47–48 (Turnhout, 1965), 48: 508.
14. Dicuil, following Pliny, Naturalis Historia 4.95, thought Hippopodes or horse-footed humans also lived in the north: see Dicuili Liber de mensura orbis terrae 7.21, ed. Tierney, p. 78.
15. See the depictions in Glosecki, "Wolf Dancers and Whispering Beasts," pp. 311 fig. 3b, 313–315; Percy Ernst Schramm, Herrschaftszeichen und Staatssymbolik: Beiträge zu ihrer Geschichte vom dritten bis zum sechzehnten Jahrhundert, in Schriften der Monumenta Germaniae Historica (Deutsches Institute für Erforschung des Mittelalters), 13.1 (Stuttgart, 1954), plate 22b. See also Ian Wood, "Christians and Pagans in Ninth-Century Scandinavia," in The Christianization of Scandinavia: Report of a Symposium held at Kungläv, Sweden, 4–9 August 1985, ed. Birgit Sawyer, Peter Sawyer, and Ian Wood (Alingsås, 1987), p. 64 [36–67].
16. See Marcia L. Colish, "Carolingian Debates over nihil and tenebrae: A Study in Theological Method," Speculum, 59 (1984): 757–95.
17. Ratramnus, epistola, ed. Dümmler, MGH:Ep. 6, p. 157.14–18.
18. Thomas, Man and the Natural World, p. 46, notes that some anthropologists believe that it is the management of animals that led to governed societies and hierarchical social life.
19. Augustine, De ciuitate dei 16.8, ed. Dombart and Kalb, 48: 508 and Isidore, Etymologiae 11.3.12–15, 12.2.32, ed. W.M. Lindsay in Isidori Hispalensis episcopi Etymologiarum siue originum libri XX (Oxford, 1911).
20. See Jan M. Ziolkowski, Talking Animals: Medieval Latin Beast Poetry, 750–1150 (Philadelphia, 1993), pp. 54–57 and Dieter Schaller, "Der junge 'Rabe' am Hof Karls des Grossen (Theodulf carm. 27)," in Festschrift

Bernhard Bischoff zu seinem 65. Geburtstag, ed. Johanne Autenrieth and Franz Brunhölzl (Stuttgart, 1971), pp. 123–41.

21. Theodulf, *carmina* 27, ed. Dümmler, MGH: Poetae Latini Aevi Carolini, 1 (Berlin, 1881; repr. 1964), p. 492.64; 25, p. 487.162; 27, p. 492.45–47.

22. Theodulf, *carmen* 27 ("Ad Coruinianum"), ed. Dümmler, MGH:PLAC 1, pp. 490–93; and trans. Ziolkowski, *Talking Animals*, pp. 269–71 and commented on p. 59.

23. See Margaret A. Sullivan, *Bruegel's Peasants: Art and Audience in the Northern Renaissance* (Cambridge, 1994).

24. Alcuin, *carmen* 5, ed. Dümmler, MGH:PLAC 1, p. 223 and n. 2.

25. Alcuin addressed many letters to Arno (the Eagle), the archbishop of Salzburg. For the calf and animal, see Alcuin, *epistolae* 88, ed. Dümmler, MGH:Ep. 4, pp. 132–33; 248, p. 401; 270, pp. 428–29; for the cuckoo, Alcuin, *carmen* 57 ("Versus de cuculo"), ed. Dümmler, MGH:PLAC 1, pp. 243–44. And see Mary Garrison, "The Social World of Alcuin: Nicknames at York and at the Carolingian Court," in *Alcuin of York: Scholar at the Carolingian Court*, ed. L.A.J.R. Houwen and A.A. MacDonald, Germania Latina, III (Groningen, 1998), pp. 59–79.

26. Alcuin, *epistola* 181, ed. Dümmler, MGH:Ep. 4, pp. 299–300 and translated by Ziolkowski, *Talking Animals*, pp. 242–44.

27. For the age-old characterization of *lupus*, see Hrabanus Maurus, *Homiliae in Evangelia et epistolas* 23, Patrologia Latina, ed. J.P. Migne, 110, cols. 187D10–12: "Quasi ergo gregem dissipat, cum fidelium populum diabolus per tentationes necat."

28. In Notker, *Gesta Karoli Magni* 1.14, ed. Hans F. Haefele, in *Notker der Stammler, Taten Kaiser Karls des Grossen*, MGH: Scriptores rerum Germanicarum, Nova series, 12 (Berlin, 1959), p. 18, Notker describes a bishop flitting around like a swallow.

29. Boethius, *Philosophiae consolatio* 4, prosa 3.17–19, ed. Ludwig Bieler, in CCSL 94 (Turnhout, 1957), p. 71; Machiavelli, *Prince* 18.2–11, ed. Giorgio Inglese, in *Niccolò Machiavelli, De principatibus*, in Istituto storico Italiano per il Medio Evo, Fonti per la storia dell'Italia medievale: Antiquitates, 1 (Rome, 1994), pp. 263–64.

30. Theodulf, *carmen* 28 ("Versus contra iudices"), ed. Dümmler, MGH:PLAC 1, p. 512.731–34.

31. Theodulf, *carmen* 28 ("Versus contra iudices"), ed. Dümmler, MGH:PLAC 1, p. 516.911–12. Dante's Ulysses (*Inferno* 26.119–20) was later to state something similar to his weary and wandering sailors:

> fatti non fostea viver come bruti,
>   ma per segur virtute e canoscenza.

> [you were not made to live as animals,
>   but to pursue virtue and knowledge.]

32. Hrabanus Maurus, *Homiliae de festis praecipuis* 58, PL 110:109A4–6.

33. Sedulius Scottus, *De rectoribus christianis* 6, ed. S. Hellmann, *Sedulius Scottus*, in Quellen und Untersuchungen zur lateinischen Philologie des

Mittlealters, 1 (Munich, 1906), p. 39. Edward Gerald Doyle, *Sedulius Scottus, On Christian Rulers and the Poems*, in Medieval and Renaissance Texts and Studies, 17 (Binghamton, 1983), p. 62, translates this as "dangerous serpents."

34. Astronomer, *Vita Hludowici imperatoris* 45 and 44.1, ed. Ernst Tremp, in MGH: Scriptores rerum Germanicarum in usum scholarum separatim editi, 64 (Hanover, 1995), pp. 462 "feralis commotio" and 456 "more canum auiumque rapatium."

35. On this, see, for instance, Joyce E. Salisbury, "Human Beasts and Bestial Humans in the Middle Ages," in *Animal Acts: Configuring the Human in Western History*, ed. Jennifer Ham and Matthew Senior (New York, 1997), pp. 9–21.

36. On hunting, see Matt Cartmill, *A View to a Death in the Morning: Hunting and Nature through History* (Cambridge, Mass., 1993), particularly pp. 28–91.

37. See *Capitulare de uillis* 36, ed. Boretius, MGH: Capitularia regum Francorum, 1 (Hanover, 1883), p. 86; *Capitulare missorum generale* (802) 39, p. 98; *Capitulare Aquisgranense* (801–813) 18, p. 172.

38. Boniface, *epistola* 78, ed. Ernst Dümmler, MGH:Ep. 3 (Berlin, 1892; repr. 1957), p. 351.14–15; see also p. 310.27–30. And see *Capitulare missorum generale* 19, ed. Boretius, MGH:Cap. 1, p. 95.

39. Erasmus, *Moriae Encomium, id est stultiae laus*, ed. Clarence H. Miller, in *Opera omnia Desiderii Erasmi Roterodami* 4.3 (Amsterdam, 1979), pp. 118–20; and Erasmus, *Praise of Folly (Moriae encomium)*, trans. Betty Radice, in *Collected Works of Erasmus*, Literary and Educational Writings, 5, ed. A.H.T. Levi (Toronto, 1986), pp. 112–113. And see Garry Marvin, "Unspeakability, Inedibity, and the Structures of Pursuit in the English Foxhunt," in *Representing Animals*, pp. 139–58.

40. See, for instance, *Capitulare missorum generale* (802) 39, ed. Boretius, MGH:Cap. 1, p. 98; *Capitulare Aquisgranense* (801–813) 18, p. 172.

41. Einhard, *Vita Karoli Magni* 30, ed. by G. Waitz after G.H. Pertz, 6th ed. overseen by O. Holder-Egger [hereafter ed. Waitz], MGH:SRGUS (Hanover, 1911), p. 34; and trans. Paul Edward Dutton, in *Charlemagne's Courtier: The Complete Einhard*, Readings in Medieval Civilizations and Cultures, 3 (Peterborough, Ont., 1998). See also Heinrich Fichtenau, *The Carolingian Empire: The Age of Charlemagne*, trans. Peter Munz (New York, 1964), pp. 42–43.

42. Ermoldus Nigellus, *In honorem Hludowici* 4, ed. Dümmler, MGH:PLAC 2, pp. 72–73.511–30.

43. Notker, *Gesta Karoli Magni* 2.8, ed. Haefele, pp. 60–61. On the case of Carloman, who died in 884, see *Annales Vedastini* 884, ed. B. von Simson, *Annales Xantenses et Annales Vedastini*, MGH:SRGUS (Hanover, 1909), p. 56; *Annales Fuldenses siue Annales regni Francorum orientalis* 884, ed. F. Kurze after G.H. Pertz [hereafter ed. Kurze], MGH:SRGUS (Hanover, 1891), p. 101.

44. Notker, *Gesta Karoli Magni* 2.8, ed. Haefele, p. 60.

45. Notker, *Gesta Karoli Magni* 2.15, ed. Haefele, pp. 79–80. On the *uenatio* in the Merovingian world, see Yitzhak Hen, *Culture and Religion in Merovingian Gaul, A.D. 481–751*, Cultures, Beliefs, and Traditions: Medieval and Early Modern Peoples, 1 (Leiden, 1995), pp. 216–219.

46. On the expectation of royal tallness, see Josiah C. Russell, "Tall Kings: The Height of Medieval English Kings," in Russell, *Twelfth Century Studies* (New York, 1978), pp. 62–75; previously printed in *The Mississippi Quarterly*, 10 (1957): 29–41.

47. Notker, *Gesta Karoli Magni* 2.15, ed. Haefele, p. 80.6.

48. Notker *Gesta Karoli Magni* 1.32, ed. Haefele, pp. 44–45.

49. Notker *Gesta Karoli Magni* 1.24, ed. Haefele, pp. 32–33.

50. *Vita Remigii episcopi Remensis*, ed. Bruno Krusch, MGH: Scriptores rerum Merovingicarum, 3 (Hanover, 1896), p. 322.

51. Theodulf, *carmen* 72, ed. Dümmler, MGH:PLAC 1, pp. 563–69.

52. *Capitulare de uillis* 40, ed. Boretius, MGH:Cap. 1, p. 86. *Etlehas* is a confusing reading, but Boretius, n. 54, allows that some German glossaries read "etliche" for a pair of swans.

    Some have speculated that this undated document may belong to Louis the Pious when he was king of Aquitaine, but like most scholars I take it to belong to Charlemagne and to come from the period prior to 800. See Klaus Verhein, "Studien zu den Quellen zum Reichsgut der Karolingerzeit," *Deutsches Archiv*, 10 (1954): 313–94; Theodor Mayer, "Das Capitulare de Villis," *Zeitschrift der Savigny Stiftung für Rechtsgeschichte*, Germanische Abteilung, 79 (1962): 1–31.

53. *Breuium exempla ad describendas res ecclesiasticas et fiscales* 25 and 31, ed. Boretius, MGH:Cap. 1, pp. 254.30 and 255.32.

54. *Capitulare de uillis* 13–14, ed. Boretius, MGH:Cap. 1, p. 84.

55. *Capitulare de uillis* 58, ed. Boretius, MGH:Cap. 1, p. 88.

56. Isidore, *Etymologiae* 12.7.48, ed. Lindsay.

57. See Cuono of St-Nabor, *carmen* line 11, "Conclamat notis sibi uocibus ingeminatis," ed. Karl Strecker, MGH:PLAC 5 (Berlin, 1937–39), p. 382 and trans. Ziomkowski, *Talking Animals*, p. 244.

58. Isidore, *Etymologiae* 12.7.48, ed. Lindsay. On the immortaility of the peacock, see Augustine, *De ciuitate dei*, 21.4, ed. Dombart and Kalb, 48: 762 and 21.7, 48: 769.

59. Apicius, *De re coquinaria* 6.5; J.M.C. Toynbee, *Animals in Roman Life and Art* (London, 1973), pp. 250–53; Augustine, *De ciuitate dei* 21.4, ed. Dombart and Kalb, 48: 762; Iris Origo, *The Merchant of Prato: Francesco di Marco Datini* (Harmondsworth, 1963; repr. 1979), p. 289.

60. Einhard, *Vita Karoli Magni* 24, ed. Waitz, p. 29. The Carolingian palace described by Hincmar of Rheims had four chief hunters and one falconer, though these were more than just suppliers of meat and were instead officers of the court administration. He also noted that there were wardens of the forests (*bersarii*), keepers of the kennels, hunters of beaver, and others. See Hincmar, *De ordine palatii* 5–6, ed. Thomas Gross and Rudolf Schieffer, MGH: Fontes iuris Germanici antiqui in usum scholarum separatim editi, 3 (Hanover, 1980), p. 64.278–79 and 282 and p. 76.395–98 and 407; the work is trans. by David Herlihy in Dutton, *Carolingian Civilization*, pp. 516–32.

61. See H.R. Loyn and J. Percival, *The Reign of Charlemagne: Documents on Carolingian Government and Administration*, Documents of Medieval History, 2

(London, 1975), p. 69, and R.P. Falkner, *Translations and Reprints from the Original Sources of European History*, 3.2, Statistical Documents of the Middle Ages (Philadelphia, 1907), p. 3: both translate "pro dignitatis causa" as "for the sake of ornament."

62. *Capitulare de uillis* 3, ed. Boretius, MGH:Cap. 1, p. 83.

63. Notker *Gesta Karoli Magni* 1.16, ed. Haefele, pp. 19–21.

64. Notker *Gesta Karoli Magni* 1.20, ed. Haefele, p. 27.12–13.

65. See Lorna Price, *The Plan of St. Gall in Brief* (Berkeley, 1982), which is based on the larger study of the same by Walter Horn and Ernest Born.

66. *Capitulare de uillis* 70, ed. Boretius, MGH:Cap. 1, pp. 90–91.

67. Walahfrid Strabo, *Liber de cultura hortorum* 1, ed. Dümmler, MGH:PLAC 2, p. 335.1. See also Walahfrid Strabo, *Hortulus*, trans. Raef Payne, commentary by Wilfrid Blunt (Pittsburgh, 1966).

68. See Notker, *Gesta Karoli Magni* 2.13, ed. Haefele, pp. 73–74.

69. Shakespeare played at a similar, but even more pointed political pastoralism in *Richard II* (III, iv, 29–107), in which the two gardeners speak of their garden as though it were like the political commonwealth of the wider world; both having noisome weeds, fair flowers choked off, and good herbs infested with bugs. Their solution was to return order to their model estate by force.

70. *Annales regni Francorum* 793 (the revised version), ed. by F. Kurze after G.H. Pertz [hereafter ed. Kurze], MGH:SRGUS (Hanover, 1895), p. 93.

71. Ermoldus, *In honorem Hludowici* 1, ed. Dümmler, MGH:PLAC 2, p. 11.197–98.

72. 3 Kings 10:22, 2 Par. 9:21.

73. For photographs of these, see Giuseppe Bovini, *Ravenna: Art and History* (Ravenna, 1978), p. 90 and J. Hubert, J. Porcher, and W.F. Volbach, *The Carolingian Renaissance*, trans. James Emmons, Stuart Gilbert, and Robert Allen (New York, 1970), plate 203, p. 222 or Friedrich Heer, *Charlemagne and His World* (New York, 1975), pp. 12–13.

74. See Charles Darwin, *The Origin of Species by Means of Natural Selection or the Preservation of Favoured Races in the Struggle for Life*, ed. with an introduction by J.W. Burrow (London, 1968), pp. 137–38 and Stephen Jay Gould, "Red Wings in the Sunset," in Gould, *Bully for Brontosaurus: Reflections in Natural History* (New York, 1992), pp. 219–22.

75. See Eriugena, *Periphyseon*, PL 122:749C and ed. Édouard Jeauneau, *Iohannis Scotti seu Eriugenae Periphyseon, Liber quartus*, in Corpus Christianorm: Continuatio Mediaevalis, 164 (Turnhout, 2000), p. 13 or ed. Jeauneau and trans. John J. O'Meara, *Iohannis Scotti Eriugenae Periphyseon (De Diuisione Naturae), Liber quartus*, Scriptores Latini Hiberniae, 13 (Dublin, 1995), p. 18 and p. 284 n. 27. See also Édouard Jeauneau, *Quatres thèmes Érigéniens*, Conférence Albert-le-Grand, 1974 (Montréal, 1978), pp. 66–69, and Jorge Luis Borges, "A Defense of the Kabbalah," trans. Eliot Weinberger, in Borges, *Selected Non-Fictions*, ed. Eliot Weinberger (New York, 1999), p. 86 n. 2.

76. *Rhythmi syllogae Sangallensis*, 76, ed. Karl Strecker, MGH:PLAC 4, pp. 610–612.

77. Theodulf, *carmen* 27 ("Ad Coruinianum"), ed. Dümmler, MGH:PLAC 1, p. 491.7–12.

78. See, in general, Paul A. Underwood, "The Fountain of Life in Manuscripts of the Gospels," *Dumbarton Oaks Papers*, 5 (1950): 42–138.

79. *Versus libris saeculi VIII adiecti* 7, ed. Dümmler, MGH:PLAC 1, p. 95.12–20.

80. On these birds, see Underwood, "The Fountain of Life," pp. 78–79. On the birds of creation, see also Ambrose, *Exameron* 5.14–15 (45–52), ed. C. Schenkl, in Corpus Scriptorum Ecclesiasticorum Latinorum, 32.1 (Prague, 1896), pp. 175–80.

81. For a color plate, see Mütherich and Gaehde, *Carolingian Painting*, plate 2.

82. The bells may be accounted for by Exod. 28:33–35 in which the priest wears a bell on his vestment so that its tinkling may be heard as he enters and leaves the Lord's presence in the sanctuary.

83. Toynbee, *Animals in Roman Life and Art*, p. 284, and Bryan Holme, *Creatures of Paradise: Animals in Art* (London, 1980), pp. 72–73.

84. Alcuin, *carmen* 23 ("O mea cella"), ed. Dümmler, MGH:PLAC 1, pp. 243–44. On the authorship of the poem, see Peter Godman, "Alcuin's Poetic Style and the Authenticity of *O mea cella*," *Studi Medievali*, 3rd ser. 20 (1979): 555–83.

85. *Karolus Magnus et Leo Papa*, ed. Dümmler, MGH:PLAC 1, pp. 369–70.137–76.

86. Ermoldus, *In honorem Hludowici* 3, ed. Dümmler, MGH:PLAC 2, p. 57.583–94.

87. Walahfrid Strabo, *De imagine Tetrici*, ed. Dümmler, MGH:PLAC 2, p. 373.107–109. And see also Michael W. Herren, "The 'De imagine Tetrici' of Walahfrid Strabo: Edition and Translation," *The Journal of Medieval Latin*, 1 (1991): 134–35, whose translation I do not follow here: I take it, for instance, that *amoena* qualifies *templa* and that the phrase *quondam tibi magnus* is explained by the next two lines of verse.

88. Walahfrid Strabo, *De imagine Tetrici*, ed. Dümmler, MGH:PLAC 2, p. 374.116–27.

89. Ovid, *Metamorphoses* 1.101–12. See also Arthur O. Lovejoy and George Boas, *Primitivism and Related Ideas in Antiquity* (1935; repr. New York, 1965) and George Boas, *Essays on Primitivism and Related Ideas in the Middle Ages* (1948; repr. New York, 1966).

90. See H. Houben, "*Visio cuiusdam pauperculae mulieris*: Überlieferung und Herkunft eines frühmittelalterliche Visionstextes (mit Neuedition)," *Zeitschrift für die Geschichte des Oberrheins* 124, NF 85 (1976): 41–42 and trans. Dutton, in *Carolingian Civilization*, pp. 203–204. See also Paul Edward Dutton, *The Politics of Dreaming in the Carolingian Empire*, Regents Studies in Medieval Culture, ed. Eugene Vance (Lincoln, Neb., 1994), pp. 67–74.

91. See G.C. Druce, "The Elephant in Medieval Legend and Art," *Archaeological Journal*, 76 (1919): 1–73.

92. In the Musée du Louvre. See Adolph Goldschmidt, *Die Elfenbeinskulpturen aus der Zeit der karolingischen und sächsischen Kaiser, viii.-xi. Jahrhundert*, 1 (Berlin, 1914; repr. Oxford, 1969), p. 77 and plate 158. Goldschmidt describes the creature beside the elephant as unidentified.

93. See Hubert et al., *The Carolingian Renaissance*, figs. 218–219, pp. 237–39 and 355.

94. For a plate, see Christopher de Hamel, *A History of Illuminated Manuscripts* (London, 1986), p. 50, plate 41. See also Henri Omont, *Peintures et initiales de la première Bible de Charles le Chauve* (Paris, 1911), plate XIV. On the Bible, see Paul Edward Dutton and Herbert L. Kessler, *The Poetry and Paintings of the First Bible of Charles the Bald*, in Recentiores: Later Latin Texts and Contexts, ed. James J. O'Donnell (Ann Arbor, 1997).

95. See Herbert L. Kessler, *The Illustrated Bibles from Tours*, Studies in Manuscript Illumination, 7 (Princeton, 1977), p. 23 and fig. 2; for a color photograph, see Hubert et al., *The Carolingian Renaissance*, p. 134, fig. 122.

96. See Toynbee, *Animals in Roman Life and Art*, pp. 37–38 and fig. 6 with the elephant as an imperial symbol on a denarius of Caesar. And see H.H. Scullard, *The Elephant in the Greek and Roman World* (Ithaca, N.Y., 1974). On the history of the elephant in the West, see Stephan Oettermann, *Die Schaulust am Elefanten: eine Elephantographia curiosa* (Frankfurt am Main, 1982), and on Charlemagne's elephant, pp. 97–99.

97. Einhard, *Vita Karoli Magni* 16, ed. Waitz, p. 19.

98. See F.W. Buckler, *Harunu'l-Rashid and Charles the Great*, Monographs of the Medieval Academy of America, 2 (Cambridge, Mass., 1931), p. 25.

99. Roger Collins, *Charlemagne* (Toronto, 1998), p. 152. In this regard it is suggestive that in 799 Charlemagne and his court were searching for a copy of Felix's debate with a Saracen, though perhaps the matter at issue was Felix of Urgel's controversial theology: see Alcuin, *epistola* 172, ed. Ernst Dümmler, MGH: Ep. 4 (Hanover, 1895; repr. Berlin, 1974), pp. 284.30–285.2.

100. *Annales regni Francorum* 801, ed. Kurze, pp. 114, 116.

101. *Annales regni Francorum* 802, ed. Kurze, p. 117.

102. Einhard, *Vita Karoli Magni* 16, ed. Waitz, p. 19.

103. *Annales regni Francorum* 810, ed. Kurze, p. 131. In 1746 J.H. Nunning told his friend J.H. Conhausen that he believed he had found the bones of Charlemagne's elephant along the Rhine: see *Commercii Litterarii dissertationes epistolicae historico-physico-curiosae clarissimorum Westphaliae duumvirorum Jodoci Hermanni Nunningii et Johannis Henrici Cohausen. . .*(Frankfurt am Main, 1746), letter 4, pp. 44–68. Whether these bones were those of Abul Abaz or some woolly mammoth is an open question. My thanks to Courtney Booker for drawing this report to my attention.

104. Buckler, *Harunu'l-Rashid and Charles the Great*, pp. 30–31.

105. And see also *Miracula et translatio Sancti Genesii martyris Hierosolymitani*, ed. G. Waitz, MGH: Scriptores 15.1 (Hanover, 1887), p. 160 and also edited in W. Wattenbach, "Die Uebertragung des Reliquien des h. Genesius nach Schienen," *Zeitschrift für Geschichte der Oberrheins*, 24 (1872): 8–21. The Reichenau author of this piece, writing between 822 and 838, said of Charlemagne's emissaries to Hārūn, "qui ab Aaron rege Saracenorum elefantem expetebant. . .," which echoes Einhard's description of Charlemagne's request.

106. See Buckler, *Harunu'l-Rashid and Charles the Great*; Richard Hodges, *Towns and Trade in the Age of Charlemagne* (London, 2000), pp. 35–67 and "Charlemagne's Elephant and the Beginnings of the Commodisation of Europe," *Acta archaeologica*, 59 (1988): 155–68. See also Michael McCormick, *Origins of the European Economy: Communications and Commerce, A.D. 300–900* (Cambridge, 2001), pp. 273, 513, 710.

107. On the collecting of exotic creatures at medieval courts, see K. Hauck, "Tiergarten im Pfalzbereich," in *Deutschen Königspfalzen: Beiträge zur ihrer historischen und archäologischen Erforschung*, in Veröffentlichungen des Max-Planck-Instituts für Geschichte, 11.1 (Göttingen, 1963), pp. 30–74.

108. Four centuries later the emperor Frederick II would assume the same demonstrative posture as king of beasts: see Ernst Kantorowicz, *Frederick the Second, 1194–1250*, trans. E.O. Lorimer (New York, 1931; repr. 1957), pp. 311, 315–316, 464, 609.

109. Charles the Bald would later possess camels, a gift of Mohammed I, the emir of Córdoba: see *Annales Bertiniani* 865, ed. F. Grat et al., in *Annales de Saint-Bertin*, p. 124.

110. See Notker, *Gesta Karoli Magni* 2.8–9, ed. Haefele, pp. 61–63. The reference to monkeys was added by Notker to the report of Hārūn's gift of an elephant.

111. Notker, *Gesta Karoli Magni* 2.8–9, ed. Haefele, pp. 60, 63–65. The emperor Nicephorus I also sent and received gifts from Hārūn: see *The History of al-Tabarī* 30, trans. and annotated by C.E. Bosworth (Albany, 1989), p. 264.

112. See Einhard, *Vita Karoli Magni* 16, ed. Waitz, p. 19; *Annales regni Francorum* 801 and 807, ed. Kurze, pp. 116 and 123, "pallia sirica."

113. Buckler, *Harunu'l-Rashid*, p. 34.

114. See, for instance, the poem about the gown of Louis the Pious worked on by Empress Judith, which was donated by Charles the Bald to Pope Nicholas I: "Hoc peplum" ed. and trans. in Paul Edward Dutton, "Evidence that Dubthach's Priscian Codex Once Belonged to Eriugena," in *From Athens to Chartres: Neoplatonism and Medieval Thought. Studies in Honour of Édouard Jeauneau*, ed. Haijo Jan Westra (Leiden, 1992), pp. 18–19.

115. See Notker, *Gesta Karoli Magni* 2.9, ed. Haefele, p. 63 (a gift of Frisian cloaks among others).

116. See Schramm and Mütherich, *Denkmale der deutschen Könige und Kaiser*, p. 95; the edition of the text having been worked on by Bernhard Bischoff. Édouard Jeauneau provided me with invaluable advice on the meaning of "diaspro" and "dio[prasium]"; for the latter he suggested that "diaprasium" would be a better reading. Johannes Heil kindly pointed me to this text.

117. See n. 111 above and the several uses of *pallia* for cloths made of silk threads and as royal cloaks in Notker, *Gesta Karoli Magni* 1.28, 1.34, ed. Haefele, pp. 39.3, 46–47.

118. The first two items in the list of Odo's removals were specifically cited as gifts by the kings Charles and Louis: see Schramm and Mütherich, *Denkmale der deutschen Könige und Kaiser*, p. 95.

119. See Ekkehard IV, *Casus sancti Galli* I, ed. I. von Arx, in MGH:SS (Hanover, 1829), pp. 88.45–89.5.

120. *Dicuili Liber de mensura orbis terrae* 7.35, ed. Tierney, p. 82.

121. An event recreated in the incised Susanna Crystal made in the mid-ninth century for Lothar II: see Genevra Kornbluth, *Engraved Gems of the Carolingian Empire* (University Park, Penn., 1995), pp. 31–48.

122. Agnellus, *Liber Pontificalis ecclesiae Ravennatis* 94, ed. O. Holder-Egger, MGH: Scriptores rerum Langobardicarum et Italicarum, saec. VI–IX (Hanover, 1878), p. 338; and trans. in Dutton, *Carolingian Civilization*, p. 56; Walahfrid Strabo, *De imagine Tetrici*, ed. Dümmler, MGH:PLAC 2, p. 371.30–45.

123. *Capitulare de uillis* 36 and 51, ed. Boretius, MGH:Cap. 1, pp. 86 and 88.

124. *Leges Burgundionum*, Liber constitutionum XLVI: De his qui tensuras ad occidendos lupos pousuerit, ed. L.R. De Salis, MGH: Legum sectio 1, Legum Nationum Gemanicarum 2.1 (Hanover, 1892), pp. 76–77 and trans. Katherine Fischer Drew, *The Burgundian Code* (Philadelphia, 1972), p. 53. See also Michel Rouche, "The Early Middle Ages in the West," in *A History of Private Life*, vol. 1: From Pagan Rome to Byzantium, ed. Paul Veyne and trans. Arthur Goldhammer (Cambridge, Mass., 1987), pp. 488–90, and Salisbury, *The Beast Within*, pp. 67–70.

125. *De uillis* 69, ed. Boretius, MGH:Cap. 1, p. 89.

126. *Capitulare Aquisgranense* 8, ed. Boretius, MGH:Cap. 1, p. 171.

127. For an example of this, see Hrabanus Maurus, *Homiliae in Evangelia et epistolas* 23, PL 110:187D6–188A1, commenting on John 10:12.

128. Frotharius, *epistola* 1, ed. K. Hampe, MGH:Ep. 5, p. 277.

129. *Rhythmi de pugna Fontanetica*, stanza 14, ed. Dümmler, MGH:PLAC 2, p. 139; and trans. in Dutton, *Carolingian Civilization*, pp. 332–33.

130. Adrevald, *Miraculorum sancti Benedicti liber primus*, PL 124:943D12-944C1 and see also the partial edition of O. Holder-Egger, MGH:SS 15.1, pp. 478–97.

131. Frotharius, *epistola* 32, ed. Hampe, MGH:Ep. 5, pp. 297–98.

132. *Annales Bertiniani* 846, ed. Grat et al., pp. 51–52.

133. See Dutton and Kessler, *Poetry and Paintings*, p. 63 and fig. 18 and Herbert L. Kessler, "An Apostle in Armor and the Mission of Carolingian Art," *Arte medievale*, 2nd ser., 4 (1990): 17–39. And see Theodulf, *carmen* 41, ed. Dümmler, MGH:PLAC 1, p. 535.97–98.

134. See Gen. 49:27; Ezech. 22:27; Matt. 7:15. See also Salisbury, *The Beast Within*, pp. 130–31.

135. *Sancti Odilonis abbatis Cluniacensis V de uita beati Maioli abbatis libellus*, ed. M. Marrier and A. Duchêne, PL 142:961–62; and trans. Paul Edward Dutton, in *Medieval Saints: A Reader*, ed. Mary-Ann Stouck (Peterborough, Ont., 1999), pp. 263–64.

136. See, for instance, Ermoldus, *In honorem Hludowici* 1, ed. Dümmler, MGH:PLAC 2, p. 6.57–58, speaking of the treacherous Basques, and *Annales Xantenses* 865, ed. B. von Simson, MGH:SRGUS, p. 24, which called Hugo, who succeeded Gunthar as bishop of Mainz, "tirranicus Hugo. . .non ut pastor, sed ceu *lupus rapax* gregem Dei inuasit"; and cf. *Annales Xantenses* 869, pp. 27–28. The poetry of Sedulius Scottus is also filled with this imagery.

137. Ermoldus, *In honorem Hludowici* 4, ed. Dümmler, MGH:PLAC 2, p. 68.370.

138. See *Annales Bertiniani* 858, ed. Grat et al., p. 76; Rodulfus Glaber, *Historiae* 2.8, ed. John France, *Rodulfi Glabri Historiarum libri quinque: Rodulfus Glaber, The Five Books of the Histories* (Oxford, 1989), p. 66. In general, see Gherardo Ortalli, "Natura, storia e mitogafia del lupo nel Medioevo," *La cultura*, 11.3–4 (1973): 257–311 and Salisbury, *The Beast Within*, pp. 162–63.

139. Bernhard Bischoff, "Ein Brief Julians von Toledo über Rhythmen, metrische Dichtung und Prosa," in Bischoff, *Mittelalterliche Studien: Ausgewählte Aufsätze zur Schriftkunde und Literaturgeschichte*, 3 vols. (Stuttgart, 1959–81), 1:296 [288–98]; Ziolkowski, *Talking Animals*, pp. 31, 48.

140. Alcuin, *carmen* 49, ed. Dümmler, MGH:PLAC 1, p. 262 and see Zilokowski, *Talking Animals*, pp. 241–44 for a translation and pp. 48–49 for commentary.

141. Dungal, *epistola* 1, ed. Dümmler, MGH:Ep. 4, p. 571.4–5 and see p. 299 n. 22 with other references to the same popular proverb.

142. *Propositiones Alcuini* 18, PL 101:1149D–1150A.

143. Alcuin, *epistola* 181, ed. Dümmler, MGH:Ep. 4, pp. 299–300.

144. Alcuin, *epistola* 174, ed. Dümmler, MGH:Ep. 4, p. 289.5.

145. Alcuin, *carmen* 45, ed. Dümmler, MGH:PLAC 1, p. 258.57–58.

146. Heito, *Visio Wettini* 11, ed. Dümmler, MGH:PLAC 2, p. 271 and Walahfrid Strabo, *Visio Wettini*, ed. Dümmler, MGH:PLAC 2, pp. 318-19.446–65. And see also, Dutton, *The Politics of Dreaming*, pp. 63–67.

147. See Simon Coupland, "The Rod of God's Wrath or the People of God's Wrath? The Carolingians' Theology of the Viking Invasions," *Journal of Ecclesiastical History*, 42 (1991): 535–54.

148. See *799: Kunst und Kultur der Karolingerzeit. Karl der Große und Papst Leo III. in Paderborn*, vol. 1: Katalog der Austellung, Paderborn 1999, ed. Christoph Stiegemann and Matthias Wemhoff (Mainz, 1999), pp. 112–113 and fig. II.70; Schramm and Mütherich, *Denkmale der deutschen Könige und Kaiser*, p. 115 and fig. 5; Peter Lasko, *Ars Sacra, 800–1200*, 2nd ed. (New Haven, 1994), p. 9; S. Beissel, "Die Wölfin des Aachener Münsters," *Zeitschrift des Aachener Geschichtsverein*, 12 (1890): 317–20.

149. On Christ trampling upon the beasts, see Paul Meyvaert, "A New Perspective on the Ruthwell Cross: Ecclesia and Vita Monastica," in *The Ruthwell Cross: Papers from the Colloquium Sponsored by the Index of Christian Art, Princeton University, 8 December 1989*, Index of Christian Art: Occasional Papers, 1, ed. Brendan Cassidy (Princeton, 1992), pp. 124–29.

150. *Karolus Magnus et Leo Papa*, ed. Dümmler, MGH:PLAC 1, p. 370.166.

151. See Schramm and Mütherich, *Denkmale der deutschen Könige und Kaiser*, p. 137 and fig. 57.

152. Alcuin, *carmen* 75.II, ed. Dümmler, MGH:PLAC 1, p. 296.7-8. This recalls Ps. 148:10 in which all God's creatures were called on to praise him.

153. Notker, *Gesta Karoli Magni* 2.12, ed. Haefele, p. 75. Sedulius Scottus called on the emperor Louis II of Italy to hunt down the Moors, the Saracen "wolves" harassing Italy: see Sedulius Scottus, *carmen* 25, ed. Traube, MGH:PLAC 3, pp. 191–92.55–58. Eriugena called the Jew a "jackdaw" (*graculus*): Eriugena, *carmen* 4.2.1, ed. Traube, MGH:PLAC 3, p. 545. On

this see, Paul Edward Dutton, "Eriugena, the Royal Poet," in *Jean Scot Écrivain: Actes du IVe Colloque international, Montréal, 28 août–2 septembre 1983* (Montréal, 1986), pp. 76–77.

154. Theodulf, *carmen* 25, ed. Dümmler, MGH:PLAC 1, p. 488.214–218. On this Scot, see Bernhard Bischoff, "Theodulf und die Ire Cadac-Andreas," in *Mittelalterliche Studien* 2:19–25.

155. Theodulf, *carmen* 35, ed. Dümmler, MGH:PLAC 1, p. 527.7.

156. See Peter Godman, *Poets and Emperors: Frankish Politics and Carolingian Poetry* (Oxford, 1987), p. 41.

157. *De conuersione Saxonum*, ed. Dümmler, MGH:PLAC 1, p. 381.47–55.

158. Gottschalk, *carmen* 1, stanza 16, ed. Karl Strecker, MGH:PLAC 6.1 (Munich, 1978), p. 91; and see Peter Godman, *Poetry of the Carolingian Renaissance*, pp. 236–37 stanza 16.

159. Walahfrid Strabo, *De imagine Tetrici*, ed. Dümmler, MGH:PLAC 2, p. 378.250–55.

160. See "Thunder and Hail over the Carolingian Countryside," chapter 7 in this book. Agobard, *De grandine* 16, ed. L. Van Acker, in *Agobardi Lugdunensis Opera Omnia*, CCCM 52 (Turnhout, 1981), pp. 14.1–15.27 (PL 104:157C4–158C3). See *Annales regni Francorum* 810, ed. Kurze, p. 182; *Capitulare missorum Aquisgranense primum* 4, ed. Boretius, MGH:Cap. 1, p. 153.11–12; *Annales Sithienses* 810, ed. G. Waitz, in MGH:SS 13 (Hanover, 1881), p. 37; and Paschasius Radbertus, *Epitaphium Arsenii* 2.1, ed. E. Dümmler, in *Philosophische und historische Abhandlungen der königlichen Akademie der Wissenschaften zu Berlin*, 2 (1900), p. 61.

161. Einhard, *Vita Karoli Magni* 32, ed. Waitz, p. 36 and chapter 4 in this book.

162. See the Utrecht Psalter, fol. 30v, in De Wald, *The Illustrations of the Utrecht Psalter*, plate 49 and the ivory book cover of the Schweizerisches Landesmuseum of Zurich, in Hubert et al., *The Carolingian Renaissance*, fig. 228, p. 248. Walahfrid Strabo, *De imagine Tetrici*, ed. Dümmler, MGH:PLAC 2, p. 371.44–45, noted that the proud demonstrated their pride by being represented in chariots and seated on horses.

163. See *Marino Marini: Complete Works*, introduction by Herbert Read, general text by Patrick Waldberg, catalogues and notes by G. Di San Lazzaro (New York, 1970), pp. 181–220.

Chapter 3   Karolus Magnus Scriptor

1. Erich Weniger, "Das deutsche Bildungswesen in Frühmittelalter," *Historische Vierteljahrschrift*, 30 (1936): 486 [446–92] regarded it as a fairy tale that Charlemagne might have been illiterate, whereas Paul Pascal, "Charlemagne's Latin," *Neophilologus*, 54 (1970): 20 [19–21] regarded it as a certainty: "It is certain, from Einhard's statement later in chapter xxv of the *Vita Karoli*, that Charlemagne was illiterate." The weakness of Pascal's case is that it was not based on substantial knowledge of Carolingian cultural history and was so criticized by Richard R. Ring, "Renovatio Karoli Latinitatis," *Res Publica Litterarum*, 1 (1978): 263–71.

2. My many thanks to John Shinners who first raised the problem with me as he was about to enter a classroom and discuss with his students the issue of Charlemagne's literacy.

3. See such fundamental studies as Ruth Finnegan, *Literacy and Orality: Studies in the Technology of Communication* (Oxford, 1988); Jack Goody, *The Domestication of the Savage Mind* (Cambridge, 1977); Carlo M. Cipolla, *Literacy and Development in the West* (Harmondsworth, 1969); Michael T. Clanchy, *From Memory to Written Record: England, 1066–1307* (London, 1979), pp. 175–91, 202–20 and repr. as "Literate and Illiterate; Hearing and Seeing: England 1066–1307," in *Literacy and Social Development in the West: A Reader*, ed. Harvey J. Graff (Cambridge, 1981), pp. 14–45; Brian Stock, *The Implications of Literacy: Written Language and Models of Interpretation in the Eleventh and Twelfth Centuries* (Princeton, 1983); Rosamond McKitterick, *The Carolingians and the Written Word* (Cambridge, 1989); Mathew Innes, "Memory, Orality and Literacy in an Early Medieval Society," *Past & Present*, 158 (1998): 3–36. I have also learned much from my discussions with David Knechtges about "literacy" in general and the situation at the Tang court (seventh to tenth centuries) where a Chinese koine, he suggested, probably served as the equivalent of court Latin.

4. Roger Collins, *Charlemagne* (Toronto, 1998), pp. 1–2, 120.

5. *The Life of Charlemagne* 25, trans. Paul Edward Dutton, in *Charlemagne's Courtier: The Complete Einhard* (Peterborough, Ont., 1998), p. 32; trans. from *Einhardi Vita Karoli Magni*, ed. by G. Waitz after G.H. Pertz [hereafter ed. Waitz] and overseen by O. Holder-Egger, in MGH: Scriptores rerum Germanicarum in usum scholarum (Hanover, 1911; repr. 1965), p. 30.

6. Edward Gibbon, *The History of the Decline and Fall of the Roman Empire* 49, ed. J.B. Bury in 7 volumes (New York, 1914; repr. 1974), 5:305.

7. Gibbon, *The History of the Decline and Fall* 49, 5:305 n. 107: "The moderns have perverted and corrected this obvious meaning. . . ."

8. F.L. Ganshof, "Einhard, biographer of Charlemagne," trans. Janet Sondheimer in F.L. Ganshof, *The Carolingians and the Frankish Monarchy: Studies in Carolingian History* (Ithaca, N.Y, 1971), p. 8.

9. Friedrich Heer, *Charlemagne and His World* (New York, 1975), p. 21 and see p. 28. The charter shown is 84a in MGH: Diplomata Karolinorum, vol. 1: Pippini, Carlomani, Caroli Magni Diplomata, ed. Engelbert Mühlbacher (Munich, 1979), pp. 120–22.

10. Einhard, *Vita Karoli Magni* 1, ed. Waitz, pp. 2–4.

11. Ian Wood, "Administration, Law, and Culture in Merovingian Gaul," in *The Uses of Literacy in Early Medieval Europe*, ed. Rosamond McKitterick (Cambridge, 1990), p. 67 [63–81]. For the charters, see Albert Bruckner and Robert Marichal, *Chartae Latinae Antiquiores: Facsimile Edition of the Latin Charters prior to the Ninth Century*, part 13: France, 1 (Zurich, 1981), no. 552 (Clothair II), pp. 16–19; no. 554 (Dagobert I), pp. 22–25; no. 555 (Clovis II), pp. 26–27; part 14: France, 2 (Zurich, 1982), no. 583 (Childebert III), pp. 38–41; no. 587 (Childebert III, but the autograph of Dagobert), pp. 55–57; no. 588 (Chilperic II), pp. 58–62; no. 593 (Chilperic II), pp. 80–82; part 17: France V (Zurich, 1984), no. 654 (Childebert III), pp. 60–63.

12. Gregory of Tours, *Liber historiarum* 5.44, ed. Bruno Krusch and Wilhelm Levison, in MGH: Scriptores reum Merovingicarum 1.1 (Hanover, 1951), p. 254 and see the manuscript representations of these letters on p. 255; Suetonius, *Vitae Caesarum*, Diuus Claudius 41.3 and D. Norberg, *La poésie latine rythmique du Haut Moyen Age* (Stockholm, 1954), pp. 31–40.

13. Gregory of Tours, *Liber historiarum* 6.24, ed. Krusch and Levison, p. 291.

14. Wood, "Administration, Law, and Culture in Merovingian Gaul," in *The Uses of Literacy in Early Medieval Europe*, p. 67.

15. See Pierre Riché, "Le renouveau culturel à la cour de Pépin III," *Francia*, 2 (1974): 59–70 and repr. in Riché, *Instruction et vie religieuse dans le Haut Moyen Age*, Variorum Reprints, CS 245 (London, 1981), item 11. See also Donald Bullough, *Carolingian Renewal: Sources and Heritage* (Manchester, 1991), pp. 125–27.

16. "Directions for Making a Birth-day Song," in *Collected Poems of Jonathan Swift*, ed. Joseph Horrell, vol. 2 (London, 1958), p. 550 and aptly quoted by Rosamond McKitterick, *The Carolingians and the Written Word*, p. 244.

17. See Pierre Riché, *Education and Culture in the Barbarian West: Sixth through Eighth Centuries*, trans. John J. Contreni (Columbia, S.C., 1976), p. 440 and n. 507.

18. See Pepin III's charter (no. 8) from Compiègne 755, ed. Mühlbacher, in MGH: Diplomata Karolinorum 1, p. 13: "Propterea in nostra mercede et remedio animae domini genitoris nostri Karoli donamus ipso loco et castello ad monasterium beati domni Dioninsiae, ubi enotriti fuimus. . ."; and Riché, "Le renouveau culturel à la court de Pepin III," pp. 61–62. Still a great deal rests on that one word, "enotriti." Max Manitius, *Geschichte der Lateinische Literatur des Mittelalters*, vol. 1: Von Justinian bis zur Mitte des Zehnten Jahrhunderts (Munich, 1911; repr. 1965), p. 244 said: "Pippin konnte nicht schreiben," but does not explain his reasoning.

19. See *Versus libris saeculi VIII adiecti* 1 (second stanza), ed. Ernst Dümmler, MGH: Poetae Latini Aevi Carolini 1 (Berlin, 1881; repr. 1964), p. 89.

20. See Riché, "Le renouveau culturel," p. 69.

21. Pachasius Radbertus, *Vita Adalhardi* 7, ed. G.H. Pertz, in MGH: Scriptores 2 (Hanover, 1829), p. 525: "Qui cum esset regali prosapia, Pippini magni regis nepos, Caroli consobrinus augusti, inter palatii tirocinia omni mundi prudentia eruditus, una cum terrarum principe magistris adhibitus . . ."; and trans. Allen Cabaniss, *Charlemagne's Cousins: Contemporary Lives of Adalard and Wala* (Syracuse, 1967), p. 29.

In the ninth-century hagiography of Charlemagne's illegitimate son Hugh the term *in tyrocinio litterari* was employed of his education, presumably to distinguish it from the normal meaning of *tirocinium* as referring to military recruits: see J. van der Straeten, "Vie inédite de saint Hugues, évêque de Rouen," *Analecta Bollandiana*, 87 (1969): 236 [215–60].

22. See Pachasius Radbertus, *Vita Adalhardi* 7, ed. G.H. Pertz, in MGH:SS 2, p. 525. And see Régine Le Jan, "Frankish Giving of Arms and Rituals of Power: Continuity and Change in the Carolingian Period," in *Rituals of Power from Late Antiquity to the Early Middle Ages*, ed. Frans Theuws and Janet L. Nelson (Leiden, 2000), pp. 282–91 [281–309].

23. Ardo, *Vita Benedicti Abbatis Annianensis et Indensis* 1, ed. G. Waitz, MGH:SS 15.1 (Hanover, 1887), p. 201: "Hic pueriles gerentem annos prefatum filium suum in aula gloriosi Pipini regis reginae tradidit inter scolares nutriendum . . ."; also trans. Judith R. Ginsburg with Donna L. Boutelle, in *Carolingian Civilization: A Reader*, ed. Paul Edward Dutton, 2nd ed. (Peterborough, Ont., 2004), pp. 176–98.

24. On military training as a stage of education, see McKitterick, *The Carolingians and the Written Word*, pp. 218–219.

25. See J.M. Wallace-Hadrill, *The Frankish Church* (Oxford, 1983), pp. 176–77, 190–91.

26. Einhard, *Vita Karoli Magni* 26 and 4, ed. Waitz, pp. 30–31, 6–7. On the issue of the verb "orare," which Einhard used to describe Charlemagne's ability to speak Latin, see Michel Richter, "Die Sprachenpolitik Karls des Großen," *Sprachwissenschaft*, 7 (1982), pp. 418–419 [412–37]. *Orare* would fit with Charlemagne's early memorization and recitation of Latin prayers.

27. Trans. Dutton in *Charlemagne's Courtier*, p. 28 from Einhard, *Vita Karoli Magni* 19, ed. Waitz, p. 23. Charlemagne's son Hugh did learn to read and studied the Liberal Arts and Catholic faith at St-Denis: see van der Straeten, "Vie inédite de saint Hugues, évêque de Rouen," pp. 236–37.

28. *Epistola Generalis* (786–800), ed. Boretius, MGH: Capitularia 1 (Hanover, 1883), p. 80.27–28. For a translation by D.C. Munro, see Dutton, *Carolingian Civilization*, pp. 91–92.

29. See Franz Brunhölzl, *Histoire de la littérature latine du Moyen Âge*, 1: *De Cassidore à la fin de la renaissance Carolingienne*, vol. 2: *L'époque carolingienne*, trans. Henri Rochais (Turnhout, 1991), pp. 12–13, 29–30. The *Vita Alcuini abbatis sancti Martini Turonensis*, ed. W. Arndt, in MGH:SS 15.1, p. 184, also claimed that Alcuin taught Charles the Liberal Arts. On the specific form of Charles's grammatical instruction, see Bullough, *Carolingian Renewal*, pp. 134–35.

30. See, for instance, Einhard, *Vita Karoli Magni* 25, ed. Waitz, p. 30; Alcuin, *epistolae* 143, 145, 155, 170, 172, ed. Ernst Dümmler, MGH: Epistolae 4 (Hanover, 1895; repr. Berlin, 1974), pp. 226–27, 232, 250–53, 280, 284–85. Dungal learned that Charlemagne had sent a letter to the abbot of St-Denis in which he inquired about eclipses and so he prepared an opinion on the matter: see Dungal, *epistola* 1, ed. Dümmler, MGH:Ep. 4, pp. 570–78. On that letter, see Bruce Stanfield Eastwood, "The Astronomy of Macrobius in Carolingian Europe: Dungal's letter of 811 to Charles the Great," *Early Medieval Europe*, 3 (1994): 117–34, and ch. 4 in this book.

31. See ch. 6 and appendix 2, in this book: Pepin the Hunchback was born ca. 770, Charles ca. 772–73, Rotrude in 775, Carloman (renamed Pepin) in 777, and Louis the Pious in 778.

32. Gottschalk noted this rare word from the *Vita Karoli Magni* in his grammatical studies, though in the Bern manuscript the word and its definition are separated by other glosses. See Gottschalk, *Opuscula de rebus grammaticis* 2, nos. 111 and 120, ed. D.C. Lambot, *Oeuvres théologiques et grammaticales de Godescalc d'Orbais* (Louvain, 1945), pp. 489–90. John Contreni kindly pointed out to me this strange transposition of glosses.

33. On the vexed question of what *orare* means here, see Richter, "Die Sprachenpolitik Karls des Großen," pp. 418–419, who would understand "to pray." But Einhard's comment on Charlemagne's inability to speak much Greek in contrast to his Latin achievement may suggest that more than just prayer in Latin was meant.

34. Donald Bullough, *Carolingian Renewal*, pp. 134–35, and see Roger Wright, "The Conceptual Distinction between Latin and Romance: Invention or Evolution?" in *Latin and the Romance Languages in the Early Middle Ages*, ed. Roger Wright (University Park, Penn., 1991), pp. 108–109 [103–113].

35. Einhard, *Vita Karoli Magni* 25, ed. Waitz, p. 30.

36. See Walter Berschin, *Greek Letters and the Latin Middle Ages from Jerome to Nicholas of Cusa*, trans. Jerold C. Frakes (Washington, D.C., 1980), pp. 102–13 and Édouard Jeauneau, "Jean Scot Érigène et le Grec," *Archivum Latinitatis Medii Aevi (Bulletin du Cange)*, 41 (1979): 5–50 and repr. in Jeauneau, *Études Érigéniennes* (Paris, 1987), pp. 85–132.

37. Suetonius, *Vitae Caesarum*, Diuus Augustus 89.1, and not in this instance Diuus Titus 3.2 as in Richter, "Die Sprachenpolitik Karls des Großen," pp. 417–418. On the use of Suetonius in the Carolingian age, see Matthew Innes, "The Classical Tradition in the Carolingian Renaissance: Ninth-Century Encounters with Suetonius," *International Journal of the Classical Tradition*, 3 (1997): 265–82.

38. For instance, according to the *Royal Frankish Annals*, in 757 the Emperor Constantine sent an organ to Pepin, presumably with Byzantine experts; in 767 the Greeks joined the Latins in a great council at Gentilly, and so on; see *Annales regni Francorum*, ed. by F. Kurze after G.H. Pertz [hereafter ed. Kurze], in MGH:SRGUS (Hanover, 1895), pp. 15–16, 24–25. See also Riché, "Le renouveau culturel," pp. 67–68; Berschin, *Greek Letters*, pp. 114–115; and Michael McCormick, "Diplomacy and the Carolingian Encounter with Byzantium down to the Accession of Charles the Bald," in *Eriugena: East and West. Papers of the Eighth International Colloquium of the Society for the Promotion of Eriugenian Studies, Chicago and Notre Dame, 18–20 October, 1991*, ed. Bernard McGinn and Willemien Otten (Notre Dame, 1994), pp. 15–48.

39. But see Pascal, "Charlemagne's Latin," who does just that.

40. See Ganshof, "The Use of the Written Word in Charlemagne's Administration," in Ganshof, *The Carolingians and the Frankish Monarchy*, pp. 125–42 and Janet L. Nelson, "Literacy in Carolingian Government," in *The Uses of Literacy in Early Medieval Europe*, pp. 258–96.

41. See Peter Godman, *Poets and Emperors: Frankish Politics and Carolingian Poetry* (Cambridge, 1987), pp. 38–92.

42. See Alcuin, *carmen* 4, ed. Dümmler, MGH:PLAC 1, pp. 221–22.36–64. On the date of the poem, see Bullough, *Carolingian Renewal*, pp. 131–32 and 153 n. 30.

43. *Libellus synodalis* (Paris, 825), ed. A. Werminghoff, MGH: Concilia aevi Karolini 1.2 (Hanover, 1908), p. 481.31. See Paul Meyvaert, "Medieval Notions of Publication: The 'unpublished' *Opus Caroli regis contra synodum* and the Council of Frankfort (794)," *The Journal of Medieval Latin*, 12 (2002): 78–89.

44. Einhard, *Vita Karoli Magni* 24, ed. Waitz, p. 30. See also Ring, "Renovatio Karoli Latinitatis," p. 264.
45. See J.K. Bostock, *A Handbook of Old High German Literature*, 2nd ed. rev. by K.C. King and D.R. McLintock (Oxford, 1976), pp. 136–68.
46. Hincmar of Rheims saw a copy of the work in the court library: see *Opusculum LV capitulorum*, Patrologia Latina 126, col. 360 and Ann Freeman, "Carolingian Orthodoxy and the Fate of the Libri Carolini," *Viator*, 16 (1985): 65–108. I would here like to thank Paul Meyvaert and Ann Freeman for exchanging ideas with me on the state of the problem.
47. On these notes and the manuscript, see *Opus Caroli regis contra synodum (Libri Carolini)*, ed. Ann Freeman with Paul Meyvaert, in MGH:Con., vol. 2 (Supplementum) (Hanover, 1998), pp. 48–50, 583, and plates 11a–b; Ann Freeman, "Further Studies in the *Libri Carolini*: III. The Marginal Notes in Vaticanus Latinus 7207," *Speculum*, 46 (1971): 597–612; Wilhelm Levison, *England and the Continent in the Eighth Century: The Ford Lectures delivered in the University of Oxford in the Hilary Term*, 1943 (Oxford, 1946), p. 156; Bullough, *Carolingian Renewal*, p. 145. There have been many who have doubted that the notes contain Charlemagne's comments: see A. Mentz, *Die Tironischen Noten* (Berlin, 1942), p. 64; Heinrich Fichtenau, "Karl der Grosse und das Kaisertum," *Mitteilungen des Instituts für österreichische Geschichtsforschung*, 61 (1953): 276; David N. Dumville, review, *Journal of Ecclesiastical History*, 51 (2000): 601 [600–603].
48. See Paul Meyvaert, "Medieval Notions of Publication."
49. A similar case of Tironian notes being used to comment on and correct as discretely as possible a finished royal manuscript can be found in Paris, Mazarine 561, the royal copy of Eriugena's translation of the *Ambigua ad Iohannem* of Maximus the Confessor: see Édouard Jeauneau, ed., *Maximi Confessoris Ambigua ad Iohannem iuxta Iohannis Scotti Eriugenae latinam interpretationem*, Corpus Christianorum: Series Graeca, 18 (Turnhout, 1988), p. lxxvi.
50. The text is, in fact, a corrected one and hundreds of erasures are evident. On the issue of (instantaneous) translation in the ninth century, see Michel Banniard, "Language and Communication in Carolingian Europe," in *The New Cambridge Medieval History*, vol. 2: *c. 700–c. 900*, ed. Rosamond McKitterick (Cambridge, 1995), p. 700 [695–708] and Rosamond McKitterick, *The Frankish Church and the Carolingian Reforms, 789–895* (London, 1977), p. 191.
51. See ch. 106, in *Asser's Life of King Alfred together with the Annals of Saint Neots Erroneously Ascribed to Asser*, ed. William Henry Stevenson (Oxford, 1904; repr. 1959), p. 95; and see *Alfred the Great: Asser's "Life of King Alfred" and other Contemporary Sources*, trans. Simon Keynes and Michael Lapidge (Harmondsworth, 1984), p. 110: "I have explained this concern for learning how to read among the young and old to give some idea of the character of King Alfred." Those were effectively the last words of Asser's work. Marie Schütt argued that Asser knew Einhard's biography: see Schütt, "The Literary Form of Asser's 'Vita Alfredi,' " *English Historical Review*, 72 (1957): 209–20.

52. 22, in *Asser's Life of King Alfred*, ed. Stevenson, pp. 19–20.

53. 75–77, in *Asser's Life of King Alfred*, ed. Stevenson, pp. 57–63.

54. 87, 81, in *Asser's Life of King Alfred*, ed. Stevenson, pp. 73, 67–68.

55. 88–89, in *Asser's Life of King Alfred*, ed. Stevenson, pp. 73–75. I am grateful for the advice Michael Lapidge gave me on this point.

56. See, for instance, the dedication of Smaragdus's *Via Regia*, ed. Ernst Dümmler, MGH:Ep. 4, p. 533: "Nomen illi 'Via regia' dedimus, et tibi regi feliciter legendum direximus, ut uelut per regia currens itinera ad regem regum et ad regiam feliciter peruenias patriam."

57. Bernhard Bischoff suspected that a circular letter had been sent out to collect these books for the royal library: see Bischoff, "Die Hofbibliothek Karls des Großen," in Bischoff, *Mittelalterliche Studien: Ausgewählte Aufsätze zur Schriftkunde und Literaturgeschichte*, 3 vols. (Stuttgart, 1959–81), 3:154–55 [149–69]; trans. as "The Court Library of Charlemagne," in Bischoff, *Manuscripts and Libraries in the Age of Charlemagne*, trans. Michael Gorman, Cambridge Studies in Palaeography and Codicology, 1 (Cambridge, 1994), p. 61 [56–75]. On the issue of the circular letter, see Bullough, *Carolingian Renewal*, pp. 139–40.

58. On the "will," see Einhard, *Vita Karoli Magni* 33, ed. Waitz, pp. 37–41 and Matthew Innes, "Charlemagne's Will: Piety, Politics and the Imperial Succession," *English Historical Review*, 112 (1997): 833–55. See also Bernhard Bischoff, "Die Hofbibliothek Karls des Großen," *Mittelalterliche Studien* 3:149–69; and trans. as "The Court Library of Charlemagne," in Bischoff, *Manuscripts and Libraries in the Age of Charlemagne*, trans. Gorman, pp. 56–75. See also the revision of Bischoff's claim (pp. 218–219 in *Manuscripts and Libraries*) that Berlin, Diez. B 66 contains the actual library list of the classical volumes in Charlemagne's library: Claudia Villa, "Die Horazüberlieferung und die 'Bibliothek Karls des Grossen': zum Werkverzeichnis der Handschrift Berlin, Diez. B 66," *Deutsches Archiv für Erforschung des Mittelalters*, 51 (1995): 29–52 and Michael Gorman, "Peter of Pisa and the *Quaestiunculae* copied for Charlemagne in Brussels II 2572, with a Note on the Codex Diezianus from Verona," *Revue Bénédictine*, 110 (2000): 248–50.

59. *Karolus magnus et Leo papa*, ed. Dümmler, MGH:PLAC 1, pp. 367–68.67–87; and trans. Peter Godman, *Poetry of the Carolingian Renaissance* (Norman, Okla., 1985), pp. 200–201. See also Angilbert, *carmen* 2, ed. Dümmler, MGH:PLAC 1, pp. 360–61.16–21.

60. *Annales de gestis Caroli Magni imperatoris* 5, ed. Paul Winterfeld, MHG:PLAC 4 (Berlin, 1899), p. 61.249–50; also trans. Mary E. McKinney, *The Saxon Poet's Life of Charles the Great* (New York, 1956), p. 92.

61. MGH:Ep. 4, p. 535.10.

62. MGH:Ep. 4, p. 542.8–28.

63. Alcuin, *epistola* 306, ed. Dümmler, MGH:Ep. 4, p. 466.4–7. See also Stephen Allott, *Alcuin of York, c. A.D. 732 to 804* (York, England), pp. 89–90.

64. Alcuin, *epistola* 172, ed. Dümmler, MGH:Ep. 4, p. 284.13–15.

65. On public reading as an aspect of Carolingian court culture, see Mayke de Jong, "Old Law and New Found Power: Hrabanus Maurus and the Old

Testament," in *Centres of Learning: Learning and Location in Pre-Modern Europe and the Near East*, ed. Jan Willem Drijvers and Alasdair A. MacDonald, Brill's Studies in Intellectual History, 61 (Leiden, 1995), pp. 164–66 [161–76].

66. See Paul Saenger, *Space between Words: the Origins of Silent Reading* (Stanford, 1997), pp. 100–119.

67. See especially McKitterick, *The Carolingians and the Written Word* and John J. Contreni, "The Carolingian Renaissance: Education and Literary Culture," in *The New Cambridge Medieval History*, 2:716–20.

68. Alcuin, *epistola* 88, ed. Dümmler, MGH:Ep. 4, p.132.35–36, and *epistola* 216, p. 360. See also *epistolae* 195 and 214, pp. 322–23, 357–58.

69. Dhuoda, *Liber manualis*, epigram, prologue, and 1.7, ed. Pierre Riché, *Dhuoda, Manuel pour mon fils*, Sources Chrétiennes, 225 (Paris, 1975), pp. 72, 80–82, 114.

70. Eriugena, *carmen* 2.4, l.19, ed. Ludwig Traube, MGH:PLAC 3, p. 533; also ed. Michael Herren, in *Iohannis Scotti Eriugenae Carmina*, Scriptores Latini Hiberniae, 12 (Dublin, 1993), p. 72. Herren's translation, p. 73, "making books with her own hands" cannot be correct: see Paul Edward Dutton, "Eriugena, the Royal Poet," in *Jean Scot Écrivain: actes du IVe Colloque international, Montréal, 28 août–2 septembre 1983*, ed. G.-H. Allard, (Montréal, 1986), pp. 67–68 [51–80]. See also Janet L. Nelson, "Women and the Word in the Early Middle Ages," *Studies in Church History*, 27 (1990): 15–25.

71. Pierre Riché, *Daily Life in the World of Charlemagne*, trans. Jo Ann McNamara (Philadelphia, 1978), p. 206.

72. Thegan, *Gesta Hludowici* 20, ed. Ernst Tremp, in MGH: Scriptores rerum Germanicarum in usum scholarum separatim editi, 64 (Hanover, 1995), p. 204.

73. Alcuin, *epistola* 172, ed. Dümmler, in MGH:Ep. 4, p. 285.12–15; trans. in *Charlemagne's Courtier*, p. 1.

74. On the shifts in orality and literacy ongoing in the Carolingian period, see Michel Banniard, *Viva Voce: Communication écrite et communication orale du IVe au IXe siècle en Occident latin* (Paris, 1992), pp. 305–422; Banniard, pp. 330–33, speculates that Charlemagne's literacy may have improved in the 790s under the impress of his resident court scholars and the volume of literary traffic around Charlemagne.

75. Alcuin, *carmen* 7, ed. Dümmler, MGH:PLAC 1, p. 227. See also Peter Godman, *Poets and Emperors*, pp. 56–59.

76. See *Annales Fuldenses siue Annales regni Francorum orientales* 844, ed. by F. Kurze after G.H. Pertz [hereafter ed. Kurze], MGH:SRGUS (Hanover, 1891), p. 35, for a contemporary warning on the difficult figures and verse forms found in Hrabanus Maurus's *De laudibus sanctae crucis*. Dhuoda felt the need to explain to her son the acrostic form in her *Liber manualis*, epigram 88–89, ed. Riché, p. 78 and 10.2 title, p. 340.

77. On the history of the form, see Ulrich Ernst, *Carmen figuratum: Geschichte des Figurengedichts von den antiken Ursprüngen bus zum Ausgang des Mittelalters* (Cologne, 1991).

78. Theodulf, *carmen* 25, ed. Dümmler, MGH: PLAC 1, p. 483.10. See D. Schaller, "Vortrags- und Zirkulardichtung am Hof Karls des Großen," *Mittellateinisches Jahrbuch*, 5–6 (1970): 14–36.

79. Bullough, *Carolingian Renewal*, p. 127.
80. Thegan, *Gesta Hludowici* 7, ed. Tremp, pp. 184, 186.
81. Thegan, *Gesta Hludowici* 19, ed. Tremp, p. 200, in commenting on Louis's linguistic abilities did carefully say that Louis did not want to read, listen to, or teach the national or barbarian poems.
82. Thegan, *Gesta Hludowici* 10 and 19, ed. Tremp, pp. 192, 202.
83. The Saxon Poet believed that this was a translation of a Carolingian Latin grammar into German: see *Annales de gestis Caroli* 5, ed. Winterfeld, MHG:PLAC 4, p. 68.547–50.
84. Alcuin, *carmen* 80.2, ed. Dümmler, MGH:PLAC 1, p. 300.3–4; and see Wilbur Samuel Howell, *The Rhetoric of Alcuin & Charlemagne* (Princeton, 1941), p. 66 and Luitpold Wallach, *Alcuin and Charlemagne: Studies in Carolingian History and Literature* (Ithaca, N.Y., 1959), pp. 29–96.
85. In the "Epitaphium Hadriani Papae," line 17, we also find "lacrimans Carolus haec carmina scripsi," but the sense of "scripsi" here may mean no more than he ordered this poem written. See "Epitaphium Hadriani Papae," 17, ed. Ernst Dümmler, MGH:PLAC 1, p. 113.
86. See Alcuin, *epistolae* 136, 145, 155, 172, ed. Dümmler, MGH:Ep. 4, pp. 205–210, 232, 250–53, 284–85.
87. Alcuin, *epistola* 136, ed. Dümmler, MGH:Ep. 4, pp. 205.17–19.
88. See *Epistolae variorum* 20, ed. Dümmler, MGH:Ep. 4, pp. 528–29.
89. See Alcuin, *epistola* 172, ed. Dümmler, MGH:Ep. 4, p. 285.
90. Alcuin, *epistola* 145, ed. Dümmler, MGH:Ep. 4, pp. 231–32.
91. These *pueri* mentioned by Alcuin were not boys, but mature servants of the king, for Alcuin referred in *epistola* 154, ed. Dümmler, MGH:Ep. 4, p. 249.12 to his assistant Fridigisus in 798 as a *puer* although he would succeed Alcuin as abbot of St-Martin's of Tours within six years.
92. See also the case of the visionary Alberic in *Visio Alberici: die Jenseitswanderung des neunjährigen Alberich in der vom Visionär um 1127 in Monte Cassino revidierten Fassung*, ed. Paul Gerhard Schmidt (Stuttgart, 1997), pp. 9–10.
93. Indeed, many presidents from John Kennedy forward have used automatic pen machines. See Charles Hamilton, *The Robot that Helped Make a President: A Reconnaisance into the Mysteries of John F. Kennedy's Signature* (New York, 1965).
94. See Albert Bruckner and Robert Marichal, *Chartae Latinae antiquiores: Facsimile edition of the Latin Charters Prior to the Ninth Century*, part 15: France 1 (Zurich, 1986), 595, 596, 602, 604, 605–607, pp. 3–11, 34–37, 46–50, 52–61.
95. For an example see Heer, *Charlemagne and His World*, pp. 21 and 28. The charter shown is 84a in MGH: Diplomata Karolinorum 1, ed. Mühlbacher, pp. 120–22. See also Peter Rück, *Bildberichte vom König: Kanzlerzeichen, königliche Monogramme und das Signet der salischen Dynastie* (Marburg, 1996), pp. 15–20 and figs. 178–89 and J. Lechner, "Das Monogramm in den Urkunden Karls des Grossen," *Neues Archiv*, 30 (1905): 702–707. David Ganz kindly discussed the question of the monogram with me. For the original hypothesis, see Theodor Sickel, *Acta regum et imperatorum Karolinorum digesta et enarrata. Die Urkunden der Karolinger*, ed. Theodor Sickel, 3 parts (Vienna, 1867–68), 1, pp. 316–317.

96. See, for instance, Bruckner and Marichal, *Chartae Latinae antiquiores*, part 15: France 1, 608 (from 13 January 769), pp. 63–65.
97. Ratpert, *Casus Sancti Galli*, 8, ed. G.H. Pertz, in MGH: Scriptores 2 (Hanover, 1829), p. 69 went to some trouble to describe Louis the German's hands-on perusal and perfection of a charter of St-Gall, perhaps in order to demonstrate its authenticity and authority.
98. Einhard, *Vita Karoli Magni* 25, ed. Waitz, p. 30.
99. John F. Collins, *Einhard, "Vita Karoli Magni"* (Bryn Mawr, 1984), p. 81, thinks the translation of "et" here should be "even," and adds "This underscoring of *scribere* is significant: apparently C. never learned to write at all." But "also" or "and moreover" may better capture the connection to the sequence of Charlemagne's linguistic abilities that preceded this one.
100. Einhard employed this diminuendo technique of moving from the better to the worse in other places including his description of Charlemagne's appearance: see Einhard, *Vita Karoli Magni* 22, ed. Waitz, p. 26. There he begins by describing his large and powerful body, but ends by noting his short neck and protruding belly.
101. See Richard H. Rouse and Mary A. Rouse, "Wax Tablets," *Language & Communication*, 9 (1989): 175–91; idem, "The Vocabulary of Wax Tablets," in *Vocabulaire du livre et de l'écriture au moyen âge: actes de la table ronde, Paris 24–26 septembre 1987*, ed. Olga Weijers (Turnhout, 1989), pp. 220–30; and a revised version of the same in *Harvard Library Bulletin*, 1 (1990): 12–19; and *Les Tablettes à écrire de l'antiquité à l'époque moderne: actes du colloque international du Centre National de la Recherche Scientifique, Paris, Institut de France, 10–11 octobre 1990*, ed. Élisabeth Lalou (Turnhout, 1992). For a scholar who can be shown to have used wax tablets, see Paul Edward Dutton, "Eriugena's Workshop: the Making of the *Periphyseon* in Rheims 875," in *History and Eschatology in John Scottus Eriugena and His Time*, Proceedings of the Tenth International Colloquium of the Society for the Promotion of Eriugenian Studies, Maynooth and Dublin, August 16–20, 2000, ed. James McEvoy and Michael Dunne, in Ancient and Medieval Philosophy, De Wulf-Maison Centre, ser. 1, 30 (Leuven, 2002), pp. 141–67.
102. Theodulf, *carmen* 25, ed. Dümmler, MGH:PLAC 1, p. 487.147–50. See also *Regula magistri* 50.12–13, ed. Adalbert Vogüe, *La règle du maître* (Paris, 1964). See also Rouse and Rouse, "The Vocabulary of Wax Tablets," p. 14.
103. See Collins, *Einhard, "Vita Karoli Magni"*, p. 81 and Joseph Cahour, *Petite Lexique pour l'étude de la "Vita Karoli" d'Eginhard* (Paris, 1928), p. 20, under "circumferre."
104. See Suetonius, *Vitae Caesarum*, Tiberius 22.42; Caligula 18.54; Claudius 29.1.
105. Dhuoda, *Liber manualis*, pref. 26, ed. Riché, p. 86.
106. *Annales de gestis Caroli Magni imperatoris* 5, ed. Winterfeld, MHG:PLAC 4, p. 61.254; also trans. McKinney, *The Saxon Poet's Life of Charles the Great*, p. 92.
107. See the *probationes pennae* printed by Bischoff, "Elementarunterricht und Probationes pennae in der ersten Hälfte des Mittelalters," *Mittelalterliche*

Studien, 1:86: "Disce, puer, tabulis, quo possis scribere kartis" [Learn, boy, on (wax) tablets so that you can write on parchment].

108. *Annales de gestis Caroli Magni imperatoris* 5, ed. Winterfeld, MHG:PLAC 4, p. 61.253–56.

109. See *Visio Karoli Magni*, ed. P. Jaffé, in *Bibliotheca rerum Germanicarum*, 4 (Berlin, 1868): 701–704; Patrick Geary, "Germanic Tradition and Royal Ideology in the Ninth Century: The *Visio Karoli Magni*," *Frümittelalterliche Studien*, 21 (1987): 274–94 and repr. in Geary, *Living with the Dead in the Middle Ages* (Ithaca, N.Y., 1994), pp. 49–76; also trans. in Dutton, *Carolingian Civilization*, pp. 456–57; and discussed in Paul Edward Dutton, *The Politics of Dreaming in the Carolingian Empire*, Regents Studies in Medieval Culture, ed. Eugene Vance (Lincoln, Neb., 1994), pp. 200–210.

110. *Capitula in synodo apud sanctam Macram ab Hincmaro promulgata*, PL 125:1085A2-11. I wish to thank David Ganz for bringing this passage to my attention.

111. Paris, Bibliothèque Nationale, lat. 10758, fols. 305–28, 337–39. See Hubert Mordek, *Bibliotheca capitularium regum Francorum manuscripta: Überlieferung und Traditionszusammenhang der fränkischen Herrscherlasse*, MGH: Hilfsmittel, 15 (Munich, 1995), pp. 587–605.

112. Ekkehard IV, *Casus sancti Galli* I, ed. I. von Arx, in MGH:SS 2 (Hanover, 1829), pp. 88.45–89.5.

113. J. Duft and R. Schynder, *Die Elfenbein-Einbände der Stiftsbibliothek St. Gallen* (Beuron, 1984), pp. 45–53.

114. *Capitulare monasticum* (10 July 817), 38, ed. Boretius, MGH:Cap. 1, p. 346.

115. On Carolingian sleep and bedrooms, see Dutton, *The Politics of Dreaming*, pp. 5–22.

116. Odilo of Cluny, *De uita beati Maioli abbatis*, in PL 142:955B–956A.

117. *Annales de gestis Caroli Magni imperatoris* 5, ed. Winterfeld, MHG:PLAC 4, p. 61.253–56.

118. Suetonius, *Vitae Caesarum*, Nero 6.4. My thanks to John Contreni for the reference.

119. See the variants provided in *Vita Caroli imperatoris*, PL 97:50 n. 37 and Collins, *Einhard*, "*Vita Karoli Magni*," p. 81. It is strange, moreover, if the root form is *effigiare*, that the word is not *effigiandis*. That alone might push us toward considering *effingendis* as the preferable reading. We should note too Suetonius, *Vitae Caesarum*, Titus 3.2, wrote: ". . .Latine Graeceque uel in orando uel in fingendis poematibus promptus et facilis ad extemporalitatem. . . ."

120. See Rouse and Rouse, "The Vocabulary of Wax Tablets," p. 18.

121. Not an "an absurd labor" as Ring translates *labor praeposterus*: see "Renovatio Karoli Latinitatis," p. 266.

122. Einhard, *Vita Karoli Magni*, pref., ed. Waitz, p. 1.18–22.

123. Robert Folz, *Le couronnement impérial de Charlemagne: 25 décembre 800* (Paris, 1964), p. 76, sees a calligraphic meaning in Einhard's statement: "il est fort possible, comme on l'a conjecturé tout récemment, qu'il ait pensé à des essais de calligraphie plutôt qu'à l'usage ordinaire de l'alphabet."

Though Folz does not supply his source, it may be suspected that he was referring to the comment by Paul Lehmann, "Das Problem der karolingischen Renaissance," in *I Problemi della civiltà Carolingia*, Settimane di Studio del Centro Italiano di Studi sull'alto medioevo, 1 (Spoleto, 1954): 336 [309–57]: "beziehe ich mehr auf das Schönschreiben als auf elementaren Gebrauch der Buchstaben." No arguments or proofs accompany either statement.

124. See Bischoff, *Manuscripts and Libraries in the Age of Charlemagne*, pp. 80, 125 and Dutton, *Charlemagne's Courtier*, pp. 184–85.

125. J. van der Straeten, "Vie inédite de saint Hugues, évêque de Rouen," p. 236.

126. *Admonitio generalis* 72, MGH:Cap. 1, ed. Boretius, p. 60.3. Bernhard Bischoff, *Latin Palaeography: Antiquity and the Middle Ages*, trans. Dáibhí Ó Cróinín and David Ganz (Cambridge, 1986), p. 81 n. 208, thought that these "notas" were Tironian notes, but the sequence in the text suggests instead a progressive or graduated basic education that leads from the memorization of the Psalms (*Psalmos*) to learning written characters (*notas*), chants (*cantus*), numbers (*compotum*), and lastly Latin grammar (*grammaticam*). It should be noted, as Bruce Eastwood pointed out to me, that Charles Jones took "notas" to be "*notas* in writing." See Charles Jones, "An Early Medieval Licensing Examination," *History of Education Quarterly*, 3 (March 1963): 20 [19–29].

127. See the chart of datable manuscripts given by David Ganz, "The Preconditions for Caroline Minuscule," *Viator*, 18 (1987): 26–27 [23–43] and see also Ganz, "Book Production in the Carolingian Empire and the Spread of Caroline Minuscule," in *The New Cambridge Medieval History*, 2:786–808.

128. Paris, Bibliothèque Nationale, Nouv. acq. lat. 1203, fols. 126v–27r and see *Versus libris saeculi VIII adiecti* 7, ed. Dümmler, MGH:PLAC 1, pp. 94–95.

129. I would like to thank Paul Meyvaert for his advice on the latter point.

130. See Bernhard Bischoff, "Die karolingische Minuskel," in Bischoff, *Mittelalterliche Studien* 3:1–4, and Bischoff, *Latin Palaeography*, pp. 112–118; Herrad Spilling, "Die Enstehung der karolingischen Minuskel," in *794-Karl der Große in Frankfurt am Main: ein König bei der Arbeit* (Frankfurt, 1994), pp. 51–54; and Ganz, "Preconditions for Caroline Minuscule."

131. See MGH:Cap. 1, ed. Boretius, p. 79 and Wallach, *Alcuin and Charlemagne*, pp. 198–226; and trans. D.C. Munro, in *Carolingian Civilization*, pp. 89–91. See the two versions of the *De litteris* edited by T. Martin, "Bemerkungen zur 'Epistola de litteris colendis,' " *Archiv für Diplomatik*, 31 (1985): 227–72.

132. See *Admonitio generalis* 72, MGH:Cap. 1, ed. Boretius, pp. 59–60. I greatly benefited from reading the relevant pages on the *Admonitio* and *De litteris colendis* of Donald Bullough's forthcoming study of Alcuin.

133. See Bischoff, *Latin Palaeography*, p. 112.

134. Ganz, "Preconditions for Caroline Minuscule," p. 37.

135. Jerome, *epistola* 107 ("Ad Laetam"), ed. I. Hilberg, in Corpus Scriptorum ecclesiasticorum latinorum, vol. 55 (Vienna, 1912), p. 294. And see also Quintilian, *Institutio oratoria* 1.1.27–28, which recommends that children use wooden stencils when learning to write.

136. Ganz, "Book Production in the Carolingian Empire," in *The New Cambridge Medieval History*, 2:790.

137. Alcuin, *epistola* 19, ed. Dümmler, MGH:Ep. 4, p. 55.23: "Qui non discit in pueritia, non docet in senectute."

138. Hibernicus Exul, *carmen* 9.1, ed. Dümmler, MGH:PLAC 1, p. 403.1 and 7–8.

139. Hrabanus Maurus, *De procinctu Romanae milicie* 3, ed. Ernst Dümmler, "De procinctu romanae milicie," *Zeitschrift für deutsches Altertum und deutsche Literatur*, 15 (1872): 444 [443–51]. See also Bernard S. Bachrach, *Early Carolingian Warfare: Prelude to Empire* (Philadelphia, 2001), pp. 120–21. Many thanks to John Contreni for supplying me with a copy of Hrabanus's text.

140. Erich Auerbach, *Literary Language and Its Public in Late Antiquity and in the Middle Ages*, trans. Ralph Manheim, Bollingen Series, 74 (New York, 1965), p. 117, noted that Einhard's "linguistic instrument is not equal to his material."

141. Remigius of Auxerre named some of the older scripts, but in general ninth-century men and women lacked a vocabulary for the scripts they used or saw: see Bernhard Bischoff, "Die alten Namen der lateinischen Schriftarten," in Bischoff, *Mittelalterliche Studien*, 1:1–5 and E.A. Lowe, *Codices Latini Antiquiores: A Palaeographical Guide to Latin Manuscripts Prior to the Ninth Century*, Supplement (Oxford, 1971), p. viii.

142. Alcuin, *carmen* 26, ed, Dümmler, MGH:PLAC 1, p. 246.27.

143. See Notker, *Gesta Karoli Magni* 2.12, ed. Hans F. Haefele, in *Notker der Stammler, Taten Kaiser Karls des Grossen*, MGH: Scriptores Rreum Germanicarum, Nova Series, 12 (Berlin, 1959), pp. 71–72 and Einhard, *Translatio et miracula sanctorum Marcellini et Petri* 2.1, ed. Georg Waitz, MGH:SS 15.1 (Hanover, 1888), p. 245.

144. Alcuin, *carmen* 26, ed. Dümmler, MGH:PLAC 1, p. 246.26.

145. See Alcuin, *epistola* 172, ed. Dümmler, MGH:Ep. 4, p. 285.

146. See Alcuin, *carmen* 94, ed. Dümmler, MGH:PLAC 1, p. 320 and *carmen* 69, ed. Dümmler, MGH:PLAC 1, p. 292.183–88.

147. *Admonitio generalis* 72, ed. Boretius, MGH:Cap. 1, p. 60 and see 68, p. 403 for the same.

148. *Capitulare missorum in Theodonis uilla datum primum, mere ecclesiasticum* 3, ed. Boretius, MGH:Cap. 1, p. 121 and see a version of the same in *Ansegisi Capitularium* 105, p. 409.

149. *Carmen* 44, ed. Dümmler, MGH:PLAC 1, p. 77.21–22. And see Ludwig Traube, *Einleitung in die lateinische Philologie des Mittelalters*, ed. Paul Lehmann, in Traube, *Vorlesungen und Abhandlungen*, ed. F. Boll, vol. 2 (Munich, 1911; repr. 1965), p. 52.

150. Though an emendation such "Confecta errore" would solve the problem of both the meter and the necessary agreement of *confecta* with the feminine singular noun *scriptio*, Dümmler left the line unemended and Traube and Paul Lehmann (in Traube, *Vorlesungen und Abhandlungen* 2:52) rightly insisted the line should be left as it is. In English it is difficult to capture the several senses of *conficio*, which can mean to make, write, and ruin or

undo. Fiducia intentionally made a mistake with the placement of "errore" and another as he played upon the several meanings of the word *conficio*. I want to thank Christopher McDonough for his considerable help in sorting out this couplet.

151. Bischoff, "Elementarunterricht und Probationes Pennae," *Mittelalterliche Studien*, 1:87.

152. Notker, *Gesta Karoli Magni* 1.8, ed. Haefele, p. 10.

153. Notker, *Gesta Karoli Magni* 1.34, ed. Haefele, p. 47.

154. Notker, *Gesta Karoli Magni* 1.3 and 1.19, ed. Haefele, pp. 4, 25.

155. Notker, *Gesta Karoli Magni* 1.7, ed. Haefele, p. 10.

156. Einhard, *Vita Karoli Magni* 26, ed. Waitz, p. 31; trans. Dutton, *Charlemagne's Courtier*, p. 33.

157. See Theodulf, *carmen* 10, ed. Dümmler, MGH:PLAC 1, pp. 464–65 and trans. in *Carolingian Civilization*, pp. 103–104. See also Jonas of Orléans, *De institutione regia* 3, ed. Jean Reviron, *Les idées politico-religieuses d'un évêque du IXe siècle. Jonas d'Orléans et son "De institutione regia,"* L'église et l'état au Moyen Age, 1 (Paris, 1930), pp. 143–44. See also Frederic Amory, "Whited Sepulchres: the Semantic History of Hypocrisy to the High Middle Ages," *Recherches de théologie ancienne et médiévale*, 53 (1986): 5–39.

158. Cited and translated in Pierre Hadot, *The Inner Citadel: The "Meditations" of Marcus Aurelius*, trans. Michael Chase (Cambridge, Mass., 1998), pp. 15–16.

159. Hrabanus Maurus, *epistola* 28, ed. Dümmler, MGH:Ep. 5 (Hanover, 1898–99; repr. 1974), p. 444.4–5.

160. This was Leonard Boyle's phrase: see Jacqueline Brown and William P. Stoneman, "Preface," in *A Distinct Voice: Medieval Studies in Honor of Leonard E. Boyle, O.P*, ed. Jacqueline Brown and William P. Stoneman (Notre Dame, 1997), p. x.

161. Procopius, *Anecdota* 6.10–17. Procopius thought it a highly unusual and lamentable thing for a Roman ruler to be illiterate.

162. See J.M. Wallace-Hadrill, *Early Medieval History* (Oxford, 1975), pp. 184–85 and Rosamond McKitterick, *The Frankish Church and the Carolingian Reforms, 789–895* (London, 1977), pp. 2–5.

Chapter 4   Of Carolingian Kings and Their Stars

1. Alcuin, *epistola* 121, ed. E. Dümmler, MGH: Epistolae 4 (Hanover, 1895; repr. 1974), pp. 176.32–177.3.

2. I take it that according to our current usage *culmen* means "ceiling" (inner roof) rather than "roof" (outer surface), that is, the inside of the dome rather than the unseen other side. See Seneca, *Naturales Quaestiones* 7.12.2, where he rejected the idea of Artemidorus that the highest region of the sky was completely solid and hardened in the manner of a roof.

3. See Pliny, *Naturalis Historia* 2.1–2 and Gen. 1–2.

4. See, for instance, Wesley M. Stevens, " 'Compotistica et astronomica' in the Fulda School," in *Saints, Scholars, and Heroes: Studies in Medieval Culture in Honor of Charles W. Jones*, vol. 2, ed. Margot H. King and Wesley M. Stevens (Collegeville, Minn., 1979), pp. 27–65.

5. Alcuin, *Disputatio Pippini cum Albino* 52, ed. Lloyd William Daly and Walter Suchier, in *Altercatio Hadriani Augusti et Epicteti philosophi* (Urbana, 1939), p. 139, and trans. Paul Edward Dutton, *Carolingian Civilization: A Reader*, 2nd ed. (Peterborough, Ont., 2004), pp. 140–46.

6. *De rectoribus Christianis*, *carmen* 11, ed. Ludwig Traube, MGH: Poetae Latini Aevi Carolini 3 (Berlin, 1881; repr. 1964), p. 159.4; and see also S. Hellmann, *Sedulius Scottus*, in Quellen und Untersuchungen zur lateinischen Philologie des Mittlealters, vol. 1 (Munich, 1906), p. 48.20.

7. Sedulius Scottus, *carmen* 4, ed. Traube, MGH:PLAC 3, p. 169.

8. Eriugena, *Periphyseon* 3, *Patrologia Latina* 122, col. 697A and ed. Édouard Jeauneau, *Iohannis Scotti seu Eriugenae Periphyseon: Liber tertius*, Corpus Christianorum: Continuatio Mediaevalis, 163 (Turnhout, 1999), p. 111; Pliny, *Naturalis Historia* 2.3.8.

9. See H. Schnitzler, "Das Kuppelmosaik der Aachener Pfalzkapelle," *Aachener Kunstblätter*, 29 (1964): 17–44; Herbert Schrade, "Zum Kuppelmosaik der Pfalzkapelle und zum Theoderich-Denkmal in Aachen," *Aachener Kunstblätter*, 30 (1965): 25–37; E. Stephany, "Das Aachener Domschatz:Versuch einer Deutung," *Aachener Kunstblätter*, 42 (1972): xx–xxii. See aslo Nigel Hiscock, "The Aachen Chapel: A Model of Salvation?" in *Science in Western and Eastern Civilization in Carolingian Times*, ed. Paul Leo Butzer and Dietrich Lohrmann (Basel, 1993), pp. 115–26.

10. See Paul Edward Dutton and Édouard Jeauneau, "The Verses of the *Codex Aureus* of Saint-Emmeram," *Studi Medievali*, 3rd ser., 24 (1983): 113–117 [75–120]; and repr. in Jeauneau, *Études érigéniennes* (Paris, 1987), pp. 593–638.

11. Alcuin, *epistola* 171, ed. Dümmler, MGH:Ep. 4, p. 283.5–6.

12. Einhard, *Vita Karoli Magni* 25, ed. by G.Waitz after G.H. Pertz, 6th ed. overseen by O. Holder-Egger [hereafter ed. Waitz], MGH: Scriptores rerum Germanicarum in usum Scholarum (Hanover, 1911; repr. 1965), p. 30; trans. Paul Edward Dutton, in *Charlemagne's Courtier:The Complete Einhard* (Peterborough, Ont., 1998), p. 32. Charlemagne also had an interest in things meteorological: see *Vita Karoli Magni* 29, ed.Waitz, pp. 33–34.

13. Einhard, *Vita Karoli Magni* 33, ed.Waitz, p. 40.18–21.

14. Thegan, *Gesta Hludowici* 8, ed. Ernst Tremp, MGH:SRGUS 64 (Hanover, 1995), pp. 188, 190.

15. *Annales Bertiniani* 842, ed. Félix Grat, Jeanne Vielliard, and Suzanne Clémencet, in *Annales de Saint-Bertin* (Paris, 1964), p. 41. See also *The Annals of St-Bertin*, translated and annotated by Janet L. Nelson, Ninth-Century Histories, 1 (Manchester, 1991).

16. See F.N. Estrey, "Charlemagne's Silver Celestial Table," *Speculum*, 18 (1943): 112–117; Stephen C. McCluskey, *Astronomies and Cultures in Early Medieval Europe* (Cambridge, 1998), pp. 140–41.

17. Seneca, *Naturales Quaestiones* 7.1.1–3.

18. Peter Brown, *Authority and the Sacred: Aspects of the Christianisation of the Roman World* (Cambridge, 1995), p. 8.

19. See Calcidius, *Commentarius* 127–36, ed. J.H.Waszink, in *Timaeus a Calcidio translatus commentarioque instructus*, 2nd ed., Plato Latinus, 4 (London, 1975),

pp. 170–77 and J. den Boeft, *Calcidius on Demons* (Commentarius Ch. 127–136), Philosophia antiqua, 33 (Leiden, 1977). The typing of the daemones as good and bad occurred in medieval commentaries on the *Timaeus*.

20. For a color illustration of this page in Paris, Bibliothèque Nationale, lat. 1141, fol. 5r, see Florentine Mütherich and Joachim Gaehde, *Carolingian Painting* (New York, 1976), p. 33. Eriugena, *carmen* 2.8, ed. Ludwig Traube, MGH:PLAC 3, p. 538.9, describes the Seraphim as "oculosa," which seems to be understood differently by Michael Herren, in *Iohannis Scotti Eriugenae Carmina*, Scriptores Latini Hiberniae, 12 (Dublin, 1993), p. 85, "you can see the Seraphim and the ones 'full of eyes' as they fly," but *oculosa* qualifies "Seraphin" and not some other angelic being. Rev. 4:8 describes six-winged creatures who "plena sunt oculis" and the *Te igitur* depiction of the Gellone Sacramentary (Paris, Bibliothèque Nationale, lat. 12048, fol. 143v) depicts two Seraphim with eye-spotted wings.

21. Note the incident reported in the *Royal Frankish Annals* for 776: while the Saxons were attacking the castle of Syburg God rendered their catapults useless and as they prepared to set fire to the castle God sent a fiery likeness of two shields wheeling over the castle. The Saxons retreated in fear. See *Annales regni Francorum* 776, ed. by F. Kurze after G.H. Pertz [hereafter ed. Kurze], in MGH:SRGUS (Hanover, 1895), pp. 44–46. For the most recent study of these annals, see Roger Collins, "The 'Reviser' Revisited: Another Look at the Alternative Version of the *Annales regni Francorum*," in *After Rome's Fall: Narrators and Sources of Early Medieval History. Essays Presented to Walter Goffart*, ed. Alexander Callander Murray (Toronto, 1998), pp. 191–213.

22. *Annales regni Francorum* 764 (revised version), ed. Kurze, p. 23 and see Collins, "The 'Reviser' Revisited," p. 208. See also *Annales regni Francorum* 807 (revised version), ed. Kurze, pp. 122–23.

23. See *Annales regni Francorum* 798, ed. Kurze, p. 104 and see Dietrich Lohrmann, "Alcuins Korrespondenz mit Karl dem Großen über Kalendar und Astronomie," in *Science in Western and Eastern Civilization*, pp. 79–114.

24. Alcuin, *epistolae* 126 and 145, ed. Dümmler, MGH:Ep. 4, pp. 185–87, 231–35.

25. See the drawing of the hemispheres from Paris, Bibliothèque Nationale, Nouv. acq. lat. 1614, fol. 81v in Patrick McGurk, "Carolingian Astrological Manuscripts," *Charles the Bald: Court and Kingdom. Papers based on a Colloquium held in London in April 1979*, ed. Margaret Gibson and Janet Nelson with the assistance of David Ganz, BAR International Series, 101 (Oxford, 1981), p. 327, and see also Hans Holländer, *Early Medieval Art*, trans. Caroline Hillier (New York, 1974), p. 88 and fig. 69.

26. Alcuin, *epistola* 148, ed. Dümmler, MGH:Ep. 4, p. 239.21–22.

27. Alcuin, *epistola* 148, ed. Dümmler, MGH:Ep. 4, p. 241.5–6.

28. See Gen. 15:5–7, Heb. 11:17, James 2:23. See also Hibernicus Exul, *carmen* 20.7, ed. Dümmler, MGH:PLAC 1, p. 410.5–6.

29. *Karolus Magnus et Leo Papa*, ed. Dümmler, MGH:PLAC 1, p. 368.80–81.

30. Sedulius Scottus, *carmen* 58, ed. Traube, MGH:PLAC 3, p. 216.41–44.

31. Alcuin, *epistola* 149, ed. Dümmler, MGH:Ep. 4, p. 242.9–14. On the Saxon wars, see now Roger Collins, *Charlemagne* (Toronto, 1998), pp. 43–57.

32. Alcuin, *epistola* 149, ed. Dümmler, MGH:Ep. 4, p. 243.9–22; not then as characterized by Heinrich Fichtenau, *The Carolingian Empire: The Age of Charlemagne*, trans. Peter Munz (New York, 1964), p. 37.

33. *Annales regni Francorum*, ed. Kurze, p. 104.

34. Alcuin, *epistola* 149, ed. Dümmler, MGH:Ep. 4, pp. 243.9–22, 245.11–16.

35. Ermoldus, *In honorem Hludowici* 1, ed. Dümmler, MGH:PLAC 2, p. 6.47–50.

36. See Ermoldus, *In honorem Hludowici* 4, ed. Dümmler, MGH:PLAC 2, p. 66.275–78. See also Peter Godman, *Poets and Emperors: Frankish Politics and Carolingian Poetry* (Oxford, 1987), pp. 110–30.

37. Alcuin, *epistola* 155, ed. Dümmler, MGH:Ep. 4, p. 250.3–6. And see Alcuin, *carmen* 74, ed. Dümmler, MGH:PLAC 1, p. 295.2 and *epistola* 171, ed. Dümmler, MGH:Ep. 4, p. 283.5.

38. Alcuin, *epistola* 155, ed. Dümmler, MGH:Ep. 4, pp. 250–53.

39. Alcuin, *epistola* 155, ed. Dümmler, MGH:Ep. 4, pp. 251.5–252.24. He had also apparently drawn up a chart on the power of the sun earlier that year: see Alcuin, *epistola* 149, ed. Dümmler, MGH:Ep. 4, p. 243.9–22.

40. See Alcuin, *epistola* 171, ed. Dümmler, MGH:Ep. 4, p. 282.13–21.

41. Alcuin, *epistola* 171, ed. Dümmler, MGH:Ep. 4, pp. 282.26–283.1.

42. See Percy Ernst Schramm, *Herrschaftszeichen und Staatsymbolik: Beiträge zu ihrer Geschichte vom dritten bis zum sechzehnten Jahrhundert*, Schriften der Monumenta Germaniae Historica, 13.2 (Stuttgart, 1955), pp. 377–417; and *Iohannis Scotti Annotationes in Marcianum*, ed. Cora E. Lutz, Medieval Academy of America, publication no. 34 (Cambridge, Mass., 1939), p. 40: "Corona Iovis rutilantium planetarum flammas significat."

43. Even Dicuil's treatise on astronomy, which was composed 814–16 and dedicated to Louis the Pious, may have had Charlemagne's cosmological interests in mind. See Mario Esposito, "An Unpublished Astronomical Treatise by the Irish Monk Dicuil," *Proceedings of the Royal Irish Academy*, 26, section C (1907), pp. 376–445; Franz Brunhölzl, *Histoire de la littérature latine du Moyen Âge*, vol. 1.2: L'époque carolingienne, trans. Henri Rochais (Turnhout, 1991), pp. 64–66; and *Dicuili Liber de mensura orbis terrae*, ed. J.J. Tierney, Scriptores Latini Hiberniae, 6 (Dublin, 1967).

44. Alcuin, *epistola* 149, ed. Dümmler, MGH:Ep. 4, p. 244.13–22 and n. 2.

45. And not Gundrada as Peter Godman, *Poetry of the Carolingian Renaissance* (Norman, Okla., 1985), p. 121 n. 41, thought or Gisela as did Pierre Riché, *Daily Life in the Carolingian Empire*, trans. Jo Ann McNamara (Philadelphia, 1978), p. 205.

46. Alcuin, *carmen* 26, ed. Dümmler, MGH:PLAC 1, p. 246.41–44.

47. Sedulius Scottus, *carmen* 3.4, ed. Traube, MGH:PLAC 3, p. 234.11–12.

48. See Collins, *Charlemagne*, pp. 144–52.

49. See Wolfram Brandes, " '*Tempora periculosa sunt*': Eschatologisches im Vorfeld der Kaiserkrönung Karls des Grossen," in *Das Frankfurter Konzil von 794: Kristillisationspunkt karolingischer Kultur*, ed. Rainer Berndt (Mainz, 1997),

pp. 49–79 and Michael Idomir Allen, "The Chronicle of Claudius of Turin," in *After Rome's Fall*, p. 318 and n. 147 [288–319]. Claudius, for instance, following Bede deliberately bypassed the problem. On the scheme itself, see Richard Landes, "The Fear of an Apocalyptic Year 1000: Augustinian Historiography, Medieval and Modern," *Speculum*, 75 (2000): 111–114 [97–145] and also David Van Meter, "The Empire of the Year 6000: Eschatology and the Sanctification of Carolingian Politics" (Ph.D. diss., Boston University, 1997).

50. *Annales regni Francorum* 807, ed. Kurze, pp. 122–23 and see Collins, "The 'Reviser' Revisited," p. 208 on this entry.

51. *Annales regni Francorum* 810, ed. Kurze, p. 133 and Dungal, *epistola*, ed. Dümmler, MGH:Ep. 4, p. 570.12–26.

52. See Bruce Stansfield Eastwood, "The Astronomy of Macrobius in Carolingian Europe: Dungal's Letter of 810 to Charles the Great," *Early Medieval Europe*, 3 (1994): 117–34. Bruce Eastwood also kindly sent me a copy of his forthcoming, "Pliny the Elder's *Natural History* : The Encyclopedia for Carolingian Astronomy and Cosmology."

53. Einhard, *Vita Karoli Magni* 32, ed. Waitz, p. 36.

54. Einhard's account of these portents was alluded to by the Astronomer, *Vita Hludowici* 20, ed. Ernst Tremp, MGH:SRGUS 64 (Hanover, 1995), p. 344.

55. It was also in 810 that a compilation of astronomical and computistical materials was assembled at Charlemagne's court. See Bernhard Bischoff, "Eine Sammelhandschrift Walahfrid Strabos," in Bischoff, *Mittelalterliche Studien: Ausgewählte Aufsätze zur Schriftkunde und Literaturgeschichte*, 3 vols. (Stuttgart, 1959–81), 2:38–41 and McGurk, "Carolingian Astrological Manuscripts," pp. 317, 321.

56. *Hibernicus Exul*, *carmen* 20.7, ed. Dümmler, MGH:PLAC 1, p. 410.1–12.

57. *Sedulius Scottus*, *carmen* 25, ed. Traube, MGH:PLAC 3, p. 190.10.

58. Cf. Acts 14:3 "signa et prodigia fieri" and 5:12: "signa et prodigia."

59. McCluskey, *Astronomies and Cultures in the Early Medieval Europe*, pp. 144–49. See also Valerie I.J. Flint, "The Transmission of Astrology in the Early Middle Ages," *Viator: Medieval and Renaissance Studies*, 21 (1990): 1–27; idem, *The Rise of Magic in Early Medieval Europe* (Princeton, 1991), pp. 87–146; Alexander Murray, "Missionaries and Magic in Dark-Age Europe," *Past and Present*, 136 (1992): 186–205.

60. See Ranee Katzenstein and Emilie Savage-Smith, *The Leiden Aratea: Ancient Constellations in a Medieval Manuscript* (Malibu, 1988) and McGurk, "Carolingian Astrological Manuscripts," pp. 317–32.

61. See McCluskey, *Astronomies and Cultures in the Early Medieval Europe*, pp. 144–49.

62. Eriugena, *Annotationes in Marcianum*, ed. Lutz, p. 165: "Haec ars uocatur Astrologia siue Astronomia. Astrologia dicitur ratio astrorum, quae ratio naturaliter est, id est que signa oriuntur uel occidunt. Astronomia uero dicitur astrorum lex, id est quando cogitantur que signa recte oriuntur uel quae oblique, et haec non est secundum naturam. . ."

63. The depiction of the quadrivium in the manuscript of the *De institutione arithmetica* of Boethius (Bamberg, Staatliche Bibliothek, Class. 5, fol. 9v),

which was made at Tours for Charles the Bald, presents personifications of the four arts and labels them as MUSICA, ARITHMETICA, GEOMETRIA, ASTROLOGIA: see Percy Ernst Schramm and Florentine Mütherich, *Denkmale der deutschen Könige und Kaiser: ein Beitrag zur Herrschergeschichte von Karl dem Großen bis Friedrich II, 768–1250* (Munich, 1962), pp. 129, 246, and fig. 41.

64. Hrabanus Maurus, *De magicis artibus*, PL 110:1095C–D.

65. See chapter 7 in this book.

66. See Pope Zacharias's answer of May 748 in Boniface, *epistola* 80, ed. Ernst Dümmler, MGH:Ep. 3 (Hanover, 1892), p. 260. On Virgil of Salzburg, see Franz Brunhölzl, *Histoire de la littérature latine du Moyen Âge*, vol. 1.1: L'époque merovingienne, trans. Henri Rochais (Turnhout, 1990), pp. 227–28, 294–95.

67. Item 8 of the *Indiculus* refers to the sacred rites of Mercury and of Jupiter; 20, to the days which that make for Jupiter and Mercury; 21, to the eclipse of the moon that they call the Triumph Moon; and 30, to the notion that women command the moon in order to take away the hearts of men. See *Indiculus superstitionum et paganiarum*, ed. A. Boretius, MGH: Capitularia regum Francroum, 1 (Hanover, 1883), p. 223.

68. Hrabanus, *Homiliae*, 42 "Contra eos qui in lunae defectu clamoribus se fatigabant," PL 110:78C–80A. Also trans. Dutton, in *Carolingian Civilization*, pp. 365–67. On the bewitched moon, see Flint, *The Rise of Magic*, pp. 99–100, 150–51, 229–30.

69. See also Jay Ingram, "The Monks Who Saw the Moon Split Open," in Ingram, *The Barmaid's Brain and Other Strange Tales from Science* (Toronto, 1998), pp. 174–84.

70. See D. Justin Schove in collaboration with Alan Fletcher, *Chronology of Eclipses and Comets, AD 1–1000* (Bury St. Edmunds, 1984), p. 295. See also Robert R. Newton, *Medieval Chronicles and the Rotation of the Earth* (Baltimore, 1972).

71. Astronomer, *Vita Hludowici* 58, ed. Tremp, p. 520. Matthias M. Tischler, *Einharts Vita Karoli: Studien zur Entstehung, Überlieferung und Rezeption*, MGH:Schriften, vol. 48.2 (Hanover, 2001), pp. 1109–111, has suggested that the Astronomer was Jonas of Orléans. On portents, see Scott Ashley, "The Power of Symbols: Interpreting Portents in the Carolingian Empire," *Medieval History*, 4 (1994): 34–50.

72. Astronomer, *Vita Hludowici*, 58, ed. Tremp, p. 522.

73. Cf. Isidore, *De natura rerum* 13, ed. Jacques Fontaine, in *Isidore de Seville, Traité de la nature*, Bibliothèque de l'École des Hautes Études Hispaniques, 28 (Bordeaux, 1960), pp. 272–74: "Haec cum nascitur, aut regni mutationem fertur ostendere, aut bella et pestilentias surgere." And see Tacitus, *Annales* 14.22: "Inter quae et sidus cometes effulsit, de quo uulgi opinio est, tamquam mutationem regnis portendat."

74. See Hrabanus Maurus, *De computo* 52, PL 107:696B–C: "Cometae quoque sunt stellae flammis crinitae, repente nascentes, regni mutationem aut pestilentiam aut bella aut uentos aestusque portendentes. . . ." He may have derived this from Bede, *De natura rerum* 24.2, ed. C.W. Jones, in *Corpus Christianorum: Series Latina*, vol. 123A (Turnhout, 1975).

75. An adaptation of Jer. 10:2.
76. Astronomer, *Vita Hludowici* 58, ed. Tremp, p. 522.
77. Lupus, *epistola* 8, ed. Léon Levillain, in *Loup de Ferrières, Correspondance*, 2 vols. (Paris, 1964) 1:60–72. See also *Servati Lupi epistulae*, ed. Peter K. Marshall (Leipzig, 1984), p. 28.
78. Lupus, *epistola* 8, ed. Levillain 1:68.
79. Einhard, *epistola* 40, ed. K. Hampe, MGH:Ep. 5 (Hanover, 1898–99), pp. 129–30 and trans. Dutton, *Charlemagne's Courtier*, pp. 160–61.
80. *Annales Bertiniani* 837, ed. Grat et al., p. 21, reports an attack on Frisia. Einhard's mention of the attack would seem to push his letter into the summer of 837.
81. See Paul Edward Dutton, *The Politics of Dreaming in the Carolingian Empire*, Regents Studies in Medieval Culture, ed. Eugene Vance (Lincoln, Neb., 1994), pp. 88–100.
82. See Einhard, *epistola* 14, ed. Hampe, MGH:Ep. 5, p. 117, and Dutton, *The Politics of Dreaming*, pp. 91–101.
83. *Annales Bertiniani* 839, ed. Grat et al., pp. 29–30 and see Dutton, *The Politics of Dreaming*, pp. 107–109, on Aethelwulf's pilgrimage to Rome.
84. Astronomer, *Vita Hludowici* 37, ed. Tremp, p. 422; and cf. *Annales regni Francorum* 823, ed. Kurze, pp. 163–64.
85. Astronomer, *Vita Hludowici* 27–28, ed. Tremp, pp. 372, 374.
86. Astronomer, *Vita Hludowici* 31, ed. Tremp, p. 388.
87. Astronomer, *Vita Hludowici* 41, ed. Tremp, p. 440.
88. The Great Winter Comet was also seen in Asia: see Schove, *Chronology of Eclipses and Comets*, p. 295. Note that *Annales Bertiniani* 838, ed. Grat et al., p. 26, identifies a lunar eclipse as the associated event.
89. Astronomer, *Vita Hludowici* 59, ed. Tremp, p. 528.
90. Astronomer, *Vita Hludowici* 62, ed. Tremp, p. 544.
91. Cf. Andreas of Bergamo, *Historia* 7, ed. Georg Waitz, MGH: Scriptores rerum Langobardicarum et Italicarum saec. VI–IX (Hanover, 1878; repr. 1964), p. 226 and for another late and complex joining of Louis's death and the solar eclipse see Agnellus of Ravenna, *Liber Pontificalis ecclesiae Ravennatis* 172, ed. O. Holder-Egger, MGH:SRL, p. 389.
92. Hrabanus Maurus, *De uniuerso* 7.7, PL 111:195C; Isidore, *Etymologiae* 11.3, ed. Lindsay.
93. Paschasius Radbertus commented at length on Matt. 16:1–4 in his *Expositio in Matthaeum* 7.16, PL 120:550C–556A.
94. Nithard 3.5, ed. P. Lauer, in Nithard, *Histoire des fils de Louis le Pieux*, in Les classiques de l'histoire de France au Moyen Age, vol. 7 (Paris, 1964), p. 108.
95. Nithard 2.10, ed. Lauer, p. 76.
96. See Janet L. Nelson, "Public Histories and Private History in the Work of Nithard," in Nelson, *Politics and Ritual in Early Medieval Europe* (London, 1986), pp. 195–237.
97. Nithard 4.7, ed. P. Lauer, p. 144.
98. Florus of Lyons, *carmen* 28, ed. Dümmler, MGH:PLAC 2, p. 562.97.
99. *Annales Bertiniani* 838, 840, 855, 859, ed. Grat et al., pp. 26, 36, 71, 81.

100. *Annales Fuldenses siue Annales regni Francorum orientalis* 839, 840, 841, 842, 855, 868, 887, ed. by F. Kurze after G.H. Pertz [hereafter ed. Kurze], in MGH:SRGUS (Hanover, 1891), pp. 30–31, 33–34, 45–46, 67, 105. On these annals, see *The Annals of Fulda*, trans. and annotated by Timothy Reuter, Ninth-Century Histories, 2 (Manchester, 1992).

101. *Annales Fuldenses* 875, ed. Kurze, p. 83.

102. *Annales Fuldenses* 882, ed. Kurze, p. 97.

103. On the authorship, see Heinz Löwe, "Studien zu den Annales Xantenses," *Deutsches Archiv für Erforschung des Mittelalters*, 8 (1951): 59–99.

104. *Annales Xantenses* 817, ed. B. von Simson, in *Annales Xantenses et Annales Vedastini*, MGH:SRGUS (Hanover, 1909), pp. 5–6.

105. Schove, *Chronology of Eclipses and Comets*, p. 273.

106. *Annales Xantenses* 832, ed. von Simson, p. 8.

107. On this last image, see Dutton, *The Politics of Dreaming*, pp. 120–21.

108. *Annales Xantenses* 868 [867], ed. von Simson, p. 25.

109. *Annales Xantenses* 867 [866], ed. von Simson, p. 25.

110. MGH:Ep. 6, ed. Dümmler, pp. 198.5–201.25. A poet writing early in June 870 noted a "flammicomus sol" with its nimbus lying in the middle of the sky. When priests asked him what such a thing portended, he answered that a nimbus was more often associated with the moon and signified rain, which was good for farmers: see *Carmina Centulensia* 107, ed. Traube, MGH:PLAC 3, pp. 338–39.

111. See also A. Dierkens, "Le tombeau de Charlemagne," *Byzantion*, 61 (1991): 156–80 and Janet L. Nelson, "Carolingian Royal Funerals," in *Rituals of Power from Late Antiquity to the Early Middle Ages*, ed. Frans Theuws and Janet L. Nelson (Leiden, 2000), pp. 145–53 [131–84].

112. Einhard, *Vita Karoli Magni* 31, ed. Waitz, p. 35. His marble sarcopahgus, with its late antique depiction of the Rape of Proserpina, "could no doubt be given a Christian reading, as symbolising the ascent of the soul to heaven": Nelson, "Carolingian Royal Funerals," p. 153.

113. Dutton, *Charlemagne's Courtier*, p. xiv.

114. See the reconstruction of the triumphal arch in Dutton, *Charlemagne's Courtier*, pp. 66–67.

115. *Life of Constantine* 4.69, translated and commented on by Averil Cameron and Stuart G. Hall, in *Eusebius, Life of Constantine* (Oxford, 1999), pp. 180–81, 345–46. And see Sabine G. MacCormack, *Art and Ceremony in Late Antiquity* (Berkeley, 1981), pp. 122–32.

116. See Holländer, *Early Medieval Art*, p. 72 plate 58.

117. For a color plate and analysis, see Mütherich and Gaehde, *Carolingian Painting*, pp. 38–39.

118. On the relation of the Sun and Moon in this painting, see Hab. 3:11: "Sol et luna steterunt in habitaculo suo. . ." Bede, *In Habacuc*, ed. J.E. Hudson, in *Beda venerabilis opera* 2, CCSL (Turnhout, 1983), p. 397, takes the sun to refer to Christ, the moon to the church.

119. See Walahfrid Strabo, *carmen* 19, "De quodam somnio ad Erluinum," ed. Dümmler, MGH:PLAC 2, pp. 364–65, and Jan M. Ziolkowski, *Talking*

Animals: Medieval Latin Beast Poetry, 750–1150 (Philadelphia, 1993), pp. 79–105, 273–74. Polachar is not, of course, Walahfrid himself as I had assumed in *The Politics of Dreaming*, pp. 44–45. A manuscript of Madrid portrays Zeus seated on his soaring eagle, see Herbert L. Kessler, *The Illustrated Bibles from Tours*, Studies in Manuscript Illumination, 7 (Princeton, 1977), p. 78 and fig. 119.

120. Eriugena, *Vox spiritualis* 1 and 14, ed. Édouard Jeauneau, in *Jean Scot, Homélie sur le prologue de Jean*, Sources Chrétiennes, 151 (Paris, 1969), pp. 200–208, 268–72; trans. John J. O'Meara, *Eriugena* (Oxford, 1988), pp. 158–76.

121. Theodulf, *carmen* 28 ("Versus contra iudices"), ed. Dümmler, MGH:PLAC 1, p. 508.556–76.

122. With Pisces in the center, that still makes only eleven, not twelve signs. Bruce Eastwood kindly pointed out to me that Martianus Capella in his *De nuptiis philologiae et Mercurii* 8.839, ed. James Willis (Leipzig, 1983), p. 316.19–21, distinguished between twelve metrically defined signs and eleven visually defined ones.

123. See Robert G. Calkins, *Illuminated Books of the Middle Ages* (Ithaca, N.Y., 1983), pp. 97–102 and plate 45. This historiated initial was presumably made for the original book before it underwent changes in the summer of 845. On those alterations, see Paul Edward Dutton and Herbert L. Kessler, *The Poetry and Paintings of the First Bible of Charles the Bald*, in Recentiores: Later Latin Texts and Contexts, ed. James J. O'Donnell (Ann Arbor, 1997), pp. 44–56.

124. See Dan. 12:3 and Wisd. 3:7. Hrabanus Maurus said that in a mystical sense the moon represents the church, the stars holy men: *De uniuerso* 9.3, PL 111:263C. Cf. Gregory the Great, *Homiliae in Hiezechihelem prophetam* 2, hom. 1, ed. M. Adriaen, in *Sancti Gregorii Magni Homiliae in Hiezechihelem prophetam*, in CCSL 142 (Turnhout, 1971), p. 209.

125. See Jerome, *epistola* 53, ed. J. Labourt, in *Saint Jérôme, Lettres*, vol. 3 (Paris, 1953), p. 12.4–5, 9–12. See also Donatien de Bruyne, *Préfaces de la Bible latine* (Namur, 1920), p. 2.

126. Paschasius Radbertus, *Vita Adalhardi* 6.2, in PL 120:1511A7–9.

127. Audradus, *Liber revelationum* 11, ed. Ludwig Traube, "O Roma nobilis: Philologische Untersuchungen aus dem Mittelalter," *Abhandlungen der philosophischen-philologischen Classe der königlich bayerischen Akademie der Wissenschaften* 19 (Munich, 1892), p. 383: "sedit in confinio aetheris et aeris." Also trans. Dutton, In *Carolingian Civilization*, pp. 351–59.

128. See Audradus, *Liber reuelationum*, ed. Traube, 1, p. 378, "sol conuersus est in tenebras. . . ," and the Lord said "Dedi hoc signum in sole. . ."; 10, p. 383: "Sequitur ibi, quod tribus continuis diebus sol obscuratus est et luna similiter."; 11, p. 383: "Tunc sol obscuratus est tribus continuis diebus et luna tribus eisdem noctibus." *Reuelatio* 10 is a variant version of 11. In general, the dates of Audradus's eclipses do not correspond to known Carolingian eclipses.

129. Sedulius Scottus, *De rectoribus Christianis* 20, ed. Hellmann, p. 89.

130. See Pliny, *Naturalis historia* 2.26.95.
131. Richmond Lattimore, *Themes in Greek and Latin Epitaphs* (Urbana, Illinois, 1962), p. 35. On the stars and astral deification in epitaphs, see idem, pp. 34–40, 310–314.
132. Pliny, *Naturalis historia* 2.5.19.
133. See Virgil, *Eclogae* 9.47; Ovid, *Metamorphoses* 15.779–870; Dio 69.11. And see Stefan Weinstock, *Diuus Julius* (Oxford, 1971) for an extensive study of the deification of Julius Caesar.
134. See Wilhelm Bousset, *Die Himmelsreise der Seele* (Darmstadt, 1901); A.F. Segal, "Heavenly Ascent in Hellenistic Judaism, Early Christianity, and their Environment," in *Aufstieg und Niedergang der Römischen Welt* 2, Principat, 23.2 (1980): 1333–94.
135. Plutarch, *De sera niminis uindicta* 563E–564A.
136. Claudian, *Panegyricus de tertio consolatu Honorii Augusti* 163–65. And see Alan Cameron, *Claudian: Poetry and Propaganda at the Court of Honorius* (Oxford, 1970), pp. 208–214.
137. But see the late fifth-century inscription at St-Martin's of Tours, which invited pilgrims to contemplate the deeds of Saint Martin and so to travel beyond the stars, touch heaven, and observe the angels in the high heaven: Paulinus of Périgeux, *De orantibus*, ed. M. Petsching, in Corpus Scriptorum Ecclesiasticorum Latinorum, 16 (Vienna, 1888), p. 165; also trans. J.N. Hillgarth, *The Conversion of Western Europe, 350–750* (Englewood Cliffs, 1969), p. 31 and rev. ed. *Christianity and Paganism, 350–750: The Conversion of Europe* (Philadelphia, 1986), p. 31.
138. Boniface, *epistola* 10, ed. Dümmler, MGH:Ep. 3, pp. 252–53.
139. *Versus libris saeculi octavi adiecti* 7.[2].3, ed. Dümmler, MGH:PLAC 1, p. 94.
140. *Karolus Magnus et Leo Papa*, ed. Dümmler, MGH:PLAC 1, p. 366.13.
141. See *Karolus Magnus et Leo Papa*, ed. Dümmler, MGH:PLAC 1, p. 367.56 and Gabriel Silagi, "Karolus—cara lux," *Deutsches Archiv*, 37 (1981): 786–91.
142. See *Karolus Magnus et Leo Papa*, ed. Dümmler, MGH:PLAC 1, p. 366.14–16.
143. See Dutton and Jeauneau, "The Verses of the *Codex Aureus*," p. 110. The spatial and symbolical parallelism of the two pages is extensive, since the baldachin of the throne roughly matches the first curved vault of heaven on the *Majestas Agni* page; Earth and Sea overlap the cornucopia-bearing attendants on Charles's page; and the Lamb of God rests perfectly above the outstretched *Dextra Dei* of the enthronement page.
144. Ermoldus, *In laudem gloriosissimi Pippini regis*, ed. Dümmler, MGH:PLAC 2, p. 80.29–32.
145. Theodulf, *carmen* 25, ed. Dümmler, MGH:PLAC 1, p. 485.67–68.
146. See Alcuin, *carmen* 72, ed. Dümmler, MGH:PLAC 1, p. 295.10; Hibernicus Exul, *carmen* 1, ed. Dümmler, MGH:PLAC 1, p. 396.24.
147. Hibernicus Exul, *carmen* 19, ed. Dümmler, MGH:PLAC 1, p. 408.13.
148. On Christ's ascension to the heavens, see Ermoldus, *In honorem Hludowici* 2, ed. Dümmler, MGH:PLAC 2, p. 34.357.

149. *De exordio gentis Francorum*, ed. Dümmler, MGH:PLAC 2, p. 144.111.
150. *Gerwardi uersus* on the presentation of Einhard's *Vita Karoli Magni* to Louis the Pious, ed. Dümmler, MGH:PLAC 2, p. 126.4 and cf. Virgil, *Aeneid* 7.99.
151. Walahfrid, *carmen* 88, ed. Dümmler, MGH:PLAC 2, p. 422.34.
152. *Epitaphium Hludowici imperatoris*, ed. Dümmler, MGH:PLAC 2, p. 653.4: "spiritus astra petit."
153. Hrabanus Maurus, *epistola* 46, ed. Dümmler, MGH:Ep. 5, p. 501.33–34.
154. *De exordio gentis Francorum*, ed. Dümmler, MGH:PLAC 2, p. 144.123 and cf. "uitamque reliquit in astris" of Virgil, *Aeneid* 5.517.
155. Sedulius Scottus, *carmen* 28, ed. Traube, MGH:PLAC 3, p. 193.1–6.
156. *Carmen Centulensia* 105, ed. Traube, MGH:PLAC 3, p. 337.48–49.
157. *De principibus Francorum*, ed. Dümmler, MGH:PLAC 2, p. 673.29.
158. *Carmina Centulensia* 92, ed. Traube, MGH:PLAC 3, p. 331.10.
159. Though not quite so many stars as found in the translation of Edward Gerard Doyle in Sedulius Scottus, *On Christian Rulers and the Poems*, Medieval & Renaissance Texts & Studies, 7 (Binghamton, 1983), who occasionally inserts a "star" where no *stella* is found in the Latin.
160. Sedulius Scottus, *De rectoribus Christianis* 9, ed. Hellmann, p. 46.
161. Sedulius Scottus, *carmen* 2.12, ed. Traube, MGH:PLAC 3, p. 180.4: "stella uenusta nitens" and see also 2.12, p. 180.13–14.
162. Sedulius Scottus, *carmen* 2.25, ed. Traube, MGH:PLAC 3, p. 191.25: "nobile lumen" and p. 192.67: "Nobile sidus."
163. Sedulius Scottus, *carmen* 2.30, ed. Traube, MGH:PLAC 3, p. 195.2: "Eximium sidus"; p. 195.24: "Resplendens sidus. . .; p. 195.28: "Sidere laetatur te quoque magnanimo"; p. 196.71–72: "Sidere Caesareo. . . ."
164. Sedulius Scottus, *carmen* 2.26, ed. Traube, MGH:PLAC 3, p. 192.13–14: "nobis concessit ab astris / Hoc sidus rutilum"; *carmen* 2.54, ed. Traube, MGH:PLAC 3, p. 212.1: "rutilans sub axe sidus."
165. Sedulius Scottus, *carmen* 2.60, ed. Traube, MGH:PLAC 3, p. 217.9–10: "Lucifer nobis rutilat uenustus / Franciae sidus super astra notum. . ."
166. Sedulius Scottus, *carmen* 2.28, ed. Traube, MGH:PLAC 3, p. 194.49: "spes aurea, nobile sidus."
167. Sedulius Scottus, *carmen* 2.14, ed. Traube, MGH:PLAC 3, p. 183.28: "angelicos uultus sidus hoc assimulat."
168. Sedulius Scottus, *carmen* 2.14, ed. Traube, MGH:PLAC 3, p. 189.7–8: "Haec noua stella micat, laus orbis, spes quoque Romae / Europae populis haec noua stella micat."
169. Sedulius Scottus, *carmen* 2.77, ed. Traube, MGH:PLAC 3, p. 228.12: "Regia stella micat."
170. Sedulius Scottus, *carmen* 2.15, ed. Traube, MGH:PLAC 3, p. 183.10: "geminae stellae" and p. 183.19–20.
171. Sedulius Scottus, *carmen* 2.24, ed. Traube, MGH:PLAC 3, p. 190.45: "Ludewicus Lucifer orbis."
172. Sedulius Scottus, *carmen* 2.61, ed. Traube, MGH:PLAC 3, p. 217.10: "Fulgens ceu rutilo splendida stella polo" and *carmen* 2.78, p. 228.2: "Stella uenustatis."

173. Sedulius Scottus, *De rectoribus Christianis, carmen* 5, ed. Traube, MGH:PLAC 3, p. 157.25–26.; and also ed. Hellmann, p. 37.

174. Sedulius Scottus, *De rectoribus Christianis* 4, ed. Hellmann, p. 31.13–20.

175. Sedulius Scottus, *carmen* 3.3, ed. Traube, MGH:PLAC 3, pp. 233–34. Traube, p. 778, identified him as an Italian noble.

176. Sedulius Scottus, *carmen* 2.67, ed. Traube, MGH:PLAC 3, p. 221.20: "sidus in orbe micat."

177. Sedulius Scottus, *carmen* 2.38, ed. Traube, MGH:PLAC 3, p. 202.11–12 and 36: "Sis decus in terra claraque stella polo."

178. Sedulius Scottus, *carmen* 2.71, ed. Traube, MGH:PLAC 3, p. 223.14: "Purpureum sidus terrigenumque decus."

179. Sedulius Scottus, *carmen* 2.6, ed. Traube, MGH:PLAC 3, p. 171.47–48.

180. Sedulius Scottus, *carmen* 2.7, ed. Traube, MGH:PLAC 3, p. 174.81.

181. Sedulius Scottus, *carmen* 2.17, ed. Traube, MGH:PLAC 3, p. 184.13–16.

182. Sedulius Scottus, *carmen* 2.18, ed. Traube, MGH:PLAC 3, p. 185.13 and 19: "lux aurea cosmi."

183. Sedulius Scottus, *carmen* 2.66, ed. Traube, MGH:PLAC 3, p. 220.1: "Aureum sidus pietate fulgens."

184. Sedulius Scottus, *carmen* 3.2, ed. Traube, MGH:PLAC 3, p. 233.9–10.

185. Sedulius Scottus, *De rectoribus Christianis, carmen* 1.3, ed. Traube, MGH:PLAC 3, p. 155.15–16; and also ed. Hellmann, p. 25.

186. Sedulius Scottus, *De rectoribus Christianis, carmen* 1.6, ed. Traube, MGH:PLAC 3, p. 156.5–8; and also ed. Hellmann, p.33.

187. Sedulius Scottus, *De rectoribus Christianis* 16, ed. Hellmann, p. 73 and see "De uariis temporibus regni," ed. Hellmann, p. 132. On the tower of Siloam and the eighteen sinners who perished when it fell, see Luke 13:4.

188. Eriugena, *carmen* 8.1, ed. Traube, MGH:PLAC 3, p. 549.2; also ed. and trans. Herren, *Iohannis Scotti Eriugenae Carmina*, p. 112.

189. Eriugena, *epistola*, ed. Dümmler, MGH:Ep. 6, p. 158.24.

190. Eriugena, *carmen* 5.4, ed. Traube, MGH:PLAC 3, p. 546.10–12.

191. Liutprand, *Relatio de legatione Constantinopolitana* 10, ed. Joseph Becker, in *Die Werke Liudprands von Cremona*, MGH:SRGUS (Hanover, 1915), p. 181.

192. Eriugena, *carmen* 2.5, ed. Traube, MGH:PLAC 3, p. 535.49–50. And yet in the *Periphyseon*, Eriugena qualifies and, indeed, undermines this talk of humans shining as stars: see Eriugena, *Periphyseon* 5 (PL 122: 988A–B), ed. Édouard Jeauneau, *Ioannis Scotti seu Eriugenae Periphyseon: Liber quintus*, CCCM 165 (Turnhout, 2003), pp. 178–79.

193. Eriugena, *carmen* 2.4, ed. Traube, MGH:PLAC 3, p. 534.51–52.

194. Eriugena, *carmen* 2.8, ed. Traube, MGH:PLAC 3, p. 537.1–5.

195. On Eriugena's role as court poet, see Paul Edward Dutton, "Eriugena, the Royal Poet," in *Jean Scot Écrivain: actes du IVe Colloque international, Montréal, 28 août–2 septembre 1983*, ed. G.-H. Allard (Montréal, 1986), pp. 51–80.

196. Eriugena, *carmen* 9, ed. Traube, MGH:PLAC 3, pp. 550–52. See also Dutton and Jeauneau, "The Verses of the *Codex Aureus*," pp. 102–13 and M. Foussard, "Aulae sidereae. Vers de Jean Scot au roi Charles," *Cahiers archéologiques*, 21 (1971): 79–88.

197. See *carmen* 1, line 3, ed. Paul Edward Dutton, "Evidence that Dubthach's Priscian Codex Once Belonged to Eriugena," in *From Athens to Chartres: Neoplatonism and Medieval Thought*. *Studies in Honour of Édouard Jeauneau* (Leiden, 1992), pp. 18–19, and, on the circumstances, pp. 20–21.

198. See Dutton, "Evidence that Dubthach's Priscian Codex Once Belonged to Eriugena," pp. 20–21.

199. Notker, *Gesta Karoli Magni* 2.6, ed. Haefele, pp. 56–57.

200. For illustrations, see J. Hubert, J. Porcher, and W. F. Volbach, *The Carolingian Renaissance*, trans. James Emmons, Stuart Gilbert, and Robert Allen (New York, 1970), pp. 147, 149.

201. Schramm and Mütherich, *Denkmale der deutschen Könige und Kaiser*, p. 95; the edition of the text was worked on by Bernhard Bischoff.

202. For a plate, see Magnus Backes and Regine Dölling, *Art of the Dark Ages*, trans. Francisca Garvie (New York, 1970), p. 150 and Sigmund Freiherr von Pölnitz, *Die Bamberger Kaisermäntel* (Weißenhorn, 1973), pp. 32–39. See also McCluskey, *Astronomies and Cultures in Early Medieval Europe*, pp. 141–45.

203. On the Mantle and its Byzantine character, see Elizabeth Caroll Waldron O'Connor, "The Star Mantle of Henry II" (Ph.D. diss., Columbia University, 1980), pp. 63–66.

204. Abbo, *Liber bellorum Parisiacae urbis* 2, ed. Henri Waquet, Abbon, *Le siège de Paris par les Normands: poème du IXe siècle*, Les classiques de l'histoire de France au Moyen Age, 20 (Paris, 1964), p. 90.331.

205. See *La Cattedra lignea S. Pietro in Vaticano*, in Memorie, 10 (Atti della Pontificia Accademia Romana di Archeologia, ser. 3; Vatican, 1971). See also Lawrence Nees, *A Tainted Mantle: Hercules and the Classical Tradition at the Carolingian Court* (Philadelphia, 1991), pp. 147–257 and Nikolaus Staubach, *Rex Christianus: Hofkultur und Herrschaftspropaganda im Reich Karls des Kahlen*, vol. 2: *Die Grundlegung der 'religion royale,'* Pictura et Poesis, 2.2 (Cologne, 1993), pp. 283–334.

206. Eriugena, *Periphyseon* 4, PL 122:752A–B and ed. Édouard Jeauneau, *Iohannis Scotti seu Eriugenae Periphyseon: Liber quartus*, CCCM 164 (Turnhout, 2000), p. 17.

207. See Kurt Weitzmann, "The Heracles Plaques of St. Peter's Cathedra," *The Art Bulletin*, 55 (1973): 1–37; Weitzmann, "An Addendum to the 'Heracles Plaques of St. Peter's Cathedra,' " *The Art Bulletin*, 56 (1974): 248–52.

208. *Periphyseon* 4 (770A), ed. Jeauneau, in *Iohannis Scotti seu Eriugenae Periphyseon: Liber quartus*, p. 42.1138–39; also edited separately by Édouard Jeauneau, in *Iohannis Scotti Eriugenae Periphyseon (De diuisione naturae), Liber quartus*, Scriptores Latini Hiberniae, 13 (Dublin, 1995), p. 68.

209. See Sedulius Scottus, *De rectoribus Christianis* 2, ed. Hellmann, p. 26.

210. See Plato, *Timaeus* 17C and Paul Edward Dutton, "*Illustre ciuitatis et populi exemplum*: Plato's *Timaeus* and the Transmission from Calcidius to the End of the Twelfth Century of a Tripartite Scheme of Society," *Mediaeval Studies*, 45 (1983): 79–102.

211. Sedulius Scottus, *De rectoribus Christianis, carmen* 1.4, ed. Traube, MGH:PLAC 3, p. 155.3–6; and also ed. Hellmann, p. 27.

212. See *La Cattedra lignea S. Pietro in Vaticano*, in *Memorie*, 10, plate 63, for the dimensions of the throne.

213. See Genevra Kornbluth, *Engraved Gems of the Carolingian Empire* (University Park, Penn., 1995). The Throne of Dagobert also has three empty oval spaces on the back of the throne.

214. See Clive N. Ruggles and Nicholas J. Saunders, "The Study of Cultural Astronomy," in *Astronomies and Cultures: Papers derived from the third "Oxford" International Symposium on Archaeoastronomy, St. Andrews, UK, September, 1990* (Niwot, Colorado, 1990), pp. 1–31.

Chapter 5   Whispering Secrets to a Dark Age

* An earlier version of this essay as a work in progress is to appear as "Keeping Secrets in a Dark Age" in *The Dragon and the Unicorn: Rhetoric and the Discourses of Power in Court Culture, East and West*, ed. David R. Knechtges and Eugene Vance (Washington: University of Washington Press). That essay was based on a talk given to the Comparative Court Cultures in Cross-Cultural Perspective conference held at the National Taiwan University in Taipei in November 1998.

1. Einhard, *Translatio et miracula sanctorum Marcellini et Petri* 2.1, ed. Georg Waitz, MGH: Scriptores 15.1 (Hanover, 1888), p. 245; and see *Charlemagne's Courtier: The Complete Einhard*, ed. and trans. Paul Edward Dutton (Peterborough, Ont., 1998), p. 83.

2. On the image of sleepless Carolingian kings, see Paul Edward Dutton, *The Politics of Dreaming in the Carolingian Empire*, Regents Studies in Medieval Culture, ed. Eugene Vance (Lincoln, Neb., 1994), pp. 5–22.

3. See *Schedula siue Libellus expostulationis* 33, Patrologia Latina, ed. J.P. Migne, vol. 126, col. 624A2–D3. Also see Eriugena's biting 'epitaph' for one of the two still living Hincmars, Hincmar of Rheims or his nephew Hincmar of Laon: full text and discussion in Paul Edward Dutton, "Eriugena, the Royal Poet," in *Jean Scot Écrivain: actes du IVe Colloque international, Montréal, 28 août–2 septembre 1983*, ed. G.-H. Allard (Montréal, 1986), pp. 56–59.

4. See Einhard's account of his dinners with the relics merchant Deusdona in Einhard, *Translatio et miracula* 1.1, ed. Waitz, p. 240.

5. See plate IV and fig. 17 in Paul Edward Dutton and Herbert L. Kessler, *The Poetry and Paintings of the First Bible of Charles the Bald*, Recentiores: Later Latin Texts and Contexts, ed. James J. O'Donnell (Ann Arbor, 1997).

6. For a useful survey of the topic, see Sissela Bok, *Secrets: On the Ethics of Concealment and Revelation* (New York, 1982). On the social history of secrets in the Middle Ages, see Karma Lochrie, *Covert Operations: The Medieval Uses of Secrecy* (Philadelphia, 1999).

7. Even Charlemagne's capitularies had force from the fact that he 'said them' in public. On issues of literacy and orality in the early Middle Ages, see Rosamond McKitterick, *The Carolingians and the Written Word* (Cambridge, 1989); *The Uses of Literacy in Early Medieval Europe*, ed. Rosamond McKitterick (Cambridge, 1990); Michel Banniard, *Viva Voce: communication écrite et communication orale du IVe au IXe siècle en Occident latin* (Paris, 1992); and D.H. Green, *Medieval Listening and Writing: The Primary Reception of German Literature, 800–1300* (Cambridge, 1994).

8. Alcuin, *Disputatio Pippini cum Albino* 95, ed. Lloyd William Daly and Walter Suchier, in *Altercatio Hadriani Augusti et Epicteti philosophi* (Urbana, 1939), p. 142 and trans. Paul Edward Dutton, *Carolingian Civilization: A Reader*, 2nd ed. (Peterborough, Ont., 2004), pp. 140–46.

9. See *Annales Bertiniani* 851, ed. Félix Grat, Jeanne Vielliard, and Suzanne Clémencet, in *Annales de Saint-Bertin* (Paris, 1964), p. 61. Also trans. Janet L. Nelson, *The Annals of St-Bertin*, Ninth-Century Histories, vol. 1 (Manchester, 1991).

10. On the sacerdotal function of kings, see Ernst Kantorowicz, *The King's Two Bodies: A Study of Mediaeval Political Theology* (Princeton, 1957).

11. Matt. 10:26. Both Mark 4:22 and Luke 8:17 take "For there is nothing hidden except to be made visible; nothing is secret except to come to light," from the Parable of the Lamp. Isidore, *Synonyma* 2.60, PL 83:859A insists upon God's capacity to penetrate and reveal all secrets: "Cognitioni eius nihil occultum est, omnia secreta uis uirtutis eius irrumpit, nulla occulta sibi latere patitur, nullis obicibus, ut penetret impeditur."

12. "Twelve Songs: VIII," in W.H. Auden, *Collected Poems*, ed. Edward Mendelson (New York, 1976), p. 119.

13. See, for instance, *Annales Xantenses* 867 (866), ed. B. von Simson, in *Annales Xantenses et Annales Vedastini*, MGH: Scriptores rerum Germanicarum in usum scholarum (Hanover, 1909), p. 24. Leidradus in a letter to Charlemagne called God "inspector conscientiarum Dominus omnipotens": *epistola*, ed. Ernst Dümmler, MGH: Epistolae 4 (Hanover, 1895; repr. 1974), p. 542.23–24.

14. See *Capitulare missorum generale* 32, ed. Alfred Boretius, in MGH: Capitularia regum Francorum 1 (Hanover, 1883), p. 97.

15. It may have been for this reason that in 799 Charlemagne and his court scholars asked Alcuin if he had a copy of the debate Felix had had with a Saracen. Charlemagne was already in contact with the court of Hārūn al-Rāshid and may have wished to know more about Saracen lands, customs, and religion. But it is just as likely that the request concerned the continuing investigation of the Adoptionist thought of Felix of Urgel. See Alcuin, *epistola* 172, ed. Ernst Dümmler, MGH:Ep. 4 (Hanover, 1895; repr. Berlin, 1974), pp. 284.30–285.2.

16. Gregory the Great, *Dialogues* 2.20, in PL 66:172B4–5. Also trans. Myra L. Uhlfelder, *The Dialogues of Gregory the Great. Book Two: Saint Benedict* (Indianapolis, 1967), p. 29. And see the examples of Benedict's powers of observation in 2.16–20 (PL 66:164A–172B).

17. Paschasius Radbertus, *Epitaphium Arsenii* 1.27–28, ed. Ernst Dümmler, in *Radbert's Epitaphium Arsenii*, in *Philosophische und historische Abhandlungen der königlichen Akademie der Wissenschaften zu Berlin*, 2 (Berlin, 1900), pp. 57–58. Also trans. Allen Cabaniss, *Charlemagne's Cousins: Contemporary Lives of Adalard and Wala* (Syracuse, N.Y., 1967).

18. See Jean-Claude Schmitt, *Le raison des gestes dans l'occident médiévale* (Paris, 1990).

19. *Regula Sancti Benedicti* 7.44–48, ed. Timothy Fry, in *RB 1980: The Rule of St. Benedict in Latin and English with Notes* (Collegeville, Minn., 1981), p. 198.

20. On Gottschalk's career, see D.E. Nineham, "Gottschalk of Orbais: Reactionary or Precursor of the Reformation," *Journal of Ecclesiastical History*, 40 (1989): 1–18 and David Ganz, "The Debate on Predestination," in *Charles the Bald: Court and Kingdom*, 2nd rev. ed., ed. Margaret T. Gibson and Janet L. Nelson (Aldershot, 1990), pp. 283–302.

21. Hincmar of Rheims, *De ordine palatii* 2 (5), ed. Thomas Gross and Rudolf Schieffer, MGH: Fontes Iuris Germanici antiqui, 3 (Hanover, 1980), pp. 42–44. Also trans. David Herlihy, in Dutton, *Carolingian Civilization*, pp. 517–32.

22. See Dutton, *The Politics of Dreaming*, pp. 11–15.

23. Notker, *Gesta Karoli Magni* 2.12, ed. H.F. Haefele, in MGH: Scriptores rerum Germanicarum, Nova Series 12 (Berlin, 1959), p. 72. Also trans. Lewis Thorpe, in *Einhard and Notker the Stammerer: Two Lives of Charlemagne* (Harmondsworth, 1969).

24. *Chronicon Laureshamense*, ed. K.A.F. Pertz, MGH:SS 21 (Hanover, 1869), pp. 357–59. Also trans. Paul Edward Dutton in Jacqueline Murray, *Love, Marriage, and Family in the Middle Ages: A Reader* (Peterborough, Ont., 2001), pp. 75–77.

25. Notker, *Gesta Karoli Magni* 1.30, ed. Haefele, p. 41.

26. Notker, *Gesta Karoli Magni* 2.11, ed. Haefele, p. 68.

27. See Notker, *Gesta Karoli Magni* 1.4, ed. Haefele, p. 6 and Jonas of Orléans, *De institutione regia* 11, ed. Jean Reviron, in *Les idées politico-religieuses d'un évêque du IXe siècle. Jonas d'Orléans et son "De institutione regia": étude et texte critique*, in L'église et l'état au Moyen Age, vol. 1 (Paris, 1930), p. 171. Also trans. R.W. Dyson, *A Ninth-Century Political Tract: The "De institutione Regia" of Joans of Orléans* (Smithtown, 1983), pp. 43–44.

28. Though Theodulf, *carmen* 27, ed. Ernst Dümmler, in MGH: Poetae Latini Aevi Carolini 1 (Berlin, 1881), p. 492.45–48 [and not as in the first printing of Dutton, *Charlemagne's Courtier*, p. 4] should, perhaps, be taken as an indication of the general sensitivities at court and the carefulness of public discourse: see Jan M. Ziolkowski, *Talking Animals: Medieval Latin Beast Poetry, 750–1150* (Philadelphia, 1993), p. 270. Dümmler suggested that this bashful Delia was a daughter of Charlemagne.

29. Paschasius Radbertus, *Epitaphium Arsenii* 1.8, ed. Dümmler, p. 33.

30. See *Pactus Legis Salicae* 30.7, ed. Karl August Eckhardt, in MGH: Legum, Sectio I: Leges Nationum Germanicarum, vol. 4.1 (Hanover, 1962), p. 120. Also trans. Katherine Fischer Drew, *The Laws of the Salian Franks* (Philadelphia, 1991). And see the revised *Lex Salica Karolina* 70.6, ed. Eckhardt, in MGH: Legum, Sectio I: Leges Nationum Germanicarum, vol. 4.2 (Hanover, 1969), p. 228.

31. *Annales Fuldenses* 858, ed. by F. Kurze after G.H. Pertz [hereafter ed. Kurze], in MGH:SRGUS (Hanover, 1891), p. 51. Also trans. Timothy Reuter, *The Annals of Fulda*, Ninth-Century Histories, vol. 2 (Manchester, 1992).

32. *Annales Bertiniani* 839, ed. Grat et al., p. 30.

33. Paschasius Radbertus, *Epitaphium Arsenii* 2.8, ed. Dümmler, p. 69.

34. *Annales regni Francorum* 823, ed. by F. Kurze after G.H. Pertz [hereafter ed. Kurze], in MGH:SRGUS (Hanover, 1895), pp. 161–62. Also trans.

B.W. Scholz and Barbara Rogers, *Carolingian Chronicles: "Royal Frankish Annals" and Nithard's "Histories"* (Ann Arbor, 1970).

35. *Constitutum Constantini* 4, ed. Horst Fuhrmann, MGH: Fontes Iuris Germanici antiqui in usum scholarum, 10 (Hanover, 1968), p. 62.

36. See William Eamon, *Science and the Secrets of Nature: Books of Secrets in Medieval and Early Modern Culture* (Princeton, 1994), especially pp. 15–90.

37. The same flow of information underlay the relationship of vassals and lords, for according to Fulbert of Chartres's set of obligations placed upon vassals, a vassal was not to harm a lord in his secrets: see *The Letters and Poems of Fulbert of Chartres, epistola* 51, ed. and trans. Frederick Behrends (Oxford, 1976), pp. 90–93.

38. *Capitulare missorum generale* 2, ed. Boretius, in MGH:Cap. 1, p. 92.

39. See Hincmar of Rheims, *De ordine palatii* 7(36), ed. Gross and Schieffer, pp. 94–96.

40. Sedulius Scottus, *De rectoribus Christianis* 6, ed. S. Hellmann, *Sedulius Scottus*, in Quellen und Untersuchungen zur lateinischen Philologie des Mittelalters, vol. 1 (Munich, 1906), p. 39. Also trans. Edward Gerard Doyle, *Sedulius Scottus: On Christian Rulers and The Poems*, in Medieval & Renaissance Texts & Studies, vol. 17 (Binghamton, 1983).

41. Lupus, *epistola* 31, ed. Léon Levillain, *Loup de Ferrières: Correspondance*, 2 vols., in Les classiques de l'histoire au Moyen Age, vols. 10 and 16 (Paris, 1964), 1:144. See also *Servati Lupi epistulae*, ed. Peter K. Marshall (Leipzig, 1984); also trans. Graydon W. Regenos, *The Letters of Lupus of Ferrières* (The Hague, 1966). The last two quotations are from Horace, *Ars Poetica* 5.390 and *Ep.* 1.18.71.

42. Lupus, *epistola* 37, ed. Levillain, 1:164.

43. Walahfrid Strabo, *Prologus*, ed. O. Holder-Egger, in *Einhardi Vita Karoli Magni*, ed. G. Waitz after G.H. Pertz, 6th ed. overseen by O. Holder-Egger [hereafter ed. Waitz], in MGH:SRGUS (Hanover, 1911), p. xxix; trans. Dutton, *Charlemagne's Courtier*, p. 8.

44. Hincmar of Rheims, *De ordine palatii* 6 (31), ed. Gross and Schieffer, p. 86.

45. Hincmar of Rheims, *De ordine palatii* 6 (31), ed. Gross and Schieffer, pp. 86, 88.

46. Hincmar, *De ordine palatii* 6 (31), ed. Gross and Schieffer, p. 88.

47. Hincmar of Rheims, *De ordine palatii* 4 (16), ed. Gross and Schieffer, p. 64. In *Annales Bertiniani* 866, ed. Grat et al., p. 130, Hincmar, the author of this portion of the annals, calls Lothar's man Walter "suum a secretis domesticum." The Eriugenian glosses (Barcelona, Archivo de la Corona de Aragón, Ripoll 59, fol. 279r) on Priscian's *Institutiones grammaticae* has the following gloss on ASECRETIS: "Sic fac asecretis a[c]caliculis, magister secreti et magister secretum; sic magister caliculi et caliculorum." On this commentary, see Paul Edward Dutton and Anneli Luhtala, "Eriugena in Priscianum," *Mediaeval Studies*, 56 (1994): 153–63.

48. See Hincmar of Rheims, *De ordine palatii* 6 (30), ed. Gross and Schieffer, pp. 84, 86.

49. *Annales regni Francorum* 793, ed. Kurze, p. 95.

50. Astronomer, *Vita Hludowici imperatoris* 59, ed. Ernst Tremp, in MGH: Scriptores rerum Germanicarum in usum scholarum separatim editi, 64 (Hanover, 1995), p. 524. Also trans. Allen Cabaniss, *Son of Charlemagne: A Contemporary Life of Louis the Pious* (Syracuse, 1961).

51. *Capitulare missorum in Theodonis villa datum secundum generale* 10, ed. Boretius, in MGH:Cap. 1, p. 124.

52. *Annales Bertiniani* 838, ed. Grat et al., p. 23 and cf. *Annales Fuldenses* 838, ed. Kurze, p. 29.

53. *Annales Fuldenses* 874, ed. Kurze, pp. 81–82.

54. *Annales regni Francorum* 788, ed. Kurze, p. 80.

55. Nithard, *Historiarum libri IIII* 1.3, ed. P. Lauer, in *Nithard, Histoire des fils de Louis le Pieux*, in Les classiques de l'histoire de France au Moyen Age, vol. 7 (Paris, 1964), p. 10. Also trans. in Scholz and Rogers, *Frankish Annals*.

56. Astronomer, *Vita Hludowici* 43, ed. Tremp, pp. 452, 454.

57. Nithard, *Historiarum* 1.3, ed. Lauer, pp. 8–10.

58. Astronomer, *Vita Hludowici* 44, ed. Tremp, p. 454–56.

59. Paschasius Radbertus, *Epitaphium Arsenii* 2.8, ed. Dümmler, p. 69.

60. Astronomer, *Vita Hludowici* 48, ed. Tremp, p. 472. The latter statement was a fulfillment of 1 Cor. 15:33.

61. See chapter 6, in this book.

62. Notker, *Gesta Karoli Magni* 2.12, ed. Haefele, pp. 71–72.

63. Hincmar of Rheims, *De ordine palatii* 5 (19), ed. Gross and Schieffer, p. 68.

64. See *Annales regni Francorum* 785 (the revised version), ed. Kurze, p. 71. Here the reviser of the royal annals reported that the conspiracy by Hardrad was quickly revealed to Charlemagne.

65. *Annales Fuldenses* 870, ed. Kurze, p. 70.

66. Notker, *Gesta Karoli Magni* 1.4, ed. Haefele, p. 5.

67. On the incident, see Janet L. Nelson, "A Tale of Two Princes: Politics, Text, and Ideology in a Carolingian Annal," *Studies in Medieval and Renaissance History*, n.s., 10 (1988): 105–40; repr. in Janet L. Nelson, *Rulers and Ruling Families in Early Medieval Europe: Alfred, Charles the Bald, and Others*, Variorum Collected Studies Series, CS 657 (Aldershot, 1999), item XVI; and Dutton, *The Politics of Dreaming*, pp. 211–215.

68. High churchmen on occasion refused to play some of these treacherous games. When Willibert, the bishop of Cologne, learned of Charles the Bald's plans to unseat the east Germanic monarchy in 876, he first asked Charles to desist and, when that proved unsuccessful, he sent a priest to inform King Louis the Younger of the ambush planned against him. See *Annales Fuldenses* 876, ed. Kurze, p. 88.

69. *Annales regni Francorum* 792 (the revised version), ed. Kurze, pp. 91, 93.

70. *Annales regni Francorum* 792 (the revised version), ed. Kurze, pp. 91, 93.

71. *Annales regni Francorum* 815, ed. Kurze, p. 142.

72. Astronomer, *Vita Hludowici* 29, ed. Tremp, pp. 380–84.

73. Astronomer, *Vita Hludowici* 25, ed. Tremp, p. 358.

74. Paschasius Radbertus, *Epitaphium Arsenii* 1.26, ed. Dümmler, pp. 55–56.

75. *Poor Richard's Almanac*, July 1735.

76. Paul the Deacon, *De gestis Langobardorum* 6.6, ed. L. Bethmann and G. Waitz, in MGH: Scriptores rerum Langobardicarum et Italicarum, saec. VI–IX (Hanover, 1878), p. 167.

77. Einhard, *Translatio* 1.1–2.3, ed. Waitz, pp. 239–46; and trans. Dutton, in *Charlemagne's Courtier*, pp. 69–87. And see Marguerite Bondois, *La Translation des saints Marcellin et Pierre: Études sur Einhard et sa vie politique de 827 à 834* (Paris, 1907).

78. We should, for instance, note that the Astronomer claimed that the pope had granted his approval for Einhard to translate the bodies of Marcellinus and Peter: see Astronomer, *Vita Hludowici* 41, ed. Tremp, p. 442.

79. See Patrick J. Geary, *Furta Sacra: Thefts of Relics in the Central Middle Ages*, rev. ed. (Princeton, 1990).

80. Herodotus 7.239 and Aulus Gellius, *Noctes Atticae* 17.9.16–17. Aulus Gellius, *Noctes Atticae* 17.9.21, also reported a variation on the same, but with the human body used as a surface: see chapter 1 in this book. See also Jocelyn Penny Small, *Wax Tablets of the Mind: Cognitive Studies of Memory and Literacy in Classical Antiquity* (London, 1997), p. 67.

81. Gregory of Tours, *Historiae* 7.30, ed. Bruno Krusch and Wilhelm Levison, in MGH: Scriptores rerum Merovingicarum 1.1 (Hanover, 1951), p. 350. Also trans. Lewis Thorpe, *Gregory of Tours, The History of the Franks* (Harmondsworth, 1974).

82. Theodulf of Orléans, *carmen* 25, ed. Dümmler, p. 487.147–50; and see Peter Godman, *Poetry of the Carolingian Renaissance* (Norman, Okla., 1985), pp. 156–57.

83. On wax tablets in the Middle Ages, see Élisabeth Lalou, "Inventaire des tablettes médiévales et présentation générale," in *Les tablettes à écrire de l'antiquité à l'époque moderne: Actes du colloque international du Centre National de la Recherche Scientifique, Paris, Institut de France, 10–11 octobre 1990*, ed. Élisabeth Lalou (Turnhout, 1992), pp. 233–80; Richard H. Rouse and Mary A. Rouse, "The Vocabulary of Wax Tablets," in *Vocabulaire du livre et de l'écriture au moyen âge: Actes de la table ronde, Paris 24–26 septembre 1987*, ed. Olga Weijers (Turnhout, 1989), pp. 220–30 and a revised version of the same in *Harvard Library Bulletin*, new series, 1 (1990): 12–19; Richard H. Rouse and Mary A. Rouse, "Wax Tablets," in *Language & Communication*, 9 (1989): 175–91.

84. *Fredegarii Chronicorum Liber quartus cum Continuationibus: The Fourth Book of the Chronicle of Fredegar with Its Continuations* 40, ed. and trans. J.M. Wallace-Hadrill (London, 1960), p. 33.

85. *Fredegarii Chronicorum Liber quartus* 41–42, ed. and trans. Wallace-Hadrill, pp. 34–35.

86. Even in the Merovingian period, some understood the risks of candid correspondence. The exiled Childeric broke a gold coin in half and gave one piece to a friend who would remain behind in the kingdom; when Childeric received the half coin and reunited the two pieces, he would know that it was safe to return. See Gregory of Tours, *Historiae* 2.12, ed. Krusch and Levison, p. 61.

87. Alcuin, *epistola* 184, ed. Dümmler, in MGH:Ep. 4, p. 309. Also trans. Stephen Allott, *Alcuin of York, c. A.D. 732 to 804: His Life and Letters* (York, 1974). On Alcuin's treatment of his correspondence, see Mary Delafield Garrison, "Alcuin's World Through His Letters and Verse" (Ph.D. diss, University of Cambridge, 1996), pp. 30–34 and Ernst Dümmler, "Alcvinstudien," *Sitzungsberichte der Königlich preussischen Akademie der Wissenschaften zu Berlin* (1891.1), Stücke I–XXVII, pp. 500–501 [495–523].

88. Lupus, *epistola* 11, ed. Levillain, 1:84.

89. See Alcuin, *epistola* 254, ed. Dümmler, p. 410.

90. Alcuin, *epistola* 112, ed. Dümmler, p. 163.5–7.

91. Alcuin, *epistola* 194, ed. Dümmler, p. 322.

92. Lupus, *epistola* 106, ed. Levillain, 2:140.

93. On the survival of medieval letters, see Giles Constable, *Letters and Letter Collections*, in Typologie des Sources du moyen âge occidentale, 17 (Turnhout, 1976) and Mary Garrison, "'Send More Socks': On Mentality and the Preservation Context of Medieval Letters," in *New Approaches to Medieval Communication*, ed. Marco Mostert (Turnhout, 1999), pp. 69–99.

94. Alcuin, *epistola* 104, ed. Dümmler, p. 151.

95. Einhard, charter of 12 September 819, in *Chronicon Laureshamense*, ed. K.A.F. Pertz, in MGH:SS 21, p. 360; see Dutton, *Charlemagne's Courtier*, p. 55.

96. See Genevra Kornbluth, *Engraved Gems of the Carolingian Empire* (University Park, Penn., 1995), pp. 76–84. For a sample of Carolingian signatures, see J. Mabillon, *De re diplomatica. . .*, vol. 1 (Naples, 1789), pp. 469–71 (tab. 54–55).

97. See Giles Constable, "Forged Letters in the Middle Ages," in *Fälschungen im Mittelalter*, vol. 5, in MGH: Schriften der Monumenta Germaniae Historica, 33.5 (Hanover, 1988), pp. 11–37.

98. See Gregory of Tours, *Historiae* 6.22 and 10.19, ed. Krusch and Levison, pp. 289–90, 510–512.

99. Einhard, *epistola* 61, ed. K. Hampe, MGH:Ep. 5 (Hanover, 1898–99; repr. 1974), pp. 139–40; trans. Dutton, *Charlemagne's Courtier*, p. 158.

100. See, in general, Michel Banniard, *Viva Voce*, pp. 307–312.

101. Frotharius, *epistola* 19, ed. K. Hampe, MGH:Ep. 5, p. 289.

102. Boniface, *epistola* 86, ed. Ernst Dümmler, in MGH:Ep. 3 (Berlin, 1892; repr. 1957), p. 751.9–11. For a full translation, see *The Letters of Saint Boniface*, trans. E. Emerton (New York, 1973).

103. Lupus, *epistola* 33, ed. Levillain, 1:150.

104. Alcuin, *epistola* 112, ed. Dümmler, p. 163.5–7.

105. Lupus, *epistola* 123, ed. Levillain, 2:188.

106. Frotharius, *epistola* 10, ed. Hampe, p. 283.

107. Lupus, *epistola* 51, ed. Levillain, 1:210.

108. Einhard, *epistola* 31, ed. Hampe, p. 125; trans. Dutton, *Charlemagne's Courtier*, p. 142.

109. Einhard, *Translatio et miracula* 1.1, ed. Waitz, p. 240.

110. Einhard, *epistola* 12, ed. Hampe, pp. 115–116.

111. Notker, *Gesta Karoli Magni* 1.26, ed. Haefele, p. 35.

112. By the same measure, a *secretum colloquium* of the sort held by Louis the German, Charles the Bald, and Lothar II at Andernach in 860 can be taken as an 'unpublicized meeting'. See *Annales Xantenses* 860, ed. B. von Simson, p. 19.

113. On medieval cryptography, see Bernhard Bischoff, "Übersicht über die nichtdiplomatischen Geheimschriften des Mittelalters," in Bischoff, *Mittelalterliche Studien: Ausgewählte Aufsätze zur Schriftkunde und Literaturgeschichte*, 3 vols. (Stuttgart, 1959–81), 3:120–48.

114. Hrabanus Maurus, *In honorem sanctae crucis*, ed. M. Perrin, in CCCM 100 (Turnhout, 1997) and, on the theology and art, see Celia Chazelle, *The Crucified God in the Carolingian Era: Theology and Art of Christ's Passion* (Cambridge, 2001), pp. 99–118.

115. See David Ganz, "The *Epitaphium Arsenii* and Opposition to Louis the Pious," in *Charlemagne's Heir: New Perspectives on the Reign of Louis the Pious (814–840)*, ed. Peter Godman and Roger Collins (Oxford, 1990), pp. 537–50.

116. See Walahfrid Strabo, *Visio Wettini*, ed. Ernst Dümmler, MGH:PLAC 2 (Berlin, 1884; repr. 1964), pp. 318–319.444–61. And see Dutton, *The Politics of Dreaming*, pp. 65–67.

117. It is not certain that Carolingian readers automatically noticed or, indeed, looked for acrostics. Dhuoda in her *Manual* for her sixteen-year-old son William employed acrostics, but was not sure he would discern them and so drew his attention to how he should read them. See Dhuoda, *Liber manualis*, epigram 88–89 and 10.2, ed. Pierre Riché, *Dhuoda, Manuel pour mon fils*, in Sources chrétiennes, vol. 235 (Paris, 1975), pp. 78, 340. Also trans. Carol Neel, *Handbook for William: A Carolingian Woman's Counsel for Her Son* (Lincoln, 1991).

118. Alcuin, *epistola* 181, ed. Dümmler, p. 299. On this letter, see Ziolkowski, *Talking Animals*, pp. 55, 242–44 and chapter 2, in this book.

    Alcuin employed the same number code in his riddle in the *Disputatio* 102–103, ed. Daly and Suchier, p. 142; trans. Dutton, *Carolingian Civilization*, pp.145–46: "ALCUIN: There were three: one never born and ever dead; another ever born and never dead; and the third ever born and twice dead. PEPIN: The first is our ambiguous birth and death on earth; the second to our Lord; the third into the condition of poverty. ALCUIN: Give me the first letters of their names. Pepin: I,V, XXX." If we should understand by 1st = A [Adam] and by 5th = E [Elijah], then a case could be made for emending XXX to XI, thus the 11th = L [Lazarus].

119. See the samples provided in *De antiquis episcoporum promotionibus*, PL 129:1381C–1398C and A. Giry, *Manuel de diplomatique* (Paris, 1893), pp. 810–812.

120. See Suetonius, *Vitae Caesarum*, Diuus Iulius 56.7 and Aulus Gellius, *Noctes Atticae* 17.9.1–5. Aulus Gellius also reports that the grammarian Probus had written a work, now lost, on the secret meaning of the letters in Caesar's correspondence.

121. *De inventione linguarum*, PL 112:1581–82; reedited by R. Derolez, *Runica manuscripta: the English Tradition* (Bruges, 1954), pp. 349–53, with an extensive description of the manuscripts and a commentary, pp. 279–383. The sample encryption supplied at PL 112:1581 contains several mistakes. It should read, once resolved, as:

INCIPIT VERSVS BONIFACII ARCHIEPI<SCOPI>
GLORIOSIQVE MARTIRIS

On Boniface and cryptography, see Wilhelm Levison, *England and the Continent in the Eighth Century: The Ford Lectures delivered in the University of Oxford in the Hilary Term, 1943* (Oxford, 1946), pp. 290–94.

122. This system too is garbled at PL 112:1581 since the replacement letters are not properly aligned below the vowels. Levison, *England and the Continent*, provides some examples of the use of this system. But see also Alcuin, *Propositiones*, PL 101:1152A: "Propositio de cursu CBNKS.BC. FVGB.LFP.RKS," which can be converted to "canis ac fuga lep<o>ris." The final dot should be replaced with 'P', that is, 'o'.

123. See Bernhard Bischoff, "Wer ist die Nonne von Hildenheim," *Studien und Mitteilungen zur Geschichte Benediktiner-Ordens und seine Zweige*, n.s., 18 (1931): 387–88.

124. See the inventory of examples supplied by Levison, *England and the Continent*, pp. 292–93 and Derolez, *Runica manuscripta*, pp. 161–65.

125. For an edition of the text, see René Derolez, "Dubthach's Cryptogram: Some Notes in Connexion with Brussels MS. 9565–9566," *L'antiquité classique*, 21 (1952): 368 [359–75] and James F. Kenney, *The Sources for the Early History of Ireland: An Introduction and Guide*, vol. 1: Ecclesiastical (New York, 1929), p. 556.

126. See H. Houben, "*Visio cuiusdam pauperculae mulieris*: Überlieferung und Herkunft eines frühmittelalterlichen Visionstextes (mit Neuedition)," *Zeitschrift für die Geschichte des Oberrheins* 124, n.s., 85 (1976): 41; also trans. Dutton, in *Carolingian Civilization*, pp. 203–204. See also Dutton, *The Politics of Dreaming*, pp. 67–80. I wish to thank Brent Hardy here for his insight into the symbolism of Ermengard's three rocks as her three sons.

127. See *Capitulare de villis* 51, ed. A. Boretius, in MGH:Cap. 1, p. 88.

128. See chapter 7 in this book.

129. See *Indiculus superstitionum et paganiarum*, ed. Boretius, MGH:Cap. 1, p. 223. Also trans. J.T. McNeill and H.M. Gamer, in Dutton, *Carolingian Civilization*, pp. 3–4.

130. Thegan, *Gesta Hludowici imperatoris* 47, ed. Ernst Tremp, in MGH:SRGUS 64 (Hanover, 1995), p. 240. Also trans. J.R. Ginsburg with D.L. Boutelle, in Dutton, *Carolingian Civilization*, pp. 176–98.

131. Astronomer, *Vita Hludowici* 56, ed. Tremp, p. 512. Cabaniss, *Son of Charlemagne*, p. 169 n. 90, wondered whether the beggar might have been the Astronomer himself, though it is not impossible that it was Atrebaldus, the abbot of Flavigny, who disguised himself and later narrated the story to Louis and the Astronomer.

132. *Annales Bertiniani* 867, ed. Grat et al., p. 138.

133. Nithard, *Historiarum* 1.3, ed. Lauer, p. 12.

134. See Walter Goffart, *The Le Mans Forgeries: A Chapter from the History of Church Property in the Ninth Century* (Cambridge, Mass., 1966).

135. See Roger E. Reynolds, "The Organisation, Law and Liturgy of the Western Church, 700–900," in *The New Cambridge Medieval History*, vol. 2: c.700–c.900, ed. Rosamond McKitterick (Cambridge, 1995), pp. 616–617.

136. Quoted in Donald G. McNeil, Jr., "Killer Songs," *The New York Times Magazine*, March 17, 2002, p. 59.

137. See Paul Willem Finsterwalder, "Eine parteipolitische Kundgebung eines Anhängers Lothars I," *Neues Archiv*, 47 (1928): 393–415.

138. James Westfall Thompson and Saul K. Padover, *Secret Diplomacy: Espionage and Cryptography, 1500–1815* (New York, 1937), p. 255, but they assume wrongly that Lothar himself was the author of the collection.

139. For a similar, though more explicit use of Scripture, see Thegan's harangue against the rebellious Archbishop Ebbo: Thegan, *Gesta Hludowici* 44, ed. Tremp, pp. 232–38.

140. See also Janet L. Nelson, "The Search for Peace in a Time of War: The Carolingian Brüderkrieg, 840–843," *Träger und Instrumentarien des Friedens im hohen und späten Mittelalter*, ed. Johannes Fried (Sigmaringen, 1996), pp. 100–101.

141. I take it here, as I did in *Charlemagne's Courtier*, pp. xxxi, 151, that Einhard, *epistola* 14, ed. Hampe, p. 117; trans. Dutton, *Charlemagne's Courtier*, pp. 151–52, was probably the letter that Einhard sent to Gerward.

142. Trans. Dutton, *Charlemagne's Courtier*, pp. 136–37; Einhard, *epistola* 52, ed. Hampe, p. 135.

143. Robert Frost, "The Secret Knows" (1945), in *The Complete Poems of Robert Frost* (New York, 1949), p. 495.

Chapter 6   A World Grown Old with Poets and Kings

*   This essay is a revised version of "Beyond the Topos of Senescence: The Political Problems of Aged Carolingian Rulers," which appeared in *Aging and the Aged in Medieval Europe*, ed. Michael M. Sheehan, Papers in Mediaeval Studies, 11 (Toronto: Pontifical Institute of Mediaeval Studies, 1990), pp. 75–94.

1. Jorge Luis Borges, "The Dialogues of Ascetic and King," trans. Eliot Weinberger, in Borges, *Selected Non-Fictions*, ed. Eliot Weinberger (New York, 1999), p. 382.

2. *King Lear* I.ii.46–51.

3. Ernst R. Curtius, *European Literature and the Latin Middle Ages*, trans. Willard R. Trask, Bollingen Series, 36 (Princeton, 1953; repr. 1973, 1990), p. 28. See also the epilogue to the 1990 edition by Peter Godman, pp. 599–653. And see James M. Dean, *The World Grown Old in Later Medieval Literature*, Medieval Academy Books, 101 (Cambridge, Mass., 1997).

4. Since the original version of this study, a number of examinations of old age in the Middle Ages have appeared: among them, see Michael Goodich, *From Birth to Old Age: The Human Life Cycle in Medieval Thought, 1250–1350* (Lanham, Md., 1989); Georges Minois, *History of Old Age from Antiquity to the Renaissance* (Cambridge, 1989); *Aging and the Aged in Medieval Europe*, ed. Michael M. Sheehan, Papers in Mediaeval Studies, 11 (Toronto, 1990); Joel T. Rosenthal, *Old Age in Late Medieval England* (Philadelphia, 1996); Shulamith Shahar, *Growing Old in the Middle Ages: "Winter Clothes us in shadow and pain,"* trans. Yael Lotan (London, 1997); *Old Age from Antiquity to Post-Modernity*, ed. Paul Johnson and Patricia Thane (London, 1998). See also Tim G. Parkin, *Old Age in the Roman World: A Cultural and Social History* (Baltimore, 2003).

5. See Robert Nisbet, *Social Change and History: Aspects of the Western Theory of Development* (Oxford, 1969), p. 3; Victor W. Turner, *Dramas, Fields, and Metaphors: Symbolic Action in Human Society* (Ithaca, N.Y., 1974), pp. 24–29; Tilman Struve, *Die Entwicklung der organologischen Staatsauffassung im Mittelalter*, Monographien zur Geschichte des Mittelalters, 16 (Stuttgart, 1978); Paul Edward Dutton, *"Illustre ciuitatis et populi exemplum:* Plato's *Timaeus* and the Transmission from Calcidius to the End of the Twelfth Century of a Tripartite Scheme of Society," *Mediaeval Studies*, 45 (1983): 79–119.

6. See Randloph Starn, "Meaning-Levels in the Theme of Historical Decline," *History and Theory*, 14 (1975): 15–16; Paul Edward Dutton, "Awareness of Historical Decline in the Carolingian Empire, 800–887" (Ph.D. diss., University of Toronto, 1981), pp. 5–12.

7. Randolph Starn, "Historians and 'Crisis,'" *Past and Present*, 52 (1971): 3–22.

8. For various uses of the metaphor, see Dutton, "Awareness of Historical Decline," pp. 19–64.

9. *The Carolingian Empire: The Age of Charlemagne*, trans. Peter Munz, Studies in Medieval History, 9 (Oxford, 1957; repr. Toronto, 1979), p. 187. It should be noted that this is not a full translation of Fichtenau's *Das karolingische Imperium: Soziale und geistige Problematik eines Grossreiches* (Zurich, 1949).

10. Fichtenau, *The Carolingian Empire*, p. 187; François L. Ganshof, "La Fin du règne du Charlemagne: Une décomposition," *Zeitschrift für schweizerische Geschichte*, 28 (1948): 533–52 [trans. Janet Sondheimer in Ganshof, *The Carolingians and the Frankish Monarchy* (Ithaca, N.Y., 1971), pp. 240–55], and "L'Echec de Charlemagne," *Académie des inscriptions et belles lettres: Comptes rendus des séances* (1947), pp. 248–54 [trans. Sondheimer in *Carolingians and the Frankish Monarchy*, pp. 256–60]. And see Roger Collins, *Charlemagne* (Toronto, 1998), pp. 171–74.

11. Astronomer, *Vita Hludowici imperatoris* 3, ed. Ernst Tremp, MGH: Scriptores rerum Germanicarum in usum scholarum separatim editi, 64 (Hanover, 1995), p. 290. The work was also edited by Georg H. Pertz, in MGH: Scriptores 2 (Hanover, 1820), pp. 607–48. The Astronomer also said that Louis and his courtiers were convinced that the body of the empire was diseased: *Vita Hludowici* 61, ed. Tremp, p. 536.

12. See *Visio Karoli Magni*, ed. P. Jaffé, in *Bibliotheca rerum Germanicarum*, 4 (Berlin, 1868): 701–704; Patrick Geary, "Germanic Tradition and Royal

Ideology in the Ninth Century: The *Visio Karoli Magni*," *Frümittelalterliche Studien*, 21 (1987): 274–294 and repr. in Geary, *Living with the Dead in the Middle Ages* (Ithaca, N.Y., 1994), pp. 49–76; also trans. in Paul Edward Dutton, *Carolingian Civilization: A Reader*, 2nd ed. (Peterborough, Oct., 2004), pp. 456–57; and discussed in Paul Edward Dutton, *The Politics of Dreaming in the Carolingian Empire*, Regents Studies in Medieval Culture, ed. Eugene Vance (Lincoln, Neb., 1994), pp. 200–210.

13. See Richard Landes, "The Fear of an Apocalyptic Year 1000: Augustinian Historiography, Medieval and Modern," *Speculum*, 75 (2000): 110–116 [97–145]; "Sur les traces du millennium: La 'Via Negativa' (2e partie)," *Le Moyen Âge*, 99 (1993): 1–26; Wolfram Brandes, " '*Tempora periculosa sunt*': Eschatologisches im Vorfeld der Kaiserkrönung Karls des Grossen," in *Das Frankfurter Konzil von 794: Kristillisationspunkt karolingischer Kultur*, ed. Rainer Berndt (Mainz, 1997), pp. 49–79; David Van Meter, "The Empire of the Year 6000: Eschatology and the Sanctification of Carolingian Politics," (Ph.D. diss., Boston University, 1997); and the helpful analysis of the issue by Michael Idomir Allen, "The Chronicle of Claudius of Turin," in *After Rome's Fall: Narrators and Sources of Early Medieval History. Essays Presented to Walter Goffart*, ed. Alexander Callander Murray (Toronto, 1998), p. 318 and n. 147 [288–319].

14. Alcuin, *epistola* 121, ed. Ernst Dümmler in MGH: Epistolae 4 (Hanover, 1895), p. 178. Alcuin here draws an allusion to Eccl. 11:6.

15. The reference is to Jerome, *epistola* 52 ("Ad Nepotianum"), ed. I. Hilberg, in Corpus Scriptorum ecclesiasticorum latinorum, vol. 54 (Vienna, 1910), pp. 413–41. Also ed. Jérôme Labourt in Saint Jérome, *Lettres*, 2 (Paris, 1951).

16. Alcuin, *epistola* 114 addressed to Eanbald, archbishop of York in 796, ed. Dümmler, p. 169: "Ecce ego duplici fatigatus molestia, id est senectute et infirmitate." See also *epistola* 229 from 801 to Charles (ed. Dümmler, pp. 373–74), where weakness and old age are again linked.

17. To give but a few examples of this persistent theme, see Candidus, *De uita Æigili* 11, ed. Ernst Dümmler in MGH: Poetae Latini Aevi Carolini, 2 (Berlin, 1883), pp. 102–103.1–5; Einhard, *epistola* 10, ed. Karl Hampe in MGH: Epistolae, 5 (Hanover, 1899), p. 114, and *epistola* 28, ed. Hampe, p. 123; the so-called *Narratio clericorum Remensium*, ed. Albert Werminghoff in MGH: Concilia 2.1.2 (Hanover, 1908), p. 813; Epistolae uariorum 31.3, ed. Ernst Dümmler in MGH: Epistolae, 6 (Hanover, 1925), p. 196.

18. Candidus, *De uita Æigili* 11, ed. Dümmler, in MGH:PLAC 2, p. 103.18.

19. See Alcuin, *epistola* 241, ed. Dümmler, p. 387; 240, p. 385; and 238, p. 383 for some of the excuses for not appearing at court. Einhard, in *epistola* 10 to Louis the Pious in 830, ed. Hampe, p. 114, line 16, describes himself as "iam senex et ualde infirmus" and pleads in a series of letters to be allowed to be absent from the court: see *epsitolae* 13, pp. 116–117; 14, p. 117; 15, p. 118; and 25, p. 122.

20. Drawing on Virgil, *Aeneid* 5.437 ff., Alcuin frequently employed this imagery. See *epistolae* 145 to Charles (ca. 798), ed. Dümmler, p. 231; 164 to Charles (799), p. 266; and *carmen* 42, ed. Ernst Dümmler, MGH:PLAC 1 (Berlin, 1881), p. 254.19–20.

21. Alcuin, *carmen* 42, ed. Dümmler, p. 254.18, and *epistola* 229 to Charlemagne (801), p. 374. In *carmen* 16, ed. Dümmler, p. 239.5–6, Alcuin asks Angilbert to help old Alcuin.

22. From Ovid, *Ars amat.* 2.670. Alcuin, *epistola* 310 to Remedius (803–804), ed. Dümmler, p. 479: "tacito pede fessa senectus ingreditur cubile nostrum." See also *epistola* 225 to Theodulf, ed. Dümmler, p. 269.

23. Theodulf, *carmen* 27 ("Ad Coruinianum"), ed. Dümmler, p. 491.37.

24. For variations of the phrase "tempora sunt periculosa," see Alcuin, *epistolae* 116, ed. Dümmler, p. 171; 74, p. 117; 193, p. 320; and *carmen* 48, ed. Dümmler, p. 261.21. See also Brandes, " '*Tempora periculosa sunt*,' " pp. 49–79.

25. Alcuin, *carmen* 9 ("De clade Lindisfarensis monasterii"), ed. Dümmler, p. 232.111–114.

26. For an analysis of the images of senescence in Alcuin's writings, see Dutton, "Awareness of Historical Decline," pp. 230–234.

27. Others thought of them in this way as well. Modoin, the young contemporary who was called Naso at court, wrote a poem in hexameters to Charles in the form of a dialogue between a *puer* and a *senex*. The young interlocutor asks for admission to the closed circle of *senes uates* (Angilbert, Alcuin, and Theodulf). See *Nasonis Ecloga*, ed. Dümmler, in MGH:PLAC 1, pp. 385–87.

    For another Carolingian dialogue based on the conflict of generations, see the one attributed to Sedulius Scottus: *Senex et adolescens*, ed. Siegmund Hellmann in his *Sedulius Scottus*, Quellen und Untersuchungen zur lateinischen Philologie des Mittelalters, 1.1 (Munich, 1906; repr. Frankfurt, 1966), p. 120.

28. See, for example, Paul the Deacon, *carmen* 12, ed. Dümmler, in MGH:PLAC 1, p. 50.12; Peter of Pisa, *carmen* 15 ("Versus Petri ad Paulum"), ed. Dümmler, MGH:PLAC 1, p. 54.45.

29. Alcuin, *carmen* 23, ed. Dümmler, p. 244.29–30. On the attribution of this poem to Alcuin, see Peter Godman, "Alcuin's Poetic Style and the Authenticity of 'O mea cella,' " *Studi medievali*, 3rd ser. 20 (1979): 555–583. Cf. also *carmen* 9, ed. Dümmler, p. 231.101–102.

30. Godman, "Alcuin's Poetic Style and the Authenticity of 'O mea cella,' " p. 577.

31. Theodulf, *carmen* 14 ("Quod multis indiciis finis proximus esse monstretur"), ed. Dümmler, p. 469.16: "fixum nil stat ut ante stetit."

32. See Cyprian, *epistola* 10.3, ed. Wilhelm Hartel, in Corpus scriptorum ecclesiasticorum Latinorum 3.1 (Vienna, 1868), pp. 352–353, and also printed in MGH:PLAC 1, p. 468 n. 2.

33. Theodulf, *carmen* 14, ed. Dümmler, p. 469.21–22.

34. Einhard, *Vita Karoli Magni* 4, ed. by G. Waitz after G.H. Pertz, 6th ed. overseen by O. Holder-Egger [hereafter ed. Waitz], in MGH:SRGUS (Hanover, 1911; repr. 1965), pp. 6–7; also trans. Paul Edward Dutton, in *Charlemagne's Courtier: The Complete Einhard* (Peterborough, Ont., 1998).

35. *Vita Karoli Magni* 22, ed. Waitz, p. 27; 19, p. 25; and 25, p. 30. On Charlemagne as a writer, see chapter 3 in this book.

36. *Vita Karoli Magni* 22, ed. Waitz, p. 26.

37. See Thegan, *Gesta Hludowici imperatoris* 7, ed. Ernst Tremp, in MGH:SRGUS 64 (Hanover, 1995), p. 186, who describes Charlemagne as "in senectute bona plenus dierum." See Gen. 25:8. See also *Nithard Historiarum libri IIII* 1.1, ed. P. Lauer, Nithard, *Histoire des fils de Louis le Pieux*, Les classiques de l'histoire de France au Moyen Age, 7 (Paris, 1964), p. 4, on Charlemagne "in senectute bona decedens. . ."

38. Ermoldus, *In honorem Hludowici* 2, ed. Ernst Dümmler in MGH:PLAC 2, pp. 24–25.3–30 and ed. Edmond Faral, *Poème sur Louis le Pieux et épitres au roi Pepin* (Paris, 1932), pp. 52–54.654–81.

39. Sedulius Scottus, *Liber de rectoribus Christianis* 20, ed. Hellmann, in *Sedulius Scottus*, p. 89.

40. Einhard, *Vita Karoli Magni* 32, ed. Waitz, pp. 36–37.

41. See Einhard, *Vita Karoli Magni*, ed. Waitz, pp. 1–2, xxviii–xxix.

42. An example of traditional imagery would be that of the *senex puer*. On this theme in Western literature, see Curtius, *European Literature*, pp. 98–101. For a few examples of its usage in the Carolingian period, see Paul the Deacon, *carmen* 2 ("Versus in laude Sancti Benedicti"), ed. Dümmler, in MGH:PLAC 1, p. 37.6–7; Alcuin, *epistola* 270, ed. Dümmler, p. 429; Einhard, *epistola* 3, ed. Hampe, p. 110; the Astronomer, *Vita Hludowici* 19, ed. Tremp, p. 340; Aimo, *Liber translationis beati Vincentii* 1.1, in PL 126:1013B9–10; and Notker, *Gesta Karoli Magni* 2.10, ed. Hans F. Haefele, in MGH: Scriptores rerum Germanicarum, Nova Series 12 (Berlin, 1962), p. 65.

43. Carolingian authors quite consciously drew on models for their understanding of senescence. As we have seen, Alcuin drew on Virgil, Ovid, and Jerome, and Theodulf on Cyprian. Paschasius Radbertus, in his preface-letter to his commentary on the Gospel of Matthew, employed Cicero's *Cato maior De senectute*: see *Epistolae variorum* 7, ed. Dümmler, in MGH:Ep. 6 (Berlin, 1925), pp. 144–47. In addition, when weighed down by old age and grief at his wife's death in 836, Einhard sought out the opinions of Cyprian, Jerome, Augustine, and perhaps Cicero: see Einhard, *epistola* 3, ed. Hampe, pp. 9–10 and also in *Loup de Ferrières, Correspondance*, 2 vols., Les Classiques de l'histoire de France au moyen âge 10, 16, ed. and trans. Léon Levillain (Paris, 1927, 1935), 1:12–18.

44. Regino of Prüm, *Chronicon* 880, ed. Friedrich Kurze in MGH:SRGUS (Hanover, 1890), pp. 116–117, claimed that the Carolingian line was dying out because of the premature deaths of the Carolingians and the infertility of their wives.

45. Two possible exceptions are Charles, son of Charles the Bald, and Carloman, son of Louis the Stammerer, both of whom died young under suspicious circumstances: see *Annales Bertiniani* 864 and 866, ed. Félix Grat, Jeanne Vielliard, and Suzanne Clémencet, in *Annales de Saint-Bertin* (Paris, 1964), pp. 105, 130; also trans. Janet L. Nelson, *The Annals of St-Bertin*, Ninth-Century Histories, vol. 1 (Manchester, 1991). And see Regino, *Chronicon* 884, ed. Kurze, p. 121.

46. Paul the Deacon, *carmen* 22 ("Epitaphium Hildegardis reginae"), ed. Dümmler, in MGH:PLAC 1, p. 59.24. On this queen, see Klaus Schreiner, " 'Hildegardis regina': Wirklichkeit und Legende einer karolingischen Herrscherin," *Archiv für Kulturgeschichte*, 57 (1975): 1–70.

47. See Einhard, *Vita Karoli Magni* 18, ed. Waitz, pp. 22–23.

48. Hrabanus Maurus, *carmen* 89 ("Epitaphium Irmingardis"), ed. Dümmler, in MGH:PLAC 2, p. 240.15–16:

> Haec quoque dum experet iuuenile hic tempus, et annos
> Maturae aetatis inciperet, iam obiit.

49. See Peter Laslett, "Necessary Knowledge: Age and Aging in Societies of the Past," in *Aging in the Past: Demography, Society and Old Age*, ed. David L. Kertzer and Peter Laslett (Berkeley, 1995), pp. 3–77 and fig. 1.1.

50. Creighton G. Gilber, "When Did a Man in the Renaissance Grow Old?" *Studies in the Renaissance*, 14 (1967): 31, makes this point for Renaissance princes and popes.

51. István Kiszely, *The Anthropology of the Lombards*, trans. Catherine Simán, B.A.R. International Series 61.1 (Oxford, 1979), pp. 163–64, on the basis of eight hundred and seventy skeletons, placed the average age of mortality for early medieval Lombard men at 34 years 9 months and for women at 34 years 2 months; but since virtually no skeletons of infants were found, the figures were lowered to 24 years 8 months and 24 years 3 months respectively. See also the parallel results provided in György T. Acsádi and Janós Nemeskéri, *History of Human Life Span and Mortality*, trans. K. Balás (Budapest, 1970), pp. 215–234; Winfried Henke and Karl-Heinz Nedder, "Zur Anthropologie der fränkischen Bevölkerung von Rubenach," *Bonner Jahrbuch*, 181 (1981): 395–419; Peter Laslett, *The World We have Lost*, 2nd ed. (London, 1971), p. 97; and Laslett, "Societal Development and Aging," in *Handbook of Aging and the Social Sciences*, ed. Robert H. Binstock and Ethel Shanas (New York, 1976), pp. 97–98.

52. Adalhard, the cousin of Charlemagne, was reputed to have lived to eighty: see *The Eclogue of the Two Nuns* appended to Paschasius Radbertus's *Vita Sancti Adalhardi* in PL 120:1555A5. Elipandus, the bishop of Toledo, claimed in a letter of 25 July 799 to be eighty-two: see Alcuin, *epistola* 183, ed. Dümmler, p. 308.2. Finally, and more scientifically datable, is the case of Egino of Verona, a relative of Queen Hildegard. A study of his skeleton has confirmed that he was indeed an octogenarian, who was born before 720 and died 26–27 February 802: see Alfred Czarnetzki, "Die Skelettreste aus dem sogenannten Egino Grab," in *Die Abtei Reichenau: Neue Beiträge zur Geschichte und Kultur des Inselklosters*, ed. Helmut Mauer (Sigmaringen, 1974), pp. 563–72, and with W. Erdmann, pp. 575–76.

53. See, for instance, Shulamith Shahar, "Who were the Old in the Middle Ages," *Social History of Medicine*, 6 (1993): 313–341.

54. Isidore, *Etymologiae* 11.2.1–8, ed. Wallace M. Lindsay, vol. 2 (Oxford, 1911); Hrabanus Maurus, *De universo* 7.1, in PL 111:179D. On age divisions in the Middle Ages, see especially John A. Burrow, *The Ages of Man: A Study in Medieval Writing and Thought* (Oxford, 1986) and Elizabeth Sears, *The Ages of Man: Medieval Interpretations of the Life Cycle* (Princeton, 1986).

55. Alcuin in his *Disputatio de rhetorica et de uirtutibus sapientissimi regis Karoli et Albini magistri* employed a four-part division (based on Cicero's *De inuentione* 1.24.35): "in aetate puer an adulescens, natu gradior an senex"; ed. Wilbur S. Howell, *The Rhetoric of Alcuin and Charlemagne* (Princeton, 1941), p. 104.609–610.

56. See Alcuin, *carmen* 1 ("Versus de sanctis Euboricensis ecclesiae"), ed. Dümmler, p. 181.528: ". . . pueros iuuenesque senesque" [also ed. Peter Godman, in *The Bishops, Kings, and Saints of York: Alcuin* (Oxford, 1982)]; Anon., *Planctus de obitu Karoli*, ed. Dümmler, p. 435, verse 4: "Infantes, senes, gloriosi praesules"; Paulinus of Aquileia (?), *carmen* 10 ("Versus de destructione Aquileiae numquam restaurandae"), verse 10, ed. Dümmler, p. 143: "iuuenes, senes, mulieres, paruulos . . ."; Aurelianus of Orléans, the postscript to his *De disciplina musicae*, ed. Ernst Dümmler in MGH:Ep. 6, p. 131: "Audiet me semper de te loquentem sexus uterque, senex, iuuenis, puer, aduena, ciues"; and Ermoldus Nigellus, *In laudem Pippini regis* 1, ed. Dümmler, in MGH:PLAC 2, p. 80.23–24, says that at the palace of Pepin in Aquitaine there were found clerics, old men (*patres*), youths (*iuuencli*), and a procession of boys (*puerile agmen*). This tripartite tendency follows a pattern of age classification into children, adults, and aged found in many societies: see Bernice L. Neugarten and Gunhild O. Hagestad, "Age and the Life Course," in *Handbook of Aging and the Social Sciences*, p. 36.

57. For example, in 830, when Lothar I was already thirty-five years old, Einhard, *epistola* 18, ed. Dümmler, p. 119.24, referred to him as "Hlotharius iuuenis augustus." Thegan, *Vita Hludowici imperatoris* 2, ed. Tremp, p. 176, refers to the twenty-nine-year-old Charlemagne in 771 as "in iuuentute."

58. On the Germanic customs of male initiation, see Tacitus, *Germania* 13; the Astronomer, *Vita Hludowici* 6, ed. Tremp, p. 300: "Ibique ense, iam appellens adolescentiae tempora, accinctus est . . ." See also Régine Le Jan, "Frankish Giving of Arms and Rituals of Power: Continuity and Change in the Carolingian Period," in *Rituals of Power: From Late Antiquity to the Early Middle Ages*, ed. Frans Theuws and Janet L. Nelson (Leiden, 2000), pp. 281–309.

59. It was as though, said the Astronomer, *Vita Hludowici* 56, ed. Tremp, p. 514, the very nerves of the land had been severed.

60. Thegan, *Gesta Hludowici* 3, ed. Tremp, p. 178.

61. See Janet L. Nelson, *Charles the Bald* (London, 1992), pp. 190–253.

62. See Collins, *Charlemagne*, pp. 141–74, on the end phase of Charlemagne's career.

63. Einhard, *Vita Karoli Magni* 29, ed. Waitz, p. 33.

64. See Theodulf, *carmen* 28 ("Versus contra iudices"), ed. Dümmler, MGH:PLAC 1, pp. 493–517.

65. See *Annales regni Francorum* 814, ed. Kurze in MGH:SRGUS (Hanover, 1895), p. 141; Thegan, *Gesta Hludowici* 13, ed. Tremp, p. 194.

66. Einhard, *Vita Karoli Magni* 32, ed. Waitz, pp. 36–37. It should be noted that an epizootic attacking both cattle and other animals raged while Charlemagne was on campaign in 810, and that his horse may have been weakened by the disease.

67. Anon., *Carmen de Pippini regis uictoria Auarica*, verse 14, ed. Dümmler, MGH:PLAC 1, p. 117. On this poem in general, see Alfred Ebenbauer, *Carmen historicum: Untersuchungen zur historischen Dichtung im karolingischen Europa*, vol. 1, Philologica Germanica, 4 (Vienna, 1978), pp. 30–33.

68. See *Lex Baiwariorum* 2.9, ed. Ernst M. von Schwind, in MGH: Leges nationum Germanicarum 5.2 (Hanover, 1926), pp. 302–303.

69. See Lupus, *epistola* 31 (to Charles the Bald), ed. Levillain, *Loup de Ferrières*, 1:142.

70. The Astronomer, *Vita Hludowici* 63, ed. Tremp, p. 550: "qui canos paternos deducit cum dolore ad mortem. . . ." And see Janet L. Nelson, "The Last Years of Louis the Pious," in *Charlemagne's Heir: New Perspectives on the Reign of Louis the Pious (814–840)*, ed. Peter Godman and Roger Collins (Oxford, 1990), pp. 147–59.

71. *The History of the Decline and Fall of the Roman Empire*, ed. John B. Bury, vol. 5 (London, 1911), p. 303.

72. See Heito, *Visio Wettini* 11, ed. Dümmler, in MGH:PLAC 2, p. 271, and the poetic rendering of Walafrid Strabo, ed. Dümmler, pp. 318–319.446–65, also ed. David A. Traill in *Walahfrid Strabo's Visio Wettini*, Lateinische Sprache und Literatur des Mittelalters 2 (Bern, 1974), p. 197. On Charlemagne's role in Carolingian dream literature, see Dutton, *The Politics of Dreaming*, pp. 50–80.

73. According to the Astronomer, the Carolingians, including Louis the Pious, were aware of this threat: see *Vita Hludowici* 21, ed. Tremp, p. 348.

74. In MGH: Capitularia regum Francorum 1, ed. Alfred Boretius (Hanover, 1883), pp. 126–30. On it, see Walter Schlesinger, "Kaisertum und Reichsteilung zur *Divisio regnorum* von 806," (1958) in *Zum Kaisertum Karls des Grossen*, ed. Gunther Wolf, Wege der Forschung, 38 (Darmstadt, 1972), pp. 116–173.

75. See Dutton, *The Politics of Dreaming*, pp. 54–80.

76. Einhard, *Vita Karoli Magni* 18–19, ed. Waitz, pp. 22–25.

77. His son Lothar I, however, knew of the practice, since after the death of his wife Ermengard in 851 he took two concubines, but never remarried: see *Annales Bertiniani* 853, ed. Grat et al., p. 67.

78. See Peter R. McKeon, "817: Une Année désastreuse et presque fatale pour les Carolingiens," *Le Moyen Age*, 84 (1978): 5–12. For the *Ordinatio imperii*, see MGH:Cap. 1, pp. 270–73, and François L. Ganshof, "Some Observations on the *Ordinatio imperii* of 817" (1955) in *Carolingians and the Frankish Monarchy*, pp. 273–88.

79. See the Astronomer, *Vita Hludowici* 32, ed. Tremp, p. 392.

80. See Thegan, *Gesta Hludowici* 36, ed. Tremp, p. 222; the Astronomer, *Vita Hludowici* 44, ed. Tremp, p. 456.

81. *Libri duo pro filiis et contra Iudith uxorem Ludovici pii*, sometimes called the *Liber apologeticus*, ed. Georg Waitz, in MGH: Scriptores 15.1 (Hanover, 1887), pp. 275–79. The work is also edited by L. Van Acker, in *Agobardi Lugdunensis Opera Omnia*, in Corpus Christianorum: Continuatio Mediaevalis, vol. 52 (Turnhout, 1981), pp. 309–312 and 315–319.

82. Hrabanus Maurus wrote a short treatise for Louis, *De honore parentibus a filiis exhibendo*, ed. Ernst Dümmler in MGH:Ep. 5, pp. 404–415.

83. On the emergence of these arguments about the obligations of fathers and sons toward each other, see Dutton, "Awareness of Historical Decline," pp. 178–86.

84. For similar retirements in England, see Clare Stancliffe, "Kings who Opted out," in *Ideal and Reality in Frankish and Anglo-Saxon Society: Studies presented to J.M. Wallace-Hadrill*, ed. Patrick Wormald with Donald Bullough and Roger Collins (Oxford, 1983), pp. 154–76.

85. Einhard, *Vita Karoli Magni* 33, ed. Waitz, p. 39.
86. They would not go quite so quietly or so completely as Purun Bhagat in Kipling's story who had one day as prime minister enjoyed the public honors of the state, wielded power, and possessed property, and the next walked into the oblivion of religious anonymity. "The Miracle of Purun Bhagat," repr. in Rudyard Kipling, *Stories and Poems*, ed. Roger Lancelyn Green (London, 1970), pp. 26–37.

Chapter 7   Thunder and Hail over the Carolingian Countryside

★ This is an expanded and revised version of an article with the same title that appeared in *Agriculture in the Middle Ages: Technology, Practice, and Representation*, ed. Del Sweeney (Philadelphia: University of Pennsylvania Press, 1995), pp. 111–137.

1. For good general introductions to this agrarian economy, see Adriaan Verhulst, *The Carolingian Economy* (Cambridge, 2002), pp. 31–84; Michael McCormick, *Origins of the European Economy: Communications and Commerce, A.D. 300–900* (Cambridge, 2001), pp. 6–12, 575–78; Georges Duby, *Rural Economy and Country Life in the Medieval West*, trans. Cynthia Postan (London, 1968), pp. 3–58; and Wolfgang Metz, "Die Agrarwirtschaft im karolingischen Reiche," in *Karl der Grosse: Lebenswerk und Nachleben*, vol. 1, ed. H. Beumann (Dusseldorf, 1965), pp. 489–500.

2. *Liber contra insulsam uulgi opinionem de grandine et tonitruis* (herafter *De grandine*) 2, ed. L. Van Acker, in *Agobardi Lugdunensis Opera Omnia*, in Corpus Christianorum: Continuatio Mediaevalis, vol. 52 (Turnhout, 1981), p. 4.7–10 [pp. 3–15] (also edited in Patrologia Latina, ed. J.P. Migne, vol. 104, cols. 148B1–C4 [147A–158C]). The relevant portions of the treatise have been translated by Paul Edward Dutton in Dutton, *Carolingian Civilization: A Reader*, 2nd ed. (Peterborough, Ont., 2004), pp. 220–23.

3. Agobard would certainly be disappointed to learn that late in the twentieth century some people have used his report as evidence that the earth was once visited by alien spaceships. See Whitley Streiber, *Communion* (New York, 1987), p. 241, 247–48. On Agobard as a rationalist, see Egon Boshof, *Erzbischof Agobard von Lyon* (Cologne, 1969), pp. 8–10, 173 and n. 14.

4. The title as it stands in the Migne (PL) edition—*Liber Contra Insulsam Vulgi Opinionem de Grandine et Tonitruis*—was taken from an addition to the sole manuscript. Van Acker emended it to "De grandine et tonitruis," which seems less descriptive of the actual contents of the work.

There has been a good deal of discussion of this text. See Jacob Grimm, *Teutonic Mythology*, vol. 2, trans. J.S. Stallybrass (London, 1883), pp. 638–39; Reginald Lane Poole, *Illustrations of the History of Medieval Thought and Learning*, 2nd rev. ed. (London, 1920; repr. New York, 1960), pp. 36–38; J.A. MacCulloch, *Medieval Faith and Fable* (London, 1932), p. 20; Allen Cabaniss, *Agobard of Lyons: Churchman and Critic* (Syracuse, 1953), pp. 24–26; Cabaniss, "Agobard of Lyons: Rumour, Propaganda, and Freedom of

Thought in the Ninth Century," *History Today*, 3 (1953): 128–34; Heinrich Fichtenau, *The Carolingian Empire:The Age of Charlemagne*, trans. Peter Munz (Oxford, 1957; repr. NewYork, 1964), pp. 174–75; Boshof, *Erzbischof Agobard*, pp. 170–76; Valerie I.J. Flint, *The Rise of Magic in Early Medieval Europe* (Princeton, 1991), pp. 111–115; and many others.

5. *De grandine* 1, ed.Van Acker, p. 3.1–3 (PL 104:147A6–9).
6. *De grandine* 1, ed. Van Acker, p. 3.4 (PL 104:147A10): "Aura leuatitia est." While *aura* in classical Latin may mean "a gentle breeze" or "air," in medieval Latin it can also mean "a violent wind" or "storm." *Leuatitia* is an unusual word that Agobard may have invented to approximate a vernacular expression.Agobard understood the phrase to mean "aura est levata": see *De grandine* 1, ed.Van Acker, p. 3.7–8 (PL 104:147B5–6) and 11, ed.Van Acker, p. 11.23–24 (PL 104:154C6–7). See also DuCange, *Glossarium Mediae et Infimae Latinitatis*, vol. 1 (Paris, 1937), p. 484: "Galli vulgo dicunt 'Il s'est élevé un Air tempestueux,' *pro* 'excitata est tempestas.' " Edward B. Tylor, *Primitive Culture: Researches into the Development of Mythology, Philosophy, Religion, Language, Art, and Custom*, vol. 1 (London, 1871), p. 84: "The phrase 'raising the wind' now passes as humorous slang, but it once, in all seriousness, described one of the most dreaded of the sorcerer's arts. . . ."
7. *De grandine* 1, ed. Van Acker, p. 3.4–8 (PL 104:147B1–6). *Tempestarius* literally means "the one associated with storms" or "stormy one," but a ninth-century council (see n. 32 later) speaks of those "qui tempestates et alia maleficia faciunt," so that Stormmaker seems a reasonable approximation of the meaning of the word. See also DuCange, *Glossarium*, vol. 8, pp. 49–50.
8. *De grandine* 11, ed.Van Acker, p. 11.19–22 (PL 104:154C1–5).
9. *De grandine* 2, ed.Van Acker, p. 4.3–7 (PL 104:148B1–8).
10. *De grandine* 7, ed.Van Acker, p. 8.11–14 (PL 104:151D2–7).
11. *De grandine* 7, ed.Van Acker, p. 8.15–24 (PL 104:151D7–152A9).
12. *De grandine* 15, ed.Van Acker, p. 14.1–12 (PL 104:156D11–157A12).
13. *De grandine* 16, ed.Van Acker, pp. 14.1–15.27 (PL 104:157C4–158C3).
14. See *Annales regni Francorum 810*, ed. by F. Kurze after G.H. Pertz [hereafter ed. Kurze], in MGH: Scriptores rerum Germanicarum in usum scholarum (Hanover, 1895), p. 182; *Capitulare missorum Aquisgranense primum 4*, ed. A. Boretius, in MGH: Capitularia regum Francorum, vol. 1 (Hanover, 1883), p. 153.11–12: "De homicidiis factis anno praesenti inter uulgares homines, quas propter puluerem mortalem acta sunt"; *Annales Sithienses 810*, ed. G.Waitz, in MGH: Scriptores, vol. 13 (Hanover, 1881), p. 37: "Boum pestilentia per totam Europam immaniter grassata est, et inde puluerum sparsorum fabula exorta"; and Paschasius Radbertus, *Epitaphium Arsenii 2.1*, ed. E. Dümmler, in *Radbert's Epitaphium Arsenii*, in *Philosophische und historische Abhandlungen der königlichen Akademie der Wissenschaften zu Berlin 2* (Berlin, 1900), p. 61: "Quːːus profecto malis precessit prior puluerem fallax adinuentio, sub qua tanta fuit uexatio et prodigium mendacii, ut prudentibus daretur intellegi, quod uniuersus orbis ad temptandum esset expositus in manibus inimici."

15. *De grandine* 13, ed. Van Acker, p. 12.1–5 (PL 104:155A10–15).
16. See *De grandine* 7, ed. Van Acker, p. 7.4–6 (PL 104:151C9–11).
17. *De grandine* 6, ed. Van Acker, p. 7.9–16 (PL 104:151A14–B8) and 7, ed. Van Acker, pp. 7.6–8.11 (PL 104:151C12–D2).
18. *De grandine* 5, ed. Van Acker, p. 6.1–13 (PL 104:150A6–B6).
19. *De grandine* 14, ed. Van Acker, p. 13.9–12 (PL 104:156C4–8): ". . . ostendunt nobis homunculos a sanctitate, iustitia et sapientia alienos, a fide et ueritate nudos, odibiles etiam proximis, a quibus dicant uehementissimos imbres, sonantia atque tonitrua, et leuatitias auras posse fieri." A copy of four of Gregory Nazianzen's sermons, translated into Latin by Rufinus, was given to Lyons by Agobard's predecessor, Bishop Leidrad (d. 815), but the "De grandinis uastatione" was not among them, or at least it is not found in the surviving manuscript, Lyons 599 (515), fols. 10v–60v. Whether or not Agobard was influenced by Gregory in this matter has yet to be established. See *Tyranni Rufini orationum Gregorii Nazianzeni nouem interpretatio*, ed. A. Engelbrecht, in Corpus Scriptorum Ecclesiasticorum Latinorum, vol. 46 (Vienna, 1910), pp. xxxv, 237–61.
20. One can follow the development of Livingstone's thought about the rainmakers in *Livingstone's Missionary Correspondence 1841–1856*, ed. I. Schapera (Berkeley, 1961), pp. 60–65, 102–103, 120–21; *Livingstone's Private Journal, 1851–1853*, ed. I. Schapera (Berkeley, 1960), pp. 239–43; and David Livingstone, *Missionary Travels and Researches in South Africa. . .*(London, 1857), pp. 22–25. One needs to note that the polished dialogue with the rainmaker that appears in *Missionary Travels* does not represent a single conversation with a single rainmaker, but a conversation that Livingstone constructed out of the various contacts he had had over several years with the Bakwains.
21. *Livingstone's Private Journals*, p. 243. Cf. Franz Boas, *The Mind of Primitive Man*, rev. ed. (New York, 1938), p. 134.
22. See *Annales regni Francorum* 814, ed. Kurze, p. 141.5–7; Nithard, *Historiarum libri IV*, 1.2, ed. and trans. P. Lauer, in *Nithard, Histoire des fils de Louis le Pieux*, in Les classiques de l'histoire de France au Moyen Age, vol. 7 (Paris, 1964), pp. 6–8; and Astronomer, *Vita Hludowici imperatoris* 21–23, 28, ed. Ernst Tremp, in MGH: Scriptores rerum Germanicarum in usum scholarum separatim editi, 64 (Hanover, 1995), pp. 346–54, 372–78; and also ed. G.H. Pertz, in MGH:SS 2 (Hanover, 1829), pp. 618–619, 621–22.
23. On Agobard's career, see Allen Cabaniss, "Agobard of Lyons," *Speculum*, 26 (1951): 50–51 [50–76]; Boshof, *Erzbischof Agobard*, pp. 20–37; Stuart Airlie, "Bonds of Power and Bonds of Association in the Court Circle of Louis the Pious," in *Charlemagne's Heir: New Perspectives on the Reign of Louis the Pious (814–840)*, ed. Peter Godman and Roger Collins (Oxford, 1990), p. 194 and n. 21 [191–204].
24. For the prohibitions against weather magic in Visigothic Spain, see Flint, *The Rise of Magic*, pp. 110–111.
25. See Alcuin, *epistola* 267, ed. E. Dümmler, in MGH: Epistolae, vol. 4 (Hanover, 1895; repr. 1974), p. 425.29–30 [425–26].
26. D.E. Nineham, "Gottschalk of Orbais: Reactionary or Precursor of the Reformation?" *Journal of Ecclesiastical History*, 40 (1989): 12 [1–18]. For a

quick tour of Frankish paganism in the Carolingian world, see Pierre
Riché, *Daily Life in the World of Charlemagne*, trans. Jo Ann McNamara
(Philadelphia, 1978), pp. 181–88; Michel Rouche, "The Early Middle Ages
in the West," in *A History of Private Life*, vol. 1: From Pagan Rome to
Byzantium, ed. Paul Veyne and trans. Arthur Goldhammer (Cambridge,
Mass., 1987), pp. 519–36; and Rosamond McKitterick, *The Frankish Church
and the Carolingian Reforms, 789–895* (London, 1977), pp. 119–22.

27. *Indiculus superstitionum et paganiarum* 22, ed. A. Boretius, in MGH:Cap. 1,
p. 223.22, and see John T. McNeill and Helena M. Gower, *Medieval Handbooks of Penance* (New York, 1965), pp. 419–21. For Cathwulf's letter, ed.
Dümmler, see MGH:Ep. 4, p. 504.12–19 [501–505].

28. *Admonitio generalis* 65, ed. Boretius, in MGH:Cap. 1, p. 58.41–59.3:
"Omnibus. Item habemus in lege Domini mandatum: 'non auguriamini'
(Lev. 19:26); et in Deuteronomio: 'nemo sit qui ariolos sciscitetur uel
somnia obseruet uel ad auguria intendat'; item 'ne sit maleficus nec incantator nec pithones consolatur.' (Deut. 18:10–11) Ideo praecipimus, ut
cauculatores nec incantatores nec tempestarii uel obligatores non fiant; et
ubicumque sunt, emendentur uel damnentur." Cf. *Capitulare missorum item
speciale* (802) 40, ed. Boretius, in MGH:Cap. 1, p. 104.5–7 [102–104];
Ansegisi abbatis capitularium collectio 1.62, ed. Boretius, in MGH:Cap. 1,
p. 402.26–30 [394–450].

29. Cathwulf, *epistola*, ed. Dümmler, see MGH:Ep. 4, p. 504.3–4.

30. Cathwulf, *epistola*, ed. Dümmler, see MGH:Ep. 4, p. 504.18–19.

31. *Statuta Rhispacensia Frisingensia Salisburgensia* (800) 15, ed. Boretius, in
MGH:Cap. 1, p. 228.9–17 [226–30] and ed. A. Werminghoff, in MGH:
Concilia 2.1 (Hanover, 1906), p. 209.18–26.

32. Council of Paris, 829 (69) 2, ed. A. Werminghoff, in MGH:Con. 2.2
(Hanover, 1908), p. 669.35–37: "Ferunt enim suis maleficiis aera posse
conturbare et grandines inmittere, futura praedicere, fructus et lac auferre
aliisque dare et innumera a talibus fieri dicuntur."

33. Council of Paris, 829 (69) 2, ed. Werminghoff, in MGH:Con. 2.2,
p. 669.37–39.

34. For a survey of this material, see McNeill and Gamer, *Medieval Handbooks*,
pp. 227 (vi.14) and n. 60, 275 (2.20), 289, and 305 (no. 33).

35. *De magicis artibus*, in PL 110:1101D1–4, 1103C11 [1095–1110]. See also
Pierre Riché, "La magie à l'époque carolingienne," in *Academie des Inscriptions et Belles-Lettres: Comptes rendus* (Paris, 1973), 134–35 [127–38] and repr.
in Riché, *Instruction et vie religieuse dans le Haut Moyen Age*, Variorum
Reprint, CS 139 (London, 1981), item XXII.

36. See n. 28 earlier and *Capitula Herardi* 3, in PL 121:764B6–10. My purpose
here is not to pursue the complex definitional and classificatory problem of
the separation of religion from magic, in part because it has been treated so
well and at such great length by others. See Keith Thomas, *Religion and the
Decline of Magic* (New York, 1971), pp. 25–50, particularly p. 41 for a series
of valuable distinctions. See also Hildred Geertz, "An Anthropology of
Religion and Magic: I," *Journal of Interdisciplinary History*, 6 (1975): 71–89

and Keith Thomas, "An Anthropology of Religion and Magic: II," *Journal of Interdisciplinary History*, 6 (1975): 91–109. For the Middle Ages, see Joseph-Claude Poulin, "Entre magie et religion. Recherches sur les utilisations marginales de l'écrit dans la culture populaire du Haut Moyen Age," in *La culture populaire au Moyen Age*, ed. Pierre Boglioni (Montreal, 1979), pp. 121–43, and Patrick Geary, "La coercition des saints dans la pratique religieuse médiévale," in *La culture populaire*, pp. 145–61.

37. For this interpretation of the word, see Grimm, *Teutonic Mythology* 2, p. 639. For another possible interpretation, see n. 89.

38. *De ecclesiasticis disciplinis et religione christiana libri duo* 2.353, in PL 132:350C2–5.

39. Burchard of Worms, *Corrector siue Medicus* 19.5, in PL 140:961D3–8. And see Cyrille Vogel, "Pratiques superstitieuses au début au XIᵉ siècle d'après le *Corrector sive Medicus* de Burchard, évêque de Worms (965–1025)," in *Études de civilization médiévale (IXe–XIIe siècles). Mélanges offerts à Edmond-René Labande* (Poitiers, 1974), pp. 751–61.

40. See *Capitulatio de partibus Saxoniae* (775–90), ed. Boretius, in MGH:Cap. 1, pp. 68–70, where Charlemagne's frustration with pagan persistence in Saxony is evident. See also J.M. Wallace-Hadrill, *The Frankish Church* (Oxford, 1983), pp. 412–419.

41. See Grimm, *Teutonic Mythology* 2, pp. 636–41, 3, pp. 1086–1089; James George Frazer, *The Golden Bough. A Study in Magic and Religion*, 3rd ed. (London, 1966), vol. 1, pp. 272–74 [244–331]; Ernest J. Moyne, *Raising the Wind. The Legend of Lapland and Finland Wizards in Literature* (Newark, 1981), esp. pp. 13–17.

42. Seneca, *Naturales Quaestiones* 4B.7.3 [4B.7.1–3]: "Rudis adhuc antiquitas credebat et attrahi cantibus imbres et repelli."

43. See Grimm, *Teutonic Mythology* 4, pp. 1769–70 and *The German Legends of the Brothers Grimm*, vol. 1 no. 251, trans. Donald Ward (Philadelphia, 1981), pp. 211–212. See also Carlo Ginzburg, *The Night Battles: Witchcraft and Agrarian Cults in the Sixteenth and Seventeenth Centuries*, trans. John and Anne Tedeschi (Baltimore, 1983), pp. xx, 22–25.

44. See Grimm, *Teutonic Mythology* 3, pp. 1086–87.

45. The almost exclusive association of women with weather-making in northern lands seems to have taken place in the eleventh century. See Pope Gregory VII, *Registrum* 7.21, ed. E. Caspar, in MGH: Epistolae selectae, vol. 2.2 (Berlin, 1955), pp. 497–98; Raoul Manselli, "Gregorio VII di fronte al paganesimo nordico: la lettera a Haakon, re di Danimarca (*Reg.* VII, 21)," *Rivista di Storia della Chiesa in Italia*, 28 (1974): 128–29 [127–32]; Manselli, *La religion populaire au moyen âge: Problèmes de méthode et d'histoire*, Conference Albert-le-Grand, 1973 (Montreal, 1975), pp. 46–47 and n. 4.

46. *Gesta Hammaburgensis ecclesiae pontificum* 4.26, 3rd ed., ed. B. Schmeidler, in MGH:SRGUS (Hanover, 1917), p. 258 (also edited in PL 146:643A6–8): " 'Thor,' inquiunt, 'presidet in aere, qui tonitrus et fulmina, uentos imbresque, serena et fruges gubernat.' "

47. The assumption that Europe even in the Middle Ages was covered by primeval forest has been called into question by F.W.M. Vera, *Grazing Ecology and Forest History* (Oxford, 2000), pp. 1–12, 28–30, 102–83.

48. *Annales regni Francorum* 820, ed. Kurze, p. 154.

49. *Annales Bertiniani* 839, ed. F. Grat, J.Vielliard, and S. Clémencet, in *Annales de Saint-Bertin* (Paris, 1964), p. 28.The description in the annal entry does not allow us to decide whether this disaster was caused by excessive rain or by storm surges. See William H.TeBrake, *Medieval Frontier: Culture and Ecology in Rijnland* (College Station, 1985), pp. 110–111. See also the account of the three hundred villagers in Thuringia who were killed in the flash flood of 889: *Annales Fuldenses siue Annales regni Francorum orientalis*, ed. by F. Kurze after G.H. Pertz [hereafter ed. Kurze], in MGH:SRGUS (Hanover, 1891), p. 118.

50. Sedulius Scottus, *carmen* 62.3–4, ed. L.Traube, in MGH: Poetae Latini aevi Carolini, vol. 3 (Berlin, 1896; repr. 1978), p. 218. And also trans. in Sedulius Scottus, *On Christian Rulers and the Poems*, trans. E.G. Doyle, in Medieval & Renaissance Texts & Studies, vol. 17 (Binghamton, 1983), p. 158.

51. See Duby, *Rural Economy*, p. 27 and Renée Doehaerd, *The Early Middle Ages in the West: Economy and Society*, trans. W.G. Deakin (Amsterdam, 1978), p. 103.

52. See H.H. Lamb, *Climate: Past, Present and Future*, vol. 2: *Climatic history and the future* (London, 1977), p. 426; Richard Hodges, *Dark Age Economics: The Origin of Towns and Trade*, A.D. *600–1000* (London, 1982), p. 139; Wendy Davies, *Small Worlds: The Village Community in Early Medieval Brittany* (London, 1988), p. 33.

For objective indications of summer storminess and heavier July to August precipitation, see H.H. Lamb, "The Early Medieval Warm Epoch and its Sequel," *Palaeogeography, Palaeoclimatology, Palaeoecology*, 1 (1965): 21–22 and fig. 1 [13–37].The dendrochronological evidence for northern Europe does not, however, seem to support the thesis that growing conditions were worse in the ninth century. See the tables printed in Emmanuel Le Roy Ladurie, *Times of Feast, Times of Famine: A History of Climate since the Year 1000*, trans. Barbara Bray (New York, 1971), pp. 386–88.

53. See Narayan R. Gokhale, *Hailstorms and Hailstone Growth* (Albany, 1975), pp. 21, 25 (fig. 2–10), 50.

54. See Benvenuto Cellini's autobiography, in *The Life of Benvenuto Cellini: A New Version*, trans. Robert H. Hobart Cust, vol. 2 (London, 1910), p. 238 [237–39].

55. *Annales Fuldenses* 882 (the continuation), ed. Kurze, p. 108. "Circumdari" should, I suppose, be translated here as "encircled" and not "spanned" as in *The Annals of Fulda*, trans. and annotated by Timothy Reuter, Ninth-Century Histories, 2 (Manchester, 1992), p. 104.

56. See Joe R. Eagleman, *Severe and Unusual Weather* (New York, 1983), p. 138.

57. Gokhale, *Hailstorms*, p. 87.

58. Gokhale, *Hailstorms*, p. 13.

59. See Einhard, *Vita Karoli Magni* 29, ed. by G.Waitz after G.H. Pertz, 6th ed. overseen by O. Holder-Egger [hereafter ed. Waitz], in MGH:SRGUS (Hanover 1911; repr. 1965), p. 33.

60. For a color plate of the Vienna Labors of the Months illumination, see Donald Bullough, *The Age of Charlemagne* (London, 1980), p. 144 plate 58.

See also Carl I. Hammer, *Charlemagne's Months and Their Bavarian Labors: The Politics of the Seasons in the Carolingian Empire*, BAR International Series, 676 (Oxford, 1997).

61. *Annales regni Francorum* 823, ed. Kurze, pp. 163–64.
62. *Annales Fuldenses* 889 (the continuation), ed. Kurze, pp. 117–118: "Grandine uero contritis frugibus mortales inopiam frugum cum miseria patiuntur."
63. See *Annales Xantenses*, ed. B. Simson, in *Annales Xantenses et Annales Vedastini*, MGH:SRGUS (Hanover, 1909), p. 31, and *Annales Fuldenses* 872, ed. Kurze, p. 76.
64. Frotharius, *epistola* 32, ed. K. Hampe, MGH:Ep. 5 (Hanover, 1898–99), p. 298.4–6.
65. See Michel Rouche, "La faim à l'époque carolingienne: essai sur quelques types de rations alimentaires," *Revue historique*, 250 (1973): 295–320, and "Les repas de fête à l'époque carolingienne," in *Manger et boire au moyen âge. Actes de Colloque de Nice (15–17 octobre 1982)*, (Nice, 1984), pp. 265–96. Rouche's conclusion, based on his interpretation of monastic provision records, that each monk ate something over three pounds of bread per day, and had an average dietary intake of approximately 6,000 calories has been called into question by Jean-Claude Hocquet, "Le pain, le vin et la juste mesure à la table des moines carolingiens," *Annales ESC*, 40 (1985): 661–86 and answered by M. Rouche, *Annales ESC*, 40: 687–88 with a rejoinder by J.-C. Hocquet, *Annales ESC*, 40: 689–90.
66. *Chronicon Moissiacense*, ed. G.H. Pertz, in MGH:SS 1 (Hanover, 1826), p. 294 [282–313]: "multi homines penuria panis perirent."
67. *Annales Bertiniani* 845, ed. Grat et al., p. 44.
68. *Annales Fuldenses* 857, ed. Kurze, p. 48.
69. *Annales Fuldenses* 875, ed. Kurze, pp. 83–84.
70. *Annales Bertiniani* 847, ed. Grat et al., p. 54.
71. On depictions of wind, rain, and lightning in the Utrecht Psalter, see Suzy Dufrenne, *Les illustrations du Psautier d'Utrecht. Sources et apport Carolingien* (Paris, 1978), pp. 74–75. For a facsimile edition, see E.T. De Wald, *The Illustrations of the Utrecht Psalter* (Princeton, 1932).
72. Nor, we should note, was this the purpose of the anonymous author of the tract *De tonitruis Libellus ad Herefridum*, PL 90:609B–614A; and trans. Dutton, in *Carolingian Civilization*, pp. 368–71. Once attributed to Bede, the work was likely written late in the ninth century, possibly at the court of Charles the Bald. It is likely a work abridged from Greek texts. See C.W. Jones, *Bedae Pseudepigrapha: Scientific Writings Falsely Attributed to Bede* (Ithaca, N.Y., 1939), pp. 45–47. Interestingly, in the introduction to the work, the author worries that his detractors might charge him with having an interest in magic. The work considers what thunder portends when it comes from one of the four directions, when it occurs in a specific month, or on a specific holy day.
73. *De grandine* 11, ed. Van Acker, p. 10.7–11.16 (PL 104:154A14–D2).
74. See "Orationes et Missa ad pluuiam postulandam" of the *Supplementum Anianense*, 92–93, ed. J. Deshusses, *Le Sacramentaire Gregorien* (Freiburg, 1971), pp. 448–49.

75. See "Missa ad repellendam tempestatem," of the *Supplementum Anianense*, 96, ed. J. Deshusses, *Le Sacramentaire Gregorien*, pp. 450–51.

76. *Vita Leobae abbatissae Biscofesheimensis* 14, ed. G. Waitz, in MGH:SS 15.1 (Hanover, 1887), p. 128 [121–31]. Also trans. C.H. Talbot, in Dutton, *Carolingian Civilization*, pp. 274–90.

77. *Vita Anskarii auctore Rimberto* 19, ed. G. Waitz, MGH:SRGUS (Hanover, 1884; repr. 1977), p. 40. The work has been translated as *Anskar: The Apostle of the North, 801–865. Translated from the Vita Anskarii by Bishop Rimbert His Fellow Missionary and Successor*, trans. Charles H. Robinson (London, 1921) and rev. in Dutton, *Carolingian Civilization*, pp. 400–51.

78. *Translatio et miracula sanctorum Marcellini et Petri* 3.16, ed. G. Waitz, in MGH: SS 15.1, p. 254 [239–64]; also trans. Paul Edward Dutton, in *Charlemagne's Courtier: The Complete Einhard* (Peterborough, Ont., 1998).

79. E.E. Evans-Pritchard, *Witchcraft, Oracles, and Magic among the Azande* (Oxford, 1937; repr. 1972), pp. 63–83.

80. See Eagleman, *Severe and Unusual Weather*, p. 150.

81. For the plausibility of this kind of general explanation for the occurrence of magical beliefs, but its insufficiency for explaining specific forms and their variation, see Thomas, *Religion and the Decline of Magic*, pp. 647–50. The position that magic and the belief in it are strong when control over the physical environment is weak derives from Bronislaw Malinowski, *Magic, Science, and Religion* (1925), repr. in Malinowski, *Magic Science, and Religion: And Other Essays* (Garden City, 1954).

82. *De grandine* 14, ed. Van Acker, p. 13.11 (in PL 104:156C6).

83. *De grandine* 11, ed. Van Acker, p. 11.19–22 (in PL 104:154C1–5).

84. *Globe and Mail*, 14 November (1987), p. A2.

85. Thomas, *Religion and the Decline of Magic*, pp. 651–54.

86. This should not be construed as an early medieval version of Luther's protest against the sale of indulgences, though both thought that these popular beliefs harmed the church and profitted the greedy (for Agobard pagan priests, for Luther a compromised church of Rome) and robbed people of monies they should put to better ends. Both Agobard and Luther were reformers, but Agobard's criticism was directed downward and was ecclesiastically conservative in nature, while Luther's was directed upward against an official, but corrupt church and his reform soon became ecclesiastically revolutionary.

87. *Vita Remigii Episcopi Remensis auctore Hincmaro* 22, ed. B. Krusch, in MGH: Scriptores rerum Merovingicarum, vol. 3 (Hanover, 1896), pp. 315. 18–316.16 [250–341]. On the resistance to paying tithes, see Giles Constable, "*Nona et Decima*: An Aspect of Carolingian Economy," *Speculum*, 35 (1960): 230, 234–35 [224–50].

88. One of the standard meanings of *canon*, and therefore, one supposes, *canonicus*, was regular tribute or measure of wheat: see *Thesaurus Linguae Latinae*, vol. 3 (Leipzig, 1906–12), pp. 273, 276.

89. See *Thesaurus linguae Latinae*, vol. 8 (Leipzig, 1936), col. 300 and R.E. Latham, *Revised Medieval Latin Word-List from British and Irish Sources* (London, 1965; repr. 1973), p. 288 where "magono" is a variant of "mango."

90. *De grandine* 2, ed.Van Acker, p. 4.14 (PL 104:148C2).
91. *Capitulare de villis* 51, ed. Boretius, in MGH:Cap. 1, p. 88.5–7: "ut sementia nostra nullatenus praui homines subtus terram uel aliubi abscondere possint et propter hoc messis rarior fiat. Similiter et de aliis maleficiis illos praeuideant, ne aliquando facere possint." See Adriaan Verhulst, "Karolingische Agrarpolitik: Das Capitulare de Villis und die Hungersnöte von 792/93 und 805/06," *Zeitschrift für Agrargeschichte und Agrarsoziologie*, 13 (1965): 181 [175–89].

Appendix 1

1. *Annales regni Francorum* 802, ed. F. Kurze after G.H. Pertz, MGH: Scriptores rerum Germanicarum in usum scholarum (Hanover, 1895), p. 117 with variants at *l*.
2. Paul Cobb will publish the results of his research in an article called "The Travails of Abu`l-`Abbas: On Caliphs, Emperors, and Elephants."

Appendix 2

1. Ed. Paul Willem Finsterwalder, "Eine parteipolitische Kundgebung eines Anhängers Lothars I," *Neues Archiv*, 47 (1928): 394–96.
2. The first instance of this saying has yet to be found. For later uses of it, see *Collectio canonum in V libris* (Lib.I–III) 1.223, ed M. Fornasari, Corpus Christianorum: Continuatio Mediaevalis, 6 (Turnhout, 1970), p. 137; Sedulius Scottus, *Collectaneum miscellaneum* 25.3, ed. Dean Simpson, CCCM 67 (Turnhout, 1988), p. 161.

INDEX

Aachen, 26, 57–58, 62–63, 66, 87, 95, 107, 112, 132, 155, 157, 161
Abul Abaz (elephant), 59–62, 189–90
acrostic poetry, 78, 118, 144, 228 n. 76, 254 n. 117, fig. 1.15
Adalhard (abbot of Corbie; ca. 752–826), 47, 72, 116
Adhemar of Chabannes (988–1034), 37
Adrevald of Fleury (d. ca. 878), 19–20
Agathias (Byzantine historian; ca. 531–80), 12–13, 17, 19
age,
  categories of, 160
  life expectancies, 158–60, 195–98
  political circumstances of, 160–67
  topoi of senescence, 152–58, 161
Agilulf (Lombard king), 22
Agilulf Visor, 4, 9, 22–23, fig. 1.5
Agnellus of Ravenna (ca. 805–54), 62
Agobard of Lyons (769–840), 146, 166, 169–72, 174–76, 181, 183–88
agriculture, 46, 48, 169–71, 176–88
Alaric (king of the Visigoths; ca. 370–410), 18–19
Alcuin (ca. 735–804), 23, 26, 30, 47, 52, 57, 65–66, 72–73, 76–80, 85, 87–89, 93–95, 97–99, 127, 140–41, 143–45, 153–56, 167, 172
Alfred (king of Wessex; 849–99), 75–76, 78, 80–81, 91–92
Ambrosius Autpertus (d. 784), 72
Andreas of Bergamo (d. after 877), 240 n. 91
angels, 97–99, 106, 113, 119, 124, 164, 236 n. 20
Angilramnus of Metz (bishop, d. 791), 89

animals,
  birds, 47, 50–59, 62, 65–68
  camels, 59, 140, 218 n. 109
  dogs, 51, 59, 61–64, 67
  elephants, 58–62
  horses, 51–52, 63, 67, 102, 140, 157
  lions, 43, 47, 58–59, 61, 63, 67
  panthers, 58, 66
  peacocks, 50–51, 54–55
  spiders, 11, 50
  wolves, 44, 58, 63–66
annals,
  of Fulda, 110, 177–78, 180
  of St-Bertin, 64, 108, 110
  of Xanten, 110–11, 180
  Royal Frankish, 60, 97, 101, 161, 177, 180, 189
Arabs, 23
Ardo (783–843), 224 n. 23
Areobindus Diptych, 59
arithmetic, 65, 77, 82
Arno of Salzburg (bishop; 746–821), 140–41, 172
Asser (d. ca. 909), 75, 78, 226 n. 51
Astronomer, the (fl. 830–45), 104–8, 126, 136–37, 153, 157
Audradus Modicus (fl. 847–53), 116
Augustine (354–430), 45–46, 51, 74
Aulus Gellius (ca. 130–80), 140, 201 n. 4, 254 n. 120
Avitus (bishop, 490–516), 15

Bede, the Venerable (672/673–735), 76, 100, 241 n. 118
Benedict of Aniane (751–821), 72
Benedict of Nursia (abbot; 480–547), 131